The Joan Palevsky  Imprint in Classical Literature

In honor of beloved Virgil—

"O degli altri poeti onore e lume..."

—Dante, *Inferno*

The publisher gratefully acknowledges the generous contribution to this book provided by the Classical Literature Endowment Fund of the University of California Press Foundation, which is supported by a major gift from Joan Palevsky.

Riot in Alexandria

THE TRANSFORMATION OF THE CLASSICAL HERITAGE
Peter Brown, General Editor

I *Art and Ceremony in Late Antiquity*, by Sabine G. MacCormack

II *Synesius of Cyrene: Philosopher-Bishop*, by Jay Alan Bregman

III *Theodosian Empresses: Women and Imperial Dominion in Late Antiquity*, by Kenneth G. Holum

IV *John Chrysostom and the Jews: Rhetoric and Reality in the Late Fourth Century*, by Robert L. Wilken

V *Biography in Late Antiquity: The Quest for the Holy Man*, by Patricia Cox

VI *Pachomius: The Making of a Community in Fourth-Century Egypt*, by Philip Rousseau

VII *Change in Byzantine Culture in the Eleventh and Twelfth Centuries*, by A. P. Kazhdan and Ann Wharton Epstein

VIII *Leadership and Community in Late Antique Gaul*, by Raymond Van Dam

IX *Homer the Theologian: Neoplatonist Allegorical Reading and the Growth of the Epic Tradition*, by Robert Lamberton

X *Procopius and the Sixth Century*, by Averil Cameron

XI *Guardians of Language: The Grammarian and Society in Late Antiquity*, by Robert A. Kaster

XII *Civic Coins and Civic Politics in the Roman East, A.D. 180–275*, by Kenneth Harl

XIII *Holy Women of the Syrian Orient*, introduced and translated by Sebastian P. Brock and Susan Ashbrook Harvey

XIV *Gregory the Great: Perfection in Imperfection*, by Carole Straw

XV *"Apex Omnium": Religion in the "Res gestae" of Ammianus*, by R. L. Rike

XVI *Dioscorus of Aphrodito: His Work and His World*, by Leslie S. B. MacCoull

XVII *On Roman Time: The Codex-Calendar of 354 and the Rhythms of Urban Life in Late Antiquity*, by Michele Renee Salzman

XVIII *Asceticism and Society in Crisis: John of Ephesus and "The Lives of the Eastern Saints,"* by Susan Ashbrook Harvey

XIX *Barbarians and Politics at the Court of Arcadius*, by Alan Cameron and Jacqueline Long, with a contribution by Lee Sherry

XX *Basil of Caesarea*, by Philip Rousseau

XXI *In Praise of Later Roman Emperors: The Panegyrici Latini*, introduction, translation, and historical commentary by C. E. V. Nixon and Barbara Saylor Rodgers

XXII *Ambrose of Milan: Church and Court in a Christian Capital*, by Neil B. McLynn

XXIII *Public Disputation, Power, and Social Order in Late Antiquity*, by Richard Lim

XXIV *The Making of a Heretic: Gender, Authority, and the Priscillianist Controversy*, by Virginia Burrus

XXV *Symeon the Holy Fool: Leontius's "Life" and the Late Antique City*, by Derek Krueger

XXVI *The Shadows of Poetry: Vergil in the Mind of Augustine*, by Sabine MacCormack

XXVII *Paulinus of Nola: Life, Letters, and Poems*, by Dennis E. Trout

XXVIII *The Barbarian Plain: Saint Sergius between Rome and Iran*, by Elizabeth Key Fowden

XXIX *The Private Orations of Themistius*, translated, annotated, and introduced by Robert J. Penella

XXX *The Memory of the Eyes: Pilgrims to Living Saints in Christian Late Antiquity*, by Georgia Frank

XXXI *Greek Biography and Panegyric in Late Antiquity*, edited by Tomas Hägg and Philip Rousseau

XXXII *Subtle Bodies: Representing Angels in Byzantium*, by Glenn Peers

XXXIII *Wandering, Begging Monks: Social Order and the Promotion of Monasticism in Late Antiquity*, by Daniel Folger Caner

XXXIV *Failure of Empire: Valens and the Roman State in the Fourth Century A.D.*, by Noel Lenski

XXXV *Merovingian Mortuary Archaeology and the Making of the Early Middle Ages*, by Bonnie Effros

XXXVI *Quṣayr 'Amra: Art and the Umayyad Elite in Late Antique Syria*, by Garth Fowden

XXXVII *Holy Bishops in Late Antiquity: The Nature of Christian Leadership in an Age of Transition*, by Claudia Rapp

XXXVIII *Encountering the Sacred: The Debate on Christian Pilgrimage in Late Antiquity*, by Brouria Bitton-Ashkelony

XXXIX *There Is No Crime for Those Who Have Christ: Religious Violence in the Christian Roman Empire*, by Michael Gaddis

XL *The Legend of Mar Qardagh: Narrative and Christian Heroism in Late Antique Iraq*, by Joel Thomas Walker

XLI *City and School in Late Antique Athens and Alexandria*, by Edward J. Watts

XLII *Scenting Salvation: Ancient Christianity and the Olfactory Imagination*, by Susan Ashbrook Harvey

XLIII *Man and the Word: The Orations of Himerius*, edited by Robert J. Penella

XLIV *The Matter of the Gods*, by Clifford Ando

XLV *The Two Eyes of the Earth: Art and Ritual of Kingship between Rome and Sasanian Iran*, by Matthew P. Canepa

XLVI *Riot in Alexandria: Tradition and Group Dynamics in Late Antique Pagan and Christian Communities*, by Edward J. Watts

XLVII *Peasant and Empire in Christian North Africa*, by Leslie Dossey

Riot in Alexandria

*Tradition and Group Dynamics in Late Antique
Pagan and Christian Communities*

Edward J. Watts

UNIVERSITY OF CALIFORNIA PRESS
Berkeley   Los Angeles   London

University of California Press, one of the most distinguished university presses in the United States, enriches lives around the world by advancing scholarship in the humanities, social sciences, and natural sciences. Its activities are supported by the UC Press Foundation and by philanthropic contributions from individuals and institutions. For more information, visit www.ucpress.edu.

University of California Press

Berkeley and Los Angeles, California

University of California Press, Ltd.

London, England

© 2010 by The Regents of the University of California

Library of Congress Cataloging-in-Publication Data

Watts, Edward Jay, 1975–.

   Riot in Alexandria : tradition and group dynamics in late antique pagan and Christian communities / Edward Watts.

     p. cm. — (The transformation of the classical heritage ; 46)

   Includes bibliographical references and index.

   ISBN 978-0-520-26207-2 (cloth, alk. paper)

   1. Alexandria (Egypt)—Intellectual life. 2. Alexandria (Egypt)—Church history. 3. Paganism—Egypt—Alexandria—History. 4. Christian communities—Egypt—Alexandria—History. 5. Asceticism—History—Early church, ca. 30–600. 6. Alexandrian school, Christian. 7. Education, Ancient—Egypt—Alexandria. 8. Riots—Egypt—Alexandria—History. I. Title.

DT154.A4W38   2010

932—dc22   2009035378

Manufactured in the United States of America

19 18 17 16 15 14 13 12 11

10 9 8 7 6 5 4 3 2 1

This book is printed on Cascades Enviro 100, a 100% post consumer waste, recycled, de-inked fiber. FSC recycled certified and processed chlorine free. It is acid free, Ecologo certified, and manufactured by BioGas energy.

To Nathaniel and Zoe . . .

CONTENTS

List of Illustrations   *xi*
Acknowledgments   *xiii*

1. The Anatomy of a Riot   1

PART ONE. HISTORICAL DISCOURSE IN INTELLECTUAL COMMUNITIES   23

2. Personal Legacy and Scholastic Identity   29
   Internal Historical Discourse and Its Transmission: The Example of Eunapius   33
   Defending Communal Historical Discourse: Porphyry's Life of Plotinus   45

3. Past, Present, and Future in Late Neoplatonic Historical Discourse   53
   The Life of Isidore and its Sources   54
   Eating, Drinking, and Learning Neoplatonic History   60
   Oral Tradition and Scholastic Identity in the Alexandrian Schools of the 480s   62
   Paralius's Beating within its Scholastic Context   65
   Fifth-Century Christian Violence in Neoplatonic Communal Memory   71
   Teaching Ethics after the Riot   78

PART TWO. THE PAST WITHIN AND OUTSIDE LATE ANTIQUE MONASTERIES   89

4. History and the Shape of Monastic Communities   95
   The Koinonia   99
   The Historia Monachorum and Visitors' Exposure to Ascetic Oral Traditions   107
   Social Relations and the Power of the Master: Barsanuphius and John   114

5.	Anti-Chalcedonian Ascetics and their Student Associates	123
	The Limits of Ascetic Influence	124
	Finding the Ascetic and Intellectual Balance	130
	The Ascetic and Sophistic Mélange of Zacharias Scholasticus	138
	A Student Riot and its Commemoration: The "Life of Paralius"	142

PART THREE. DEFINING THE ALEXANDRIAN BISHOP — 155

6.	Creating the Legend of the Alexandrian Bishop	163
	Mechanisms of Episcopal Power	165
	Athanasius and the Politics of Self-Definition	172
	Athanasius's Restoration and Redefinition	175
	The Athanasian Historical Legacy	182
7.	Theophilus and Cyril: The Alexandrian Bishop Triumphant	190
	Theophilus and the Historical Character of Athanasius	191
	The Legacy of Theophilus	205
8.	Peter Mongus Struggles with the Past	216
	Chalcedon and the Redefinition of the Alexandrian Bishop	217
	Peter Mongus and Resistance in an Age of Compromise	229
	Peter Mongus and the Beating of Paralius	234
	A Riot's Aftermath	243
9.	Conclusion	254

Appendix 1. Dating the Riot — 263
Appendix 2. How Much Should We Trust Zacharias Scholasticus? — 265
Bibliography — 269
Index — 285

ILLUSTRATIONS

MAP

Late antique Alexandria   *xvi*

FIGURES

1. Theater, auditoria, and portico, Kom el-Dikka   *6*
2. Auditorium K, Kom el-Dikka   *7*
3. Auditoria, baths, and latrine, Kom el-Dikka   *9*
4. Serapeum site, Alexandria   *194*
5. Theophilus standing atop bust of Serapis   *206*

ACKNOWLEDGMENTS

This project began in late 2004 as an exploration of the role played by oral communication in the most literate segments of late antique society. I first worked through texts written by pagan intellectuals, the most ostentatiously literate figures in the late Roman world. When this material proved fertile, I then moved on to ascetic circles, with bishops my next intended target. Because it brought together intellectuals, students, and a bishop, I originally imagined that the riot at the core of this book would conclude a larger, more diffuse study of orality and literacy in late antiquity. After conversations with colleagues and friends, I came to see that the riot offered a unique micro-history through which I could trace the interaction of oral and written traditions as well as their influence on actual events. The work that has resulted investigates these traditions and the way that intellectual, ascetic, and ecclesiastical communities preserved, adapted, and transmitted them.

A project like this would be impossible without a great deal of institutional and personal support. Indiana University has generously backed my work with a series of research awards. These include a fellowship from the College Arts and Humanities Institute in 2005, an Outstanding Junior Faculty award in 2007, and two summer research fellowships. The History Department too has been both generous and accommodating to me. Laura Cerruti, Stephanie Fay, Kate Toll, Cindy Fulton, and the University of California Press have been encouraging and helpful throughout this process. I owe Laura particular gratitude for her early advice and suggestions about how to make this study leaner and more focused.

Many students, colleagues, friends, and family members have helped to inspire and improve this study. Diane Fruchtman, David Maldonado, and Brad Storin as well as the graduate students in various ancient history seminars have served as willing (or, perhaps, only captive) audiences and occasional critics of some of the ideas and interpretations expressed here. Brad and Ellen Muehlberger are owed particular gratitude for spending a summer reading the Coptic *Life of Longinus*. Hopefully this book now convinces them that it was not an entirely fruitless enterprise.

Conversations and correspondence with Glen Bowersock, Deborah Deliyannis, Jeff Gould, Veronika Grimm, Walter Kaegi, Matthias Lehmann, Noel Lenski, Scott McGill, David Michelson, Joe Pucci, Samuel Rubenson, Cristiana Sogno, Jan Eric Steppa, Dennis Trout, Michael Kulikowski, Tina Shepardson, and audiences at Oxford University, Villanova University, Rice University, the University of Illinois, Princeton University, the University of Chicago, and the University of Tennessee have helped me separate good ideas from bad. John Matthews lent me the encouragement and enlightenment for which he is justly famous. My colleagues John Hanson and Danny James each opened my eyes to the study of oral traditions. John Dillon turned me on to the wonderful material surviving from the Old Academy. At an early stage in this project, Christopher Haas provided a succinct and extremely useful introduction to the newest finds at Kom el-Dikka. On several occasions, Michael McGerr offered sage advice about how to structure this sort of study. Grzegorz Majcherek twice welcomed me to the Kom el-Dikka site in Alexandria and each time taught me more in a few hours than I could otherwise have learned in weeks. Craig Gibson and Han Baltussen were kind enough to share relevant forthcoming material with me.

A number of colleagues have read all or part of the manuscript and offered extremely useful suggestions for improvement. Matt Christ and Bert Harrill guided my forays into Classical and Hellenistic philosophy. Eric Robinson focused my view of the elusive Gessius. At a very early stage in this project, Cam Grey provided succinct and insightful commentary that helped me conceive of the book's larger shape. Susan Harvey, who introduced me to hagiography in the mid-1990s, continued to show me new ways to probe these texts. Anthony Kaldellis infused more blood into my language and led me towards a fine, software-foiling title. Tina Sessa brought me out into the wider world of late antique bishops. And two anonymous readers gently offered ways to strengthen and expand many of my arguments.

I owe special debts of gratitude to two friends, whose assistance and support enabled me to extend myself in the ways that this study demanded. In addition to being a fantastic teacher of Coptic, David Brakke was always willing to answer questions, discuss ideas, suggest bibliography, read materials, and put up with odd Syriac queries. One could not ask for a better colleague. Peter Brown too has been extremely generous with his time and expertise. Our conversations always stimulated my thought, pushed my inquiries in new directions, and gave me a sense of what this research could yield. It will be impossible to think of this project without also remembering the tea, orange juice, and good company I found at Small World.

The final words of thanks must be reserved for my family. In the four years that this book took shape, both my son and my daughter were born. My family has been as determined as I to see this project through to its conclusion. My parents Dan and Karen Watts and my in-laws Brij and Sunanda Bhargava each helped to make possible the trips to Egypt that this project necessitated. The strength and determination of my wife Manasi inspired me throughout this process. This book led her to brave sandstorms, hostile Bedouin, tortured prose, and daily meals at the Trianon, to offer fresh ears and a photographer's eye to the sites and sounds of late antique and contemporary Egypt. Words cannot capture my gratitude.

This book is dedicated to my son, Nathaniel, and my daughter, Zoe. Nathaniel grudgingly allowed me to interrupt his meals of pureed green beans and oatmeal in order to review Coptic flash cards. Zoe drank her bottles calmly and patiently while Constantine of Siout and the *Storia della Chiesa* sat open on the arm of the rocking chair. I will never forget their roles in this process—even if they already have.

Bloomington
December 29, 2008

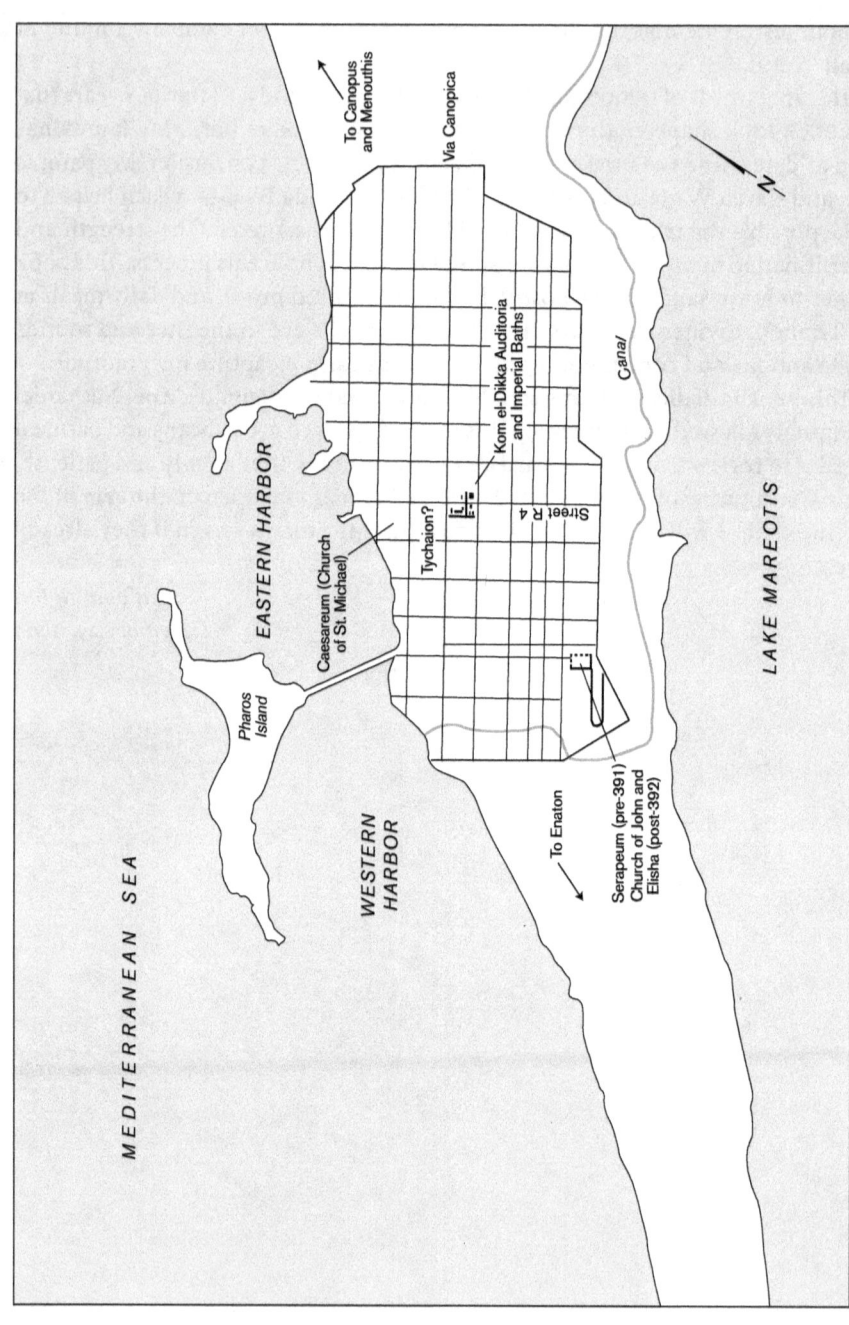

Late antique Alexandria

1

The Anatomy of a Riot

In the fall of 485, a teenager named Paralius arrived in Alexandria to study under the grammarian Horapollon.[1] The youngest of four brothers, Paralius had grown up a child of some privilege in the pleasant city of Aphrodisias, the inland capital of the Roman province of Caria and an important center for pagan intellectual pursuits in the later fifth century.[2] Paralius belonged to one of the families contributing to the city's cultural vibrancy. Although his parents had died while he was still a child, Paralius's brothers Proclus and Democharus ensured that he received a high-quality education.[3] Proclus, who taught rhetoric in the city, probably handled Paralius's training when he reached the appropriate age for grammatical instruction to begin.[4]

---

1. For the dating of Paralius's arrival and the subsequent events, see appendix 1. Details of his life are taken from Zacharias Scholasticus's *Life of Severus*, the only surviving source that speaks about him. All references to this text refer to the edition and translation prepared by M. A. Kugener (Zacharias of Mytilene, *Vie de Sévère*, PO II, Paris, 1907; rev. ed., Belgium, Turnhout, 1971). The references to the text will refer to the pagination of Kugener's first edition. The translations from the *Life of Severus* used in this book are based upon those of L. Ambjörn, *The Life of Severus by Zachariah of Mytilene* (Piscataway, NJ, 2008). In places they have been amended for clarity.

2. For Paralius's origins see Zacharias Scholasticus, *Life of Severus*, 14. For the importance of pagan intellectuals in fifth-century Aphrodisias see, for example, C. Roueché, *Aphrodisias in Late Antiquity* (London, 1989), inscriptions 53 and 54, as well as her discussion of Asclepiodotus of Aphrodisias on pp. 86–92.

3. Implied by *Vit. Sev.* 14–15.

4. On their positions in Aphrodisias, see *Vit. Sev.* 39. Instruction in grammar could begin as early as age seven or eight, though Paralius seems to have been considerably older than this (cf. R. A. Kaster, *Guardians of Language: The Grammarian and Society in Late Antiquity* [Berkeley, 1988], 11).

The trip to Alexandria represented the next stage in Paralius's education. Like his brothers before him, Paralius was in line to receive the most complete and socially respectable education that the late Roman world offered. This consisted of a solid background in basic letters followed by formal instruction in grammar. In his late adolescence, Paralius would graduate to a school of rhetoric. By the fifth century it had become popular to cap this education either with some philosophical study or with a more practical legal training.[5]

Their own educational background suggests that Paralius's brothers expected him to progress through each of these educational levels—and he was to do it at the best schools available. Paralius's trip to Alexandria represented a natural step in this process. In the late 480s, Alexandria stood out as the finest center for grammatical and rhetorical teaching in the eastern Mediterranean. This is not to say that it was the only such center. We know that, in 485, Paralius's brothers could have sent him to well-regarded teachers in Athens, Gaza, or Damascus as well as any number of other places whose teachers have passed unremembered into silence.[6] At this point in time, however, the brightest and most ambitious children of the eastern Mediterranean elite congregated in Alexandria. Paralius's family was closely joined to the social and intellectual network that linked the major teaching centers of the eastern Mediterranean and must certainly have worked through the delicate calculus of campus rankings familiar to many ambitious American families today.[7] The Alexandrian grammatical and rhetorical schools were the Harvard or Yale of their day and the opportunities they afforded to their graduates more than offset their considerable financial and emotional cost.[8]

When Paralius arrived in Alexandria he would have met fellow students who came from areas as diverse as Gaza, Pisidia, and Syria.[9] The fame of Alexandria's schools certainly drew these young men, but the powerful reputation of some Alexandrian teachers also exerted a considerable attractive force. In the case of Paralius, the teacher with whom he was most familiar was Asclepiodotus. The son-in-law of a prominent city councilor in Aphrodisias, Asclepiodotus had lived

---

5. For details of this educational progression see E. Watts, *City and School in Late Antique Athens and Alexandria* (Berkeley, 2006), 3–5; as well as R. Cribiore, *The School of Libanius in Late Antique Antioch* (Princeton, 2007), 29–41, 207–13.

6. On teaching in Athens see Watts, *City and School*, 79–110, as well as the profiles of various Athenian teachers in Damascius's *Life of Isidore*. For Gaza, note the teaching career of Aeneas of Gaza. Damascus was where Damascius began rhetorical training.

7. On the influence of these networks see E. Watts, "Student Travel to Intellectual Centers: What was the Attraction?" in *Travel, Communication and Geography in Late Antiquity*, eds. L. Ellis and F. Kidner, 13–23 (Aldershot, 2004); and R. Cribiore, *School of Libanius*, 83–110.

8. On the educational opportunities see Watts, *City and School*, 11–12. On the substantial cost, see Cribiore, *School of Libanius*, 185–88.

9. Zacharias Scholasticus came from Gaza (*Vit. Sev.* 24). Severus was from Pisidia (*Vit. Sev.* 10). Damascius was from Syria (Photius, *Bib.* Cod. 181.1).

in that city for a number of years.[10] An Alexandrian by birth, Asclepiodotus and his wife spent the first part of their married life in Caria before moving back to Alexandria in order to get fertility treatments at a local shrine to Isis.[11] News about Asclepiodotus and his Alexandrian colleagues continued to reach Aphrodisias during Paralius's childhood. He and his brothers heard about the miraculous conception of Asclepiodotus's child and learned, possibly again from an Alexandrian source, about the brewing revolt of the Isaurian general Illus.[12] Indeed, the connections between his family and Alexandria seem to have been extensive and, when the time came to send Paralius abroad, his brothers entrusted him to the teacher Horapollon.[13] After an exchange of letters introducing Paralius to him, Horapollon accepted Paralius into the school and assumed general responsibility for the youth's spiritual and intellectual well-being.[14]

A late antique school enabled this sort of personal supervision. Even in a large teaching environment like Alexandria, professors handled a manageable number of students, probably never more than one hundred and usually far fewer than that.[15] Often professors worked to foster a degree of cohesion within their cohort of students. Some schools conducted elaborate initiation rituals during which a new arrival would swear an oath to study under a certain teacher or group of teachers. In some cases, he would also promise to stay away from the classes of rivals.[16] Once he had formally agreed to join the school, the intellectual community initiated the new arrival. While the specifics of the rituals probably varied between

10. On Asclepiodotus and his first stay in Aphrodisias see Damascius, *Life of Isidore*, fr. 86A–G in the edition of P. Athanassiadi, *Damascius: The Philosophical History* (Athens, 1999).

11. Described by Zacharias in *Vit. Sev.* 16–19 and possibly alluded to by Damascius in *Vit. Is.* 86D.

12. For Illus, see *Vit. Sev.* 40. Though Caria was not far from Illus's base of support in Isauria, the *Life of Severus* is clear that the revolt was known about from the activities of Pamprepius (cf. Zacharias, *Vit. Isaiae*, 7.15–26 = Syr. 10–11).

13. *Vit. Sev.* 15. Such arrangements were common (e.g., Libanius, *Or.* 1.20) and need not suggest a particularly close relationship between the family and the teacher.

14. On the application process to a school see Cribiore, *School of Libanius*, 112–14.

15. Philostratus (*VS* 591) says casually that Chrestus of Byzantium had over one hundred paying pupils in Byzantium, a number that is probably close to the maximum a professor could handle. Libanius claims to have had classes of around eighty students (*Or.* 1.37). For a more realistic discussion of Libanius's numbers, see Cribiore, *School of Libanius*, 96–97. The complex of lecture halls recently excavated at Kom el-Dikka in Alexandria includes at least twenty fifth- and sixth-century auditoria that could comfortably hold between twenty and thirty students. For more details on the site see the important volume of T. Derda, T. Markiewicz, and E. Wipszycka, eds., *Alexandria: Auditoria of Kôm el-Dikka and Late Antique Education*, *Journal of Juristic Papyrology*, Supplement 8 (Warsaw, 2007). For the capacity of the site see G. Majcherek, "The Late Roman Auditoria: An Archeological Overview," in *Alexandria: Auditoria*, 45.

16. These oaths are best attested in the fourth century. See, for example, Libanius, in *Or.* 1.16, *Or.* 18.14; Himerius, *Oration* 48.37; and Eunapius, *VS* 485–87.

(and even within) intellectual centers, there does seem to have been a similar format to them. The new student was initially treated as an outsider and mocked as an inferior by the older students. In fourth-century Athens, for example, this involved both verbal mockery and the threat of physical violence (if not an actual beating).[17] Elsewhere the hazing was probably confined to taunts and teasing that reinforced an initiate's lowly status within the scholastic community.

Once the new arrival passed through this ritual entry, he would be accepted as a legitimate member of the school.[18] In some cases, he would be given the privilege of wearing a distinctive scholarly robe.[19] Though the threat of violence receded after a student's initiation, taunts and teasing apparently continued to reinforce his inferior status within the scholastic community for much of his first year.[20] Despite their lower status, many new students like Paralius found their schools neither unwelcoming nor unfamiliar. In fact, it was common for teachers and students alike to describe their relationship to others in the school in familial terms. Students described their teachers as "parents" and their peers as "brothers."[21] This personal intimacy was fostered by a curriculum that emphasized the value of close friendships and it was sustained by other, less savory, communal activities. Throughout antiquity, students studying abroad were known for their ability to squander large sums of money on parties that, put charitably, enhanced the cohesion of a student body.[22] Older students also displayed a more alarming tendency to brawl with the members of other schools in collective expressions of loyalty that either defended the honor of their professor or enhanced the profile of his school.[23]

What is important about such things, however, is not that ancient students were a wild bunch but that, in most cases, these actions were performed as a part of a group.[24] If a new student like Paralius accepted this environment and the terms of his initiation, he would find a close-knit group of peers led, at least in theory, by a supportive professor.[25] This taught him to value new relationships with people

---

17. On this see E. Watts, "The Student Self in Late Antiquity," in *Religion and the Self in Antiquity*, ed. D. Brakke, M. Satlow, and S. Weitzman (Bloomington, 2005), 238.

18. The initiation of students can be seen to follow the classic three-stage template first described by A. van Gennep, *The Rites of Passage*, trans. M. B. Vizedom and G. Caffee, 2nd ed. (Chicago, 1960).

19. Olympiodorus of Thebes, fr. 28.

20. E.g., Gregory Nazianzen, *Or.* 43.17; Zacharias, *Vit. Sev.*, 47.

21. E.g., Libanius, *Ep.* 931, 1009, 1070, 1257; Synesius, *Ep.* 16. For a discussion of these terms see Petit, *Les Étudiants de Libanius* (Paris, 1957), 35–36; and Cribiore, *School of Libanius*, 138–43.

22. For students spending large sums of money, see Cicero *ad Atticum* xii.32.2; xv.15.4; xv.17.4; and Libanius, *Or.* 1.19

23. Such behavior is alluded to by Himerius (*Or.* 4.9; *Or.* 69) and, in an Antiochene context, Libanius (*Or.* 19).

24. On this see Watts, "Student Self," 240–41.

25. Libanius (*Or.* 1.17) describes the personal isolation a nonconformist could feel in this environment.

who did not share his familial and regional background. It also illustrated to him that, within an academic environment, a distinctive code of behavior existed that could render acceptable behaviors that were normally unacceptable (like street fighting) if they either enhanced a student's integration into the school or furthered the school's interest.

While most late antique students failed to exhibit the sort of loyalty to their schools that ancient sources idealize, the physical setting in which teaching occurred influenced scholastic loyalties and interscholastic rivalries.[26] This was particularly true of the space in which Horapollon taught Paralius. Horapollon shared what seems to have been a complex of classrooms with the philosophers Heraiscus, Isidore, Ammonius, Paralius's family friend Asclepiodotus,[27] and, probably, the grammarian John Semeiographos and the rhetorician Sopater.[28] Some of these teachers also shared students with one another. Horapollon certainly cooperated with his father, Asclepiades, and his uncle Heraiscus.[29] He may have allowed students to work with Isidore and Ammonius as well. It also seems that John Semeiographos and Sopater had some sort of arrangement for student exchange.

Alexandria encouraged this sort of professorial exchange. It was a large city, perhaps the third largest in the empire in 485, and its compact geography placed a premium on urban space.[30] Possibly because of this, teaching in Alexandria apparently took place in rather confined quarters. In the mid- to late fifth century, perhaps as many as twenty-five lecture halls were constructed in the center of the city abutting a late Roman bath.[31] A richly decorated public latrine separated the

---

26. Student loyalty to professors was often uncertain or of short duration. Libanius and Augustine both describe problems with students who transferred to other teachers, despite the agreements they made (e.g., Aug., *Conf.* 5.12; Libanius, *Or.* 43). Financial and physical difficulties also could cut short a student's time at school (e.g., Libanius, *Epp.* 379, 1371; and Cribiore, *School of Libanius*, 177–80). On rivalries, note, for example, Libanius's struggles to take over teaching space in Antioch (described in *Or.* 1.100–3).

27. *Vit. Sev.* 16. Athanassiadi (*Damascius*, 20–21) has suggested that these teachers were all a part of one school.

28. *Vit. Sev.* 12–13.

29. This is suggested by J. Maspero, "Horapollon et la fin du paganisme Égyptien," *BIFAO* 11 (1914), 166 line 15.

30. The Alexandrian population has been estimated to be around 500,000 people during the Roman imperial period and perhaps slightly less by the fifth century. For a survey of the various numbers suggested over time see D. Delia, "The Population of Roman Alexandria," *TAPA* 118 (1988), 275–92. For a sense of the congestion of the city note C. Haas, "John Moschus and Late Antique Alexandria," in *Alexandrie Medievale II, Études alexandrines 8*, ed. C. Décobert (Cairo, 2002), 51–52; and J. McKenzie, *The Architecture of Alexandria and Egypt, 300 B.C.–A.D. 700* (New Haven, 2007), 218.

31. The remains are described and analyzed in detail by Majcherek, "The Late Roman Auditoria," 11–50; and placed in their urban context by J. McKenzie, "The Place in Late Antique Alexandria 'Where the Alchemists and Scholars Sit . . . Was Like Stairs,'" in *Alexandria: Auditoria*, 53–83. On the larger

FIGURE 1. Theater, auditoria, and portico, Kom el-Dikka, Alexandria, fifth or sixth century. Photo by Manasi Watts.

lecture halls from the bath house. These seem to have been part of a larger scholastic quarter in the city that included a public theater, a colonnaded portico, and a large open space in which people could congregate. Intriguingly enough, all of the lecture halls were entered from the portico. Evidently it was supposed to serve as a sort of common hallway.

The number of classrooms found at Kom el-Dikka and the unique nature of the space around them leads one to suspect that Paralius may have taken lessons in this space.[32] Even if he did not, the lecture halls and their general environment

---

complex of auditoria see Z. Kiss, "Les auditoria romains tardifs" in *Fouilles Polonaises à Kôm el-Dikka (1986–1987), Alexandrie VII*, eds. Z. Kiss, G. Majcherek, H. Meyza, H. Rysiewski, and B. Tkaczow (Warsaw, 2000), 8–33; and G. Majcherek, "Kôm el-Dikka. Excavations and Preservation Work, 2002/2003," *Polish Archaeology in the Mediterranean* 15 (2004), 25–38, as well as "Kom el-Dikka. Excavation and Preservation Work, 2003/2004," *PAM* 16 (2005), 17–30. I thank Professor Majcherek for the final two references. Note now the detailed reconstructions in McKenzie, *Architecture of Alexandria*, 208–20.

32. It is worth noting here the spatial similarity between the Kom el-Dikka complex and that used by Libanius in Antioch. The Antiochene setting is described in Libanius, *Or* 22.31; *Or*. 5.45–52;

FIGURE 2. Auditorium K, Kom el-Dikka, Alexandria. Photo by Manasi Watts.

provide a good general idea of the space in which his classes would have met. In fact, they offer a setting not unlike what one would find in a modern American secondary school. There were classrooms, a latrine, and a covered hallway linking the space. One must imagine that each teacher followed something of a class schedule and was on campus only when he was scheduled to teach.[33] His students too would have been present only when their lessons were scheduled, with either their primary teacher or another teacher with whom he cooperated. Like all students, they also would have loitered in the halls before and after class discussing any number of things related (or unrelated) to their scholastic life.

---

cf. Cribiore, *School of Libanius*, 44. The scale and layout of the Kom el-Dikka site, however, distinguishes it from other teaching spaces. For an analysis see R. Cribiore, "Spaces for Teaching in Late Antiquity," in *Alexandria: Auditoria*, 143–50. In fact, there are few other late antique sites that contain analogous remains. See, for example, K. Welch, "Some Architectural Prototypes for the Auditoria at Kom el-Dikka and Three Late Antique (fifth century AD) Comparanda from Aphrodisias in Caria," in *Alexandria: Auditoria*, 115–33.

33. Suggested by *Vit. Sev.* 23.

One should not discount the significance of these hallway conversations. It was here, quite literally just outside of the controlled environment of the classroom, that students like Paralius worked with one another to make sense of their educational experience. The schools of Horapollon and his colleagues attracted an extremely diverse group of students. Both pagan and Christian students listened to lectures in these halls and had discussions in the adjoining portico. Surviving texts preserve a number of fictional and semi-fictional discussions that took place in the open areas around Horapollon's classroom.[34] Many of these touch upon subjects more or less related to the content of classroom lectures. Students discussed contentious elements of a professor's teaching,[35] the religious achievements of Alexandrian intellectuals, and even the prophecies that students received from shrines.[36] Each of the participants in these discussions brought a distinct point of view to the encounter. While pagan students could argue that Plato agreed with the Aristotelian doctrine of the eternity of the world, Christian students could counter that Plato's *Timaeus* seems to say very much the opposite.[37] When pagan students spoke about their own and their teachers' trips to the shrine of Isis in the Alexandrian suburb of Menouthis, Christian students could counter with a description of the miraculous cures performed at the shrine of St. Cyrus and John in the same suburb.[38] Despite such discussions' incendiary potential, the social cohesion created within scholastic circles ensured generally respectful and civil interactions between pagan and Christian students.[39] Indeed, religiously heterogeneous intellectual circles like those of Ammonius Saccas and Hypatia show that Alexandria had long successfully nurtured this sort of tolerant culture.[40]

---

34. These texts will be discussed in much more detail below.

35. Such is the case with the fictionalized discussion between Zacharias Scholasticus and Gessius, each students of the philosopher Ammonius, about the eternity of the world (Zacharias, *Ammonius* 370–925).

36. E.g., *Vit. Sev.* 20–22.

37. Zacharias, *Ammonius* 670–94; cf. Aeneas of Gaza, *Theophrastus* 40.2.

38. The pagan Menouthis shrine is known only from Christian polemical texts (primarily Zacharias's *Life of Severus*, Cyril of Alexandria's *Orations on St. Cyrus and John* [PG 77 1100], and Sophronius's *Encomium to the Holy Cyrus and John, the Martyrs* [PG 87]). However, these texts make it clear that the wonders performed at that shrine were discussed in the city. J. Gascou, "Les origines du culte des saints Cyr et Jean," *Analecta Bollandiana* 125 (2007), 1–35, has recently argued that the shrine of Cyrus and John dates later than the fifth century. The presence of the iatrosophist Gessius (an older contemporary of Paralius) in the *miracula* associated with the shrine suggests, however, that the shrine was probably operative in the later fifth or early sixth century.

39. An exception to this is the anti-pagan speech given before a religiously mixed audience by Zacharias Scholasticus at the funeral of his friend Menas (*Vit. Sev.* 45). Evidently, this speech outraged many of the students in attendance.

40. On the circles of Ammonius Saccas and Hypatia see Watts, *City and School*, 151–68, 187–203, as well as M. Dzielska, *Hypatia of Alexandria*, trans. F. Lyra (Cambridge, MA, 1995).

FIGURE 3. Auditoria, baths, and latrine, Kom el-Dikka, Alexandria. Photo by Manasi Watts.

When Paralius arrived in Alexandria, he found himself immersed in this world. Though acquainted with his teacher Horapollon and his colleague Asclepiodotus, Paralius had a hard time adjusting to his new environment. Perhaps sensing this, Horapollon took an interest in making Paralius feel at ease, even going so far as to accompany him to religious services. Nevertheless, Paralius remained uncomfortable and decided to take a step that his brothers Democharus and Proclus dreaded. Paralius sought out his third brother Athanasius.[41] His older brothers treated Athanasius as a pariah. Despite a solid classical education including professional training at the renowned law school of Berytus, he had converted to Christianity while on a business trip to Alexandria.[42] He proceeded to renounce the world and take up residence at the Enaton, a large anti-Chalcedonian monastery so named because it was located nine miles west of Alexandria.[43]

41. *Vit. Sev.* 15.
42. *Vit. Sev.* 14.
43. *Vit. Sev.* 15. The "monastery" of the Enaton was actually a conglomeration of smaller *koinobia*, each with its own church and interests. On the Enaton, see P. van Cauwenbergh, *Étude sur les moines*

Before he left for Egypt, Paralius's brothers forbade him to contact Athanasius, an injunction that one must assume they had communicated to Horapollon as well.[44] Despite this ban, Paralius sought out his brother. During the visit, the two brothers were joined by Athanasius's friend and fellow ascetic Stephen, a former sophist responsible for Athanasius's conversion to Christianity. As one would expect, their conversation turned to theology and the two monks raised a series of objections to Paralius's pagan beliefs. Paralius could not respond to these points and Stephen encouraged him to seek guidance from Horapollon and his colleagues Ammonius, Isidore, Heraiscus, and Asclepiodotus.[45]

When Paralius next visited his brother, he admitted that he had found his teachers' answers to Stephen's comments unpersuasive. However, the story that Asclepiodotus's child had been conceived through the intervention of the shrine of Isis in Menouthis still made Paralius trust in the power of the old gods.[46] This popular miracle story was evidently repeated in the Alexandrian schools and in the communities to which the students who attended them returned.[47] The Enaton monks asked Paralius to request from his teacher written proof that Asclepiodotus's wife was lactating; if such a statement could not be gotten, they held that the account of this event must be false.

Despite these conversations, Paralius continued to behave in much the same way as other members of Horapollon's school. Some time after his second visit to Athanasius, probably in the spring of 486, Paralius visited the incubation shrine of Isis in Menouthis, which was popular among Alexandrian students.[48] While he was there, the goddess appeared to him in a vision and identified one of his classmates as a magician.[49] When Paralius mentioned this to his fellow students, he was told that the student he had so identified had a similar vision in which Paralius was marked as a magician. Paralius then traveled back to the Isis shrine, made the appropriate sacrifices, and asked for clarification. The goddess, however, failed to reappear.

Enraged, Paralius returned to Alexandria and launched into a series of attacks

---

d'Égypte: depuis le Concile de Chalcédoine, jusqu'à l'invasion arabe (Paris-Louvain, 1914), 64–72. See also J. Gascou, "The Enaton," *Coptic Encyclopedia* 954–57.

44. *Vit. Sev.* 15.
45. *Vit. Sev.* 16.
46. *Vit. Sev.* 16–19.
47. This is suggested by *Vit. Sev.* 36–37.
48. For this practice within the larger religious context of later Roman Egypt see, in particular, the comments of D. Frankfurter, *Religion in Roman Egypt: Assimilation and Resistance* (Princeton, 1998), 40–41, 162–69. Note the objections of Alan Cameron, "Poets and Pagans in Byzantine Egypt," in *Egypt in the Byzantine World, 300–700*, ed. R. Bagnall (Cambridge, 2007) 26–28; as well as the comments about Zacharias's account in appendix 2.
49. *Vit. Sev.* 20–21.

against pagan gods and his teachers who worshipped them. He publicly mocked Horapollon, Asclepiodotus, Heraiscus, Ammonius, and Isidore for their devotion to the gods and, specifically, for their interest in the shrine of Isis at Menouthis. The shrine itself received particular criticism. He said its priestess was no more than a common prostitute who behaved lubriciously with anyone who approached her.[50]

These verbal attacks cut to the core of the scholarly community to which Paralius belonged. He had assailed the reputations of the teachers to whom he and his fellow students were bound and for whose interests they were expected to fight. His use of rather crude sexual innuendos to characterize the priestess of the Menouthis Isis shrine was both more vulgar and potentially more widely offensive.[51] His peers knew of this temple from the stories about Asclepiodotus that were circulating, but some of them also had personal experiences with the priestess. With these personal attacks, Paralius had clearly overstepped the bounds of scholastic decorum.

Paralius's behavior provoked a predictable response. On the following Friday, a day when Horapollon lectured from his home and the lecture halls were used for philosophical discussions, the students of Horapollon who had heard of Paralius's outbursts set upon him and beat him. Paralius just managed to escape them and fled into a small crowd of Christian students who were waiting for their philosophy lecture to begin.[52] Three of these were student-*philoponoi,* Christian associates of the Enaton, the monastery to which Paralius's brother belonged. These students were well known in the porticos surrounding the lecture halls. They seem to have asked their classmates about their religious affiliations and rhetorical preferences and, if these students answered unsatisfactorily, the student-*philoponoi* then offered religious instruction as well as appropriate Christian rhetorical models.[53] This exercise, they believed, helped to counteract the pagan influences in the curriculum and religious environment of the Alexandrian schools. Consequently, when Paralius fled to the group of student-*philoponoi,* Horapollon's outraged students perhaps sensed that a tangle with a group of outsiders tied to the Enaton would cause significantly more trouble than the beating of an insolent first-year student. They permitted the *philoponoi* to whisk Paralius away.

With Paralius in their hands, these Christian students set about transforming his beating from punishment of an obnoxious teenager into a religious persecution launched by a hostile pagan intellectual establishment. Such a view of the recent events was, of course, consistent with their natural suspicion of pagan teachers,

50. *Vit. Sev.* 22–23.
51. The iconography associated with the Isaic function of ensuring marital happiness and fertility often involved nude images of the goddess, the sexual significance of which could be deliberately misinterpreted. On Isis in Roman Egypt see Frankfurter, *Religion in Roman Egypt,* 99–106.
52. *Vit. Sev.* 23.
53. *Vit. Sev.* 13.

but it is notable nonetheless how brazenly the circumstances of the beating were altered. Writing later about the event, Zacharias Scholasticus, one of Paralius's *philoponoi* rescuers, blamed Horapollon for the beating and described wresting Paralius from the "murderous hands" of his attackers.[54] He also praised the wounds Paralius had suffered for Christ. Each charge was plainly untrue. Paralius, who had never gone to a church service, could hardly be said to be a Christian and the beating was deliberately scheduled so that it occurred at a time when Horapollon was away from the classrooms (and could easily deny any involvement). Nevertheless, the inconvenient reality of the situation was ignored in the *philoponoi* portrayal of Paralius.

Once this group arrived at the Enaton, the monks came to agree that Paralius had suffered unjust injuries for Christ. Led by the head of the monastery, they sent a delegation to explain the situation to the Alexandrian bishop, Peter Mongus. This was a significant step because Peter had become an extremely suspect figure among the anti-Chalcedonian leadership of the city. Indeed, he had at times faced open revolts of anti-Chalcedonian clergy and ascetics. The Enaton had long been a stronghold of anti-Chalcedonian opinion in Alexandria's western suburbs.[55] Peter welcomed the opportunity to cooperate with them in order to turn Christian attention away from the Christological division of the city and towards a common pagan enemy.

In Peter Mongus's hands, Paralius's beating underwent a further interpretation. Initially, Peter supported the student-*philoponoi* line by sending Paralius and a crowd of Christian supporters to the prefect of Egypt with a written endorsement of their complaint. In the meantime, the head of the Enaton spread word in the city about the "persecution" of Paralius and the anti-Christian actions of the Alexandrian teachers. By that afternoon, even before the court heard Paralius's complaint, elements of the Christian population of the city had risen up against Horapollon and his colleagues. The teachers fled in the face of this popular outcry and, following Paralius's hearing, the prefect refused to call them back to the city (presumably for their own safety).[56]

On Friday, Peter Mongus simply put his authority behind the student-*philoponoi* version of events. On Saturday, however, he began to take ownership of this event for himself. That morning, Paralius and the Enaton monks returned and offered to show Peter the Isaic shrine in Menouthis. Seizing upon this unique opportunity, Peter Mongus organized a Saturday raid against the Menouthan temple. Paralius was pressed into service as a guide and led a crew of anti-Chalcedonian

---

54. *Vit. Sev.* 24. Note the phrase ܐܝܕܝܐ ܕܩܛܘܠܐ.

55. For this perspective see *Vit. Long.* 29–37, text in T. Orlandi, ed., *Vite dei Monaci Phife Longino*, Testi e Documenti per lo Studio dell'Antichita 51 (Milan, 1975).

56. *Vit. Sev.* 26–27.

monks from the Enaton and Chalcedonian monks from the eastern suburb Canopus to the small house-temple.[57] By the end of Saturday afternoon, this mob had sacked the shrine, captured the priest in charge, and sent a written description of the idols contained within it to Peter Mongus.[58] Some members of the raiding party stayed behind in Menouthis to wait for a convoy that would take the objects back to Alexandria the next morning. The rest returned to the city.

On Sunday morning, Peter Mongus treated the assembled crowd to a magnificent spectacle. He walked into the church to hear the congregation chanting "Psychapollon," a play on Horapollon's name that poked fun at his soul-destroying teaching.[59] When it came time for the sermon, the patriarch recounted the "persecution" of Paralius by pagans and glorified the Christian reaction to this. He spoke about the raid on the Isis shrine in Menouthis, a pagan temple that was anything but unknown in nearby Alexandria, and read the description of the idols that had been sent to him.[60] He then led the congregation outside and supervised as they "brought out all of the pagan idols that they could find in the baths or in private houses, placed them down and burned them."[61]

At the conclusion of this bonfire, the camel convoy from Menouthis arrived. Peter ordered the camels to proceed into the center of the city, unload their cargo and display it to the excited mob of Christians that had assembled.[62] Peter was joined by the prefect of Egypt, the chief of the corps of guards, the municipal senate, and the wealthy property owners of the city.[63] When the parade and display of Menouthis miscellany finished, Peter ordered the captured priest of Isis forward to endure the jeers of the crowd and to undergo a mocking inquisition from Peter. As Sunday afternoon came to a close, the crowd lavished praises on Peter, the civic notables, and the emperor Zeno before dispersing.[64]

---

57. In a recent article questioning the veracity of Zacharias's account, Alan Cameron has argued that Zacharias "does not characterize the building as a temple" ("Poets and Pagans in Byzantine Egypt," 26–27). The Syriac is, however, ambiguous. It says simply that the company of monks and students "came to a certain ܒܝܬܐ" (ܐܝܟ ܠܒܝܬܐ ܗܢܐ). ܒܝܬܐ can mean "house," but it also can mean "temple," "church," or, more abstractly, simply "place" or "room." (Payne Smith, 43 col. 1). The context in which Zacharias uses the term suggests that "temple" is certainly a possible interpretation. It is also worth noting that the late antique concept of a temple differed from ours. In the fourth century, a register of buildings in the five districts of Alexandria listed 2,478 "temples" within the city limits (P. M. Fraser, "A Syriac *Notitia Urbis Alexandrinae*," *JEA* 37 [1951], 103–8). This number is inconceivable without including smaller temples like that described by Zacharias.

58. *Vit. Sev.* 32–33.

59. *Vit. Sev.* 32.

60. *Vit. Sev.* 33. On the reputation of the shrine among Alexandrian Christians see, particularly, Sophronuis, *Miracles of St. Cyrus and John*, 24–25.

61. *Vit. Sev.* 33.

62. *Vit. Sev.* 33–35.

63. The crowd is described in *Vit. Sev.* 33.

64. *Vit. Sev.* 35.

In the end, Peter Mongus and his supporters had capitalized upon Paralius's Friday confrontation with his student peers to present an impromptu weekend of anti-pagan activity. Once Peter saw the chance to raid the Menouthis Isis shrine, it seems that he carefully stage-managed the entire affair. In fact, this followed an old and familiar script, evoking the events of Theophilus's famous raid on the Alexandrian Serapeum in 391.[65] In both cases, the temples were patronized by pagan intellectuals and their sack was precipitated by pagan student violence against Christians.[66] Both sacks were authorized by the bishop of the city and each culminated in a parade and public destruction of the religious objects found on site, which were led by the bishop and prominent members of the community. The Serapeum destruction had helped to establish bishop Theophilus's ferocious anti-pagan reputation, and Peter Mongus, whose political position was far from secure in 486, evidently hoped to bask in some reflected glory.[67]

This sequence unfolded in a short forty-eight-hour span. In that time, one can witness a progression of events that escalated intercommunal tensions in the city and transformed the meaning of Paralius's encounter with his classmates. On Friday afternoon, the punitive beating of an overly assertive and disruptive first-year student served merely to defend the scholastic hierarchy that held a small group of students together. By Sunday evening, however, this isolated incident had evolved from a disciplinary beating within a scholastic setting into an act of religious violence with implications for the Christian and pagan communities in Alexandria and its suburbs. What is more remarkable, however, is the way the meaning of these events had been constructed. When hands were first placed upon Paralius on that Friday afternoon, the reason for and meaning of this assault must have been clear to both Paralius and his attackers. When Paralius fled from his attackers to the student-*philoponoi* and agreed to accompany them to the Enaton, he permitted the events to be redefined, first as religious persecution of a Christian by pagan students, and later as an act sanctioned by "soul-destroying" pagan teachers. The scope of the event again expanded when Peter Mongus intervened. The beating of Paralius now represented a link in the chain of pagan-Christian confrontations that had helped to define the Alexandrian patriarchate.

The speed of this evolution is particularly impressive. In two days' time, Paralius, a previously nondescript teenager, had become a figure whose importance resonated because of the preexisting communal histories that illustrated the par-

---

65. For a description see Socrates, *HE* 5.16 and, more vividly, Rufinus, *HE* 11.22. For a survey of the ancient accounts of the fall of the Serapeum and its aftermath see J. Schwartz, "La fin du Serapeum d'Alexandrie," *American Studies in Papyrology*, vol. 1, *Essays in Honor of C. Bradford Welles* (New Haven, 1966), 97–111.

66. On the teachers involved in the Serapeum incident, see Watts, *City and School*, 188–92.

67. For Peter's position in 486, see Watts, *City and School*, 219; and C. Haas, *Alexandria in Late Antiquity: Topography and Social Conflict* (Baltimore, 1997), 328–29.

ticular virtues, vices, and modes of behavior appropriate for students, lay Christians affiliated with monasteries, and the Alexandrian bishop. The students of Horapollon knew Paralius to be an aggressive and disrespectful student who questioned the integrity of respected teachers and institutions in a particularly vulgar manner. According to the informal code of scholastic behavior, these attacks merited an aggressive, even violent response. Under different circumstances, Paralius's beating would have been ignored beyond the schools. However, to the student-*philoponoi*, a group with an inimical relationship to pagan teachers and their students, Paralius's narrow escape from a murderous mob of his peers confirmed their historical suspicion of Alexandrian pagan intellectuals. Peter Mongus, by contrast, saw Paralius through a lens fashioned by the historical traditions of the Alexandrian patriarchate. Peter saw that this pagan violence could be presented as a moment like that faced by his great predecessor Theophilus. He was interested in making the reality of his contemporary situation correspond to the paradigms established by previous patriarchs. In this way, Peter was both responding to the historical traditions of the community he headed and reshaping the present to resemble this idealized past.

At various times, the members of Horapollon's intellectual circle, the student-*philoponoi*, and the leadership of the Alexandrian church all relied upon the historical foundations of their communities and the value structures these supported to shape their interpretations of present events.[68] The contradictions between these interpretations highlight the differences between the historical traditions that defined these groups. Nevertheless, in each context, the reaction to Paralius's situation was quick and the communal understanding of its significance was almost immediately appreciated. This shows a remarkable awareness within each group of the way in which past (and present) events supported the core values each group held.

Perhaps just as interesting as the ways in which these group identities shaped perceptions of present events is the way in which the events surrounding Paralius were later incorporated into communal historical narratives. Despite the pageantry of the parade of idols from Menouthis, Peter Mongus's anti-pagan activities in 486 did little to shape his historical legacy. Later literary sources, including a history written by the former *philoponos* Zacharias Scholasticus, remember Peter

---

68. It is important to distinguish between the formative processes at work during and after this riot and Halbwachs's concept of "collective memory." As this study will show, these communal histories are both more fluid and less totalizing than that proposed by Halbwachs. Indeed, one of the most intriguing facets of this riot is the degree to which one can see negotiation between two distinct sets of values illustrated by communal histories (see chapter 5, below). For the general theoretical debates surrounding the conception of "collective memory," see M. Halbwachs, *Les Cadres Sociaux de la Mémoire* (Paris, 1925); J. Assmann, *Das kulturelle Gedächtnis: Schrift, Erinnerung und politische Identität in frühren Hochkulturen* (Munich, 1992); E. Castelli, *Martyrdom and Memory: Early Christian Culture Making* (New York, 2004), 11–32.

instead as a controversial and misunderstood champion of anti-Chalcedonian orthodoxy.[69] The legacy of the riot lived on within the circle of student-*philoponoi*. In the early 490s, Zacharias Scholasticus wrote a text designed to assert their ownership of this event.[70] He reflects particularly upon the student-*philoponoi* and the religious situation in the schools. For the pagan philosophers, sophists, and grammarians who taught in Alexandria, this riot and the events that followed it forced them to reconsider the roles they played in the world. As time passed, their focus turned to an imperial investigation that followed the riot and its use of torture and coercion to persecute Alexandrian pagan teachers.[71] This led to a dramatic recalibration of the communal past within this group of intellectuals. Alexandrian traditions about passive pagan philosophical resistance to Christian persecution became popular and even influenced some of the teaching done in Neoplatonic classrooms.

Paralius's beating is of little significance to the larger history of the eastern Mediterranean. No great empires fell, no cities changed hands, no one died, and much of what transpired was quickly forgotten even by the general Alexandrian population. Nevertheless, our record of the events of those few days in 486 sheds considerable new light upon the functioning of late antique intellectual and spiritual communities. Paralius's experiences make it possible to appreciate what could initially attract a person to a community, how one joined, and the importance of conformity within these groups. We can also see how these groups used the past to provide practical illustration of the ideals, beliefs, and behaviors they valued. We can further

---

69. On his legacy see Zacharias, *HE* 6.4–6. Originally written in Greek, Zacharias's *Ecclesiastical History* has come down to us in a Syriac epitome. It makes up books 3–6 of a larger Syriac historical work, first edited and published by E. W. Brooks, *Historia Ecclesiastica Zachariae Rhetori vulgo adscripta*, CSCO vol. 83–84; 87–88 (Louvain-Paris, 1921–29). For additional bibliography see G. Krüger and K. Ahrens, *Die sogenannte Kirchengeschichte des Zacharias Rhetor* (Leipzig, 1899); P. Allen, "Zachariah Scholasticus and the *Historia Ecclesiastica* of Evagrius Scholasticus," *JTS* n.s. 31 (1980), 471–88; and P. Blaudeau, *Alexandrie et Constantinople (451-491): de l'Histoire à la Géo-Ecclésiologie* (Rome, 2006), 581–617. Ancient evidence differs as to the exact nature of Zacharias's text—a confusion that extends even to the Syriac *Chronicle* that contains the epitome of his work. In an appendix to Book Two, Zacharias's work is described as "the *Chronicle* of Zachariah, a rhetor, which he wrote in Greek to a man named Eupraxius." The words "*Ecclesiastical History* of Zachariah" are found at the top of the pages in Books Three through Six of this same manuscript, however. In addition, Brit. Mus. Add. MS. 12154, fol. 151 and 158 preserve two fragments of Zacharias's text that are described as from the "*Ecclesiastical History* of Zachariah." Although Zacharias's historical work evidently resembled and is often described as a *Chronicle*, I will, for the sake of clarity, use the title *Ecclesiastical History* in this study.

70. This has come down as the first section of the *Life of Severus*. For this material and its distinction from the rest of the text see E. Watts, "Winning the Intracommunal Dialogues: Zacharias Scholasticus' *Life of Severus*," *JECS* 13 (2005), 437–64.

71. Damascius's view on this material is expressed in *Vit. Is.* 117A–C and discussed in chapter 3 below.

witness the degree to which inclusion in the community relied upon an acceptance of a shared interpretation of the past. It also becomes clear, however, that a high degree of interpretative flexibility existed. If social conditions changed, almost forgotten traditions could be revived or new ones created that better conveyed a set of virtues and ideal behaviors appropriate to the present circumstances.

While this discussion has summarized Paralius's scholastic career, much remains to be said about the groups involved in these events and the ways in which traditions about the past shaped their behavior.[72] At least since the work of Edward Gibbon, the interaction of classically-trained intellectuals, Christian ascetics, and bishops has preoccupied many scholars of the later Roman world.[73] This is with good reason. In their own distinct ways, people belonging to each of these groups created, sustained, and challenged many of the structures that made the late antique world functional. Of these three, intellectuals enjoyed the most long-standing positions of influence. Since the advent of the Roman imperial system, teachers provided the education (*paideia*) that shaped the minds and characters of the Roman cultivated class. The value of this training was widely recognized. *Paideia* armed students with an arsenal of rhetorical skills and literary references shared, at least ostensibly, by the elite of the Roman world. It also bestowed upon its possessors a certain refined sensibility and awareness of the essential virtues that defined one as a gentleman.[74] Later Roman intellectuals provided their charges with an outline of how they were to act, how they were to treat other men, and what role they were to play in their communities. By creating a mode of expression and set of social expectations common to the Roman imperial elite, *paideia* and the intellectuals who passed along its values helped to sustain the cohesion of the empire.

The formative role played by intellectuals was an occasional source of tension. Intellectuals stood out as some of the most outspoken pagans in the Roman East and, as Christianity became increasingly important in the Roman world, the interests and values of pagan teachers seemed increasingly out of step with the goals of a Christian empire. In absolute terms, their numbers may have been small,[75] but their social position, literary habits, and intellectual authority made these pagan intellectuals disproportionately influential.[76] Most refrained from using their positions to publicly advocate for polytheism or defend specific cultic prac-

---

72. For the role of tradition in linking past and present in a way that gives past experience meaning in present circumstances see D. Lowenthal, *The Past is a Foreign Country* (Cambridge, 1985).

73. E.g., Edward Gibbon, *The Decline and Fall of the Roman Empire*, 1.37.

74. For this line of thought see P. Brown, *Power and Persuasion: Towards a Christian Empire* (Madison, WI, 1992), 122; M. Bloomer, "Schooling in Persona: Imagination and Subordination in Roman Education," *Classical Antiquity* 16.1 (1997), 59–63.

75. Alan Cameron, "Poets and Pagans," 21–46.

76. It is notable, for example, how much of P. Chuvin's *Chronicle of the Last Pagans*, trans. B. A. Archer (Cambridge, Mass., 1990) focuses upon intellectuals. Even the ecumenical survey of F. Trom-

tices, but the environment they fostered provoked some Christian students to complain that, in their schools, "it is hard to avoid being carried away by (the gods') devotees and adherents."[77] Emperors too recognized that teachers could affect the religious attitudes of their students and regulated the activities of intellectuals in order to further their own religious agendas.[78] To survive in this environment, pagan intellectuals needed to maintain a balance between their personal theological ideas and the larger social role they were expected to play.

Ascetics often seem as emblematic of late antiquity's dynamic Christian social order as pagan intellectuals are of its classical cultural traditions. Ascetics, late Roman Christian authors tell us, lived the life of angels on the earth by "forsaking their homes and families . . . in order to be anxious only about the things of the Lord."[79] The supposed purity of their thought and spiritual inspiration of their actions allowed monks to claim great authority within Christian communities. They are often described as spiritual mentors and mediators who encouraged individual Christians to be pious and offered to intervene on their behalf with the divine. A range of late antique sources speak of ascetics playing a concrete social role as well. Authors speak about monks who resolve disputes, advocate for the poor, intervene with imperial administrators, and even advise the emperor.[80] While it is often quite difficult to disentangle the real activities of Christian ascetics from the literary treatments that idealize their conduct, there can be little doubt that some ascetics played these important public roles at least some of the time.[81]

The public involvement of Christian ascetics was not always for the best. The

---

bley (*Hellenic Religion and Christianization AD 320–529*, 2 vols. [Leiden, 1993–94]) spends more time on intellectuals than on any other late pagan group.

77. Gregory Nazianzen, *Panegyric on Basil* 21. This complaint is echoed over a century and a quarter later by Zacharias Scholasticus in *Amm.* ll. 27–32.

78. The two most notable instances occur under Julian and Justinian. For Julian see J. Matthews, *Laying Down the Law: A Study of the Theodosian Code* (New Haven, 2000), 274–77 and T. Banchich, "Julian's School Laws: *Cod. Theod.* 13.3.5 and *Ep.* 42," *The Ancient World* 24 (1993), 5–14. For Justinian see E. Watts, "Justinian, Malalas, and the End of Athenian Philosophical Teaching in A.D. 529," *JRS* 94 (2004), 168–82.

79. Theodoret, *Cure of Hellenic Maladies*, 3.91–92. On the *Cure of Hellenic Maladies* see now the important study of N. Siniossoglou, *Plato and Theodoret: The Christian Appropriation of Platonic Philosophy and the Hellenic Intellectual Resistance* (Cambridge 2008).

80. For resolving disputes see, for example, *Life of Theodore of Sykeon* 114; advocacy for the poor: Theodoret, *RH* 17.3; intervening with imperial officials: Theodoret, *RH* 12.7, 13.7, cf. John Chrysostom, *Homilies on the Statues* 17.2.6; advising the emperor: *Life of Daniel the Stylite*, 51, 55, 56, 71. For analysis of this phenomenon see P. Brown, "The Rise and Function of the Holy Man in Late Antiquity," *JRS* 61 (1971) 80–101; as well as his later reassessment, "The Rise and Function of the Holy Man in Late Antiquity, 1971–1997," *JECS* 6.3 (1998), 353–76.

81. On the variety of activities presented in literary portraits of holy men see, for example, M. Whitby, "Maro the Dendrite: An Anti-Social Holy Man?" in *Homo Viator: Classical Essays for John Bramble*, ed. Michael Whitby, Philip Hardie, and Mary Whitby (Bristol, 1987), 309–17.

same purity of spirit that enabled monks to play a public role also could be construed as liberating them from the bonds of social convention. For this reason, monks sometimes served as shock troops in late antique Christian battles against heresy and paganism. Many such incidents feature in the exaggerated and formulaic literary creations that celebrate ideal ascetic behavior.[82] Often these texts describe somewhat restrained demonstrations and protests, but credible accounts of ascetic religious violence also come down from late antiquity. They range from the Egyptian abbot who burglarized and threw urine at the house of a local noble suspected of pagan activity[83] to the bands of monks held responsible for destroying temples and terrorizing villagers in the Syrian countryside in the 380s.[84] The achievements of leading monks brought new recruits to monasteries and prompted laymen to incorporate ascetic discipline into their lives in the world. Taken to extremes, these new sets of social behaviors threatened to disrupt the basic rhythms of social life. In much the same way that pagan intellectuals could seem to be holding back the development of a new Christian order, so too did Christian ascetics sometimes appear overly eager to press for the emergence of an orthodox, fully Christian empire. Like pagan intellectual circles, ascetic communities needed to strike a balance between the particular ideas that were valued inside their group and the actions that their members and associates took in the wider world.

Bishops, too, represent essential but problematic fixtures of the later Roman social and religious landscape. Some bishops had an ascetic background,[85] but most could not claim the sort of charismatic authority that belonged to ascetics. Episcopal authority derived instead from the recognition that the ecclesiastical establishment bestowed upon individual leaders. Often these men were already figures of considerable local political importance and were expected to advocate publicly for the interests of their congregations. The real authority of a bishop, however, derived from the role that he played within a Christian community. The bishop supervised Christians' religious growth by welcoming newcomers into the church, presiding over their baptisms, and preaching sermons that guided their conduct.

Christians expected leadership from their bishops. This could have a political

---

82. On the formulaic nature of some such mentions see D. Brakke, *Demons and the Making of the Monk: Spiritual Combat in Early Christianity* (Cambridge, MA, 2006), 213–39.

83. This occurred during the controversial interactions between the abbot Shenoute and Gessius. Important in understanding this conflict is S. Emmel, "From the Other Side of the Nile: Shenute and Panopolis," in *Perspectives on Panopolis: An Egyptian Town from Alexander the Great to the Arab Conquest*, ed. A. Egberts, B. Muhs, and J. van der Vliet (Leiden, 2002), 95–113.

84. E.g., Libanius, *Or.* 30.46–47.

85. John Chrysostom of Constantinople and John the Almsgiver in Alexandria are two of the best known such bishops. For a Western parallel note the bishops who came from the ascetic community at Lérins (e.g., Hilary, *Vita Honorati* 17.24).

component, but any such activity could not conflict with more important ecclesiastical duties. Some of this was because, in spite of many premature obituaries, the old civic order continued to function effectively in the late antique Roman East.[86] In most cases, bishops worked alongside this old power structure and were either supported or restrained by it. More important, however, was the Christian belief that the spiritual authority of a bishop derived from the inspiration of the Holy Spirit. If the bishop truly enjoyed this spiritual connection, his personal conduct would reflect a similar divine inspiration. Too great an involvement in political affairs could make a bishop look base or power-hungry. His social role was thus constrained both by political circumstances and by a set of Christian expectations that he could influence but not completely reshape.

Communal history helped intellectuals, ascetics, and bishops distinguish between appropriate and inappropriate behaviors. By the 480s, these groups all enjoyed extremely long histories and had developed sophisticated mechanisms for both preserving and communicating their collective pasts. Indeed, it is important to emphasize how deep into late antiquity we are when Paralius's beating takes place. The Christian empire inaugurated by Constantine was then only a few decades younger than the American Republic of Washington is now. In 486, the Western Roman Empire no longer existed as a political entity, the last openly pagan emperor had died nearly a century and a quarter before, and ascetics (the youngest of these three groups) had been a presence in the cities and countryside of Egypt and the East for two hundred years. And yet the Alexandria in which the deep pasts of intellectuals, ascetics, and bishops intersected with present realities remained a religiously heterogeneous place. It was a city in which pagan philosophers fascinated by a lock of the goddess Isis's hair floating down a Nile canal walked by Christian ascetics mulling the consequences of the Council of Chalcedon. When these men passed each other, they carried with them the memory of previous generations of intellectuals, ascetics, and bishops who had interacted with one another in both exemplary and shameful ways.

On one level, the riot is then an idiosyncratically Alexandrian story born from the unique dynamics of an old and crowded city. And yet there are two reasons that one should not discount the wider historical significance of this event or dismiss it as yet another example of Alexandrian (or Egyptian) exceptionalism. First, excluding the Alexandria bishop, the figures involved in the riot are largely non-Egyptian. Paralius is from Aphrodisias. His teacher Horapollon and his colleagues are from places as diverse as Caria, Egypt, Syria, and Greece. Paralius's student rescuers and their supporters in the Enaton monastery come from a wide

---

86. For premature obituaries of the traditional civic elite see Libanius, *Or.* 49. For a modern corrective see A. Laniado, *Recherches sur les notables municipaux dans l'empire protobyzantin* (Paris, 2002).

range of cities across the Levant and Asia Minor. Alexandria represented the site of this conflict, but the people involved arrived there from a host of other locations and brought with them a broad set of interests.

There is also nothing specifically Egyptian about the notions of the past that influenced these groups or the mechanisms through which they were passed along. As this study will show, intellectual circles across the Mediterranean had used many of the same mechanisms to preserve historical traditions and instill a sense of community among students since at least the fourth century B.C. The Alexandrian riot may represent a particularly clear moment of conflict between these traditions and the ideas of the wider world, but neither the traditions themselves nor the process of their transmission are particularly exceptional.

The same is broadly true of the historical material that circulated among the ascetics and their associates involved in the riot. As will be shown in chapter 5, there is considerable overlap between the ideas and traditions that circulated in late fifth-century Alexandrian and Palestinian anti-Chalcedonian monasteries. In addition, the sharing of this material within monastic circles and the transmission of it to a wider public followed patterns that can be documented as early as the second quarter of the fourth century. Here too, the Alexandrian riot reveals not an exceptional community but only a particularly clear instance in which these traditions influenced behavior.

The Alexandrian episcopate, of course, poses a different challenge. It did, in fact, create a distinctive historical discourse that centered on the actions of leading Egyptians and defined the scope of episcopal action in Egyptian terms. Even here, though, Alexandrian bishops faced popular expectations and constraints on their behavior much like those encountered by bishops elsewhere. While Alexandrians drew upon a specifically Egyptian discourse to define the appropriate spheres of episcopal action, bishops elsewhere shared their broader concerns and strategies.

This suggests that the intellectuals, ascetics, and Alexandrian bishop involved in the riot must be appreciated against the larger backdrop of late Roman society. Consequently, before embarking upon a specific study of these actors, it is important first to understand the ways in which similarly constituted intellectual, ascetic, and ecclesiastical groups used the past to shape their communities in late antiquity. Such an approach allows one to understand how, broadly speaking, communal histories contributed to the architecture of later Roman social and religious groups. At the same time, it will permit a better understanding of the relevance of these small actors to general trends in the larger cultural history of late antiquity.

While each section of this study ultimately focuses upon the Alexandrian environment of the 480s, Paralius's beating will serve as a framework around which to construct a discussion of the ways in which traditions of the past assisted in the cultural construction of late antique intellectual, ascetic, and ecclesiastical communities. Though distinct, these three studies will proceed in a similar fashion; they will begin with a general exploration of the place of historical traditions within communities of the sort found in late-fifth-century Alexandria. They will then move to a more specific discussion focusing upon the traditions operative in the Alexandrian communities active in the events of 486.

This study will serve two purposes. First, a more developed understanding of the personalities and communities involved in this riot should make clear how communal ideas about a shared past helped to shape the interactions between pagan intellectuals, Christians involved with monasteries, and the Alexandrian church. Second, and most importantly, this discussion will show that the social and religious changes that seized the late Roman world did little to disrupt the patterns of interpersonal communication that enabled individuals to identify with a particular community. Despite the rise of Christianity and the greater institutional organization that is often seen as characteristic of the later Roman Empire, personal connections and individual interactions remained the most important ways that people came to understand their proper place in the world. Ultimately, it is hoped that this study can bring us a bit closer to the ordinary human faces and human voices that played such an important part in the gradual evolution of late antique society.

PART ONE

Historical Discourse in Intellectual Communities

Paralius returned to Alexandria . . . He mocked Horapollon, Asclepiodotus, Heraiscus, Ammonius, and Isidore (who finished his life being recognized as a magician and troublemaker) . . . But the students of Horapollon, who were subject to the folly of paganism, could not support the sarcasms and reproaches of Paralius. So they set upon him in the school where they all studied.

ZACHARIAS, VIT. SEV. 22–23

AS ZACHARIAS DESCRIBES IT, a modern reader may be forgiven for thinking of Paralius's beating as a petty over-reaction to a rather insignificant set of perceived slights. An ancient audience would have seen things differently. The education of elite students took place within a hierarchical social environment that ensured the stratification of teachers, teaching assistants, and students through formal rites of passage and informal hazing. While intellectual achievement was prized, loyalty to the teachings of the school, the person of the teacher, and one's fellow students represented the foremost social virtue in this environment. Neither Zacharias nor his audience would have quarreled with this basic scholastic value structure (indeed, in a later section of the *Life of Severus,* Zacharias explains how a Christian study circle created a similar scholastic hierarchy).[1] Instead, as shown by the passage with which this section begins, Zacharias levels a more nuanced criticism. He objects not to the loyalty that Horapollon's students showed to their teacher but to the fact that loyalty to teachers like Horapollon and the "magician" Asclepiodotus was misplaced.[2] Zacharias hoped his readers would appreciate that the personal corruption of these professors corresponded to the corruption of their teachings. Horapollon's students, who were "subject to the follies of paganism,"[3] worked as unwitting agents of disreputable men and their violence naturally

---

1. Zacharias's description of the Christian reading circle he set up with Severus in Berytus seems to evoke a school (*Vit. Sev.* 55–56).

2. For this idea, note E. Watts, "Winning the Intracommunal Dialogues: Zacharias Scholasticus' *Life of Severus,*" *JECS* 13 (2005), 437–64.

3. ܗܘܘ ܐܝܠܝܢ ܕܛܥܝܘܬܐ ܕܚܢܦܘܬܐ ܗܘܢ (*Vit. Sev.* 23).

grew out of a misplaced loyalty to flawed ideas. They were corrupted youths and, as such, their teachers bore responsibility for their actions.

Zacharias's comments highlight the degree to which the behavior of teachers and their students was thought to reflect their teaching. By connecting the bad behavior of Horapollon's students with the bad doctrines that they were taught, Zacharias reprises an old, well-tested method of attacking an intellectual circle. In his criticisms, Zacharias does not reach particularly far back—he speaks only about events of the past decade or so—but the pattern he follows highlights an important part of ancient intellectual life. Though we tend to examine ancient philosophy in doctrinal terms and ancient rhetoric in practical terms, their study was a profoundly personal experience in which the doctrines and skills taught were often difficult to disentangle from the character of the teacher.[4] In essence, the successful teacher explained ideas about the world and one's ideal actions in it while simultaneously serving as a living exemplar of the doctrines he taught. If a teacher lived ethically, his way of life illustrated the practical application of abstract notions that he explained in class. However, if his behaviors did not correspond to the ideals he explained, a professor could reasonably expect the contradiction to be noticed and pointed out. Indeed, from a very early point in the history of Greek education, teachers appreciated the correlation between their personal reputations and their scholarly credibility.

The establishment of schools that remained intact for generations lent an additional importance to historical traditions about the actions and moral character of past scholastic leaders. Within the Academy, for example, the legacy of Plato served to validate the Academic intellectual project.[5] At the same time, differently constructed historical legacies of Plato and his successors were used by Peripatetics to undercut the legitimacy of contemporary Academic ideas.[6] As Zacharias Scholasticus, the early Academics, and the Peripatetics all realized, information about the character and achievements of a school's leaders (both past and present) defined perceptions of the institution and its doctrines. For this reason, the historical traditions that contained this information were worth preserving in a reliable fashion and worth defending with vigor.

This section of our study will explore how representations of the past communicated the distinct identities and achievements of ancient intellectual groups. This examination will have two parts. The first chapter discusses the importance of historical traditions within a range of ancient intellectual environments. Begin-

---

4. A connection between professorial behavior and effectiveness in teaching was made most famously in the emperor Julian's teaching legislation (*C. Th.* 13.3.5; cf. Quintilian, *Inst. Or.* 12.1.1).

5. On this point see E. Watts, "Creating the Academy: Historical Discourse and the Shape of Community in the Old Academy," *JHS* 127 (2007), 106–22.

6. Ibid.

ning with Plato's Academy in the fourth century B.C. and ending with the schools of Iamblichus and Chrysanthius three-quarters of a millennium later, it shows how the leadership of ancient schools used their own personal histories as well as those of their predecessors to advertise the unique and positive aspects of the teaching circles they headed. While these narratives helped to develop the public profile of an institution, they also played the more important role of cementing student allegiances to the school. In many cases, teachers first exposed students to illustrative personal anecdotes about their intellectual ancestors in intimate private conversations. This tied institutional history to the unique teacher-student personal bond that, in theory at least, lent a familial air to a scholastic life. Because students were both personally and emotionally invested in these stories, they worked doubly hard to defend the integrity of their own school's traditions while, at times, attacking the credibility of those associated with rival schools.

The second chapter will apply this basic interpretative framework to the Alexandrian intellectual circles that came to be involved in the events of 486. After demonstrating the nature of the anecdotes that circulated within the school of Horapollon and its associated intellectual circles, the study establishes that his school encouraged interpersonal ties that caused students to become invested in these traditions. Of particular interest, however, is the fate of these traditions after Paralius's beating. This act of violence and its aftermath frayed the strong personal relationships between teachers and students, while also changing the nature of communal discourse. As the community splintered, so too did its collective sense of the past. Among some philosophers, old traditions celebrating pagan resistance to Christian imperial power were disavowed silently while others glorifying social withdrawal and a passive response to political pressure became more prominent. This process of development, which is on display within the various narrative levels of Damascius's *Life of Isidore,* created a number of distinct views of the ethical values appropriate for a pagan intellectual. As subsequent events would show, these ideals shaped not only the personal behavior of Neoplatonic leaders but also the eventual fate of Platonic teaching in late antiquity.

2

Personal Legacy and Scholastic Identity

In 339 B.C., Speusippus, Plato's nephew and successor as the head of the Academy, died after a long illness.[1] In his absence, a major crisis fell upon the school. Though it would ultimately become the institution that first showed ancient schools how to ensure scholastic continuity, the Academy that Plato founded and Speusippus administered was very different from the well-established institution that Crantor or Arcesilaus would eventually head. The very early Academy served more as a space within which interesting and compelling philosophical discussion could take place than as a center with a defined set of doctrines and methods of inquiry.[2] Only the great reputation of Plato and the universal respect students felt for Speusippus had kept this diverse philosophical community together for the past two scholastic generations.

When Speusippus died, however, he left no appointed successor and no mechanism for choosing one from among the various middle-aged philosophers who formed the next Academic generation. Upon his passing, the earliest Academy, which had often been known simply as the school of Plato, lacked a personally

---

Parts of this section reprise arguments first presented in E. Watts, "Creating the Academy: Historical Discourse and the Shape of Community in the Old Academy," *JHS* 127 (2007), 106–22; and "Orality and Communal Identity in Eunapius' *Lives of the Sophists and Philosophers*," *Byzantion* 75 (2005), 334–61.

1. For the death of Speusippus see L. Tarán, *Speusippus of Athens: A Critical Study with a Collection of the Related Texts and Commentary* (Leiden, 1981), 7, as well as Diogenes Laertius, 4.3.

2. The diversity of intellectual approaches within the Platonic and Speusippan Academy is remarkable. On this see Watts, "Creating the Academy: Historical Discourse and the Shape of Community in the Old Academy," *JHS* 127 (2007), 106–14; as well as J. Dillon, *The Heirs of Plato: A Study of the Old Academy (347–274 B.C.)* (Oxford, 2002), 1–29.

distinctive scholarch for the first time in its history.³ This was a significant organizational problem because, historically, intellectual circles had been closely identified with their founder and tended to disperse upon their founder's death; in the mid-fourth century B.C. there was little precedent for choosing a second generation of leaders and none for choosing a third.⁴ Attached to this practical concern, however, was the equally important but less well-defined issue of how one understood the significance of the third-generation Academy. To survive in the long term, the Academy needed to establish an institutional identity that built upon the legacy of its founder while simultaneously demarcating the distinct advantages of an Academic (as opposed to simply a Platonic or Speusippan) training. In short, it needed both to create a new organizational structure and (to use a modern concept) to define the Academic educational brand.

Xenocrates, the successor chosen by the inner circle of the Academy, skillfully addressed this situation.⁵ He crafted a unique Academic scholastic identity that wedded his ethical teachings to historical traditions recording his own and his mentor's exemplary lifestyles. These narratives particularly highlighted the virtue of temperance. For Xenocrates, temperance represented a form of personal moderation and its importance derived from the practical application of his ethical theory that *eudaimonia* arose in part from seeking only the minimum physical resources necessary to service our proper needs.⁶ Temperance then represented a powerful notion that defined both Xenocrates' ethical system and his personal reputation.⁷ Discourse in and around the Academy began to advertise its power to regulate good conduct and reform bad behavior. These discussions centered upon the temperate character of Xenocrates and celebrated his ability to redeem even the most dissolute characters.

---

3. For the Platonic Academy as simply the "school of Plato" see, for example, Aelian, *VH* 4.9.10–13.

4. Direct institutional succession seems not to have been a concern in sophistic schools of the fifth and early fourth centuries B.C. One exception to this may be the Sicilian sophists Corax and Tisias, the former of whom is credited with the first rhetorical handbook, but too little is known of them to suggest that they established a line of intellectual succession. On them, note De Romilly, *Les grands sophistes dans l'Athènes de Périclès* (Paris, 1988), 93; and T. Cole, *The Origins of Rhetoric in Ancient Greece* (Baltimore, 1991), 22–27.

5. Xenocrates was chosen to head the school in a contentious vote of its inner circle (Philodemus, *Hist Acad.* VI–VII = Isnardi Parente, *Senocrate*, fr. 1.15–24 = Tarán, *Speusippus*, Test. 2.14–31). Following his election, Aristotle, Menedemus, and Heraclides (the men who ran against him) all seem to have left the Academy.

6. Clement, *Strom.* 2.22 = Isnardi Parente, *Senocrate*, fr. 232. For discussion of this idea see Dillon, *Heirs of Plato*, 141–49.

7. As Dillon has suggested (*Heirs of Plato*, 136–37), Xenocrates' ethical system likely owes much to his understanding of Plato's teaching, with some attempts to further develop these ideas in his own direction.

Extant sources preserve a small but not insignificant array of Xenocratean anecdotes, the general tenor of which one can appreciate from three of the most notable examples.[8] The first recounts a drinking contest held at the court of Dionysius of Sicily. The prize for this was a golden crown and, when Xenocrates won the contest, he showed his contempt for worldly goods by placing his prize atop a statue of Hermes and walking off.[9] A second group of anecdotes emphasizes Xenocrates' insusceptibility to carnal temptation by recounting the failure of various courtesans who tried to seduce him.[10] The third focuses upon the popular trope of the interaction between a philosopher and a king. There are a number of variations on this theme among the *testimonia* related to Xenocrates, but the most notable concerns a large gift of money sent by Alexander the Great. Xenocrates took from this a small amount and sent the rest back, saying that it was of more need to a king than a philosopher.[11] Consistent with his ethical theory of moderation, Xenocrates accepted only the amount of Alexander's gift that was required to meet his basic needs.

Each of these anecdotes demonstrates particular ways in which Xenocrates' lifestyle illustrated his ethical teachings, but the best-known and most memorable story told about Xenocrates concerns the philosophical conversion of Polemo. It presents both Xenocrates' own personal qualities and the effect that they had on students.[12] Polemo was a wealthy young Athenian infamous for his dissolute lifestyle.[13] One morning, fresh from a night of drinking, he came upon a lecture being conducted by Xenocrates. Polemo burst in, sat down, and attempted to raise Xenocrates' ire by heckling him. "Xenocrates, without changing countenance, dropped the topic on which he was discoursing and began to speak of modesty and temperance. The gravity of his words brought Polemo to his senses . . . he stripped away luxury in its entirety and, healed by the salutary medicine of a single speech, from notorious debauchee, he ended up a great philosopher."[14]

These anecdotes illustrated Xenocrates' temperance, but they also made a clear statement about the unique character of an Academic training. They marked the

8. On these, note M. Isnardi Parente, "Per la biografia di Senocrate," *RFIC* 109 (1981), 129–62.

9. This story appears often (e.g., Philodemus, *Hist. Acad.* VI; Diog. Laert. 4.8; Athenaeus, *Deipno.* 10.437 b–c; cf. Isnardi Parente, "Senocrate," 132–33).

10. See, for example, Valerius Maximus 4.3. ext. 3a and Diog. Laert. 4.7.

11. Diog. Laert. 4.8; Cicero *Tusc. Disp.* 5.32.91; Stobaeus *Flor.* 3.5.10; Valerius Maximus, 4.3 ext. 3b; cf. Isnardi Parente, "Senocrate," frs. 23–29.

12. For versions of this story see Isnardi Parente, *Senocrate*, frs. 43–47 and, more exhaustively, M. Gigante, *Polemonis Academici Fragmenta* (Naples, 1977), frs. 15–33. The most detailed versions of the anecdote are found in Diog. Laert. 4.16 = Gigante fr. 16 and Valerius Maximus 6.9 ext. 1 = Gigante fr. 20. This tradition was so memorable that, in the Roman period, it became emblematic of the transformative effect of Academic teaching (e.g., Lucian, *Double Indictment* 17 = Gigante, fr. 25).

13. On his background see Gigante, frs. 10–12 (on his family) and 13–14 (youthful vices).

14. Valerius Maximus, 6.9 ext. 1 (trans. D. R. Shackleton Bailey, LCL).

Academy as an institution that prized temperance and taught this virtue so effectively that its instruction could transform even the most vicious and dissolute characters. This was a distinctive discourse constructed to capitalize upon the unique characteristics that Xenocrates brought to the Academy and designed to emphasize the practical advantages of Academic philosophical teaching. Indeed, Academic historical traditions would later claim that not just Xenocrates but Plato and Speusippus too had manifested the same personal commitment to temperance. This communal history then represented a powerful, and somewhat novel, solution to the problem of defining the character of a multi-generational educational institution. Through Xenocrates' initiative, the Academy could be seen to have an institutional identity that was consistent across intellectual generations. Its history then validated its current shape.

Opponents from other philosophical schools, notably Peripatetic and Eretrian writers, attempted to demonstrate the intemperate character of current and former Academic leaders. Their efforts reveal Xenocrates' success in using the school's history to highlight the power of its ethical teachings. These anti-Academic authors leveled attacks against the scholarchs Polemo, Xenocrates, Speusippus, and even Plato himself. In general terms, they attacked Plato for pride, gluttony, and even plagiarism.[15] Speusippus was presented as emotionally unstable and devoted to pleasure.[16] Xenocrates was stupid, clumsy, and disloyal.[17] And Polemo was ridiculed with stories about his vicious past.[18] Though different criticisms are leveled at each scholarch, these hostile traditions are collectively designed to cut away specifically at the attributes that made the Academy a unique institution under Xenocrates and Polemo.

In most cases, this material is either undatable or clearly attributed to much later authors (like Hermippus).[19] However, the literary remains of the Hellenistic authors Aristoxenus of Tarentum (b. 370 B.C.) and Antigonus of Carystus (fl. 240 B.C.) suggest quite strongly that an anti-Academic historical tradition quickly arose in response to the claims coming out of the Academy. Of particular interest

---

15. Plato's pride is largely the subject of Cynic attacks. See A. S. Riginos, *Platonica: The Anecdotes concerning the Life and Writings of Plato* (Leiden, 1976), anecdotes 46, 71. His gluttony is suggested by the Peripatetic Hermippus (in Diog. Laert. 3.2); note on this also the Cynic traditions about Plato that make up Riginos, anecdotes 68, 69. Hermippus is the immediate source for the plagiarism charge (in Diog. Laert. 8.85), though Aristoxenus may be the ultimate source.

16. Note, for example, Diog. Laert. 4.1.

17. On his clumsiness see Diog. Laert. 4.6 and Plutarch, *Coniug. praecept.* 28.141 = Isnardi Parente, *Senocrate*, fr. 5. On the charges of stupidity, see Plutarch, *De recta ratione audiendi* 18.47e = Isnardi Parente, *Senocrate*, fr. 4. For discussion see Isnardi Parente, "Senocrate," 130–31.

18. Some of this emphasis can be seen in Diogenes Laertius's account of his early life (Diog. Laert. 4.16). Note as well the account of Philodemus, *Hist. Acad.* IV–XIII and the discussion of Dillon, *Heirs of Plato*, 156–57.

19. Diog. Laert. 4.6 = Isnardi Parente, *Senocrate*, fr. 2.

are the different ways in which these responses are crafted. Antigonus, a former student at the school of Menedemus, chose to focus upon the immoral character of Xenocrates' successor Polemo, the most famous example of a dissolute man supposedly converted to a temperate life by Academic teaching.[20] Aristoxenus, a former student of Aristotle, directed his attacks against the intemperance and poor character of Socrates and Plato, in his mind the earliest links in the Academic historical tradition.[21] Though the work of each is extremely fragmentary, their writings suggest that, by the time of Polemo, the notion of an Academic institutional history emphasizing the temperance of its leaders (both current and former) was influential enough to merit a response from followers of Xenocrates' displaced rivals. Quite early on, rival philosophers realized that attacks upon the Academy's institutional history could undermine the integrity of the school's teaching. As the fourth- and early third-century explosion of philosophical biographies shows,[22] Peripatetics and others also seem to have first copied and later improved upon the Academic methods of drawing upon the legacy of past leaders to illustrate the potency of a particular brand of teaching. Xenocrates and his contemporaries thus created a technique that came to shape the way later schools publicly defined the significance of their teaching.

INTERNAL HISTORICAL DISCOURSE AND ITS TRANSMISSION: THE EXAMPLE OF EUNAPIUS

Xenocrates' efforts show how an intellectual circle could draw upon its past to illustrate the unique attributes and practical effects of its current teaching. More than eight centuries separate the Academy of Xenocrates and the school of Horapollon but, in this time, the revolutionary methods used by the Old Academy to create a collective identity by drawing upon its communal past became conventional. Academics, Peripatetics, Stoics, and Epicureans all succeeded in establishing intellectual communities that endured for centuries while looking back to

---

20. On Antigonus generally see A. Momigliano, *The Development of Greek Biography*, 2nd ed. (Cambridge, MA, 1993), 81. The best larger study of Antigonus remains that of U. von Wilamowitz-Möllendorf, *Antigonos von Karystos*, 2nd ed. (Berlin, 1965).

21. On Aristoxenus, note the thorough treatment of Momigliano, *Greek Biography*, 73–76. Aristoxenus attacks Plato as a plagiarist, a parasite, and a book-burner (Aristoxenus, fr. 67 [Wehrli]). Cf. Riginos, *Platonica*, 165n3; Riginos, *Platonica*, 71, drawing upon Aristoxenus, fr. 62 [Wehrli]; and Riginos, *Platonica*, 166, drawing upon Aristoxenus, fr. 131 [Wehrli]. His Socrates "showed himself fully a slave to pleasures." Not only was he frequently angry, but Socrates was also "most eager to partake in sexual pleasures" (Aristoxenus, fr. 54b [Wehrli] = Theodoret, *Graec. affect. curatio* XII 61. Cf. Aristoxenus, fr. 56 = Synesius *Encomium calvitatis* 81 a cap. 17).

22. For the role of Peripatetics in shaping ancient biography see F. Leo, *Die griechisch-römische Biographie nach ihrer literarischen Form* (Leipzig, 1901), as well as Momigliano, *Greek Biography*, 17–20.

founders who defined the group's basic principles. The Roman imperial period, however, saw the decentralization of these institutions. Platonists offer perhaps the best known and most easily reconstructed example. The Academy founded by Plato ended when Antiochus of Ascalon successfully challenged the authority of its last scholarch, a man named Philo, in the 80s B.C.[23] Philo was the last of the Academic Skeptics, while Antiochus offered students a dogmatic Academic training that looked back to the doctrines and ideas of Plato, Speusippus, Xenocrates, and Polemo. Each man, however, justified his Academic leadership by claiming fidelity to the true principles laid out by Plato, the community's founder.[24] Antiochus's dynamic personality and his attractive system of thought won out, but the Academy he inaugurated possessed none of the material resources of the original and probably perished by 44 B.C., within a generation of his own death.[25] Platonism, of course, endured for at least another six centuries—but no Academy remained at its center.

I will explore the implications of Antiochus's Academy for the larger Platonic intellectual community in more detail in an upcoming study, but at this point it is worth noting that Antiochus's challenge was not an anomaly. It grew out of a world in which the appeal of Greek philosophy extended across the Mediterranean while the Athenian caretakers of philosophical traditions gradually lost their ability to control them. Even a quick glance at the writers and thinkers who originated from Antiochus's home region in the first century B.C. shows how ecumenical Greek intellectual culture had become. In addition to Antiochus himself, Palestine and Syria produced the Stoic philosophers Posidonius and Sosus, the Epicurean Philodemus, and the poet Meleager.[26] The spread of Greek learning to the wider Hellenistic world resulted in a more decentralized cultural environment in which people continued to identify with major intellectual traditions but came to know them through individual teachers and schools. The result was a sort of franchising out of intellectual learning in which local teachers followed an intellectual "brand" and taught their own versions of it. Students then identified with a long-standing thought tradition as well as a much more ephemeral school or group of thinkers.

The eccentric Epicurean philosopher Diogenes of Oenoanda offers a representative example of this trend. Sometime in the mid-second century A.D., Diogenes paid to have a collection of philosophical texts inscribed on the wall of a stoa in

---

23. For Antiochus, his challenge, and the result see J. Glucker, *Antiochus and the Late Academy* (Göttingen, 1978) and J. Dillon, *The Middle Platonists, 80 B.C. to A.D. 220*, 2nd ed. (Ithaca, 1996), 52–62. Although its date of disappearance cannot be as accurately discovered, the Peripatetic school too lost its Athenian center in the Roman imperial period. On this see J. P. Lynch, *Aristotle's School: A Study of a Greek Educational Institution* (Berkeley, 1972).

24. This reprises the important argument of Glucker, *Antiochus*, 15–31.

25. Antiochus probably died in 69 B.C. His final known successor is last heard about in 44 B.C.

26. For discussion of these characters see Dillon, *Middle Platonists*, 52.

the Lycian city of Oenoanda.²⁷ While Diogenes often identifies himself as a follower of Epicurus, his works provide an idiosyncratic group of Epicurean doctrines. These include a conception of universal citizenship,²⁸ some doubts about the predictive power of dreams,²⁹ and a set of odd polemics against other philosophical schools that contrast with Epicurus's generally non-polemical tone.³⁰ Chronology may explain some of this idiosyncrasy, but it is also important to note that Diogenes belonged to a regional Epicurean community (probably centered on Rhodes) with a distinct set of interests.³¹ Indeed, if Platonic circles in the second century A.D. are a good guide, the proliferation of intellectual "franchises" like the one to which Diogenes belonged generated distinctive ideas that differentiated even philosophical communities that claimed a common intellectual heritage.³²

A similar sort of decentralization of intellectual culture can be seen in the rhetorical schools of the imperial period. Unlike philosophical circles, schools of rhetoric historically offered neither strictly defined doctrinal profiles nor particular institutional centers. Athens retained a sort of pride of place into late antiquity,³³ but important centers of sophistic study proliferated across the Mediterranean. An abundance of historical traditions created by these individual sophistic schools have been preserved in Philostratus's *Lives of the Sophists*. Philostratus's work presents anecdotes that highlight distinctive attributes of individual teachers while simultaneously profiling groups of sophistic families, in both the literal and metaphorical sense.³⁴ This suggests that, by the Roman imperial period, sophistic

---

27. For discussion of Diogenes see M. F. Smith, *The Philosophical Inscription of Diogenes of Oinoanda* (Vienna, 1996) and idem, *Supplement to Diogenes of Oinoanda The Epicurean Inscription* (Naples, 2003). Smith (*Philosophical Inscription*, 39–40) argues convincingly for a second-century date because the hand used to carve the inscription resembles that used in a similar Oenoandan inscription dated to the 120s. On this second inscription see S. Mitchell, "Festivals, Games, and Civic Life in Roman Asia Minor," *JRS* 80 (1990), 183–93.

28. "While the various segments of the earth give different people a different country, the whole compass of this world gives all people a single country, the entire earth, and a single home, the world." (Diogenes, Fr. 30.1.12–2.1). On the Stoic notions resembling this idea see Smith, *Epicurean Inscription*, 139; cf. C. W. Chilton, *Diogenes of Oenoanda, The Fragments: A Translation and Commentary* (Oxford, 1971), 70.

29. Fr. 9.6.6–8; 53.

30. Smith, *Epicurean Inscription*, 137–40.

31. The Rhodian base is suggested by Fr. 62, Fr. 63. On this, see Smith, *Epicurean Inscription*, 35.

32. Note, for example, the distinct ideas presented by second-century Platonists like Atticus, Gaius, and Albinus. For discussion see Dillon, *Middle Platonists*, 231–340.

33. E.g., Libanius, *Or.* 1.12; Synesius, *Ep.* 136.

34. On the nature of Philostratus's text see K. Eshleman, "Defining the Circle of Sophists: Philostratus and the Construction of the Second Sophistic," *CP* 103 (2008), 395–413. S. Swain, "The Reliability of Philostratus' *Lives of the Sophists*," *CA* 10.1 (1991), 148–63; as well as the more critical perspective of P. A. Brunt, "The Bubble of the Second Sophistic," *BICS* 39 (1994), 25–52.

and philosophical circles had come to use many of the same tools to craft and present their communal histories.

The intellectual decentralization characteristic of the later Hellenistic and early Roman imperial periods did not change the basic techniques that rhetorical and philosophical schools used to communicate their collective pasts. In the later Roman Empire, as in classical Athens, particular schools and intellectual circles cultivated public reputations that defined the nature of their teaching and illustrated the great legacies of their leadership. Libanius, for example, grew up in the fourth century A.D. hearing stories about "Callinicus and Tlepolemos and not a few other sophists [which] described their orations and how they vanquished or were vanquished by one another."[35] These in turn made him passionate about attending the Athenian schools that featured in these stories.[36] Indeed, Libanius's career is filled with instances in which he and his rivals worked to shape a positive public perception of their teaching by advertising the elite status of their followers and floridly describing their victories in rhetorical competitions.[37] Efforts to shape public perceptions of a teacher's past even entered into rhetorical performances, as evidently was the case when Himerius used the occasion of his visit to the court of the emperor Constans to contrast himself with Prohaeresius.[38] Teachers who ineffectively defended their reputations experienced a great decline in student numbers. In one case, a skilled teacher with an unfortunate tendency to lose his composure found that his "eloquence availed him of nothing because his general behavior was held in disrepute . . . he became a laughing-stock throughout the city."[39] He was reduced to paying a few young men to attend his classes while those with a reputation for evincing the ideals of sophistic conduct captured most of the city's genuine students.[40]

These brief notices show the power that scholastic reputations had in attracting students to individual schools. However, they provide only the most memorable and publicly available elements of this historical discourse; they are of limited use in allowing us to see how a student came to identify personally with an individual teacher or his school. So, for example, they do not reveal how discussion of the personal history of a scholarch and the institutional history of a school helped

---

35. Libanius, Or. 1.11.
36. E.g., Libanius, Or. 1.12.
37. See, for example, Or. 1.79 (on Libanius's pride in having attracted the sons of local notables); Or. 1.72 (on a governor sending a son to study with Libanius); Or. 1.49–50, 87–90 (on his various rhetorical triumphs). Note on this Cribiore, *The School of Libanius in Late Antique Antioch* (Princeton, 2007), 84–88.
38. Himerius, Or. 41.2. On this see T. D. Barnes, "Himerius and the Fourth Century," *CP* 82 (1987), 208.
39. Libanius, Or. 1.65.
40. For paying students, see as well Themistius, Or. 23.290c.

ancient intellectual circles to command the devotion of their students. To see this, it is necessary to turn our attention to intellectual communities with richer historiographic legacies.

In the late antique period, few groups of intellectuals are more richly described than those presented by Eunapius in his *Lives of the Sophists and Philosophers*. Writing in the late fourth century, Eunapius preserves historical traditions that circulated within intellectual communities and describes the circumstances under which he came to learn about these traditions. His text, then, shows how the historical discourse within a school illustrated the specific values emphasized in its teaching. It also explains why students developed such loyalty to these ideas.

The *Lives of the Philosophers and Sophists* is, obviously enough, a collective biography in which the author has a rationale for including and excluding certain figures. A proper understanding of the text then demands an assessment of its basic organizational principles.[41] In its preface, Eunapius describes the work as a "narrative of the main achievements of distinguished men" who were either sophists or philosophers.[42] Despite this rather ecumenical claim, almost all of the individuals whose lives he describes shared elements of a common intellectual lineage with Eunapius.[43] Eunapius's ties to these men are crucial because his philosophy instructor, Chrysanthius, his rhetorical supervisor, Prohaeresius, and his informal medical tutor, Oribasius, are the nexuses through which Eunapius is linked to most of the philosophers, sophists, and iatrosophists he describes.[44] In a sense, the *Lives of the Sophists and Philosophers* represents Eunapius's reconstruction of his own intellectual family tree, but he enlivened this genealogical exercise with anecdotes that reflected his own understanding of his intellectual ancestors and their achievements.[45] Throughout the text, Eunapius chooses to include accounts of the actions taken by his subjects that he thought proved most meaningful within his intellectual circle.

---

41. On this point, see the discussion of P. Cox Miller, "Strategies of Representation in Collective Biography: Constructing the Subject as Holy," in *Greek Biography and Panegyric in Late Antiquity*, ed. T. Hägg and P. Rousseau (Berkeley, 2000), 220–21. For more discussion of the organizational principles of Eunapius's text see Watts, "Orality and Communal Identity," 334–61; and R. Penella, *Greek Sophists and Philosophers: Studies in Eunapius of Sardis* (Leeds, 1990).

42. *VS* 453.

43. This concern with scholastic family trees is notably missing from Libanius, a fact with leads Cribiore (*School of Libanius*, 84) to suggest that "a school was a certain teacher and ceased to be or fell into decline when he disappeared." Libanius, however, represents a special case because his difficult relationships with his teachers Diophantus and Zenobius would have made such a dynastic emphasis seem odd and unpersuasive.

44. For Eunapius's connections to these men, see *VS* 502–3 (Chrysanthius); 493 (Prohaeresius); and 488–89 (Oribasius).

45. P. Athanassiadi, "The Oecumenism of Iamblichus: Latent Knowledge and its Awakening," *JRS* 85 (1995), 244–45 has noted the importance that Eunapius placed upon establishing an extremely

His portrait of Iamblichus vividly illustrates the degree to which Eunapius used anecdotes to demonstrate the practical significance of the sometimes esoteric study that a philosophical circle demanded. Eunapius provides three stories about Iamblichus. First, he describes how Iamblichus sometimes worshipped in private and, consequently, was forced to deny a rumor that he levitated when he prayed. Second, Eunapius tells how Iamblichus sensed the presence of a dead body while on a walk with his students. Finally, Eunapius records how, on a visit to the baths at Gadara, Iamblichus produced the spirits Eros and Anteros (in the form of two boys) from two of the springs on the site.[46]

Eunapius learned of each of these events from accounts that circulated orally within schools headed by Iamblichus's intellectual descendants. Eunapius is particularly explicit about this when he describes how he learned of Iamblichus's reported levitation. "The report of [this event] came to the author of this work through Chrysanthius of Sardis. This man was a pupil of Aedesius, and Aedesius was one of the inner-circle of Iamblichus, and he reported these things to Chrysanthius."[47] Eunapius then continues, "he also said that there occurred the following manifestation of (Iamblichus's) divine nature," and the discussion of Iamblichus's premonition of the dead body then commences.[48] Following this incident, Eunapius prefaces his final anecdote about Iamblichus with a statement that "they testified also to a still more marvelous incident," presumably again a reference to the oral testimony of Aedesius which was conveyed to him through Chrysanthius.

These anecdotes began to be shared among Iamblichus's own students during the teacher's lifetime. They continued to circulate in the teaching circles set up by Aedesius and other Iamblichan students, and were further perpetuated by Chrysanthius and Aedesius's other students. While Eunapius admitted to the existence of "even more astonishing and marvelous" testimony about Iamblichus, he chose not to report it "since (he) believed it a dangerous and sacrilegious thing to introduce corrupt and fluid oral testimony into a stable narrative."[49] Instead, Eunapius chose only to accept testimony that came to him from Chrysanthius about events that were actually witnessed by Aedesius. Eunapius's allusion to another (fluid and corrupt) set of oral traditions about Iamblichus is particularly significant given his claim in the preface of the *Lives* that a primary aim of the work was to "give stability" to oral testimony

---

simple Platonic succession. It is important to note that the emperor Julian shared many of Eunapius's philosophical and medical ancestors. Aside from his antagonism towards Prohaeresius, Julian has no connection to the main rhetoricians in the text. It cannot then be argued that the text set out to trace Julian's intellectual genealogy.

46. On this site note Y. Hirschfeld, *The Roman Thermae at Hammat-Gader* (Jerusalem, 1997).
47. *VS* 458.
48. *VS* 459. Aedesius is Eunapius's ultimate source.
49. *VS* 460.

that was likely to be confused by the passage of time.⁵⁰ This implies that Eunapius had access to two sets of oral traditions about Iamblichus, one that he judged to be stable and another that he judged corrupt. His exclusive reliance upon the oral testimony of Chrysanthius suggests that Eunapius understood the "texts" of oral anecdotes passed from teacher to student to be more secure than other types of historical materials.⁵¹ These internal narratives had a particular value because they grew out of the personal relationships at the heart of a philosophical circle.

The anecdotes told about Iamblichus among his students tended to emphasize the ways in which his activities reinforced his teachings.⁵² This was particularly true of his theurgic teaching. Theurgy was, in its most basic form, a set of rituals designed to assist the human mind in apprehending something of the ineffable divine presence. For Iamblichus, theurgy purified a philosopher's soul and enabled his mind to overcome the limitations of the material world and ascend to a world of pure thought.⁵³ So the student account of Iamblichus's levitation, which he himself denied, was nonetheless preserved as an important demonstration of the master's teaching that the theurgist became man and god simultaneously.⁵⁴ Iamblichus's ability to discern the presence of corpses from an extreme distance and his skill at drawing forth divine figures respectively showed the theurgist's capacity to sense with his mind and his superior skill in uniting the divine aspect of his soul with related divine figures.⁵⁵ As these were central features of Iamblichus's

---

50. *VS* 453.

51. This idea of valuing oral testimony differently depending upon the status of its source dates back at least to Herodotus. On this, see S. Lewis, *News and Society in the Greek Polis* (London, 1996), 85–89. This prejudice extended into the legal realm as well (on which see P. Garnsey, *Social Status and Legal Privilege in the Roman Empire* [Oxford, 1970], 207; and the comments of P. A. Brunt, review of Garnsey, *JRS* 62 [1972], 169). While teachers and their students were presumably of the same social status, the elevated position of a teacher within the intellectual community made his accounts more authoritative.

52. For an excellent explanation of how the Iamblichan anecdotes functioned within the text, see P. Cox Miller, "Strategies of Representation," 242–44. A more general discussion of the importance such anecdotes had in illustrating both the character of a teacher and the character of his teaching is found in P. Cox, *Biography in Late Antiquity: A Quest for the Holy Man* (Berkeley, 1983), 9–20.

53. The best (though far from most accessible) description is that of Iamblichus, *De Myst.* 2.11.98, 3.7.114–8.117, 25.158–59. Among the many contemporary scholars who have written about theurgy are P. Athanassiadi, "The Chaldean Oracles: Theology and Theurgy," in *Pagan Monotheism in Late Antiquity*, ed. P. Athanassiadi and B. Frede (Oxford, 1999), 149–84; G. Shaw, "Theurgy: Rituals of Unification in the Neoplatonism of Iamblichus," *Traditio* 41 (1985), 1–28; A. Sheppard, "Proclus' Attitude to Theurgy," *CQ* 32 (1982), 212–24; A. Smith, *Porphyry's Place in the Neoplatonic Tradition: A Study in Post-Plotinian Neoplatonism* (The Hague, 1974), 81–99.

54. P. Cox Miller, "Strategies of Representation," 242; and G. Shaw, *Theurgy and the Soul: The Neoplatonism of Iamblichus* (University Park, Pennsylvania, 1995), 51. For this idea, see Iamblichus, *De myst.* 148.

55. G. Shaw, *Theurgy and the Soul*, 121–26; and P. Cox Miller, "Strategies of Representation," 243.

teaching, it is only natural that the individuals learning from him would focus upon examples of his conduct that illustrated these doctrines.[56] This was probably particularly true for new students who were struggling to understand the tangible application of the ideas expressed around them.

Eunapius similarly describes how Maximus of Ephesus applied Iamblichan-inspired philosophical ideas. Maximus, a human oracle, an accomplished theurgist, and a man whose arrogance dangerously exceeded acceptable bounds,[57] revealed both the electrifying near-divinity and the personal susceptibility of Eunapius's Neoplatonic ancestors. In his account, Eunapius focuses upon Maximus's spectacular spiritual and political successes as well as his acute real-life failures. He writes about things like Maximus's travels to Julian's court,[58] his accompaniment of Julian on his Persian campaign,[59] his punishment under the emperor Valens,[60] his partial political rehabilitation,[61] and his execution by Valens in 371.[62] While Eunapius provides some additional details about these events, they were already well-known. Indeed, many of these events are similarly described by Ammianus Marcellinus.[63]

The same cannot be said for the elements of Eunapius's narrative that reflect upon Maximus's specific philosophical and theurgical activities. Although Eunapius acknowledges not having any real personal interaction with the philosopher,[64] he had access to some quite specific information about Maximus's theurgical activities. He knew about an occasion when, in front of his fellow students, Maximus performed a ritual that made a cultic statue smile and caused temple torches to light up.[65] He also knew about Maximus's efforts to manipulate auspices related

---

56. Eunapius's attempt to illustrate the ways in which the character of his philosophers supports their teachings has deep literary roots (on this, see Leo, *Die griechisch-römische Biographie*, 259–61). Xenophon's *Memorabilia*, for example, is a defense of Socrates' character as well as an illustration of his teachings (cf. Momigliano, *Greek Biography*, 52–54). For the relationship Eunapius's work had to this tradition, see D. F. Buck, "Eunapius' *Lives of the Sophists*: A Literary Study," *Byzantion* 62 (1992), 141–57.

57. P. Cox Miller, "Strategies of Representation," 245.

58. VS 477.

59. VS 478.

60. VS 478–79.

61. VS 480.

62. VS 480.

63. Eunapius, for example, heard of Maximus's initial imprisonment while studying under Prohaeresius in Athens (VS 478). The similarities to Ammianus are striking and there has been much discussion about whether Ammianus made use of Eunapius's writings. On this, see, T. D. Barnes, "The *Epitome de Caesaribus* and its Sources," *CP* 71 (1976), 265–67; Penella, *Greek Sophists*, 73–75; G. W. Bowersock, *Julian the Apostate* (Cambridge, MA, 1978), 7; J. Matthews, *The Roman Empire of Ammianus* (London, 1989), 175; and C. Fornara, "Julian's Persian Expedition in Ammianus and Zosimus," *JHS* 111(1991), 1–15.

64. VS 473.

65. VS 475.

to his departure to Julian's court[66] and Maximus's ability to sense that a spell had been put on the female philosopher Sosipatra.[67]

As previous generations of Neoplatonists used the figure of Iamblichus to define the standards of their intellectual community, the generation to which Eunapius belonged looked, at least in part, to Maximus for similar clarification. While Maximus had a far more ambiguous legacy than Iamblichus, the stories told about him illustrated the spectacular spiritual potential of theurgy.[68] These tales came to Eunapius in much the same way as the earlier accounts of Iamblichus's deeds; Chrysanthius again seems to have been Eunapius's main source.[69]

In fact, at the end of the text, Eunapius even seems to explain how Chrysanthius passed this information to him. When discussing his teacher's death, Eunapius mentions that, as a part of his daily routine, Chrysanthius would take walks. "He would take along the author of this text. He would stretch these into long and leisurely walks. And one would forget the soreness of his feet, because he would become enchanted by the stories Chrysanthius told."[70] This is clearly one of Eunapius's fonder memories of his teacher, but this habit was not peculiar to Chrysanthius. Indeed, it was also a favorite activity of Aedesius and, possibly, Iamblichus as well.[71] Such personal interactions (and the transmission of anecdotes that they enabled) formed an integral part of a student's relationship with his teacher. It should not be surprising that they also helped to shape Eunapius's portraits of his intellectual ancestors.

Eunapius also shows that the same mechanisms that enabled the transmission of oral traditions in philosophical schools served a similar purpose in late antique schools of rhetoric. His account of the lives of his rhetorical teachers combines facts about his subjects with anecdotes he heard as a student to illustrate the particular virtues of their scholastic character. This becomes most clear in Eunapius's discussion of the career of his teacher Prohaeresius. Though Prohaeresius is himself treated extensively in a biography devoted solely to his accomplishments, Euanpius actually begins to shape his audience's view of Prohaeresius in his biography of Prohaeresius's teacher, Julianus. In this chapter, he includes one long

---

66. *VS* 476–77.
67. *VS* 469–70.
68. The force of such anecdotes is shown by Eunapius's suggestion that the emperor Julian was drawn to Maximus because his display of theurgic ability at the temple of Hecate revealed the power of Neoplatonic teaching (*VS* 475).
69. On this point see Watts, "Orality and Communal Identity," 349–50.
70. *VS* 502.
71. In Aedesius's case (*VS* 481), Eunapius suggests that the walks also were designed to teach his students how to behave toward others. As for Iamblichus, his encounter with the dead body may have occurred during such a walk. On this, see G. Fowden, "The Platonist Philosopher and his Circle in Late Antiquity," *Philosophia* 7 (1977), 374.

anecdote "as a sample of Julianus's learning and prudence."[72] It centers upon a court case in which students of Julianus were prosecuted by the students of a rival. On this occasion, Prohaeresius delivered a stunning extemporaneous defense speech that not only led to the acquittal of Julianus's student cohort but even generated tears among the members of the audience and applause from the trial judge.[73] What Eunapius hoped this anecdote would show about Julianus's skills is unclear, but he does make it quite plain that, on this day, Prohaeresius won a spectacular rhetorical triumph against extremely long odds.

This theme reappears a number of times in Eunapius's proper treatment of Prohaeresius. He recounts a set of anecdotes describing rhetorical triumphs that Prohaeresius earned despite difficult conditions. For example, he explains how Prohaeresius was forced into exile by his jealous rivals.[74] When his return to Athens had been arranged, Prohaeresius triumphed in a great rhetorical competition.[75] Not long after this, Eunapius describes the successful speech that Prohaeresius gave on a difficult theme before the proconsul Anatolius.[76]

Prohaeresius's rhetorical school valued a set of skills and achievements that differed significantly from those of the Iamblichan Neoplatonic schools, and Eunapius's discussion of his teacher's achievements reflects this difference.[77] Instead of focusing upon theurgy and its use (which was largely irrelevant to success in a rhetorical school), the anecdotes Eunapius records about Prohaeresius present him as an example of all that finely tuned rhetorical ability could allow one to achieve. Each of Prohaeresius's three great rhetorical performances was remembered as occurring despite extremely challenging conditions. Indeed, the speech given at the trial of Julianus's students and that given upon Prohaeresius's return from exile were presented as marvelous improvisational performances.[78] A great sophist

---

72. VS 483.

73. VS 483–85. On Prohaeresius's status in the school of Julianus at the time of the trial, see E. Watts, *City and School in Late Antique Athens and Alexandria* (Berkeley, 2006), 49–53.

74. VS 487–88.

75. VS 488–91.

76. VS 492. On the career of this Anatolius see S. Bradbury, "A Sophistic Prefect: Anatolius of Berytus in the Letters of Libanius," *CP* 95 (2000), 181–84.

77. P. Cox Miller ("Strategies of Representation," 237–40) has attempted to downplay the different focal points of Eunapius's anecdotes. Instead she has argued that both his philosophical and sophistic lives are designed to emphasize the link between *paideia* and divinity. The evidence for this from the sophistic lives is slight. It is true that Eunapius uses the term θειότατος to refer to Prohaeresius (at VS 468, 483, and 492) and he mentions Prohaeresius consulting the shrine at Eleusis (VS 493), but this does not suggest that Prohaeresius was connected to a Neoplatonic circle. Eunapius has distinguished his philosophers and sophists from the beginning of the text and the anecdotes he records about Prohaeresius illustrate sophistic and not Neoplatonic skills.

78. Eunapius underlines the technical skill that Prohaeresius displayed at the trial. His speech included an *encomium* of Julianus as well as a memorable *gnomē* about Themistocles. On the impor-

needed to be dispassionate when performing under duress and also needed to possess the ability to speak extemporaneously.[79] Eunapius's descriptions of Prohaeresius's speeches highlight the teacher's superior command of these skills.

These anecdotes further communicate Prohaeresius's great sophistic skill by highlighting public reaction to the teacher's defining orations. When Prohaeresius began speaking before the proconsul in Corinth, the official "bowed his head and was overcome with admiration for the force of the arguments, his weighty style, and sonorous eloquence."[80] Upon the conclusion of the oration, "the proconsul jumped up and, shaking his purple-edged cloak, that serious and unshakable judge applauded Prohaeresius like a schoolboy."[81] Similar emphasis upon the power that Prohaeresius's arguments had over an audience appears in Eunapius's accounts of his other two career highlights.[82] These emphases are not incidental; inventive argumentation, an effective style of speaking, and a forceful self-presentation were all important qualities that a rhetorical school developed in its students. Prohaeresius's complete mastery of these qualities simultaneously illustrated the potential power of his teaching and communicated its proper application to his students.[83]

In the same way that the testimony of Chrysanthius shaped Eunapius's philosophical portraits, that of Tuscianus, a teaching assistant of Prohaeresius, informed his most substantial biographies of sophists.[84] When Eunapius describes the defense speech Prohaeresius delivered at his teacher's trial, he states that "Tuscianus, who was present at the trial, reported these things to the author."[85] Conversations with Tuscianus similarly inform Eunapius's discussion of Prohaeresius's

---

tance of *encomia* in the curriculum, see R. Cribiore, *Gymnastics of the Mind: Greek Education in Hellenistic and Roman Egypt* (Princeton, 2001), 228–30. For the *gnomē* about Themistocles, see G. Kennedy, *Greek Rhetoric under Christian Emperors* (Princeton, 1983), 9–10.

79. The ability to speak eloquently in difficult or unexpected situations was particularly prized, though not always adequately cultivated by sophists (Kennedy, *Greek Rhetoric under Christian Emperors*, 140–41).

80. *VS* 484.

81. *VS* 484–85.

82. On the occasion of his speech before the proconsul, Prohaeresius was so spectacular that everyone "declared him to be a god or the very model of Hermes, the god of eloquence" (*VS* 490).

83. While it was considered bad form to play to an audience and try to induce applause (e.g., Quintilian, *Inst.* 12.9), an audience's approval of a high-quality speech was highly valued.

84. Tuscianus was one of the *hetairoi* (an advanced student with teaching duties) of both Julianus and Prohaeresius. It has been assumed by R. Penella (*Greek Sophists*, 137–38, 138 n49) that Tuscianus left teaching for a career in government in the 350s, but it seems more likely that he was still a *hetairos* of Prohaeresius in 362. Although Cribiore (*School of Libanius*, 109) sees this term working somewhat differently in the Libanian corpus, the existence of long-term assistants who carry over from a teacher to his successor can be seen in Libanius's school as well (e.g., *Or.* 31; cf. *School of Libanius*, 35). One such assistant, Gaudentius, evidently continued in this role past the age of eighty (Libanius, *Ep.* 745).

85. *VS* 484.

other triumphs.[86] It appears, then, that oral testimony about the rhetorical achievements of Prohaeresius circulated among members of his school. Like the stories that Eunapius heard about the successors of Iamblichus, these tales focused less upon Prohaeresius's biographical details and more upon his virtues and triumphs as an intellectual.

This feature strongly suggests that oral traditions about teachers played a significant role in giving meaning to the projects undertaken by late antique intellectual communities. These anecdotes illustrated the potential benefits of a particular school's rhetorical or philosophical training, but they also conferred a sense of identity upon the students who heard and retold them. While most students could never hope to achieve the things that Iamblichus, Maximus, or Prohaeresius did, their education gave them a personal connection to these figures and allowed students to take pride in the glory of their ancestors. In fact, the later Roman educational system perpetuated a culture in which the student's self-identity was tied to his teacher during (and often following) the period of his education.[87] This was especially true of the Athenian rhetorical schools that Eunapius attended, in which familial language and ritualized scholastic rites of passage defined the rhythms of intellectual life.[88] Though defined in a different way, late antique schools of philosophy also emphasized the close relationship between master and student.[89]

As the next chapter will show, this suggests a broader pattern that helps to explain the dynamics in the Alexandrian school that Paralius attended. While many of the oral traditions that circulated in schools explained how one could practically apply the ideas a school taught, they had a more personal element that went beyond simple questions of doctrine. This testimony enabled a student to claim his or her place, on a personal level, alongside a teacher to whom he or she had grown attached. Individually, students had close personal bonds with their teachers. Collectively, they belonged to a corps of students that felt a common loyalty to their scholastic "father" and to the intellectual family tree to which he belonged. The relatively inflexible rhetorical and philosophical curricula of the time meant that anecdotes conveying the personality and personal achievements

---

86. E.g., *VS* 488, 491.

87. For this connection holding even after schooling finished, see Cribiore, *School of Libanius*, 104; and Libanius, *Or.* 58.33. See also P. Wolf, *Vom Schulwesen der Spätantike: Studien zu Libanius* (Baden, 1952), 56.

88. For discussion see E. Watts, "The Student Self in Late Antiquity," in *Religion and the Self in Antiquity*, ed. D. Brakke, M. Satlow, and S. Weitzman (Bloomington, 2005), 236–41.

89. Proclus, for example, referred to his teachers Plutarch and Syrianus as his grandfather and father (*Vit. Proc.* 29) and also shared a tomb with Syrianus (*Vit. Proc.* 36). It also worth noting the joint tomb of the Old Academic scholarchs Polemo and Crates (Diog. Laert. 4.21), though this may have been indicative of a different sort of personal connection.

of a master and his intellectual ancestors seldom emerged in formal teaching settings. Instead, the stories that captured the personal side of a teacher and a teacher's teachers were communicated orally to students, usually through conversations between members of the intellectual family. These stories came to define the collective struggles the community endured, the collective triumphs it achieved, and the common standards to which its members aspired. The social circumstances of a school then rendered such narratives valuable commodities whose integrity needed to be defended.

DEFENDING COMMUNAL HISTORICAL DISCOURSE: PORPHYRY'S LIFE OF PLOTINUS

Eunapius distinguishes between two types of historical traditions about intellectuals. One category, the anecdotes and ideas that passed from master to student within a school, provided reliable information about the deeds of a mentor. Another, less credible category of material contained the rumors and other stories told by individuals outside of the scholastic family. Eunapius trusted ideas about the past that were controlled by a scholastic hierarchy and suspected those that circulated freely, but he does not show how students responded when rumors from outside a scholastic circle developed into criticisms of a professor. Such comments were, of course, judged to be unreliable and unpersuasive but, because they reflected negatively upon the school, they could not always be ignored. To see how members of a scholastic circle reacted to outside criticism, one can turn to another late antique biography, Porphyry's *Life of Plotinus*. The *Life of Plotinus* does occasionally address the views of its subject held by outsiders, and an examination of these instances shows how an intellectual community blunted attacks on its leadership.

Porphyry intended the *Life of Plotinus* to serve many overlapping purposes. Like many ancient biographies, the text illustrates the ways in which Plotinus's lifestyle manifested his philosophical ideas, but Porphyry aimed for something more complicated than a basic study of Plotinus's life when he composed this work. The *Life* also served as the preface to Porphyry's edition of Plotinus's writings, the *Enneads*.[90] Authors like Porphyry often used notable biographical details about a thinker to make a reader predisposed towards accepting his philosophical system, but some aspects of Plotinus's life presented Porphyry with significant challenges.[91] From all evidence, Plotinus had been a controversial figure whose often innovative philosophical teachings disregarded some foundational ideas held by other philos-

---

90. M. Edwards, "Birth, Death, and Divinity in Porphyry's Plotinus," in *Greek Biography and Panegyric*, 66.
91. Watts, *City and School*, 178–80.

ophers. His opponents frequently attacked him and, in the three decades between Plotinus's death and Porphyry's publication of the final version of the *Enneads*, a number of hostile traditions about Plotinus had begun to circulate.[92] Plotinus was attacked as a plagiarist, a charlatan, and a man whose extreme hubris was divinely punished by a horrific death. Because the *Life* worked to introduce the greatness of Plotinus's ideas by illustrating their power in the world, these charges forced Porphyry to show that hostile rumors about Plotinus were untrue.[93]

Porphyry responded to these charges by drawing heavily upon the internal discourse, both written and oral, of Plotinus's circle of followers. Porphyry's literary reaction to the charge that Plotinus plagiarized the work of Numenius is typical. This accusation apparently originated from Greece, perhaps from the circle of Eubulus, and it reached the Plotinian group through a philosopher named Trypho.[94] After the death of Plotinus, Amelius, a long-time member of the Plotinian school, wrote a response to this charge that systematically differentiated Plotinus's thought from that of Numenius.[95] He addressed a copy of this to Porphyry, with a rhetorical request that Porphyry suggest changes in instances where Amelius's arguments did not conform to those of Plotinus. Though it may have circulated more widely, the refutation that Amelius wrote stands out primarily as a composition inspired by Porphyry's own concerns for Plotinus's reputation.[96] It was an internal document designed simply to reiterate Plotinus's philosophical ideas for an already appreciative audience of his followers.

If Porphyry had intended to refute plagiarism accusations against Plotinus, Amelius's text could have been a useful tool, as useful to Porphyry's case perhaps as Longinus's praise of Plotinus, which he later quotes.[97] Nevertheless, Porphyry chose not to draw upon Amelius's philosophical counterarguments in the *Life of Plotinus*. He also does not suggest that his readers consult Amelius's writings. Instead, he reminds his readers that a work exists refuting the charge that Plotinus had plagiarized and then quotes the text of Amelius's cover letter to Porphyry explaining his reasons for writing. Indeed, far from providing evidence countering the accusation that Plotinus plagiarized his work, Porphyry simply points his

---

92. Plotinus died in 270 A.D. and Porphyry seems to have finished work on the *Life of Plotinus* in c. 300. On this dating, see Edwards, "Birth, Death, and Divinity," 66–67; cf. M. Edwards, *Neoplatonic Saints: The Lives of Plotinus and Proclus by their Students* (Liverpool, 2001), xxxiv.

93. Edwards, "Birth, Death, and Divinity," 63.

94. *VP* 17. For Eubulus as a possible source see Edwards, *Neoplatonic Saints*, 30n168. Note as well Porphyry's previous interaction with Eubulus described in *VP* 15.

95. For Amelius's role in the school see *VP* 1. In the cover letter to this treatise Amelius speaks of being far away from the school and asks that Porphyry correct the elements of the treatise that conflict with Plotinus's own thoughts. This seems to suggest a date of composition after the death of Plotinus, probably during the period when Porphyry was editing the *Enneads*.

96. *VP* 17.

97. This is *VP* 19.

readers back to a text outlining the essential contents of the Plotinian system that circulated among Plotinus's followers. In essence, his defense of Plotinus consisted of appeal to the internal literature of Plotinus's circle. It would likely be persuasive only to those who had already begun to appreciate Plotinus's singular genius.

A more interesting example concerns Porphyry's efforts to blunt the criticism of Plotinus leveled by astrologers.[98] Plotinus had come to the conclusion that, though the stars exerted some power in this life, astrology was an unreliable predictor of the future.[99] Devotees of astrology saw this as the highest form of arrogance and did not hesitate to point out that the fates had taken their revenge on Plotinus by afflicting him with a horrible final illness. Perhaps the best example of this comes from Firmicus Maternus. He described in gruesome detail how disease progressed through Plotinus's putrefying flesh and liquefying internal organs while contrasting it with the idealized, peaceful deaths of Socrates and Plato.[100] Indeed, the situation appeared doubly damaging to Plotinus's reputation because his followers, evidently repulsed by Plotinus's condition, had left him to die largely alone.

The use of an inconvenient or unpleasant death to question the integrity of famous men has many parallels in ancient literature, but this need not suggest that such criticism was unpersuasive to ancient audiences.[101] Indeed, given his habit of arguing against widespread popular beliefs, some people might have assumed that such a gruesome death was appropriate for Plotinus. Though exaggerated, Maternus's potent description suggests the circulation of polemical traditions explicitly highlighting the doctrinal causes of Plotinus's unpleasant and seemingly unphilosophical death.

If Porphyry wished for his readers to see the potency of Plotinus's thought reflected in his life, the horrifying nature of Plotinus's final illness demanded that Porphyry redefine it in a positive light. It is telling that he again drew upon the internal discourse of the Plotininan circle to make this defense. Porphyry lays out a sophisticated explanation extending through many of the first few chapters of the *Life of Plotinus*.[102] He first establishes a broad philosophical foundation upon which his narrative can be constructed. Through the deliberate inclusion and

---

98. This particular line of argument owes much to M. Edwards's compelling analysis of *VP* 2 and related passages in Edwards, "Birth, Death, and Divinity," 56–63.

99. *VP* 15. Cf. Edwards, "Birth, Death, and Divinity," 56.

100. F. Maternus, *Mathesis* 1.20–21; cf. Edwards, "Birth, Death, and Divinity," 57. Of course hemlock poisoning was far more horrific than the peaceful drift to sleep that Plato describes.

101. For inconvenient deaths, note the hostile tradition that Plato died from a lice infestation (Diogenes Laertius, 3.40–41). For other gruesome deaths see Lucian, *Alex*. 59 (on the death of Alexander of Abonoteichus), Lactantius, *De Mortibus* 33 (on the death of Galerius), and, perhaps most memorably, Socrates, *HE* 1.38 (on the death of Arius).

102. The centerpiece is *VP* 2, though Edwards ("Birth, Death, and Divinity," 55–61) sees this defense shaping some of what Porphyry writes in *VP* 1 as well.

omission of details about Plotinus's life, Porphyry emphasizes that Plotinus had no interest in commemorating or even noting his day of birth and little concern for his body.[103] In Porphyry's account, Plotinus's death represented only a stage in the migration of his soul to the heavens, with the probable implication that a long illness was more conducive to this ascent than a quick death.[104]

Once he had laid this philosophical foundation, Porphyry crafted an account of Plotinus's last days that revealed a sage living out his final illness in a way that was consistent with his teachings. He claims to base his account on the testimony of Eustochius, the member of Plotinus's inner circle who last saw the master alive. Eustochius described a malady that began with vocal hoarseness and progressed to blurred vision and ulcerations of the feet and hands. At some point, Eustochius continued, Plotinus's habit of kissing his followers made them uncomfortable and they stopped visiting. Plotinus then left Rome and retired to a villa owned by the widow of Zethus, one of his former students. This widow and Castricius, another former member of the inner circle, then tended to his needs. When Plotinus neared death, Eustochius came to him. He reported to Porphyry that "Plotinus said, 'I am still waiting for you,' adding that he was trying to raise the divine in himself to the divine in all. As a snake crept under the bed in which he was lying and slipped out through a hole that was there in the wall, his spirit left him."[105]

While actual circumstances made it difficult to suggest that Plotinus died nobly, Porphyry's carefully crafted account of his teacher's final illness enables him to emphasize that, at each stage of his affliction, Plotinus was in full control of his activities.[106] At his condition's outset, Plotinus decided to stop taking massages. As he deteriorated, Plotinus again made the decision to leave Rome and distance himself from his followers. Indeed, Porphyry even implies that Plotinus chose the moment when his death was to occur.[107] This sense of self-determination also extends to the inconvenient abandonment of Plotinus by his followers. Such a thing was highly irregular, at least within literary presentations of ancient intellectual circles, and it suggests that Plotinus's followers had become particularly disenchanted with their master.[108] Here again, the testimony of Eustochius presents a different picture. Because it was Plotinus who decided to leave his main

---

103. Edwards, "Birth, Death, and Divinity," 57.
104. Edwards, "Birth, Death, and Divinity," 57. Cf. VP 2.26–27.
105. VP 2. The translation is that of Edwards, slightly amended.
106. Edwards, "Birth, Death, and Divinity," 57.
107. Ibid.
108. It seems to have been something of a literary convention to describe how the followers of a great teacher attended him on his deathbed. Note, for example, Plato, *Phaedo* 116b–118a on the death of Socrates (Plato was, however, absent; for discussion of his illness see G. Most, "A Cock for Asclepius," *CQ* 43 [1993], 96–111); Eunapius, *VS* 505 on the death of Chrysanthius; and Marinus, *Vit. Proc.* 20, 26 as well as Damascius, *Vit. Is.* 125A–B for the presence of companions around Proclus before his death.

group of followers in Rome, one could not say that they had abandoned him or his teaching. Furthermore, Plotinus stayed in a house that had belonged to one former member of his inner circle, he lived on resources provided by another, and a third, Eustochius, attended to him at the moment of his death. Plotinus's followers presented his final retirement to Campania not as the abandonment of a teacher by his students but as the master's deliberate move away from a large group of followers to a smaller group so that he could be housed in surroundings that facilitated the gradual disentangling of soul and body.

One final element of Eustochius's report bears examination. When Eustochius arrived at Plotinus's bedside, he saw a snake crawl under the bed and out a hole in the wall. This odd detail has proven difficult to understand. The snake has been variously identified as Plotinus's daemon, Hermes Trismegistus, or the animal into which his soul transmigrated.[109] Recently Mark Edwards proposed that we understand the snake to represent Asclepius who, in this instance, has come to Plotinus, given him the opportunity to choose his own cure for his ailment, and granted his request to be cured of the mortal condition by effecting the separation of his body and soul.[110] Porphyry then juxtaposes Eustochius, who was a physician by training, with the divine physician Asclepius and, to borrow Edwards's phrase, stations a human doctor "to gather up the mortal wrappings" after Asclepius has freed his soul.[111]

In sum, Porphyry provides a narrative of Plotinus's death that emphasizes his freedom of action, shows the devotion of his followers, and even validates his claim that "the gods should come to me."[112] Remarkably, when the narrative is read as an accompaniment to Plotinus's own teachings in the *Enneads,* Porphyry almost convinces that Plotinus's death need not reflect badly upon his teaching.[113] Porphyry's artful presentation deserves some credit for this, but one should not disregard the fact that Porphyry's information derives from oral testimony that circulated within the school. Just as Porphyry's account becomes more persuasive as one becomes better aware of Plotinus's teaching, Eustochius constructed his testimony around his own understanding of the practical application of the Plotinian system. He likely understood Plotinus's death in much the same way that Porphyry explains it to his readers. When Eustochius spoke of these events to other members of Plotinus's school, they too would have relied upon Plotinus's

---

109. On this note the discussion of Edwards, "Birth, Death, and Divinity," 59–61 as well as "Two Episodes in Porphyry's *Life of Plotinus," Historia* 40 (1991), 456–64.

110. Edwards, "Birth, Death, and Divinity," 61. Compare this to the line of interpretation surrounding *Phaedo* 116a7–8 (e.g., Damascius, *Commentary on the Phaedo,* 285 in L. G. Westerink, ed., *The Greek Commentaries on Plato's Phaedo, Vol. II, Damascius,* [Amsterdam, 1977]).

111. Ibid.

112. *VP* 10. Note the comments of Edwards, ibid. 61n28.

113. Edwards, ibid 63.

philosophical system to craft their understanding of its significance. Until Eustochius's report appeared in Porphyry's text, his words circulated internally among Plotinus's followers. All of them were schooled in Plotinus's system and presumably understood Eustochius's account of his death in much the same way that Porphyry's text presents it.

Porphyry's discussion of the plagiarism charges against Plotinus and his picture of Plotinus's final illness suggest the degree to which members of intellectual circles reacted to criticism by turning back to their own internal traditions. In a sense, a challenge to the integrity of an intellectual group seems to have prompted members to look inward for traditions or testimony that validated their belief in the importance of the group's ideas and its leaders. It is this dynamic that Porphyry's text here typifies, but Porphyry is not alone in behaving this way. In his biography of Proclus, Marinus similarly blunts anticipated criticism by drawing upon oral testimony that circulated within the school. In the fifteenth chapter of the *Life of Proclus*, Marinus presents Proclus's forced exile to Lydia not as a political failure but as a divinely-ordained opportunity to become initiated into a new set of ancient mysteries. Of more immediate relevance to our discussion, Marinus explained away Proclus's long descent into senility by describing a vision that suggested that this was preordained. For obvious reasons, Proclus's dementia presented his devotees with an even more severe credibility problem than Plotinus's bodily disintegration. To make sense of the dramatic decline in Proclus's mental capacities, Marinus mentioned a vision in which Proclus's revered master Plutarch of Athens appeared to Proclus and foretold that he would live for seventy years. Proclus "lived seventy-five years, as we said before, but for five years he was no longer in good health . . . Indeed, he marveled whenever he remembered the dream and each time it came to mind he said he had lived only seventy years."[114] Because the community had accepted that Proclus experienced divinely inspired visions throughout his life (a point Marinus established earlier in the text), Proclus's followers would accept the plausibility of Plutarch's prediction.[115] Members of Proclus's inner circle would recognize that, far from being a sign of personal or spiritual failure, the master's unfortunate descent into senility actually confirmed the elevation of his spirit and his deep connection with the divine. As Porphyry had done with Plotinus, Marinus transformed Proclus's inconvenient death into a proof of his authority.

The above examination of community formation in the Old Academy, the internal oral traditions of the Iamblichan and Prohaeresian intellectual circles, and the

---

114. *Vit. Proc.* 26.
115. On Proclus's divinely inspired visions see *Vit. Proc.* 6, 27, 28, 30–31, 32. An interesting parallel is *Vit. Proc.* 36, in which his second teacher Syrianus appears to him.

inwardly reflexive defenses of Plotinus and Proclus correspond to a broader picture of the personal experience of scholars in the ancient world. In antiquity, successful intellectual circles established a particular, widely-known institutional identity that attracted students. Once a student joined such a group, he would become privy to specific details of a scholastic past to which he was now joined. Communal elders passed this information to new initiates in intimate settings that enhanced the personal ties binding master and student. This private information often confirmed and further developed the public reputation that the school worked to establish. In fact, one must probably imagine that the members of late antique intellectual circles spent much of their time outside of the classroom recounting illustrative anecdotes about past and current leaders of the community.[116] As Eunapius seems to suggest, these centered upon a cluster of distinctive and important themes that lent cohesion to the group of students and illustrated the intellectual community's special status.[117]

As followers came to identify strongly with a particular school, the ideals and behaviors communicated by that school's internal traditions became a part of their identity. Indeed, some intellectuals, like Porphyry and Marinus, reached the point where their primary social identity was tied to membership in a particular intellectual community.[118] This made defense of the traditions used to sustain these communities important. In moments where these traditions came under attack, it was natural for intellectuals to respond by vigorously reaffirming their confidence in their school and its leadership. Marinus and Porphyry show that such defenses often drew upon the internal historical and literary traditions of a school, a seemingly odd choice given that these traditions often simply reiterated the very themes whose credibility was threatened. Nevertheless, external criticism often reinforced an individual's identification with an intellectual circle by encouraging him to recall the communal history that gave emotional and historical meaning to his own membership in the group.[119]

---

116. This is, at any rate, implied by Eunapius's relationship with Tuscianus. Contemporary parallels are perhaps also instructive here. In *Saint and Sufi in Modern Egypt: An Essay in the Sociology of Religion* (Oxford, 1973), Michael Gilsenan's important study of the Sufi Order *Hamidiya Shadhiliya*, the author describes how discussions of the karamat or "grace acts" of the Order's founder dominate the internal discourse of the circle's membership. Gilsenan comments: "His acts are perhaps the major topic of conversation among the brothers when they gather for meetings after special occasions or when they sit together in coffee shops" (33). These anecdotes are important because they emphasize the special characteristics of the community to which the brothers belong.

117. Cf. Gilsenan, *Saint and Sufi*, 29.

118. Borrowing the paradigm of Gilsenan, *Saint and Sufi*, 70.

119. Cognitive neuroscience has recently shown how decisions that people make about the reliability of data are constrained in part by the emotional significance of the decision (see, for example, D. Westen and G. O. Gabbard, "Developments in Cognitive Neuroscience: 1. Conflict, Compromise, and Connectionism," *Journal of the American Psychoanalytic Association*, 50 [2002], 85–87). So, in

These case studies, then, show how membership in an intellectual community could be shaped. They trace this formative process from one's initial acquaintance with the group through to his or her intense identification with a school and its traditions. They reveal that intellectual circles understood the value of their traditions about the past and, once students had come to identify with a particular circle or teaching tradition, they had little inclination to accept criticism of the school or its leadership. In fact, the defense of an intellectual circle's historical legacy seems to have been a recognized requirement of membership in such a group.

---

an interesting study (described in Westen and Gabbard, "Developments," 86), it was shown that people's feelings about the reliability of vote-counting measures in Florida following the 2000 Presidential election were directly tied to their feelings about the different candidates. The conclusion was that only "when affective constraints are minimal [do] cognitive constraints tend to influence people's judgments."

3

Past, Present, and Future in Late Neoplatonic Historical Discourse

This section of our study began with Zacharias Scholasticus's description of students who were "subjected to the follies of paganism" by their teachers and reacted to criticism of their scholastic culture with violence. The preceding chapter has shown how personal and structural elements of the ancient intellectual environment encouraged students to become attached to the historical traditions that shaped their communities. It has also demonstrated that students frequently responded to criticisms of their teachers by rallying to defend their reputations. This chapter explores the historical traditions that circulated in the Alexandrian intellectual environment in which Paralius studied. It will then consider how Paralius's criticism of them triggered a violent response. Our analysis will conclude by describing how the events of the late 480s changed the ideas emphasized in Alexandrian and Athenian scholastic traditions.

This discussion must begin, however, with an introduction to our sources. The surviving source that best describes the history of late-fifth-century Alexandrian intellectuals is Damascius's *Life of Isidore*.[1] Unfortunately, Damascius's text is not

---

1. P. Athanassiadi (*Damascius: The Philosophical History* [Athens, 1999], 39–40) has argued that this work should be called the *Philosophical History* instead of the previously accepted title, *Life of Isidore*. I am not convinced that this change is necessary. Two Byzantine authors mention the work explicitly. One, Photius, twice says that he "read Damascius regarding the *Life of Isidore the Philosopher*" (Cod. 181.125b30 and Cod. 242.335a21). In Codex 181, Photius also discusses the oddity of the work being so entitled when it covers a whole host of other intellectuals as well. The second notice is found in the Suda's problematic biographical entry for Damascius (an entry that begins by describing him as a "Stoic philosopher"). This lists a set of publications by Damascius including "commentaries on Plato, *On First Principles*, and a philosophical history." The *Suda* seems to offer a description of

as straightforward as, say, Eunapius's *Lives of the Sophists*. As it currently stands, the *Life of Isidore* exists only in fragments preserved in Photius's *Bibliotheke* and the Suda, a situation that obscures much of the text's original narrative purpose.[2] Nevertheless, the fragments that remain demonstrate that Damascius used the text to discuss the life and career of his friend and teacher Isidore. Damascius placed Isidore within a broad eastern Mediterranean intellectual world and described how his philosophical virtues compared to those of his contemporaries.[3] The *Life of Isidore*, then, provides a composite measure of many philosophers that was based upon their intellectual skill, personal behavior, and willingness to maintain philosophical integrity in the face of outside pressure.

While Damascius's methods present a challenge to anyone attempting to undertake a thorough literary analysis of the *Life of Isidore*, his digressive discussion reveals a number of the historical traditions that shaped the intellectual communities to which Damascius belonged. In fact, as Damascius notes at the outset, the various anecdotes he tells about Isidore and his associates are "those things which I believe to be true and which I have heard from my master."[4] Like Eunapius, Damascius presents glimpses of the past that were transmitted to him orally by his teacher. As the text proceeds, however, Damascius makes it clear that he has also drawn upon conversations and anecdotes that he heard from other members of the Alexandrian Neoplatonic network.[5] His text then provides a survey of the historical discourse in circulation within the Alexandrian intellectual environment.

THE LIFE OF ISIDORE AND ITS SOURCES

Damascius assembled the *Life of Isidore* in the 520s from raw narrative materials he had been collecting for much of his adult life.[6] This material ranges from the reports that he heard in the early 470s to recollections of his own experience of

---

the work and not its specific title. Because Photius reproduces and then engages critically with the title *Life of Isidore*, he seems both more confident and better informed. Furthermore, Isidore is the central figure in the text, from beginning to end, and the scope of Damascius's project is much narrower than that of Numenius to which Athanassiadi has compared it.

2. On this, note the comments of Athanassiadi, *Damascius*, 61–62.
3. On Damascius's aims, note Athanassiadi, *Damascius*, 24–27.
4. *Vit. Is.* 6A. Note as well *Vit. Is.* 84E.
5. Among the Alexandrians he mentions as sources for such traditions are the ex-consul Severus (*Vit. Is.* 7, 51A–E), the philosopher Theosebius (*Vit. Is.* 45B), an older contemporary philosopher named Hierax (*Vit. Is.* 58B), Asclepiodotus (*Vit. Is.* 96D), as well as the Athenian Marinus (*Vit. Is.* 98B) and the Damascene Severianus (*Vit. Is.* 108).
6. The date of composition is generally placed between 517 and 526. On this, see Athanassiadi, *Damascius*, 43 and 58.

events in the 510s, but Damascius does seem to have tried to remain relatively faithful to the content and themes conveyed by his original sources.[7] Within the *Life of Isidore,* Damascius includes anecdotes indicative of the intellectual and spiritual achievements of individuals as well as descriptions of significant places and accounts of marvelous tales.[8] He also identifies a small number of respected mentors upon whom he relies for many of these stories.

One of his most notable sources was Flavius Messius Phoebus Severus, a consul in 470.[9] Although defined by his high public office, Severus abandoned his political career after the fall of the western emperor Anthemius in 472 and moved to Alexandria in order to cultivate a personal interest in philosophy. Once he arrived, Severus established an Alexandrian intellectual salon in which he read philosophical works from his personal library and discussed ideas with the many intellectuals who called upon him.[10] On one occasion, Damascius heard Severus describe the visit of certain Indian Brahmans.[11] Severus told his listeners about the diet of his Indian guests, their political role at home, and their ability to use prayer to cure droughts, famines, and epidemics. He further fascinated his listeners with tales of seven-headed snakes, root vegetables shaped like Gorgons, and Italian battles in which the souls of long-dead combatants continued their fight.[12]

Some of the most interesting material that Severus discussed with Damascius highlighted pagan political resistance to Christian religious domination. Severus suggested to Damascius that the western emperor Anthemius (467–72) was a pagan and Severus claimed that he served as consul under Anthemius as part of a secret plan to restore paganism.[13] He also described portents and omens that directly correlated to political events, both Roman and foreign. Severus told Damascius that his horse emitted sparks until he took consular office, and indicated that a similar thing had happened to the Ostrogoth Valamir.[14] Furthermore, though Damascius is less explicit about this, Severus may also have been the source for some of the later discussion of pagan plots to assassinate various Christian emperors.[15]

---

7. Athanassiadi (*Damascius,* 60) rightly comments that much of this material is deliberately presented in the voice of the original narrator.

8. For the genre to which this material belongs, note Athanassiadi, *Damascius,* 59–61.

9. Consul of the West in 470 (*PLRE* II 1005–6; cf. R. S. Bagnall et al., *Consuls of the Later Roman Empire,* [Atlanta, 1987], 470). On his general reputation see Malchus, fr. 5 (Blockley).

10. *Vit. Is.* 51C.

11. *Vit. Is.* 51D.

12. *Vit Is.* 50, 51E. Though Damascius does not attribute the Italian battle narrative explicitly to Severus, nearly all of his knowledge of Western affairs seems to come from Severus.

13. *Vit. Is.* 77A.

14. This is *Vit. Is.* 51A. Damascius here misidentifies Valamir as a companion of Attila and the father of Theoderic.

15. Aside from the actions of Anthemius (about which Severus must be the source), the most notable examples of this concern Marcellinus of Dalmatia (*Vit. Is.* 69A–D) and a general historical

This sort of political discussion was not new to intellectual pagans like Damascius. Before he arrived in Alexandria, Damascius had heard similar things from Severianus, his first teacher of rhetoric. Like Severus, Severianus had once served in the imperial government but saw his career end prematurely, in large part because of his paganism.[16] In fact, Severianus proudly advertised his refusal to convert to Christianity, on occasion even passing around an imperial letter in which he was promised high office in exchange for his nominal conversion. Severianus also took part in a plot to kill the emperor Zeno and restore paganism. The conspiracy was divulged by Aspar and Severianus barely escaped execution, but Severianus spoke freely and openly about his involvement not even five years after it was uncovered.[17] One must then imagine that the scholastic environment saw the circulation of a number of contemporary traditions celebrating high-level pagan attempts to regain political influence.[18]

A different, less hopeful sort of political narrative circulated in Alexandria as well. Instead of lionizing prominent pagans who tried to change the political conditions of the Empire, these traditions focused upon pagan intellectuals who refused to compromise their behaviors when pressured by Christians. Damascius seems to have heard many of these traditions from Theosebius, the period's best-known scholar of Epictetus. Among Alexandrian intellectuals, Theosebius stood out for the virtuousness of his private life. Though he had a slight public profile, Theosebius worked privately to "regulate his outward way of life and the life within" and reform the personal behaviors of others.[19] Theosebius shared stories with Damascius about his personal chastity, including a remarkable account of his decision to stop having sexual intercourse when it became clear that his wife was infertile.[20] In addition, Damascius heard about an exorcism that Theosebius performed by calling upon Helios and the God of the Jews.[21]

Theosebius's Epictetan inclinations revealed themselves most clearly in the

---

survey at *Vit. Is.* 115. Because the Marcellinus material includes references to Salustius, an Athenian source is preferable to Severus. The general survey involves Severianus, another of Damascius's teachers, and he seems to have described the most notable pagan actions. Severus may have described some of the earlier attempts such as that of the unnamed "great general of the East." On this material, see as well R. von Haehling, "Damascius und die heidnische Opposition im 5 Jahrhundert nach Christus." *JAC* 23 (1980), 82–95.

16. *Vit. Sev.* 108.

17. Damascius seems to have left for Alexandria around 478 (on the basis of Photius's comments in *Bib.* 181.81–89), meaning that he would likely have heard about this from Severianus sometime between 476 (Zeno's restoration) and 478.

18. Also notable are a third set of traditions describing the involvement of the philosopher Salustius with Marcellinus, the independent military leader of Dalmatia in the 470s. On this see *Vit. Is.* 69D.

19. *Vit. Is.* 46D.

20. *Vit. Is.* 46E.

21. *Vit. Is.* 46B; note as well the comments of Athanassiadi, *Damascius*, 135n104.

narratives emphasizing the private acts of virtuous resistance performed by past pagan philosophers. One such tradition, which concerned Theosebius's teacher Hierocles, can be traced explicitly from the *Life of Isidore* to Theosebius. "Once in Byzantium, he gave offence to the ruling party and, being taken to court, he was savagely beaten up. As he flowed with blood he gathered some of it into the hollow of his hand and sprinkled it over the judge, exclaiming: 'There, Cyclops, drink the wine now that you have devoured the human flesh.' He was condemned to exile and after returning to Alexandria some time later he continued to teach philosophy to his disciples just as before."[22]

This short anecdote about Hierocles forms part of a larger collection of narratives that describe pagan intellectuals virtuously resisting Christian pressure. These include an account of the murder of Hypatia and a discussion of Olympus's brave rallying of the faithful during the Christian siege of the Serapeum in 391.[23] Each recalls a scene of Alexandrian pagan victimization at the hands of Christians and emphasizes how, despite extremely difficult circumstances, a particular philosopher maintained his or her composure and dignity. These traditions about philosophical resistance join with other testimony describing Hierocles' behavior as well as Theosebius's own personal moderation and chastity to illustrate Epictetan ethical behaviors.[24] Here, as in Xenocrates' Old Academy or Eunapius's *Lives of the Sophists*, we can see a teacher using his own personal history as well as those of his intellectual ancestors to illustrate the practical application of the ethical theories he taught.

Less politically potent but even more remarkable material came to Damascius from Isidore, his philosophical mentor and the man responsible for his decision to embrace a philosophical life.[25] The most memorable tales concerned the Egyptian brothers Heraiscus and Asclepiades, two of Isidore's philosophy teachers who were particularly accomplished theologians.[26] Damascius knew each of these men personally and had read their hymns and theological treatises, but Isidore's statements still largely informed his assessment of their achievements. The stories that he told emphasized their skill at incorporating Egyptian religious rituals within the Neoplatonic philosophical system.[27] Damascius includes two pieces of information about Asclepiades that seem to come from Isidore. The first de-

---

22. *Vit. Is.* 45B (trans. Athanassiadi). This material must have come to Damascius from Theosebius, his only named source for materials related to Hierocles.

23. These are *Vit. Is.* 43A–E (Hypatia) and 42A–F (Olympus). The Hypatia material certainly comes from more than one source, with some elements coming from "ignorant legends" (fr. 43A) and others from a more secure scholastic tradition.

24. Note in this context Simplicius, *In Ench.* 32.186–91.

25. Isidore likely told Damascius many of these tales in the course of their eight-month-long journey from Alexandria to Athens in 488/9.

26. *Vit. Is.* 72A.

27. It is, of course, open to debate how traditional the Egyptian religion practiced by Asclepiades and Heraiscus was. On the development of Egyptian religion in the Roman period see the important

scribes a long lock of hair that Asclepiades once saw floating in the Nile and understood to be hair of the goddess Isis (it may in fact have been an extremely long piece of a papyrus plant).[28] Damascius also recorded a number of marvelous anecdotes about Asclepiades' experiences with the holy meteorites called baetyls in Syria.[29] More amazing tales circulated about Heraiscus.[30] He had extraordinary powers of sense perception that allowed him to distinguish sacred statues in which gods dwelled and to discern when a woman was menstruating.[31] Some said that his birth prefigured his holiness because he was born with his finger physically joined to his mouth in the same way as Horus and Helios.[32] One extremely clipped fragment even mentions a dream in which it was prophesized that Heraiscus would become a Bacchus, an Orphic term indicating a truly accomplished philosopher.[33]

The most impressive stories that Isidore shared with his young friend concerned his spiritual mentor, Serapio.[34] A sort of urban ascetic, Serapio embodied the Pythagorean notion of living unnoticed.[35] According to Damascius, Serapio lived alone in his house and had contact with a few neighbors only when necessary. Though he would visit holy places during the appropriate seasons for festivals, he spent most of his time at home praying and singing hymns. These behaviors were consistent with his philosophical inclinations. Because he concerned himself with the spiritual elements of philosophy, Serapio had little interest in technical elements of the discipline and even less use for books. Damascius, surely working from Isidore's personal knowledge of Serapio's lifestyle, says that he possessed only

---

discussions of D. Frankfurter, *Religion in Roman Egypt: Assimilation and Resistance* (Princeton, 1998); and, more particularly, Frankfurter, "The Consequences of Hellenism in Late Antique Egypt: Religious Worlds and Actors," *Archiv für Religionsgeschichte* 2 (2000), 184–92.

28. *Vit. Is.* 72E. Note here the reasonable explanation of Athanassiadi, *Damascius*, 187n169.

29. *Vit. Is.* 72F. In concluding his paraphrase of this section Photius says: "he says that he himself and Isidore saw these same things at a later time." It is likely, then, that Asclepiades' experiences were brought up by Isidore when he and Damascius shared them.

30. Heraiscus may be identified with the unnamed mentor whose every word Isidore recorded (*Vit. Is.* 35A; for Heraiscus as the subject see C. Zintzen, *Damascii Vitae Isidori Reliquae*, [Hildesheim, 1967] 62; compare, however, Athanassiadi, *Damascius*, 115n74).

31. *Vit. Is.* 76D–E.

32. *Vit. Is.* 76E.

33. *Vit. Is.* 76A. On this Orphic language see Athanassiadi, *Damascius*, 57 and 195n185, as well as Orphic fr. 5 (Kern).

34. Isidore must be the source for these stories. On this, see as well P. Athanassiadi, *La Lutte pour L'Orthodoxie dans le Platonisme Tardif: Du Numénius á Damascius* (Paris, 2006), 207.

35. λάθε βιώσας (*Vit. Is.* 111). This (originally Epicurean) expression is paralleled in *Vit. Proc.* 15. See on this the comments of Athanassiadi, *Damascius*, 265n284; M. Edwards, *Neoplatonic Saints: The Lives of Plotinus and Proclus by their Students* (Liverpool, 2001), 81n157.

two or three heavily worn books.[36] In fact, Serapio seems to have preferred Orphic texts above all others and spent much of his time reading these works, pondering their meanings, and directing any unresolved questions to Isidore. Damascius makes it clear that Serapio did this in silent anonymity for most of his later life.[37]

To understand the significance of these testimonies it helps to consider them alongside the similar material that Damascius harvested from Theosebius. Whereas Theosebius defined the real-world applications of Epictetan teaching, Serapio inhabits Alexandrian intellectual discourse as a different sort of ethical exemplar. His religious and spiritual dedication reflected both Neo-Pythagorean ethical dictums and Neoplatonic teaching about spirituality.[38] Historical traditions about Serapio and Theosebius then function in a complementary fashion, with each man becoming emblematic of different doctrinal strands within the ethical teachings of Alexandrian Neoplatonists.

Beyond the explicit testimony of his teachers, Damascius's profound sensitivity to traditions associated with holy places further shaped his view of the Alexandrian intellectual world of the 470s and early 480s. Indeed, the rich Egyptian spiritual environment had a tendency to spill into the conversations of Alexandrian intellectuals. To Damascius and his mentors, the gods remained present and active, if one knew where to find them. Heraiscus, for example, found a sacred statue of Aion that had been lost amidst the bustle of Alexandria.[39] Other teachers knew about hidden shrines in which ancient rituals could still be practiced, and remembered locations where the remains of long-gone temples could still be found.[40] Teachers even tried to keep alive their own rather peculiar allegorized reading of Egyptian hieroglyphs.[41] Alexandrian intellectuals also shared tales describing the continued power of divine places in and around Alexandria. Sometimes they mentioned supernatural appearances and encounters with holy figures, while other discussions illustrated the tangible benefits of a divine presence.[42] In the same way that the personal legacies of Hierocles, Theosebius, and Serapio

36. Compare here Proclus's statement (at *Vit. Proc.* 38): "If I were a king, I would bring it about that the Chaldean Oracles and the *Timaeus* alone of all ancient books were preserved."

37. *Vit. Is.* 111.

38. Damascius sets his interpretation of Serapio as an exemplar of the Cronian life against the competing idea that Pamprepius, the arch-villain of the *Life of Isidore*, embodied the Typhonian life (*Vit. Is.* 112A). As will be discussed below, this is probably a revisionist view of Pamprepius.

39. *Vit. Is.* 76E.

40. For hidden shrines see *Vit. Is.* 53B as well as the discussion of Frankfurter, *Religion in Roman Egypt*, 40–41. For the rediscovery of a lost temple see *Vit. Is.* 53D.

41. The *Hieroglyphica* of Horapollon stands out as a particular example of this genre. Note as well *Vit. Is.* 74A–E. For discussion of Horapollon's project, see H.-J. Thissen, *Vom Bild Zum Buchstaben–Vom Buchstaben Zum Bild. Von Der Arbeit an Horapollons Hieroglyphika* (Stuttgart, 1998).

42. E.g., *Vit. Is.* 75F.

illustrated Neoplatonic ethical teachings, so too did traditions about holy places reflect the idea that certain blessed locations facilitated access to the divine.[43] Here again we see real-world illustrations lending depth and color to the abstract ideas presented within Neoplatonic classrooms.

EATING, DRINKING, AND LEARNING NEOPLATONIC HISTORY

Damascius's text also captures some of the private moments when professors told students about their scholastic predecessors. Teacher-student meals represented one of the most important settings in which these stories could be shared. It was during such a meal that Isidore learned that Asclepiades had seen a "lock of Isis" in the Nile.[44] Similarly it seems to have been at another dinner that Severianus spoke to Damascius and his brother Julian about his public career and Zeno's offer of high office in exchange for his conversion to Christianity.[45] One also suspects that the long, spiritually rich conversations that Damascius and Isidore shared with Asclepiodotus after their short trips to sacred spots around Aphrodisias may have occurred over leisurely dinners.[46]

One should not underestimate the impact that these meals had on students. The simple invitation to dine with a teacher represented a significant reward for a student and bestowed upon him an elevated status within the community. Damascius describes his brother's invitation to dine with Severianus as "a reward for his enthusiasm that was befitting a member of his inner circle."[47] Other schools in other periods accorded the same status to an invitation to dine with a teacher. Herodes Atticus offered intellectually stimulating lunches to his most promising pupils[48] while two of Proclus's early teachers gave him standing dinner invitations in recognition of his scholastic achievements.[49] At the same time, these meetings often engendered a bond between teacher and student that brought tangible meaning to the familial language of a school. When Proclus first received a dinner invitation from Leonas, his Alexandrian teacher of rhetoric, it meant that Leonas would not only share "his knowledge with Proclus but [that] he even deemed

---

43. Proclus, *In Rem.* 77.13–78.24; cf. Athanassiadi, *La Lutte*, 195n12.
44. *Vit. Is.* 72E. For a discussion of the identity of these "hairs" note the comments of Athanassiadi, *Damascius*, 187n169 as well as D. Bonneau, *La crue du Nil, divinité égyptienne à travers mille ans d'histoire, 332 av. – 641 ap. J.-C.* (Paris, 1964), 259–63.
45. Though not made explicit, such is the implication of *Vit. Is.* 108.
46. *Vit. Is.* 87A, 96D.
47. *Vit. Is.* 108. I am here interpreting ἑταῖρος as "member of a school's inner circle," the most common meaning in the *Life of Isidore*. The word could also simply mean "companion."
48. Philostratus, *VS* 585–86.
49. *Vit. Proc.* 8, 9.

Proclus worthy to share his house and dine together with his wife and children, as if he were his own legitimate child."[50]

The conversations and anecdotes exchanged in these intimate personal settings often acquired the same emotional power as oral traditions shared within families.[51] Indeed, these traditions were doubly valuable as tools to communicate the historical identity of an intellectual community. Not only did they draw upon the authority of the professor, the highest level of the scholastic hierarchy, but they were also selectively transmitted to the most promising new members of an intellectual community in a setting that specifically recognized their accomplishments.[52] This experience linked together a student's pride in his own achievements, his affection for his teacher, and the experience of learning about his own intellectual forefathers. It could not better nurture his emotional attachment to the community's view of its past.

While many of the anecdotes that flowed through the Alexandrian scholastic environment seem to have been transmitted within these intimate contexts, the late antique commentary tradition suggests that elements of Neoplatonic historical discourse occasionally leaked out in less selective settings. Despite the volume of late antique commentaries that survive, anecdotal discussion of the past remains rare within these texts. Commentators occasionally introduce the exegetical perspectives of their teachers in discussions about a particular text, but they rarely discuss the personality or deeds of a philosophical mentor.[53] One text, Olympiodorus's *Commentary on the Gorgias*, stands out as a notable exception. This seems to have been Olympiodorus's first attempt at a commentary and, as such, it owes significant debts to Olympiodorus's teacher Ammonius. He drew upon Ammonius for exegetical approaches[54] but, as the commentary progresses (and, perhaps, as the young professor finds himself stretching to fill class time), the Ammonian material becomes more frequent. In fact, after completely neglecting to mention Ammonius in the first half of the commentary, Olympiodorus includes six informal comments or anecdotes that Ammonius shared with him in the text's second

50. *Vit. Proc.* 8.
51. On familial oral traditions in antiquity see, for example, R. Thomas, *Oral Tradition and Written Record in Classical Athens* (Cambridge, 1989), 9, 94–154. Also note the discussion of similar traditions with the anthropological category of "esoteric tradition" in J. Vansina, *Oral Tradition: A Study in Historical Methodology* (Harmondsworth, 1973), 34.
52. For the authority attached to ideas coming from teachers see the discussion of Eunapius above. Note as well the comments of Damascius, *Vit. Is.* 6A and 98B.
53. Simplicius serves as an excellent example of this tendency. Despite calling upon his teachers Damascius and Ammonius as sources for interpretative ideas on a number of occasions (e.g., *in Ph* 9.59.24, 9.193.2, 10.1363.9 [for Ammonius] and *in Ph* 9.630.35, 9.778.27 [for Damascius]) , he gives no significant anecdotes about either one. In fact, the closest he comes to this is his description of an astrolabe experiment that Ammonius conducted while he was present (*in Cael* 7.462.20–31).
54. E.g., 32.2, 41.9.

half.⁵⁵ These moments show that teachers occasionally introduced small selections of the historical traditions of Alexandrian intellectual circles into their classrooms. In this way, some elements of the closed, internal, oral traditions of philosophical circles slipped into public view. Although a classroom discussion lacked the emotional impact of a teacher-student dinner, these rare glimpses into a communal scholastic past would still have been impressive to students steeped in the familial culture of a late antique school.

ORAL TRADITION AND SCHOLASTIC IDENTITY IN THE ALEXANDRIAN SCHOOLS OF THE 480S

The physical environment of the Alexandrian schools becomes relevant when considering the broader power of these traditions. The remains unearthed at Kom el-Dikka may be (or at least strongly resemble) the classrooms, porticoes, and courtyards in which Ammonius, Isidore, Asclepiades, and their colleagues taught.⁵⁶ Even if they are not, the writings of Zacharias Scholasticus describe a space that corresponds to that found at Kom el-Dikka.⁵⁷ It included a complex of multiple lecture rooms that bordered a portico in which students milled about, chatting with each other while they waited for class to start. Zacharias Scholasticus's *Ammonius* further describes an area called "the *temenos* of the Muses," in which "poets, rhetors, and students of grammar make their declamations" as well as an area away from this in which students could go to further discuss difficult issues raised in class.⁵⁸ This seems to have been located near the classrooms, but it remained a distinct and less-trafficked space to which students went only on occasion. Here again the vast open block of gardens next to the classrooms at Kom el-Dikka provides a useful parallel, if it is not in fact the same space that Zacharias describes.⁵⁹

---

55. *In Gorgiam* 24.2, 39.2, 40.5, 44.5, 44.6, 48.5. On this, note the comments of Jackson, Lycos, and Tarrant, *Olympiodorus' Commentary on Plato's Gorgias* (Leiden, 1998), 252n739.

56. For these classrooms, see chapter 1, above.

57. *Vit. Sev.* 23. The unique nature of the school rooms found at Kom el-Dikka further supports the identification of these remains with those used by Horapollon and his colleagues. For other teaching spaces see R. Cribiore, "Spaces for Teaching in Late Antiquity," in *Alexandria: Auditoria of Kôm el-Dikka and Late Antique Education*, ed. T. Derda, T. Markiewicz, and E. Wipszycka (Warsaw, 2007), 143–50.

58. Zacharias, *Amm.* ll. 361–69.

59. On this space see G. Majcherek, "The Late Roman Auditoria: An Archeological Overview," in *Alexandria: Auditoria of Kôm el-Dikka and Late Antique Education*, ed. T. Derda, T. Markiewicz, and E. Wipszycka (Warsaw, 2007), 14–15; J. McKenzie, "The Place in Late Antique Alexandria 'Where the Alchemists and Scholars Sit,'" in *Alexandria: Auditoria*, 79. Elsewhere McKenzie equates the *temenos* of the Muses explicitly with the teaching complex of Kom el-Dikka (*The Architecture of Alexandria and Egypt, 300 B.C.–A.D. 700* [New Haven, 2007]), 214).

One can imagine this teaching area to be a public space in which students of various ages from a number of different schools circulated freely and through which interesting stories told during the previous night's dinner or that day's teaching quickly spread. So, if Olympiodorus filled the last minutes of class with an anecdote about Ammonius, his audience of young men would spill out into a crowded public space excitedly sharing these stories.[60] As these crowds of students leaving the supervised environment of the classroom mingled and scattered off to the baths, neighboring shops, or even the lavatory,[61] they carried with them the most memorable of these historical snippets. Though perhaps distorted or embellished by the active minds and imprecise vocabulary of students, these excited conversations could nevertheless introduce small pieces of the internal historical discourse of intellectual communities into the wider world.[62]

In the same way that stories about Xenocrates helped to define the Old Academy, the tales that leaked out of Neoplatonic classrooms figured into the general perception of late-fifth-century Alexandrian schools. Many Alexandrians knew about the oracles given by the Menouthis Isis shrine and the story of the conception of Asclepiodotus's miraculous child was known within pagan communities as far away as Aphrodisias.[63] People were also well aware of their teachers' enthusiasm for high-level actions designed to restore an imperial regime more friendly to pagan concerns. Students, both pagan and Christian, knew of the support that pagan intellectuals lent to Illus's coup in 484 and understood the general tendency within the community to respond favorably to such initiatives.[64] In fact, the quick dissemination of interesting stories about teachers likely contributed to the outrage Horapollon's students felt when they heard Paralius's criticisms. They must have feared that such criticisms would quickly destroy their teacher's reputation.

60. This student-to-student transmission would likely fall into the category of "corrupt and fluid oral testimony" that Eunapius hesitated to use in his *Lives* (see *VS* 460).
61. If one uses Kom el-Dikka as a model, baths, a taverna, a theater, and a sort of agora space are all associated with classrooms. For the bath see B. Tkaczow, *Topography of Ancient Alexandria: An Archaeological Map* (Warsaw, 1993), 97–98; for the taverna see Tkaczow, 98; for the theater see Tkaczow, 85, as well as the important reinterpretation of G. Majcherek, "Kôm el-Dikka: Excavations and Preservation Work 2002/2003," *Polish Archaeology in the Mediterranean* 15 (2004), 33; and "Kom el-Dikka: Excavations and Preservation Work 2003/2004," *Polish Archaeology in the Mediterranean* 16 (2005), 22. See as well McKenzie, *Architecture of Alexandria*, 206–20. She reconstructs a complex of workshops but no taverna.
62. For purpose of comparison, again note the comments of M. Gilsenan (*Saint and Sufi in Modern Egypt: An Essay in the Sociology of Religion* [Oxford, 1973], 33) about the nature of conversations among members of Sufi orders.
63. For divine visions see *Vit. Sev.* 20. For the conception of Asclepiodotus's child see *Vit. Sev.* 18.
64. For Christian student knowledge of the support for Illus among pagan intellectuals see Zacharias, *Vita Isaiae* 10. Among pagan students, see *Vit. Sev.* 40.

They feared this because, once in circulation, this type of oral testimony could influence the opinion of outsiders. Indeed, in fifth-century Alexandria, these traditions had powerful effects on their hearers. Damascius describes two men, Euprepius and Epiphanius, both experts in Egyptian mystical rites, who "were not born into the traditional way of life, but they overlapped with and met those who had been and, having benefited from their company, they became for their contemporaries the source of many blessings and, among other things, the powerfully voiced messengers of many tales."[65] Euprepius and Epiphanius were attracted to paganism because of their personal interactions with Neoplatonists,[66] and became converts whose views of the divine were reshaped by social interactions. They are of additional interest because, once they converted and became experts in Egyptian theology, Epiphanius and Euprepius became centerpieces of a pagan social network that perpetuated the same stories they had once found so attractive.

Damascius himself shows the influence that such stories could have on a student. In the nine-year span extending from his initial encounter with Severianus until his flight from Alexandria with Isidore, Damascius worked as a rhetorician.[67] This was a demanding profession that involved daily practice of rhetorical exercises and Damascius seems to have been a dedicated practitioner convinced of the positive transformative effect of rhetoric.[68] But Damascius's view of rhetoric changed as his friendship with Isidore developed. During the eight months that they spent traveling together in 488/9, Damascius heard Isidore celebrate the accomplishments of men who had focused all of their attention on union with the divine. As a result, Damascius grew to think of philosophy as an ideal pursuit while rhetoric became for him a "pernicious activity that focused all of his attention on the mouth and turned it away from the soul."[69] The stories exchanged within the context of his new friendship with Isidore progressively diminished Damascius's attachment to rhetoric until he turned to philosophy, Isidore's own passion. The growing intimacy between Damascius and Isidore paralleled Damascius's blossoming love of philosophy. Damascius's experiences, then, show the connection between the power of Neoplatonic discourse and the natural respect and affection that students had for their mentors.

The Christian Zacharias Scholasticus's *Life of Severus* provides even more evidence for the broader potency of Neoplatonic communal history in an Alexandrian context. Though ostensibly a presentation of the early life of Severus, the

---

65. *Vit. Is.* 41, trans. Athanassiadi.
66. Epiphanius's interest in Aion particularly suited an Alexandrian Neoplatonic environment in which Heraiscus was praised for his ability to discern the god's presence in a statue (*Vit. Is.* 76E).
67. Photius, *Bib.*, 181.80; cf. *Vit. Is.* 137B.
68. Note here Damascius's description of the required preparation at *Vit. Is.* 137B.
69. *Vit. Is.* 137B.

anti-Chalcedonian bishop of Antioch, the text contains a long section in which Zacharias aggressively attacks some of the historical traditions that circulated orally within Alexandrian schools.[70] Zacharias understood that the same social relationships that allowed positive anecdotes about teachers to spread rapidly among students could also facilitate the quick dissemination of negative traditions. He thus astutely directed his attack against the personal integrity of the philosophers who featured in and circulated the best known of these stories. Zacharias particularly focuses upon the story of Asclepiodotus's child and repeatedly highlights the unreliability of this account. Asclepiodotus is introduced as a man who attracted the admiration of pagans only through his magical skill. Zacharias then describes him futilely stumbling through ever more elaborate pagan infertility treatments (including sexual unification with an idol of Isis) until he is rendered an object of ridicule.[71]

Zacharias hopes to use this narration to destroy the reputation of Asclepiodotus. At the same time, Zacharias also takes care to emphasize that Isidore, Asclepiades, Heraiscus, Ammonius, and Horapollon helped to spread and defend the tale about Asclepiodotus's child.[72] This enabled Zacharias to expand his specific attack on Asclepiodotus into a credible assault on all of the stories that spread out from Neoplatonic inner circles. His efforts reveal a fundamental understanding that, in the extremely hierarchical world of ancient education, these stories could create or reinforce a student's identification with the faith of his teachers. Zacharias's attack on the reputations of leading Alexandrian Neoplatonists, then, represents a deliberate and well-developed attempt to counteract the power of these tales.

PARALIUS'S BEATING WITHIN ITS SCHOLASTIC CONTEXT

The historical traditions that characterized Alexandrian teachers of the 470s and 480s grew out of a social environment in which personal intimacy, collective rites of passage, and distinctive doctrinal teaching combined to shape the ideals and behaviors of students. It is against this backdrop that one can begin to appreciate the acute tension that Paralius managed to generate within the school of Horapollon. In a few short months, his distrust of the communal past and his disrespect

---

70. On the complicated nature of this text see chapter 5 as well as appendix 2.
71. Although it reprises an old charge of religious excess (cf. Philostratus, *Vit. Ap.* 6.40), this claim may have been plausible to Christians familiar with Isaic iconography. The Isis *anasyrmene* images in which the goddess raises her clothing to expose her vulva may raise the possibility of sexual union with an idol among non-pagans. On this iconography see Frankfurter, *Religion in Roman Egypt*, 104, as well as the list of figurines he presents in n. 27.
72. *Vit. Sev.* 22.

for professorial authority strained the social bonds that kept Horapollon's community of students together. Paralius's criticism of his teachers proved so explosive because it threatened both the public profile and the social cohesion of the school.

This can be seen more easily by reviewing Paralius's behavior in the time leading up to his assault. Paralius's initial conversation with his brother and the sophist Stephen at the Enaton exposed him to a set of arguments highlighting pagan religious failures.[73] These could have been (and probably were) generic criticisms drawn directly from Christian polemical literature,[74] possibly resembling the critiques Olympiodorus would later confidently refute in his commentary on the *Gorgias*.[75] They had no particular relevance to Paralius's own experiences and, consequently, they would have done little to shake his identification with the theological ideas of his teachers. Nevertheless, when Stephen instructed Paralius to return to school, "submit questions of this type to Horapollon, Heraiscus, Asclepiodotus, Ammonius, Isidore, and to the other philosophers who were among them," he did as he was asked.[76]

It is reasonable to consider what motivated Paralius to behave in this way. Zacharias's text, however, presents a set of thorny problems that makes it difficult to recover even the barest outlines of Paralius's motivations. In Zacharias's account, Paralius has become a hagiographic protagonist whose spiritual conflicts and motivations have been largely obscured by the literary role that he performs.[77] For this reason, Zacharias has no interest in exploring Paralius's psychology. He says little about what prompted Paralius to visit the Enaton (aside from brotherly affection) and nothing about why Paralius thought it a good idea to aggressively interrogate his teachers. For a Christian author writing for a Christian audience it may have seemed essential to assume that pagans naturally moved towards Christianity but, as we have seen, movement from Christianity to paganism also occurred in Alexandrian schools. We can only wish that Zacharias had provided more discussion of this broader social and religious context.

Despite Zacharias's obscurity, it is possible to recover some of the broader outlines of Paralius's motivations. First, it is clear that his visit to the Enaton was motivated in part by the desire to see his middle brother, Athanasius, evidently the family member closest in age to Paralius. Second, Paralius's behavior

73. *Vit. Sev.* 16.

74. *Vit. Sev.* 16. Similar criticisms are found, for example, in Athanasius, *Contra Gentes* 1.8–26 and Theodoret, *Cure of Hellenic Maladies*, bk. 10. The latter work would not have been affectionately embraced by anti-Chalcedonian monks.

75. Olympidorus, *In Gorgiam*, 47.2–4.

76. *Vit. Sev.* 16.

77. The nature of Zacharias's text and the thematic goals it advances are treated in more detail in chapter 5 and appendix 2.

fits in with a broader social context in which religious experimentation and questioning occurred with some regularity. We can see this in a scholastic context in an incident recounted in a later section of Zacharias's *Life of Severus*. When describing events in the law schools of Berytus around 490, Zacharias tells of a Christian named John who, because of his unrequited love for a woman, fell in with a group of law students who were experimenting with paganism.[78] On certain occasions, they would assemble and carry out pagan rites. When Zacharias and his friends found out about their activities, John confessed and thanked God for delivering him "from the servitude and error of demons. He declared he was, in fact, a Christian and the son of Christian parents but he had erred and had worshipped idols."[79]

John's story of coming to Berytus as a Christian and falling in with a group of fellow students who were experimenting with paganism was not unique. In a homily given during his Antiochene episcopate, Severus himself confirms the impression that this sort of religious experimentation was common in the school of Berytus. "I know many of the young men who devoted themselves to Roman law in that turbulent city, that is Berytus, and they went off to [Tripoli] to pray and speedily left their vain erudition and way of life and purified their minds of Hellenic myths."[80] Beyond late antique schools, texts like the *Miracles of Thecla* and the *Miracles of Saint Cyrus and John* describe similar religious questioning occurring at shrines throughout the late antique East.[81] It is important too to remember that Paralius came from a religiously mixed family. His background may have rendered him more inclined to this sort of experimentation than some of his peers.

Whatever his motivations, Paralius continued his exploration by making a second trip to the Enaton. When he returned there, Paralius acknowledged that his teachers had not refuted Stephen's arguments. At the same time, Paralius resisted accepting Stephen's larger criticisms of paganism. He could not do so, he said, because he had heard about the miraculous birth of Asclepiodotus's child. For Paralius "this demonstration provided a more compelling proof than any argument and he glorified it as an obvious pagan miracle."[82] This particular wonder differed from the generic oracles and other pagan marvels that Stephen had

---

78. *Vit. Sev.* 62. For discussion of this incident see, for example, P. Chuvin, *Chronicle of the Last Pagans*, trans. B. A. Archer (Cambridge, MA, 1990), 112–13.

79. *Vit. Sev.* 62.

80. G. Garitte, "Textes hagiographiques orientaux relatifs à S. Leonce de Tripoli: II. L' homélie copte de Sevère d'Antioche," *Le Muséon* 79 (1966), 335–86.

81. E.g., *Miracles of Cyrus and John*, *Mir.* 29, 30. *Miracles of Thecla* 17, 39, 40. For discussion of the Thecla miracles see S. F. Johnson, *The Life and Miracles of Thekla: A Literary Study* (Washington, D.C., 2006), 153–60.

82. *Vit. Sev.* 19.

criticized because powerful personal relationships lay behind Paralius's faith in this tale. Indeed, this tradition circulated in both the Alexandrian schools Paralius now attended and the Aphrodisian pagan community in which he was raised.[83] Because the reputations of his respected Alexandrian and Aphrodisian mentors stood behind the tale, Paralius had a personal attachment to this story and the divine principles it illustrated.

When Paralius brought Asclepiodotus's story back to the Enaton, the monk Stephen encouraged him to evaluate its truth by selecting a well-known Alexandrian woman who could check to see if Asclepiodotus's wife was lactating. Foolishly, Paralius brought this request to the philosophers.[84] Paralius was told delicately that such a test was both unnecessary and insulting because, as a student, he ought to have faith in the character of his teachers and the truthfulness of their words. This comment should have served to end the discussion. It ought to have reminded Paralius of his place within the scholastic hierarchy, emphasized that his teachers stood as polished exemplars of values being taught within the school, and suggested that Paralius be more respectful of his elders.

Of course, Paralius did not find this answer satisfactory. After he received a deceptive vision of his own from the Menouthan Isis shrine, his suspicion of his teachers turned into hostility against the religious ideas they presented. Zacharias describes Paralius's intellectual conversion in illuminating terms. Paralius "recalled that Stephen and Athanasius had both held long discussions with him about the perversities of evil demons, telling him that they have the habit of exciting men against one another."[85] After he returned to the shrine and found the goddess unwilling to answer his prayers for some direction, "he praised the great Stephen who had truly spoken the truth and he prayed, as he had been counseled to do."[86]

Zacharias wrote this section of the *Life of Severus* in order to associate Paralius's conversion and the sacking of the Menouthis Isis shrine with the monks of the Enaton and their student affiliates.[87] One must then expect that he would emphasize (and perhaps overemphasize) the role in Paralius's conversion played by Stephen, apparently one of the main liaisons between the Enaton monastery and Alexandrian students. However, while one may legitimately question some of the

---

83. For Asclepiodotus's efforts to circulate the story in Alexandria, see *Vit. Sev.* 18–19. The *Life of Severus* makes clear (*Vit. Sev.* 17) that Asclepiodotus of Aphrodisias, the father of Asclepiodotus's wife, Damiane, and a wealthy man of high rank, knew of this story and believed it. Interestingly, Zacharias simply describes him as "one who was deceived."

84. *Vit. Sev.* 19–20.

85. *Vit. Sev.* 20.

86. *Vit. Sev.* 21.

87. On this point see Watts, "Winning the Intracommunal Dialogues: Zacharias Scholasticus' *Life of Severus*," *JECS* 13 (2005), 454–59; and appendix 2.

details Zacharias provides, the general pattern that he suggests seems sound. Zacharias describes Paralius slowly moving from complete acceptance of the communal religious and philosophical values exemplified by Asclepiodotus, Isidore, and Horapollon to a different set of Christian ascetic ideals illustrated by Stephen. It is only natural that, as his personal convictions evolved, Paralius's faith in and attachment to the exemplars of each community would reflect his spiritual development. In a sense, he had been transformed from a student of Horapollon into a disciple of Stephen.

Paralius's subsequent actions underline the degree to which personal attachments shaped his confessional perspective. When Paralius returned to his school from Menouthis, he mocked his teachers Horapollon, Asclepiodotus, Heraiscus, Ammonius, and Isidore as well as the priestess of the Isis shrine in Menouthis.[88] These were direct attacks on the integrity of Horapollon and his colleagues but, just as importantly, they also represented Paralius's first action to distance himself from their intellectual community. Indeed, Paralius's fellow students understood the significance of his criticisms. By publicly attacking the credibility of men like Horapollon, Paralius had also undermined powerful stories about the immediate and remote past that teachers told to favored students. Loyal students could not accept the public "sarcasms and reproaches of Paralius" that cut so deeply into the foundations for their community.

For centuries, students had reacted violently to those who challenged the integrity and prestige of their teachers. Philostratus, for example, describes how the students of the sophist Hadrian had one of their teacher's critics beaten to death.[89] Libanius equates this sort of battle with that fought by soldiers for their country.[90] Later in his life, Libanius even speaks fondly about the fathers who used to take pride when they saw "on their sons' bodies the evidence of the battles they fight on their teacher's behalf, the scars on the head, face, hands, and on every limb."[91] Following in this longstanding tradition of student combat, Horapollon's corps of students decided to use violence to defend Horapollon's honor and reassert his personal authority. Hoping perhaps to avoid implicating their teacher in their actions,[92] the students waited until Friday, a day when Horapollon was away. They then set upon Paralius with the apparent goal of beating some sense into him. This

88. *Vit. Sev.* 22.
89. Philostratus, *VS* 587–88. The critic was a devotee of Hadrian's rival, Chrestus of Byzantium.
90. *Or.* 1.19.
91. *Or.* 3.22. Other scholastic riots in the fourth century may have been motivated by a similar desire to win prestige for teachers. See, for example, Eunapius, *VS* 483; Himerius, *Or.* 67; and Libanius, *Or.* 1.21 on the great riot.
92. In rare cases, teachers whose students committed acts of violence on their behalf were charged as participants (e.g., Eunapius, *VS* 483–85).

was a corrective action motivated by a specific academic code of conduct that required loyal students to defend the personal reputations of their teachers.[93]

Unfortunately for the students of Horapollon, what began as a corrective action within the boundaries of a scholastic circle soon expanded into a wider conflict. Paralius's specific offence against the Alexandrian Neoplatonic community was his public belittling of the integrity and religious practices of his teachers. His peers' violent response, however, provided Christian opponents with an opportunity to deliberately misrepresent Paralius's beating as an anti-Christian persecution. Zacharias Scholasticus witnessed the beating and joined with other student-*philoponoi* to stop it.[94]

Due in large part to their own experiences with Alexandrian Neoplatonism, Zacharias and his *philoponoi*-influenced compatriots immediately interpreted Paralius's beating as an unprovoked attack on a young man who had legitimately questioned the integrity of his teachers.[95] To them, this was fundamentally a religious action designed to prevent Paralius from becoming a Christian. When Zacharias said this to Paralius's attackers, Horapollon's students responded, quite legitimately to their mind, that they had no quarrel with Zacharias in particular or Christianity in general.[96] The beating was simply an isolated punishment motivated by Paralius's disrespectful behavior. Perhaps Zacharias even knew that this claim was true, but this explanation was easy enough to dismiss and, in the hands of the student-*philoponoi*, Paralius's beating lost its peculiarly scholastic meaning. The corrective action of Horapollon's inner circle of students suddenly acquired a wider and more dangerous religious significance.

As we know, Zacharias and his colleagues quickly succeeded in convincing many Alexandrian Christians that the assault upon Paralius constituted an anti-Christian persecution. Once this idea took root, Horapollon, his students, and his colleagues lost control over events. In rapid succession, the beating was followed by a legal complaint against Horapollon and, a day later, by the sack of the Menouthis shrine of Isis. The following year saw an investigation in which the imperial official Nicomedes tortured Horapollon and Heraiscus. Asclepiades died in hiding during this inquisition and Isidore, Damascius, and Asclepiodotus all fled the city. Ammonius and Horapollon remained in Alexandria but each succumbed to Christian pressure; Ammonius was forced to tone down the pagan content of his teaching, while Horapollon later converted to Christianity.[97] These seem to

---

93. E. Watts, "The Student Self in Late Antiquity," in *Religion and the Self in Antiquity*, ed. D. Brakke, M. Satlow, and S. Weitzman (Bloomington, 2005), 239.

94. *Vit. Sev.* 23–24.

95. Their perspective will be analyzed in more detail in chapter 5.

96. They even commented to Zacharias, "We have nothing against you but we are taking vengeance upon Paralius as an enemy" (*Vit. Sev.* 24).

97. Note the comments of Damascius, *Vit. Is.* 118B on the philosophical compromises made by Ammonius and 120B on the religious compromise of Horapollon. For discussion of the compromises

have been necessary actions under the circumstances, but such compromises were inconsistent with the ideal of proud philosophical resistance to political pressure. In the eyes of their less malleable contemporaries, the willingness of Ammonius and Horapollon to stray from strict pagan confessional and philosophical principles demonstrated profound character flaws.

Horapollon's students set upon Paralius that Friday in order to defend the reputation of their teachers and reinforce the cohesion of their student corps. Their actions ultimately had a far different result. This scholastic punishment evolved, first into an intercommunal religious riot, and ultimately into an imperially-sponsored investigation. It eventually shattered the unity of the Alexandrian Neoplatonic community. Some leading philosophers fled the city in fear. Others showed themselves unable to duplicate the philosophical resistance to political pressure celebrated by historical traditions circulating within the Alexandrian scholastic community of the 470s and 480s. In any case, no one fully succeeded in exhibiting the philosophical virtues that were supposed to animate the behaviors of the community's leaders. In the riot's aftermath, some Neoplatonists recognized that they belonged to a community that had proven unable to live up to the models celebrated in its history. They then began to craft practical ethical systems that one could actually follow under contemporary conditions.

FIFTH-CENTURY CHRISTIAN VIOLENCE IN NEOPLATONIC COMMUNAL MEMORY

The *Life of Isidore* allows us to see how the riot ultimately changed the lessons that some Neoplatonists found in their past. Although of questionable value for the community's immediate reaction to the events of the late 480s, Damascius's later recollections of the period and its aftermath do have immense utility as cultural documents illustrating how Neoplatonic discourse evolved over the next generation. When he composed the *Life of Isidore* in the late 510s or early 520s, Damascius had already placed Paralius's beating, the subsequent riot, and Nicomedes' investigation into a larger historical narrative that highlighted both ideal philosophical behaviors and instances in which philosophers failed to measure up to ethical standards.[98] Damascius presented this history through a series of short morality tales that highlighted philosophical virtues at work and had clear moral and pedagogic purposes. He drew these tales from his own experiences as well as the

---

see E. Watts, *City and School in Late Antique Athens and Alexandria* (Berkeley, 2006), 222–25; and R. Sorabji, "Divine Names and Sordid Deals in Ammonius' Alexandria," in *The Philosopher and Society in Late Antiquity*, ed. A. Smith (Swansea, 2005), 203–14.

98. Note here the comments of Athanassiadi (*Damascius*, 26–27) about goals of the *Life of Isidore*.

oral traditions he heard in the 470s and 480s. By the time that he wrote of them, Damascius had long since decided on the lessons that they would convey.[99]

Damascius is largely silent about the events of the riot itself. Paralius and the *philoponoi* merit no mention in the surviving fragments and Damascius alludes only briefly to the sack of the Isis shrine.[100] Instead, Damascius spends a great deal of time talking about the investigation launched by the imperial official Nicomedes in either 487 or 488.[101] This investigation arose from a complicated set of events. The first cause was likely the support that Alexandrian philosophers had given to the failed revolt launched against the emperor Zeno by the Isaurian general Illus and his associate Leontius in 484.[102] Prior to launching the rebellion, Illus actively courted the support of a broad coalition of Isaurians, pagans, and Chalcedonian Christians. Pamprepius, an Egyptian rhetorician and poet, came to Alexandria in 481/2 and succeeded in building considerable pagan support for the undertaking both within and outside of the city.[103]

This is not to say, however, that Nicomedes was sent by Zeno to investigate the teachers of Alexandria solely because of their favorable outlook towards Illus. Alexandrian pagans were not unique in their support for Pamprepius and his patron. Pamprepius's appeals and his prophecies were just as influential among pagans in Aphrodisias and Gaza, but no corrective action is known to have been taken in either of those cities.[104] In fact, imperial authorities seem not to have been particularly concerned about pagan support for Illus. Isaurians and Chalcedonian bishops were the only supporters initially punished for their involvement and this punishment was meted out quickly following the rebellion's failure.[105] Alexandrian philosophers, by contrast, were punished years after the fact.

---

99. For discussion of how thematic elements of oral discourse reflect a community's cultural values see J. Vansina, *Oral Tradition as History* (Madison, 1985), 18–21, as well as the comments of B. Nasson, "Abraham Esau's War, 1899–1901: Martyrdom, myth, and folk memory in Calvinia, South Africa," in *The Myths We Live By*, ed. R. Samuel and P. Thompson (London and New York, 1990), 124–25.

100. Athanassiadi sees a connection between the events described in *Vit. Sev.* 28–29 and the difficulties Damascius describes in *Vit. Is.* 53B. An even stronger correlation exists between *Vit. Sev.* 19 and *Vit. Is.* 53D. On each of these parallels see Athanassiadi, *Damascius*, 151–52nn126–27.

101. For this date see appendix 1.

102. For a discussion of this defeat see H. Elton, "Illus and the Imperial Aristocracy under Zeno," *Byzantion* 70 (2000), 399; as well as the earlier treatment of E. Stein and J. M. Palanque, *Histoire du Bas-Empire*, vol. II (Paris, 1949), 19–31.

103. *Vit. Is.* 77B, 113A–C.

104. For Aphrodisias see *Vit. Sev.* 40–41. For the revolt's implications in Gaza, see Zacharias, *Vit. Isaiae* 10 (Syr.), 7.14–26 (trans.).

105. Calandion, the Chalcedonian bishop of Antioch, was punished for his support of Illus and deposed along with nine other Chalcedonian supporters of Illus. Their fates are described by Theophanes, *Chron.* AM 5982 and Evagrius, *HE* 3.16.

Two additional features of Nicomedes' investigation suggest that he was not exclusively (or even primarily) concerned with flushing out treasonous attitudes among Alexandrian pagans. In his account of the events, Damascius indicates that Nicomedes began his inquiry by closing down the Alexandrian schools.[106] While pagan teachers had supported Illus, they are unlikely to have been his only, or even most important, partisans in Alexandria. Shutting down the schools would have made little sense unless Nicomedes had decided from the outset that teachers were his main target. In addition, Damascius makes it clear that the Alexandrian patriarch, Peter Mongus, both played a role in summoning Nicomedes and had the ability to exonerate individuals Nicomedes had targeted.[107] Such intervention would be highly irregular in a treason case but much more comprehensible had the bishop himself called for the inquiry.

Instead of a simple treason investigation, Nicomedes' probe of the activities of Alexandrian teachers happened because they had shown themselves willing to disturb the peace on two recent occasions. The disruptive tendencies that led these men to support Illus resurfaced two years later in the civil unrest that Paralius's beating provoked. While one instance of bad judgment could be overlooked in a small community of relatively little political consequence, a second incident could not be ignored. The combination of support for Illus and involvement in the Paralius affair made Alexandrian intellectuals unique among Illus's supporters. Paralius's beating can then explain why these Alexandrians were both the only pagans known to be punished for supporting Illus and his only supporters outside of the fortress of Papirius who were punished as late as 488.

Nicomedes' calamitous investigation occurred because Illus's rebellion and the Paralius affair combined to elicit extraordinary imperial concern about the activities of Alexandria's pagan intellectuals. Damascius, however, chose to separate his sparse account of the riot from his larger narration of Alexandrian events in the 480s. He had a good thematic reason for doing this. In the *Life of Isidore*, he describes this period as one of steady communal decline in which the moral failings of individual teachers endangered and ultimately destroyed the community of pagan intellectuals in and around Alexandria. In Damascius's eyes, this process began well before the riot with the arrival of Pamprepius in Alexandria in 481/2. Although Damascius suggests that the leaders of Alexandria's philosophical schools found Pamprepius to be a dangerous figure,[108] he admits that Pamprepius's ideas affected the behavior of many of these supposedly virtuous men.[109] He describes Pamprepius as "an effective instrument of the Necessity which opposes

106. *Vit. Is.* 116E.
107. *Vit. Is.* 118B.
108. *Vit. Is.* 113 J–K, Q. Isidore, for example, "avoided him as a man pursued by the Furies."
109. For the effect of Pamprepius's ideas on the larger community see Damascius's comment at *Vit. Is.* 113L as well as the remarks of Zacharias Scholasticus (*Vita Isaiae* 10 and *Vit. Sev.* 40).

the good" and makes clear that his rise had profound consequences.[110] Not only would the community's involvement with Pamprepius eventually attract unnecessary imperial attention to its activities, but it also began a process of ethical decay. The ascendancy of such a morally flawed character prefigured a general ethical descent in which the leadership of Cronian figures like Serapio and Isidore was replaced by the Typhonian tendencies of Pamprepius and the moral relativism of philosophers like Ammonius and Horapollon.[111]

Damascius understood that this ethical decline had a real and detrimental long-term effect upon behavior. Damascius objected most to Pamprepius's attempt to generate excitement for Illus's rebellion while simultaneously discouraging pagans from doing anything substantial to support it.[112] In Damascius's view, Illus's revolt needed active support to succeed. The prophecies and stories told by Pamprepius, however, made the philosophers "always waste opportunities"[113] and caused pagans, both within and outside of the charmed Neoplatonic intellectual circle, to avoid taking necessary but uncomfortable actions to save the community. Indeed, Pamprepius had already earned a reputation for counseling inaction based upon his understanding of "the decrees of Providence," knowledge many thought he "divined from some hidden foreknowledge."[114]

To Damascius, the false oracles of Pamprepius and the quietism they encouraged ran counter to the very foundations of philosophical virtue. Damascius describes this tendency with profound disgust:

> Men tend to describe as virtue a life of despising action, but this does not agree with my judgment. For the virtue which engages in the midst of public life through political activity and discourse fortifies the soul ... Indeed, politics offers great possibilities for doing what is good and useful; also for courage and firmness. That is why the learned, who sit in their corner and philosophize at length and in grand manner about justice and moderation utterly disgrace themselves if they are compelled to take some action. Thus, bereft of action, all discourse appears vain and empty.[115]

With careful retrospection, Damascius had come to believe that Pamprepius set in motion a dangerous course of events that began with Illus's revolt and culminated in Nicomedes' investigation. These circumstances demanded courageous philosophical activity, but Pamprepius's ideas discouraged the weak-willed from

110. *Vit. Is.* 113D (trans. Athanassiadi).
111. *Vit. Is.* 112A.
112. If the general seemed too close to pagans, he likely would have undercut his support among the larger and more powerful community of Chalcedonian Christians. On this point, note as well the comments of A. Cameron, "Poets and Pagans in Byzantine Egypt," in *Egypt in the Byzantine World, 300–700*, ed. R. Bagnall (Cambridge, 2007), 35–36.
113. *Vit. Is.* 113L.
114. Malchus, fr. 23 (Blockley).
115. *Vit. Is.* 124 (trans. Athanassiadi).

taking this necessary action. Some men, like Isidore, rose above these circumstances and showed themselves to be true philosophers.[116] Others, however, accepted the excuses that Pamprepius offered (though they hypocritically claimed to disavow the man himself) and sat back as crisis enveloped Alexandrian pagan intellectuals.

Damascius goes on to describe how the ethical rot begun by Pamprepius ultimately toppled the Alexandrian Neoplatonic community. Nicomedes' investigation played an important part in this but, in Damascius's mind, the passive and ethically slack behaviors encouraged by Pamprepius ultimately proved even more destructive. He shows this by chronicling the actions of a number of different men, each of whom responded uniquely to the challenges presented by Nicomedes' inquisition. Like other scholastic histories, Damascius's recollection of these events was personality-driven, with ethical exemplars and hypocritical villains clearly identified.

Although he is elsewhere critical of Isidore, Damascius saw Isidore's actions under these circumstances as exemplary.[117] When Nicomedes issued his order suspending teaching, Isidore showed himself to be "no less than Socrates in the pursuit of truth. He too, when ordered by the thirty tyrants not to hold discussions, was unable to obey their command."[118] Isidore further showed himself to be above the political pressures of the time by writing a warning letter to Harpocras when he learned that Nicomedes had begun searching for him.[119] Finally, when the situation in Alexandria became unbearable and Isidore saw no cure for the city's corruption, he decided to flee to the more religiously and philosophically amenable environment of Athens.[120] For Damascius, Isidore's behavior in this time of extreme difficulty marked him as an ideal philosophical exemplar.

Damascius's presentation of his former teacher Ammonius provides a powerful contrast to Isidore's measured philosophical response. Ammonius was very much Isidore's superior as a technical philosopher, but Damascius felt that Nicomedes' investigation showed Ammonius to be far inferior when it came to living in accordance with philosophical ideals. Despite being "a supremely dedicated worker and the greatest commentator who ever lived,"[121] Ammonius "came to an agree-

---

116. *Vit. Is.* 26B.
117. E.g., *Vit. Is.* 17, 32B, 37D. For Damascius's critiques of Isidore, see the discussion of Athanassiadi (*Damascius*, 33–34).
118. *Vit. Is.* 116E.
119. *Vit. Is.* 117B.
120. Isidore seems to have tried this twice. The first attempt, by ship, was detected (*Vit. Is.* 119A–D, 121). The second, his long land journey with Damascius, is described in *Vit. Is.* 122A–C and 132–44. As Peter Brown suggested to me, Damascius's description of this reads a bit like a pagan *de Fuga* justifying a flight from state-sponsored punishment.
121. *Vit. Is.* 57C (trans. Athanassiadi, slightly amended).

ment with the overseer of the prevailing doctrine"[122] that required him to amend his teaching and adapt its theological content. Ammonius may have been sufficiently influenced by the quietistic notions advanced by Pamprepius that he was simply looking for a way to survive in Alexandria until the arrival of the better conditions Providence decreed. Damascius, however, saw a baser motivation. Ammonius, according to Damascius, sacrificed his integrity for money,[123] a serious indictment of a philosopher who was expected to remain true to his principles even in the most difficult of circumstances.

Although Nicomedes' investigation uncovered the moral failings of accomplished Alexandrian teachers like Ammonius, it also revealed exemplary behavior in some of the city's more philosophically middling characters. The best such example is Gessius, an iatrosophist who had only perfunctory philosophical training.[124] Despite his medical achievements, Gessius was a below-average and indifferent philosopher whose love of pomp usually prevented him from living an appropriate philosophical life.[125] But Nicomedes' persecution revealed a surprising strength of character in Gessius. While Damascius thought the doctor lacked conventional philosophical virtues, he "applauded the noble courage of his virtuous soul. For, when Heraiscus was wanted by the emperor Zeno, [Gessius] hid him in his own house exposing himself to danger and, as Heraiscus fell ill in his place of refuge and died, Gessius buried him properly, wrapping his body and rendering it the customary rites."[126] Despite Gessius's inadequate philosophical training, Damascius portrays him as a moral exemplar whose virtues of personal resistance make him an ideal figure. This contrasts with Ammonius who, despite his trappings of philosophical knowledge, proved unable to live up to philosophical ideals.

Damascius's narrative of events in Alexandria from the arrival of Pamprepius until his own departure in 488 highlights his personal disappointment with the city's philosophical community and its leadership. Damascius explicitly credits Pamprepius with laying the initial groundwork for these moral failings and establishing the negative political climate that enabled Nicomedes' investigation. But he focuses particularly upon the crumbling of the community of scholars and what this showed about the ethical integrity of its leading thinkers. In a way, the political pressures and physical tortures that led to this moral rot are secondary to the fact that the rot occurred at all; they serve as mere background to the more significant personal psychic dramas that Damascius describes. To Damascius, a

---

122. *Vit. Is.* 118B (trans. Athanassiadi).
123. *Vit. Is.* 118B.
124. On Gessius in general see E. Watts, "The Enduring Legacy of the Iatrosophist Gessius," *GRBS* 49 (2009), 113–34.
125. *Vit. Is.* 128.
126. *Vit. Is.* 128 (trans. Athanassiadi).

real philosopher remained true to his convictions regardless of external circumstances. The events taking place between Pamprepius's Alexandrian arrival and the conclusion of Nicomedes' investigation are important because they separated out the genuine philosophers from the merely learned.

Once we understand this to be Damascius's narrative intent, it becomes clear why Paralius's beating does not figure prominently in his retelling. Although the beating and subsequent riot helped to focus Alexandrian ecclesiastical attention upon the city's pagan teachers, the machinations of Christian students, monks, and clergy had little direct relevance to Damascius's discussion of the personal virtue of individual philosophers. He was narrating the triumphs and failings of philosophers as philosophers; Christian figures only operated in the background as instruments who helped to illuminate the true character of Damascius's pagan subjects. Even Peter Mongus, the Alexandrian instigator of Nicomedes' investigation, ultimately comes across as a minor figure who enters the text only to provide Ammonius with a material incentive to betray his convictions and reveal his true moral character.[127]

In the same way that Damascius's thematic concerns obscure the importance of Christian figures, they also cause him to overemphasize the significance of Pamprepius. While Pamprepius's actions may have set in motion the moral decline of Alexandrian pagan intellectuals, it is hard to argue that they directly precipitated Nicomedes' investigation. There are a number of reasons for this. First, the chronology does not suggest any direct connection. Pamprepius appeared in Alexandria six years before the inquisition, and Illus's revolt had failed almost four years earlier; imperial officials had ample opportunity to respond to charges of Alexandrian pagan disloyalty before 488. Furthermore, despite Damascius's claim that Pamprepius "seemed like one who would betray" the Roman Empire,[128] his plotting did not represent a unique or particularly egregious act when seen within its historical context. One must remember that Damascius describes three other moments in the 470s when pagan intellectuals worked alongside military or political figures to try to change the direction of Roman political life. Although the project of Pamprepius and Illus had less chance of success than that of the consul Severus, their rebellion certainly had more promise than Severianus's bungled assassination of Zeno or Salustius's ill-fated association with Marcellinus of Dalmatia.[129] Nevertheless, Damascius, to a greater or lesser degree, respected the intellectuals involved in these other attempts and saw no negative moral consequences

---

127. He appears twice, once as the somewhat ambiguously defined "altogether evil" leader of the Christians and again as the man with whom Ammonius makes his treacherous agreement (*Vit. Is.* 113I-J and 118B).

128. *Vit. Is.* 113P.

129. On Marcellinus see, *Vit. Is.* 69 A-E. Note as well P. MacGeorge, *Late Roman Warlords* (Oxford, 2002), 15-68; and Athanassiadi, *Damascius*, 181n157.

arising out of their failure. Looking back from the 510s, Damascius saw Pamprepius as a more sinister character whose actions had much worse consequences.

In the years following Paralius's beating and the investigation of Nicomedes, the attitude of Neoplatonists towards active political resistance seems to have changed. Damascius ceases to speak favorably about attempts to overturn the Empire's pro-Christian order and even criticizes pagans who practice their religion with too much public zeal. In an exemplary passage, Damascius criticizes the Athenian scholarch Hegias for restoring religious rites "with an enthusiasm that was more hazardous than pious."[130] To one who had experienced Nicomedes' investigation, this brazen behavior had predictable consequences. "From these actions scandal arose in the city and [Hegias] attracted angry hatred."[131] Instead of highlighting activities designed to change Roman political dynamics, the post-488 historical testimony recorded by Damascius idealized Epictetan ethical behaviors of the sort once championed by Theosebius. Isidore, of course, serves as Damascius's most developed exemplar of these virtues under pressure but others, like Gessius, Harpocras, and Heraiscus, also provided practical illustrations of proper philosophical behavior. This reveals an important, yet subtle, shift in ethical emphasis.

TEACHING ETHICS AFTER THE RIOT

The increasing prominence of Epictetan study within the philosophical curriculum of Damascius's school paralleled the embrace of Epictetan ethics within Damascian historical discourse. Although the Stoic Epictetus was read by many influential fifth- and sixth-century Neoplatonists,[132] none of these men seems to have given great weight to his writing and there is no sign that his work played a major role in the fifth-century Neoplatonic philosophical curriculum. Even Hierocles, the teacher of Theosebius, largely ignored Epictetus in his teaching of practical ethics; he preferred instead the Pythagorean *Carmen Aureum*.[133]

If his disciple Simplicius is any guide, Damascius's students had a different view of Epictetus. Simplicius calls his words "very effective and moving so that anyone not totally deadened would be goaded by them, become aware of his own afflictions, and be energized to correct them."[134] Tellingly, Simplicius also praises the

---

130. *Vit. Is.* 145B.
131. Ibid.
132. Hierocles, Proclus, and Olympiodorus all knew the *Encheiridion*. For discussion of this see T. Brennan and C. Brittain, "Introduction" in *Simplicius: On Epictetus' Handbook 1–26*, trans. idem (Ithaca, 2002), 4 and 28n18, as well as the larger discussion of G. Boter, *The Encheiridion of Epictetus and its Three Christian Adaptations: Transmission and Critical Edition* (Leiden, 1999).
133. Brennan and Brittain, "Introduction," 5.
134. Simplicius, *Comm. in Epict. Ench.* 1.30–33 (trans. Brennan and Brittain, with slight adaptation).

Epictetan tactic of illustrating abstract values with concrete examples.[135] In fact, Simplicius found this teaching so powerful that he undertook to write a commentary on the Epictetan *Encheiridion* while still an associate of Damascius.[136] His commentary frames the text as an essential introduction to Neoplatonic philosophy designed to inculcate in students the ethical and political virtues necessary for higher philosophical study.[137]

Simplicius faced a particular challenge in using a Stoic work as an entry point to the Platonic philosophical curriculum. Although a powerful and memorable text, the *Encheiridion* took some positions that a Platonist could not support and remained silent on other ideas that, to Simplicius's mind, belonged in a proper introduction to Platonic education. Simplicius, then, found himself side-stepping problematic doctrines expressed by Epictetus and adding long sections describing various sorts of practical ethics not mentioned by Epictetus.[138]

For our purposes the most interesting of these additional essays concerns the appropriate behavior for a philosopher living in a morally corrupt state.[139] Although it is loosely related to Epictetus's discussion of the need for a philosopher to be unconcerned about political position or state honors,[140] this essay is purely a Simplician insertion. In proper Platonic fashion, it holds out a political role for the philosopher as "a father and teacher for all in common, their corrector, counselor, and guardian."[141] As Simplicius continues, however, the connection between Simplician theory and Damascian anecdotal illustration becomes even tighter. After describing the political role of a philosopher in a functioning state, Simpl-

---

135. *In Ench.* 83.12.

136. On the dates of composition for the *Encheiridion* see the discussion of Alan Cameron, "The last days of the Academy at Athens," *PCPS* 195 (1969), 13; and I. Hadot, *Simplicius: Commentaire sur le Manuel d'Épictète* (Leiden 1996), 8–24. Note as well the comments of Brennan and Brittain, "Introduction," 2–4.

137. *In Ench.* 3.1–2. On the Neoplatonic scale of virtues and the place of political and ethical virtues on this scale see J. Pépin, *Théologie cosmique et théologie chrétienne* (Paris, 1964), 380–86; D. O'Meara, *Pythagoras Revived* (Oxford, 1989), 97–99; and the extensive discussion of L. G. Westerink (ed. and trans.), *Prolégomènes à la Philosophie de Platon* (Paris, 1990).

138. So, for example, Simplicius has to dance around the Epictetan position that the soul is mortal (e.g., *In Ench.* 1.47–2.14; see the discussion of Brennan and Brittain, "Introduction," 5). He also added seven essays to the commentary in order to introduce important Platonic ideas that were otherwise missing. For discussion of this feature of the text, see Brennan and Brittain, "Introduction," 7–18. Nevertheless, his ability to engage the text in this way was perfectly consistent with the conventions of Neoplatonic commentary. On these, see H. Baltussen, "From Polemic to Exegesis: The Ancient Philosophical Commentary," *Poetics Today* 28 (2007), 273–75.

139. For a detailed discussion of this section of the text see D. O'Meara, "Simplicius on the Place of the Philosopher in the City (*In Epictetum* Chap. 32)," *Mélanges de l'Université de Saint Joseph* 57 (2004), 89–98.

140. This discussion is found in ch. 24 of the *Encheiridion*.

141. *In Ench.* 65.3

icius moves on to consider his proper response to an irredeemably unjust government.[142] "In a corrupt state," he writes, the philosopher will "abstain from public affairs. . . . Indeed, he ought to ask to be an exile from these incurable affairs, and, if indeed it is possible, he will go to another, better state."[143]

Simplicius also describes another, less dramatic, course of action. Under these conditions, he says, "it is also fine to present yourself as moderate . . . It is also fine to keep far away from offending people in power and from tasteless frankness in these circumstances."[144] One must keep in mind, he says, that such states "entirely impede from beginning the proper education of the souls as well as the ultimate fixing of this education in them."[145] At the same time, if a soul can be found that withstands such a political arrangement "it is shown to be more perfect in virtue."[146]

Simplicius's interjections on this point are eye-catching and, when one overlays his thoughts on this matter with the anecdotes contained within Damascius's *Life of Isidore*, it becomes apparent that he has here described the practical ethical system illustrated by many of Damascius's stories.[147] Damascius' Isidore, for example, embodies these values nearly perfectly. Isidore played as great a role in public affairs as the age allowed.[148] He provided guidance to those who he felt had erred and actively criticized vice,[149] but he refrained from any contact with Christian leadership because of their pollution.[150] When political conditions were most reasonable, in the 470s and early 480s, Isidore behaved with the modesty and relative restraint that Simplicius suggested a philosopher ought to display in an unjust but not utterly corrupt state. After the riot that Paralius inspired and the subsequent investigation of Nicomedes, however, it was no longer possible to live philosophically in Alexandria. Then, just as Simplicius recommends, Isidore left Alexandria for Athens, a city in which local conditions permitted him to live according to his principles.[151]

---

142. A. Kaldellis argues (*Procopius of Caesarea: Tyranny, History, and Philosophy at the End of Antiquity* [Philadelphia, 2004], 105) that this line of argument too is Platonic and derived from *Republic* 496d–e and 620c–d.

143. *In Ench* 65.35.

144. *In Ench.* 65.7–13, trans. Brennan and Brittain.

145. *In Ench.* 66.29.

146. *In Ench.* 66.30–33.

147. Cf. O'Meara, "Simplicius on the Place of the Philosopher," 97. It is also worth noting, as Kaldellis (*Procopius of Caesarea*, 101–4) and others have, that this system is on most prominent display when Damascius, Simplicius, and their associates leave the Roman Empire for Persia.

148. *Vit. Is.* 26B.

149. *Vit. Is.* 15A.

150. *Vit. Is.* 20A–B.

151. On the Athenian conditions at this time see Watts, *City and School*, 111–23. It is worth noting that this resembles Theosebius's account of Hierocles' flight from Constantinople to a more hospitable Alexandrian environment in the 430s.

Simplicius also enables us to appreciate Damascius's particular fixation on a man's behavior as the best mark of his philosophical aptitude. If, as Simplicius states, only the rarest and most perfectly virtuous soul shows itself able to withstand life in a corrupt *politeia*, the Alexandrian philosophers who maintained their integrity throughout the difficult events of 486–8 were particularly notable figures. They represented the few men who remained philosophical in spite of the pressure of tyrants. In Damascius's narrative, this bleak social backdrop made the political virtue of men like Gessius shine forth with such intensity that it obscured their undistinguished pursuit of higher virtues. But Isidore blazed the brightest in these circumstances. His ability to preserve "faith and modesty" during the persecution spotlighted not only his great political virtues but also the general loftiness of his mind and his higher philosophical accomplishments.[152]

By the same token, Damascius's narratives also provide real-world illustrations of Simplicius's notion that a corrupt political order could prevent many extremely gifted men from holding to an appropriate ethical course. Ammonius stands as the best example of a man who failed to behave philosophically despite a first-rate philosophical education. Damascius emphasizes that Ammonius was the son of a virtuous philosopher and a pious mother who was herself a philosophical adept.[153] He was educated by Proclus, the foremost Platonic teacher of his generation, and Proclus doted on him as a favored son.[154] In spite of Ammonius's solid education and long, intimate exposure to men and women whose daily conduct displayed perfect virtue, Damascius characterizes him as a man whose education was corrupted by the environment in which he lived. He began well enough and, at one point, earned Damascius's deep respect.[155] But, as the Alexandrian ethical climate changed in the 480s, Damascius saw that Ammonius had, to appropriate Simplicius's phrase, "betrayed his own freedom . . . lost his ethical disposition and was expelled from the Olympian path."[156] In much the same way that Isidore became emblematic of the rare philosopher who showed perfect virtue in a corrupt society, so too did Ammonius serve to illustrate the potential for such a society to rip a soul from even the sturdiest ethical moorings.

Simplicius's theoretical discussion of the proper expressions of philosophical political virtues seems to parallel many of the ideal behaviors illustrated by

---

152. Cf. *Vit. Is.* 34A.

153. Damascius describes Ammonius's father, Hermeias, as "deficient in his ability to argue . . . but so well exercised in virtue that not even Momus himself would have found fault with him" (*Vit. Is.* 54, trans. Athanassiadi). Aedesia, for her part, was "pious and holy" and "her virtue was admired by the entire chorus of philosophers and their leader Proclus" (*Vit. Is.* 56, trans. Athanassiadi).

154. *Vit. Is.* 57B.

155. Their close relationship is suggested by the fact that Damascius was chosen to give the funeral oration for Ammonius's mother Aedesia (*Vit. Is.* 56).

156. *In Ench.* 66.20–24.

Damascius in the *Life of Isidore*. Although one should certainly hesitate to propose a direct textual link between the comments of Simplicius and the anecdotes of Damascius, it is also certain that the ideas expressed by each man grew out of the same social and intellectual milieu. Indeed, the two texts were written in relatively close chronological proximity. They highlight the important, mutually reinforcing interplay between formal doctrinal teaching, historical discourse, and social interaction in forming ethical sensibilities and shaping behavior in Damascius's school.

The utility of Simplicius's text exceeds even this point, however. His commentary not only shows the thematic convergence of classroom teaching and historical tradition. It also helps to illustrate the evolution of some communal historical traditions in the aftermath of Nicomedes' investigation. Simplicius's discussion of the ideal political behaviors of a philosopher corresponds in large part to the themes Damascius emphasized when describing the events between Pamprepius's revolt and Isidore's flight from Alexandria. At the same time, there is no space in Simplicius's system for the political assertiveness displayed by pagan intellectuals in the 470s and early 480s. Indeed, although Damascius and his mentors celebrated the attempts by Severus, Severianus, and Salustius to use political power or assassination to overturn a corrupt Christian political order, such actions fly in the face of Simplicius's notion that a philosopher ought to remain quiet and humble in such circumstances. Simplicius's doctrinal discussions, then, reflect the same shift in emphasis that we saw in Damascius's anecdotes. In both contexts, active political opposition stopped being an ideal indication of one's political virtues; Simplicius does not even mention it among the possible expressions of these virtues.[157] One is then left with the unmistakable impression of a shift in Neoplatonic political ideals.

By the early sixth century, the glorious historical traditions describing intellectuals who worked to restore pagan leadership had become fossils of a past age in which great political actions were still possible. Though they were mentioned by Damascius, these anecdotes had little practical significance after 488. Pamprepius's machinations, Paralius's riot, and Nicomedes' investigation had collectively convinced Damascius and his followers that such behavior was no longer feasible. The only ethical path that remained was an Epictetan one, explained in texts like the *Encheiridion* and illustrated by historical traditions like those passed along to Damascius by Theosebius. In the aftermath of Paralius's beating, the once broad spectrum of ideal political behaviors had become constricted.

This shift in the thematic focus of communal discourse had a very real effect on the shape of intellectual circles in the Eastern Mediterranean. To see this, one

---

157. Note, however, Simplicius's qualification that some actions may be found that need a "companion in danger" (*In Ench.* 65.44).

needs only to compare the fates of two schools—the Alexandrian circle run by Ammonius and the Athenian Platonic academy ultimately controlled by Damascius. After Nicomedes' investigation, Ammonius remained in Alexandria. He seems to have adapted his teaching slightly while maintaining a reasonably high public profile.[158] Ammonius chose to disregard the ideal of social withdrawal later championed by Damascius and Simplicius in order to continue to play an active role as a teacher and public figure. Isidore, by contrast, took a different approach. By choosing to leave Alexandria and its corrupt political environment, he remained absolutely true to his philosophical convictions. At the same time, he abandoned any political or pedagogic role he could play in the city.

Both courses of action had consequences that affected not only Neoplatonic ethical teaching but also the shape of philosophical education in the late antique eastern Mediterranean. Ammonius's decision to accept some restriction on his activity led him to craft a distinctive teaching style that proved popular in Alexandria. In addition, it seems that Ammonius's followers remained politically engaged, if not particularly active.[159] We cannot know how he described the riot and investigation to followers (if he presented it to them at all), but the behaviors of Ammonius and his successors do suggest how they might have understood its aftermath. After Paralius's riot and Nicomedes' investigation, Ammonius seems to have made the continuity of philosophical teaching in Alexandria his top personal priority. If embracing a somewhat flexible set of ethical principles allowed him to adapt and continue his teaching, this seems to have been a price he was willing to pay. This was not a heroic position to take, but it did enable his circle to survive not just the investigations of Zeno but the much more severe Justinianic political climate. In fact, his school continued for at least three and possibly as many as five academic generations after his death. Perhaps because of Ammonius's willingness to forsake inflexible ethical doctrines, the teaching tradition that he once headed proved to be the last known active Platonic circle in antiquity.[160]

On the other side, Isidore's flight to Athens highlighted his stubborn and principled Epictetan resistance to Christian pressure. Perhaps more significantly, it also served as a vehicle that conveyed the future scholarch Damascius to the city. The young philosophical convert fetched up on Athenian shores filled with the conviction that Isidore had acted most philosophically in fleeing Alexandria.

---

158. On the adaptation of his teaching see Watts, *City and School*, 222–30. For his high public profile, note *Vit. Is.* 78E for his conflict with Erythrius, a prefect under Zeno (cf. Malchus, fr. 7 [Blockley]).

159. Olympiodorus, for example, seems to have been familiar with the events surrounding the ceremonial *adventus* of the governor Hephaistus (*In Alcibiadem* 2.80–82, ed. Westerink).

160. Watts, *City and School*, 257–61. On the fate of Platonic teaching in the sixth and early seventh centuries see more generally E. Watts, "Where to Live the Philosophical Life in the Sixth Century? Damascius, Simplicius, and the Return from Persia," *GRBS* 45 (2005), 307–15.

Damascius conveyed these ideas to his followers, evidently both in his teaching and in informal conversations about their philosophical ancestors. It is little surprise that, when Damascius himself ultimately faced similar Christian pressure, he showed no interest in political compromise.

The political values that Isidore exemplified made the establishment of a sustainable Neoplatonic community difficult in the later Roman context. Isidore's commitment to these values, after all, forced him to flee his city, his school, and most of his students in a time of crisis. His was an act of principle that privileged his own personal integrity above the needs of his students and the demands of the school to which he belonged. And, when the situation in Athens proved too politically fraught, Isidore fled from it as well.[161] By choosing to idealize a solitary philosopher who guarded his philosophical ideals above all else, Damascius put himself in a situation where the needs of his school and circle of followers would, by necessity, be secondary to the demands of his own philosophical principles.

For Damascius, these principles clashed violently with contemporary realities in the late 520s. The Athens to which he and Isidore fled in the 480s was, as they expected, a place in which the influence of a significant pagan community made it possible for Neoplatonists to live as they saw fit. By the late 510s, administrative and social changes had eroded the power of Athenian pagans.[162] In the 520s, these local conditions combined with assertive imperial anti-pagan actions to threaten the existence of the Athenian philosophical community that Damascius headed. This process culminated in 529 when an edict was issued forcing the closure of Damascius's school.[163] In the real world there were, of course, many ways in which Damascius could respond to this pressure. However, the rigid ethical system and uncompromising historical traditions of his school left Damascius no room for compromise. In good Epictetan fashion, Damascius sat by while authorities proscribed his teaching. Then, when his property was threatened by a subsequent round of legislation in the early 530s, Damascius and his followers apparently resolved that the corruption of Roman society had reached such a point that they had no choice but to leave for the more hospitable Persian empire.[164] In this they emulated the historical example of Isidore and forsook their home city and the dwindling institution that Damascius headed.

Damascius and his associates eventually returned to the Roman world under

---

161. On this see *Vit. Is.* 151A–E as well as the discussion of Watts, *City and School*, 122–23.

162. For discussion of these changes see Watts, *City and School*, 129–31. For an assessment of the role of councils under Justinian, see A. Laniado, *Recherches sur les notables municipaux dans l'empire protobyzantin* (Paris, 2002), 47–62.

163. For the nature of this edict and the particular path it followed, see E. Watts, "Justinian, Malalas, and the End of Athenian Philosophical Teaching in A.D. 529," *JRS* 94 (2004), 168–82.

164. Agathias, 2.30.3–4.

the protection offered by a clause in the Roman-Persian peace treaty of 532.[165] Intriguingly, Damascius's school seems to have dissolved; we know of no students who were trained by the exiled philosophers after their return.[166] In the same way that Ammonius's response showed some of the ethical problems a teacher faced when he privileged scholastic continuity over inflexible philosophical conviction, Damascius's unfailing loyalty to the ethical ideals exemplified by his teacher helped to kill his school. Indeed, it is notable that, even when Damascius and his followers returned from Persia with full legal protection for their religious activities, the old scholarch proved unable to reconstitute a school. Instead, he and his followers continued living a steadfast and philosophically appropriate life until they, and the scholastic tradition they represented, ultimately died without institutional heirs.

Scholars studying ancient intellectual circles have a natural inclination to consider them as centers of doctrinal teaching. Consequently, much has been made of the importance of the formal doctrinal instruction that went on in this context. The

---

165. Agathias, 2.30.5–2.31.4. For discussion of the protections offered the philosophers by the treaty of 532 see Kaldellis, *Procopius of Caesarea*, 106.

166. In the last century, Alexandria, Athens, Asia Minor, and Harrān (the Greek Carrhae) have all been suggested as sites to which the philosophers returned, with Harrān now the most popular choice. For Harrān and the establishment of a multi-generational school there, see M. Tardieu, "Sābiens Coraniques et 'Sābiens' de Harrān," *Journal Asiatique* 274 (1986), 1–44; and *Les Paysages reliques. Routes et haltes syriennes d'Isidore á Simplicius* (Louvain, 1990). Against Tardieu, see J. Lameer, "From Alexandria to Baghdad: Reflections on the Genesis of a Problematic Tradition," in *The Ancient Tradition in Christian and Islamic Hellenism*, ed. G. Endress and R. Kruk (Leiden, 1997), 181–91; C. Luna, Review of R. Thiel, *Simplikios und das Ende der neuplatonischen Schule in Athen*, *Mnemosyne* 54 (2001), 482–504; R. Lane Fox, "Harran, the Sabiens, and the late Platonist 'Movers,'" in *The Philosopher and Society in Late Antiquity*, 231–44; and now K. van Bladel, *The Arabic Hermes: From Pagan Sage to Prophet of Science* (Oxford, 2009), 70–79. I have elsewhere argued for the scattering of the circle ("Where to Live the Philosophical Life," 307–15). While it is compelling in parts, I remain unconvinced by the general thrust of I. Hadot's renewed arguments for Harrān ("Dans quel lieu le néoplatonicien Simplicius a-t-il fondé son école de mathématiques, et où a pu avoir lieu son entretien avec un manichéen?" *International Journal of the Platonic Tradition* 1 [2007], 42–107). It is difficult to assert that the philosophers returned to Harrān when no explicit statement connecting Simplicius and others to the city is made in any ancient or medieval text. In addition, these arguments for long-term scholastic continuity would be more compelling if one could identify any students or successors of these men in contemporary or nearly contemporary texts. Hadot ("Dans quel lieu," 76ff., 102) suggests the existence of a school of mathematics founded by Simplicius on the basis of a couple of remarks in much later Arabic sources (most notably the thirteenth-century historian Ibn al-Qifti). Against her suggestion, see the important arguments of van Bladel, *The Arabic Hermes*, 75n52. The only member of the circle whose post-Persia location can be fixed is Damascius, who penned an epitaph in the city of Emesa in 538 (*Greek Anthology* 7.553; for the stone itself see Cameron, "Last Days," 21–22).

previous two chapters have attempted to broaden our understanding of these environments by emphasizing the power that the personalities and personal histories of scholastic leaders had to shape an institution's public perception and the behaviors of its students. Much of this power derived from the specific contours of the Roman scholastic environment. Student life often began with a process of initiation that heightened a student's sense of belonging to a privileged and exclusive group. Most schools also developed a strict hierarchy which rewarded a student's intellectual advancement and personal relationship with a teacher. Students consequently prized personal contact with a professor, especially in informal social settings.

Eunapius provides a revealing glimpse into this environment. He describes the devotion that many students had for their teachers as well as the rituals and other scholastic customs that produced such strong personal attachments. Eunapius had something of a unique scholastic experience. Although he clearly revered his teacher of rhetoric, Prohaeresius, Eunapius seems to have had little personal interaction with him. Indeed, Eunapius came to know of Prohaeresius's personality and achievements largely through the reports of older members of his school.[167] By contrast, Chrysanthius, Eunapius's teacher of grammar and philosophy, was a close friend. Chrysanthius often invited Eunapius to accompany him on anecdote-filled walks just as his own teacher, Aedesius, and Aedesius's teacher, Iamblichus, had done with their favorite students. Eunapius, then, shows two ways in which formative anecdotes circulated among students. In both cases, these stories had the effect of bolstering Eunapius's pride in the intellectual lineage to which he belonged while simultaneously illustrating the practical applications of the doctrines and techniques taught in each school. Eunapius, then, describes the dynamic process through which personal relationships, historical traditions, and formal doctrinal teaching worked together to shape a student's appreciation of his intellectual heritage.

Eunapius writes with deep conviction and displays an obvious love for his mentors and the institutions they headed, but he does not reveal how students responded when outsiders attacked the people, traditions, and doctrines that engendered these feelings. For this we must turn to other late Roman sources. Unsurprisingly, they show that intellectuals did not respond favorably to the negative comments of outsiders. Members of a school tended to react to such criticism by reaffirming their personal faith in the integrity of their mentors and the historical testimony that defined their careers. Furthermore, as shown by Porphyry's defense of Plotinus, this could be done in a way that simultaneously undercut an opponent's charges and reiterated important elements of a school's teaching.

---

167. On this point, see E. Watts, "Orality and Communal Identity in Eunapius' *Lives of the Sophists and Philosophers*," *Byzantion* 75 (2005), 350–52.

This general background explains some of the particular tensions that helped to prompt Paralius's beating. Christian and pagan sources emphasize the degree to which the Alexandrian schools of Horapollon and his associates defined the personalities and personal legacies of Alexandrian teachers through their philosophical and spiritual accomplishments. Our sources also indicate that Alexandrian students learned about these achievements under many of the same conditions that Eunapius earlier described. The exceptional members of a student corps often heard stories from their teachers over dinner or in other relatively intimate social settings. For the student guests these stories became, in essence, souvenirs of the experience as well as reminders of the high communal status and personal intimacy that the occasions represented. For this reason, when these and other anecdotes flowed into the broader student population, they would have retained much of their power.

This was the environment into which Paralius entered. Although the product of a respected pagan intellectual family, Paralius did not prove adept at negotiating this complicated social world. Instead of building relationships with his fellow students and competing with them to win his teacher's affection, Paralius seems to have spurned the school in order to spend time with his brother, a monk at the Enaton monastery. This was an uncommon but not unprecedented decision; Libanius, for example, disengaged from the student corps of his own teacher.[168] Indeed, Paralius's aloofness would not even have been particularly problematic had he not chosen to rebel against the scholastic social hierarchy. Paralius, however, also publicly assailed the character of his teachers. His outburst inspired Horapollon's corps of students to rally around their mentor and attack Paralius in order to silence his criticism. In so doing, they reaffirmed their own loyalty to Horapollon.

As even Zacharias seems obliquely to acknowledge, the beating that Paralius received represented a normal corrective action. Indeed, such things happened with some regularity throughout the later Roman Empire. But Paralius's beating had unexpected consequences. It did not so much defend the actions and reputations of Alexandrian pagan teachers as it called attention to their activities. Ultimately this led to an imperial investigation of the teachers and their schools. When this investigation came, Alexandrian teachers were challenged to rise to the ethical standards demanded by the doctrines they taught and exemplified by the stories they told. Unsurprisingly, many proved unable to do this. Not only were some of the doctrines contradictory but others were revealed to be unworkable in the Alexandrian political context of the late 480s. Some teachers, like Ammonius, evidently decided that a compromise with the authorities represented the best way out of an extremely difficult situation. Others, most notably Isidore, chose a pious self-segregation in which they quietly resisted all outside pressure.

168. On Libanius, see *Or.* 1.20–23.

In the end, Illus's rebellion, Paralius's beating, and the subsequent investigation of Nicomedes had a profound effect upon the community of Alexandrian philosophers. They produced an immediate split that separated the teachers who remained in Alexandria from those who fled. They also changed the way teachers and students thought about their community's common history. Although seemingly limited in their effect, these developments resonated widely. In Alexandria, they ultimately determined the shape of Neoplatonic teaching for most of the next century. In Athens, they helped chart the path for Neoplatonism's eventual dislocation. Paralius's beating helped to set in motion a process of engagement with the past that forced the last generations of Neoplatonists to face the practical limitations of a colorful but sometimes irrelevant communal memory. It left a splintered philosophical community in which a shared communal history and the personal bonds that supported it scattered across the eastern Mediterranean along with its squabbling members.

PART TWO

The Past Within and Outside Late Antique Monasteries

When the three of us, myself and Thomas the sophist (from my city Gaza), who loves Christ in every way, and Zenodotus of Lesbos came by—for we were constantly in the holy churches together with those called the philoponoi *(those who, in some places, were called "the diligent" and in others "companions") we seemed somehow to intimidate [the pagan students] . . . With difficulty, due to some rioters, we managed to save Paralius from their murderous hands. We then took him to the place called Enaton to be among the monks. We showed them the bruises which he had received for the Christian religion, we made them to understand how much he had suffered unjustly for having abused the error of the pagans.*

VIT. SEV. 23–24

THE STUDENT-PHILOPONOI WHO RESCUED Paralius enjoyed a unique status within Alexandria. Within the schools, Zacharias, Thomas the sophist, and Zenodotus were fearsome and powerful figures because of their affiliation with Christian churches and monasteries. Beyond the schools, however, the connection between these students and Christian monasteries appears much less impressive. While Zacharias and his friends easily entered the physical space of the Enaton, they remained outsiders within the monastery's walls. The monks knew these three students but felt no obvious obligation to them and had to be convinced to take action on their behalf. This suggests that the scholastic-*philoponoi* enjoyed a sort of dual identity. In secular contexts, they distinguished themselves through their extraordinary commitment to Christian service and advertised their affiliation with the Alexandrian bishop and the monastery of the Enaton. In the ascetic environment, these young men enjoyed a casual familiarity with the monks, their monastery, and their collective spiritual priorities, but they were accorded no special recognition.

With feet in both the secular and monastic worlds, the student- *philoponoi* are part of a broader category of people who tried to mix a worldly vocation with an ascetic affiliation. In a society that often experienced ascetic life only indirectly, Zacharias and other laymen affiliated with monasteries qualified as monastic insiders who evoked the piety of monks and could summon the great spiritual and political power of these holy men. Within a monastery, however, these men never fully participated in community life. Pious visitors often took part in discussions with monks and benefited from their spiritual guidance, but a clear line separated them from the regular members of the community. Most monks had a distinct physical appearance, a definable habit, and a well-regulated daily schedule that distinguished them. Many ascetic leaders also restricted the times and places in which laity and monks could interact. Monastic affiliates like the student-*philoponoi,* then, could become intimately aware of practices and ideas that excited monks while remaining unaffected by the particular rhythms that organized their daily life.

The Christian students who shaped the second phase of the Alexandrian riot of 486 straddled these two distinct worlds. They devoted much of their time to the study of Plato, Aristotle, and techniques of rhetorical composition, but they also identified with the teaching of leading anti-Chalcedonian ascetics. Although Classical learning and anti-Chalcedonian polemics are two very different things, they represented the most important ideological influences upon Zacharias and his friends. Throughout their time in Alexandria, these students worked to create a common intellectual ground between anti-Chalcedonian ascetic and Classical sophistic traditions.

This section of our study examines the mechanisms by which ascetically-inclined laymen like Zacharias Scholasticus came to identify with the ideas and traditions that defined monastic life. Monasteries, like pagan schools, explained ideals of conduct abstractly and illustrated them with historical anecdotes. The first chapter of this section considers how this ascetic discourse affected the behaviors of monks in monasteries and, ultimately, how these ideas spread beyond closely controlled late antique ascetic groups. It does this by looking at a series of short case studies. The discussion begins by examining the organization of daily life in Egyptian monasteries in the fourth and fifth centuries, with particular attention paid to late-fourth-century Pachomian communities. In each Pachomian monastery, regular assemblies punctuated a daily routine in which leaders spoke about the Scriptural foundations of the community's unique lifestyle. Surviving Pachomian biographical material suggests that the brothers also heard about the history of their community and the deeds of its leaders in some of these communal assemblies. These regular history lessons influenced the values and behaviors of Pachomian monks. In addition, sources describing the apprenticeships through which communal elders individually supervised the spiritual development of junior monks suggest that these ascetic master-disciple relationships also facilitated the transmission of particularly potent historical traditions. Personal ties and shared communal experiences, then, helped monks to identify with these stories and the ideals they illustrated.

Texts as diverse as the *Historia Monachorum* and the *Plerophories* of John Rufus show that visitors to monasteries were also exposed to some of the same illustrative anecdotes that circulated among monks. These oral testimonies exercised particular influence over certain lay Christians, some of whom came to see leading monks as personal spiritual instructors. Surviving sources (most notably the letters of the

Gazan ascetics Barsanuphius and John) show that these intimate spiritual discipleships helped laymen to identify with the historical traditions that defined ascetic communities while also affecting their behavior in the outside world.

The second chapter in this section focuses upon anti-Chalcedonian ascetic communities in Alexandria and Gaza. Although these communities bear no direct connection to the groups discussed in the preceding chapter, a similar set of master-disciple and ascetic-layman relationships characterized their organizations and enabled the transmission of historical materials. This chapter will show that a number of Christian students, Zacharias Scholasticus foremost among them, were affiliates of the Enaton monastery in Alexandria and related ascetic communities in Gaza. By the 480s, the Alexandrian and Gazan monasteries to which these students were tied had become important centers of resistance to the Council of Chalcedon. The anecdotes heard by students and other visitors to these ascetic circles celebrated monastic political resistance to imperial pressure and described divinely inspired visions that associated the Council of Chalcedon with the imminent end of the world. These eschatological ideas conflicted directly with the important Neoplatonic teaching that the world was eternal. They consequently forced Alexandrian students of philosophy to choose between the ascetic discourse to which they had become attached and the ideas presented by their teachers. This environment caused some students, like the Alexandrian student-*philoponoi,* to become extremely hostile towards pagan professors whose teachings they thought pulled students away from Christianity. These students gradually became conditioned to look for anti-Christian activity in the scholastic environment. Their misrepresentation of Paralius's beating as a religious "persecution" and their vigorous response to it grew out of a fundamental conflict between ideas presented by Neoplatonists and the beliefs sustained by their personal relationships with anti-Chalcedonian ascetics. The riot they promoted also changed the pagan-Christian dynamic within the schools and gave Christian students greater confidence to assert their ideas. It marked a turning point in the communal history of the student-*philoponoi* and, as such, it came to occupy a central position in the communal narratives underpinning this new Christian assertiveness.

4

History and the Shape of Monastic Communities

In 350, the leaders of the eight monasteries that made up the Pachomian ascetic system (the *Koinonia*) traveled to Phbow, the headquarters of the federation, to greet Apa Theodore, the new head of their order.[1] Their visit came at the end of a particularly difficult time for the Pachomian community. Pachomius, the founder of the *Koinonia* and the visionary responsible for its organization, had died in May of 346 during a plague that took away many of the group's other most senior leaders. Petronius, the scion of a wealthy Egyptian family and Pachomius's appointed successor, died that July.[2] His replacement, a diligent but ineffectual leader named Horsiesios, lasted just over three years before a revolt by the leadership of the Pachomian monastery at Thmoušons forced him to step down. The elders of the *Koinonia* then nominated Theodore to replace Horsiesios.[3]

Theodore was a natural choice. Before he had a falling out with Pachomius in 343, Theodore had been Pachomius's designated successor and he enjoyed good relations with the heads of individual Pachomian monasteries.[4] His elevation

---

1. The number of Pachomian communities at this time is debatable, with seven being the minimum. See the map included in P. Rousseau, *Pachomius: The Making of a Community in Fourth-Century Egypt*, 2nd ed. (Berkeley, 1999), 56, as well as Rousseau, "Pachomius" in *Late Antiquity: A Guide to the Postclassical World*, ed. G. W. Bowersock, P. Brown, and O. Grabar (Cambridge, MA, 1999), 624–25. The Sahidic text describing this meeting is clear that ⲙⲡⲉϣⲙⲟⲩⲛ ⲛ̄ϩⲏⲅⲟⲩⲙⲉⲛⲟⲓ were present.

2. *Bohairic Life of Pachomius* (henceforth *Bo.*), 130; cf. *First Greek Life of Pachomius* (henceforth G¹), 117b. For discussion of Petronius and his position, see Rousseau, *Pachomius*, 153, 183–84.

3. *Bo.* 139; G¹ 127–29. The *Vita Prima* does not explicitly state that this assembly included the heads of all of the Pachomian monasteries. The Bohairic text, however, is more clear.

4. This is made clear by *Bo.* 94 and G¹ 106–7a.

under these difficult conditions restored him to the high status that many thought he deserved, gave the rest of the *Koinonia* a leader in whom they could express their confidence, and seemed to promise more friendly relations between the abbot and the community elders. For this reason, the Pachomian elders cheerfully journeyed to Phbow with the expectation that Theodore would welcome them and, collectively, they could amicably end the crisis enveloping their community.

Their hopes were quickly disappointed. As soon as he saw them, Theodore "became very angry and they almost had to compel him to embrace them."[5] Instead of the warm reception they hoped to receive, Theodore's expression registered both rage and sadness. When they had all arrived, Theodore sat before them and began to speak. Everything from the sorrowful tone of Theodore's voice to his decision about how to address his new subordinates conveyed the seriousness of the situation. These details also had a more subtle, yet equally clear, meaning within a Pachomian context. By sitting among his visitors, Theodore emphasized that this was not a ceremonial occasion when a new authority figure first received his subordinates. Instead, this was to be a moment of instruction and discussion in which Theodore would teach these elders about the proper behavior of Pachomian ascetics.[6] Discussion groups like these occurred often among Pachomian monks and occupied an important part of the Pachomian daily routine. Every evening, the monks would assemble in small groups to hear a communal leader teach about Scripture. The groups would then discuss his teaching, offer mutual support for their ascetic endeavors, and, on occasion, offer a rebuke to a monk who had committed a misdeed.[7]

According to the Bohairic *Life of Pachomius*,[8] Theodore imitated this setting

---

5. *Bo.* 142 = *S. Pachomii Vitae Sahidice Scriptae*, ed. L. T. Lefort, CSCO 99–100 (Louvain, 1952), 274.31–33. The translations of Pachomian texts are those of A. Veilleux, *Pachomian Koinonia, The Lives, Rules, and Other Writings of Saint Pachomius and his Disciples*, vols. 1–3 (Kalamazoo, MI, 1980–83), unless otherwise noted. The best example of this most interesting section of the "Bohairic Life" survives only in Sahidic. Given its importance to this study, the translations of *Bo.* 139–42 are my own and based upon this Sahidic text.

6. The context here matches the description of Theodore's informal discussion sessions in *Bo.* 188. This contrasts with his more formal sermons during which everyone stood silently.

7. For these evening rituals see, for example, the discussion led by Pachomius at G^1 77 and the general picture provided by G^1 58. For discussion, see as well Rousseau, *Pachomius*, 85–86; for rebukes on such occasions, ibid., 97–98; cf. Pachomius, *Precepts* 121.

8. The account of this address in the Bohairic life differs in significant ways from the events described in the Greek *Vita Prima*. The Bohairic life mentions two addresses that Theodore gave, one to the brothers of Phbow and another to the elders in charge of the other Pachomian monasteries (*Bo.* 141–42). The *Vita Prima* (G^1 131) seems to suggest that Theodore spoke only to the brothers at Phbow and then visited privately with the leaders of the other monasteries in the system. On the relationship between these two texts, see Rousseau, *Pachomius*, 37–48 as well as the longer and more detailed discussions of A. Veilleux, *La Liturgie dans le cénobitism pachômien au quatrième siècle*,

when giving his initial address to the heads of the various Pachomian monasteries. He also planned an appropriate lesson for the occasion. Theodore suggested to the assembled elders that their revolt against Horsiesios threatened to bring the anger of God down upon the community. Horsiesios was a truly good man "whom God and our father [Pachomius] installed in his holy place" and serious consequences awaited those who disregarded this divine plan.[9] To illustrate these consequences, Theodore drew upon a series of scriptural passages that highlighted moments when men acted in ways contrary to God's will.[10]

His lesson then turned back to the contemporary situation. He urged the elders to repent and seek forgiveness for the contempt that they had shown for God's plan. They had "raised [their] hands to destroy the holy place which the Lord bestowed upon our holy father Pachomius because of his tears and prayers."[11] Indeed, Theodore continued, their behavior was all the more revolting because God had sent a vision warning Pachomius of the turmoil that would engulf the monastery. Theodore then reminded his visitors of this vision, which Pachomius had shared with them. "When the Lord opened his eyes in a vision, he saw the greater part of the brothers—some in the mouths of crocodiles, others in a fire, some in the mouths of wild beasts. Others, about to be drowned in the middle of the river, were crying out seeking help. At once [Pachomius] stood praying for the salvation of these men."[12]

Theodore then came to the point of his lesson. He urged all of the elders to remember the example of Pachomius, repent of their arrogance, and agree to "govern our lives in humility of heart and effort." If everyone agreed to this, "our souls shall become worthy to see the holy ones."[13] To confirm this promise, Theodore then introduced another set of biblical passages illustrating divine anger towards the contemptuous and compassion towards the repentant. He concluded by returning to the present situation:

> My brothers, you who are leaders of the holy places of God which he gave to our righteous father, I hear perverted words issuing from your mouths. Some in fact are saying, "This monastery is mine," others, "This object is mine." Now things of this sort ought not to take place here. But if you truly are prepared with all your heart

---

Studia Anselmiana 57 (Rome, 1968), 1–159; and *Pachomian Koinonia*, 1.1–21. As with all Pachomian biographical materials, it is hazardous to assume the historicity of any one event. Nevertheless, the general course of events described in the Bohairic life seems plausible and therefore suggestive of the way Theodore may have exercised authority within the community.

9. *Bo.* 142 = Lefort, 275.5–6.
10. These include allusions to Genesis 50:19; Esther 4:17; Isaiah 40:17; Luke 19:14; Micah 6:3; and Matthew 13:27.
11. *Bo.* 142 = Lefort, 275.22–25, trans. Veilleux, amended.
12. *Bo.* 142 = Lefort, 275.28–276.1.
13. *Bo.* 142 = Lefort, 276.10–14.

to act in a spirit of renunciation like our righteous father, then agree with this: "We are not the leader of a community but we are prepared to submit to anything that you impose upon us."[14]

As the setting demanded, the brothers then were given the chance to discuss Theodore's lesson with him. They immediately answered him with the words of repentance that he sought. They proclaimed themselves ready to act as he had requested and urged Theodore to quickly reestablish the rules which Pachomius had laid down for them. They further emphasized that they understood his teaching by telling Theodore, "the Lord has exalted you so that you might nourish all of us in the blessed wisdom and the traditions of our father who gave them to us for the health of our souls."[15] Then, with the lesson and discussion concluded, Theodore "left the eight leaders of the monasteries in Phbow weaving mats like all of the brothers."[16] The time for teaching had passed and all the monks, regardless of rank, now moved on to the next part of their daily routine.

One cannot know how accurately our hagiographer described Theodore's audience, but we can see that the power of this story derived from its author's acute awareness of the rhythms of Pachomian ascetic life. In his reconstruction, when the heads of the constituent Pachomian monasteries arrived to congratulate Theodore on his elevation, they understood their visit to be a special occasion during which Theodore's new subordinates would affirm their loyalty to him. By making this trip, these eight fathers were tacitly inviting Theodore to acknowledge a particular sort of authority structure for the larger Pachomian community that seemed likely to end the power struggle between the leader of the Pachomian federation and the individual heads of its constituent monasteries. After deposing Horsiesios, the fathers were now, in essence, proposing that one monk would serve as the leader of the whole community but he would do so only with the consent of the heads of each monastery. Their mission, then, resembled that of aristocrats congratulating a new king while simultaneously reminding him of their own prerogatives. However, Theodore's carefully calibrated response destroyed any illusion that the Pachomian monasteries had entered a new era. By inducing the visiting fathers to sit down and listen to his instruction, Theodore had robbed the visit of any extraordinary significance. It had been transformed from the coronation of a new ascetic monarch to another mundane moment in the well-ordered Pachomian day.

From this incident, it should already be clear that Scripture and the historical traditions attached to Pachomius represented two important ways in which the members of the *Koinonia* came to understand the nature of their discipline and the limits of appropriate behavior within their community. This was a feature of

---

14. *Bo.* 142 = Lefort, 277.17–26.
15. *Bo.* 142 = Lefort, 278.7–10.
16. *Bo.* 143 = Lefort, 278.11–13, trans. Veilleux, amended.

Pachomian life that Theodore apparently appreciated. In fact, the appeal to these twin pillars of Pachomian communal identity became an important feature of Theodore's leadership. In the texts of Theodore's surviving *Instructions* one sees him repeatedly weaving together Scripture and references to Pachomius to illustrate the practical significance of his teachings for members of the Pachomian community. So, for example, Theodore's third *Instruction* emphasizes the need for the monks of the *Koinonia* to make common cause and work collectively for the spiritual and ascetic improvement of all of their fellows.[17] After a long series of specific recommendations about improving behavior, Theodore introduces a set of biblical allusions that support his ideas. He then tells the brothers that because they now understand "the exact meaning of all of this according to the knowledge of the Scriptures, the breath of God," they are to become "imitators of Apa Pachomius' life."[18] Within the *Koinonia*, Pachomius represented an ascetic exemplar whose conduct showed the practical application of God's word.

Other Pachomian sources describe the impact that Theodore's rhetorical fusing of biblical materials and the historical legacy of Pachomius could have on monks under his charge. On one occasion, Theodore publicly named a group of insolent monks and warned them that, if they did not repent, they would undergo great punishment.[19] These monks sneered at his warning and he expelled them from the monastery. Theodore then addressed the rest of the monastery in order to explain his decision. Quoting Matthew 13.42, Theodore told them that this insolence was a serious matter and the punishment of God would be severe. He then recalled for his audience a moment when Pachomius said that a brother who had behaved dishonorably would receive great blows from the Lord.[20] "When the brothers heard this additional testimony from our father Theodore, namely that of our father Pachomius, they were alarmed and took steps to make greater efforts to escape painful blows."[21] With Theodore's action now supported by both Scripture and Pachomian precedent, the once-skeptical brothers accepted the necessity of his expulsion order.

THE *KOINONIA*

To appreciate why Pachomian monks responded so strongly to Theodore's well-crafted appeals to Scripture and communal history, one must understand the role

---

17. The text of Theodore's *Third Instruction* is found in L. T. Lefort, ed., *Oeuvres de s. Pachôme et de ses disciples*, CSCO 159 (Louvain, 1956), 40–60. For an English translation, see Veilleux, *Pachomian Koinonia*, 3.92–119.

18. Theodore, *Instruction* 3.35, trans. Veilleux.

19. *Bo*. 149. Here too one may question the degree to which our hagiographer has enhanced Theodore's actions in order to push forward a particular theme.

20. This perhaps alludes to the vision described in *Bo*. 88.

21. *Bo*. 149, trans. Veilleux.

that these materials played in establishing the rhythm of life within Pachomian monasteries. Their importance was made clear from the very first moment that a monk sought to join the *Koinonia*. All men wishing to enroll in a Pachomian monastery would turn up at the gatehouse that separated it from the outside world. There they would wait, perhaps for as long as a few days, until they could be examined by the head of that particular monastery.[22] While they waited, these new arrivals were taught the Lord's Prayer and a few psalms by the monks in charge of the gatehouse.[23] After a few days had passed, the head of the monastery would question the new arrival about his willingness and ability to commit to the monastic life. If he found the man's answers satisfactory, the father would then clothe him in the monk's habit, a symbolic act that welcomed him to the community.[24] This would be followed by an intense period of study in which the novice was taught about the rules of Pachomian life.[25] In this period he was also required to learn a number of psalms and other passages of Scripture by heart. If he could not read, he was taught to do this so that he could better engage in the study of biblical texts.[26]

Learning Scripture and the principles on which Pachomius had organized his community comprised a novice monk's first experiences with the *Koinonia* because these things set the basic cadence to which daily life in Pachomian monasteries marched.[27] The monks slept in private cells in individual houses that usually contained around twenty monks. These houses formed the basic building block of the Pachomian community and also constituted the monk's main social world.[28] Each house had a superior who supervised both the spiritual progress of each

22. The initial process of initiation is somewhat obscure, though its nature is suggested by the accounts of Pachomius's initiation of his early followers. See, for example, G¹ 24 and *Bo.* 23 (on Pachomius's early disciples), G¹ 36 and *Bo.* 30 (on Theodore's initial moments in the community). For discussion, note Rousseau, *Pachomius*, 70. On the process in the later fourth century see the detailed description in *Praeceptum* 49.

23. On this instruction, see *Pr.* 49 and Rousseau, *Pachomius*, 70. For the porters and their teaching responsibilities, note *Bo.* 26. The learning of the psalms is also perhaps suggested by *Bo.* 15 and *Bo.* 23.

24. This entire process is described by Rousseau, *Pachomius*, 70–71. For the clothing in monastic habit, see *Bo.* 26. For the questioning of a new arrival, note *Bo.* 23 and G¹ 24.

25. The learning of these traditions is suggested by *Bo.* 23 and *Pr.* 49. Although this purports to describe Pachomius's training of his first disciples, the pattern of initiation described here likely resembles that of the broader Pachomian community at the time this description was written.

26. *Pr.* 49, 139. Note as well Rousseau, *Pachomius*, 70.

27. The following description of the daily routine in the *Koinonia* draws heavily upon the reconstruction of Rousseau, *Pachomius*, 77–85. While one can question how well this represents life under Pachomius, one can confidently use these sources to illustrate patterns of life under the supervision of Theodore and Horsiesios.

28. On these houses and the important role they played in both Pachomian social and economic life, see E. Wipszycka, "Contribution à l'étude de l'économie de la congrégation Pachômienne," *JJP* 26 (1996), 167–210.

monk and the daily work he performed. At dawn a horn or gong would sound and each monk would leave his cell to assemble with his housemates before the entire house set off for the *synaxis,* the ritual morning prayers.[29] From the time that he left his cell until he entered the *synaxis,* each monk was to "recite something from the Scripture."[30] When the entire monastery had assembled, the monks would "stand house by house, according to its rank and order, with each housemaster standing in front of his men. The seconds would also stand behind each of them, checking on the brothers to make sure no one was absent. This is how they stood, in order, listening to the words of God."[31] The assembly itself included a great deal of reading from the Scriptures as well as collective prayers and time for silent reflection among the monks. This may also have been the time when individual monks performed penance for various transgressions.[32] While monks were expected to be attentive, they did not remain idle. The floor of the space in which the *synaxis* took place seems to have been covered with damp rushes and the monks plaited ropes with these rushes while prayers went on.[33]

This basic pattern of working while reciting texts, praying, and contemplating God's word continued throughout the day. After prayers, the monks were assigned their daily work by the housemaster, who communicated to them the instructions of the superior of the monastery.[34] Once the necessary tools were assembled, the monks of each house processed to their worksite in orderly lines led by their housemaster. They would then set to these tasks, again working to the rhythm of scriptural recitation and directing their thoughts through silent contemplation.[35] The workday was interrupted by a midday meal, which the monks would take in silence, and it concluded with a smaller evening meal.[36] The hours following the meal were for instruction, communal prayer, and discussion within the individual houses. On certain days of the week the superiors of each monastery presented a short lesson to all of the monks before leading them in common prayer.[37] On other days, this lesson seems to have been presented in the houses by the various headmasters.[38] As they withdrew, the monks again did so while repeating passages

---

29. Note *Leg.* 2 as well as *Pr.* 3, 9.
30. *Pr.* 3.
31. *Bo.* 188, trans. Veilleux.
32. Rousseau, *Pachomius,* 80n15.
33. *Pr.* 4.
34. *Pr.* 19, 24. Note as well Rousseau, *Pachomius* 81–82 and Veilleux, *Liturgie,* 127. For the relationship between individual houses and the tasks assigned to the monks, see Wipszycka, "Économie de la congregation Pachômienne," 167–79.
35. *Pr.* 28. Note here the comments of Rousseau, *Pachomius,* 82n28.
36. For meal time see the description of Palladius, *HL* 32.6
37. There seem to have been three such lessons scheduled each week, with the superiors leading the collective instruction on Saturdays and Sundays (*Bo.* 26; cf. G^1 58 and Rousseau, *Pachomius,* 85).
38. G^1 28; *Bo.* 26. See as well the discussion of Rousseau, *Pachomius,* 85.

from Scripture. The evening concluded with discussion of the night's catechesis in the houses.

Pachomian monks spent their days engaged in near-constant recitation and contemplation of Scripture. This recitation not only dictated the cadence to which they worked but also helped to occupy the monks' minds as they passed through the monastery on their way to and from scheduled tasks. Quite literally, Scripture regulated the way that Pachomian monks thought, the pace at which they worked, and the manner in which they moved through the day. One cannot overstate the power that properly deployed biblical allusions could have in shaping the practices of Pachomian monks.

As we have already seen in pagan intellectual circles, much of the influence of communal historical traditions derives not from the doctrines a community claims to uphold but from the personal interactions and relationships that give tangible meaning to membership in such a group. The same was true within Theodore's Pachomian system. Although the *Koinonia* was designed as a collective ascetic enterprise in which the efforts of all monks helped to further the individual practice of each member, the organization possessed a clear and well-developed hierarchy of offices.[39] Spiritual and political authority cascaded down from the leader of the *Koinonia* to the stewards of its constituent monasteries and from them to the masters and seconds of the individual houses. In many but not all cases, this hierarchy reflected individual monks' seniority as much as their organizational and ascetic aptitude. This rigid hierarchy was constantly reinforced by the pattern of life in the monastery. When the entire monastery assembled for *synaxis*, for example, the houses entered individually, each led by its housemaster and his second.[40] The rules of the *Koinonia* even stated explicitly that "no one may walk ahead of his housemaster and his leader."[41] Once the *synaxis* began, "no one was allowed to sing Psalms apart from the housemasters and the elders of the monastery, who are of some reputation."[42] Such was the respect that average monks were to show to these elders that, if anyone was absent when the elders chanted, he was punished publicly and immediately.[43] So much importance was placed upon the monastic hierarchy that only the superior of the monastery could give a monk permission to be excused from a gathering of all the brothers.[44]

Within each house, the housemasters and their seconds exerted an even more

---

39. For the collective purpose see, for example, *Bo.* 105, 127–29; G¹ 120b–c. These passages will be discussed in more detail below.
40. *Pr.* 59.
41. *Pr.* 130.
42. *Pr.* 16.
43. *Pr.* 17.
44. *Pr.* 18, 23.

pervasive influence on the lives of individual monks. They controlled not only the tasks that the monks performed but even the most mundane aspects of their lives. So, for example, one monk could not receive property from another without the housemaster first approving the exchange.[45] He could not shave his head or change his wardrobe without permission.[46] And if a monk was pricked with a thorn he could not even draw the thorn out with tweezers unless the housemaster or second approved.[47] It should not be surprising that the housemaster also determined much of the teaching that shaped the practice of monks under his charge. He delivered thrice-weekly instructions in the house[48] and, on occasions when the superior taught before the entire monastery, the housemaster apparently led the discussions in which the brothers sought to interpret the meaning of the day's teaching.[49] He also had responsibility for the practical application of this teaching and the punishment of monks who did not obey the monastery's rules.[50] The housemaster, then, effectively controlled most elements of an ordinary monk's life.

The correlation of rank and ascetic experience within the Pachomian community means that knowledge of the institutional history of the *Koinonia* collected at the highest levels of its hierarchy. The biographers of Pachomius admit freely that their sources for the events of his life were "the fathers of old who lived a long time ago with him. For [Pachomius] would often recount these things to them after explaining the words of the Holy Scriptures."[51] These communal elders knew about more than Pachomius's deeds; they claimed that, in his *Instructions*, Pachomius explained to them what thoughts motivated his behavior.[52] In informal conversations, Pachomius also described for the most advanced monks in the community any visions that he had.[53] Pachomius evidently expected that, once this material became known to communal elders, they would use it to teach the monks over whom they had authority.

The Pachomian biographers approached their task of collecting the oral traditions describing Pachomius's life with seriousness and solemnity. Because most of the material resided in the minds of communal elders and circulated on occasions when they thought it most useful, the younger monks "saw that it was neces-

---

45. *Pr.* 106.
46. *Pr.* 97–98.
47. *Pr.* 96; cf. *Pr.* 82.
48. *Pr.* 50.
49. A fact perhaps suggested by *Pr.* 122–23, though this may actually refer to teaching done by the housemaster within the house.
50. *Pr.* 133.
51. G^1 10.
52. G^1 46.
53. G^1 99.

sary to [collect the material], so that we might not forget altogether what we had heard about this perfect monk who is our father after all of the saints."[54] When he headed the community, Theodore helped to push this process along. During his final illness, Theodore began to speak to his followers about the life of Pachomius. He described Pachomius's childhood, he cataloged the labors Pachomius underwent in establishing the *Koinonia*, and shared everything that he remembered hearing from Pachomius's mouth.[55] Following Theodore's lead, the authors of Pachomian biographies trusted completely the recollections of the community's elders. In fact, they characterized their own collecting and recording of anecdotes surrounding Pachomius as that of "children eagerly desiring to recall the memory of the fathers who brought us up."[56] They were writing what was, in effect, a family history that defined the struggles and achievements of a multi-generational ascetic enterprise. Their elders had taught these men that, as current members of the *Koinonia*, they too could share in the glory of Pachomius's ascetic victories by preserving and retelling illustrative stories about him.

A number of different traditions circulated within the community that illustrated how the collective efforts of the *Koinonia* generated a higher level of ascetic discipline than a solitary ascetic could achieve. Some of these concerned the initial visions that inspired Pachomius's project. In these, he was given divine assurances that his service to fellow ascetics would bring them great collective benefits.[57] Other traditions claimed to preserve the teaching of Pachomius himself. One, a parable that Pachomius framed as a rebuke to some talkative monks, lays out a specific view of the advantages of a shared ascetic life. "I will show you as well that the honor and the glory of men of the *Koinonia*, who have a good way of life together with the excellence of the toils which they impose on themselves, are superior to those men who lead an anchoritic life."[58] This happens because "he who makes progress in the *Koinonia* with purity, obedience, humility, and submissiveness . . . will grow rich forever in imperishable and enduring riches."[59] An ascetic who practices his discipline as a solitary "does not bear the responsibility of other ascetics, but neither does he see those who practice exercises . . . such a man will not rank high in the kingdom of heaven."[60] Elsewhere Pachomian traditions highlight the dangers faced by monks who live an ascetic life without the help of others. One tradition, which seems to have originated with Pachomius's own mentor, Palamon, describes a solitary ascetic who became so proud of his achievements

54. G^1 98.
55. *Bo.* 193–94.
56. G^1 99.
57. E.g., *Bo.* 17.
58. *Bo.* 105.
59. *Bo.* 105.
60. *Bo.* 105.

that he challenged Palamon to recite a prayer on burning coals. When Palamon refused to do this, the solitary performed the feat and walked proudly away. With no associates to moderate his practices, the ascetic was soon consumed by his pride and sinned. Unable to bear the shame, he then threw himself into a fire.[61] The behavior of this monk stands out against the discipline of the loose community of monks over whom Palamon watched and contrasts powerfully with the cohesive community that Pachomius would create. Pachomius's system, then, promised greater rewards to ascetics than the more spectacular but more dangerous practices of solitary ascetics.

Members of the *Koinonia* also shared with one another historical traditions that used non-Pachomian figures to celebrate and sanction the achievements of the community. The best known examples involve Antony, the prototypical solitary ascetic. One popular story describes a visit that Theodore and Zaccheus, another Pachomian monk, supposedly paid to Antony not long after the death of Pachomius.[62] The two monks arrived at Antony's enclosure and, when they were announced as members of the Pachomian community, Antony greeted them warmly. He told them not to be grieved by the death of Pachomius "because you have become his body and you have received his spirit."[63] Antony was then said to express his admiration for what Pachomius had created. "The fact that he gathered souls around himself in order to present them as holy to the Lord reveals that he is superior to us and that it is the path of the Apostles that he took."[64] The Greek *Life* is even more explicit in recording Antony's praise for the communal organization of the *Koinonia*. Antony is said to have told his visitors, "When I became a monk, there was no community to nurture other souls; each one of the ancient monks after the persecutions practiced his *askesis* alone."[65] He then continued, "Concerning your father, I often heard how well he walked according to the Scriptures."[66]

The traditions describing Theodore's encounter with Antony serve to validate the Pachomian version of a communal ascetic life. As Antony was the individual commonly recognized as the founder of Christian asceticism, his praise offered an authoritative view on what constituted ideal practice. Indeed, the Pachomian community was not alone in using the figure of Antony to sanction novel or controversial claims about ascetics and their practice. Jerome, Athanasius, and the circle of Didymus the Blind all drew upon the popular figure of Antony to establish

61. *Bo.* 14; G¹ 8.
62. *Bo.* 126–29; G¹ 120. On Antony's appearance in these traditions, see D. Brakke, *Athanasius and Asceticism,* 2nd ed. (Baltimore, 1998), 214–16.
63. *Bo.* 126.
64. *Bo.* 126.
65. G¹ 120.
66. G¹ 120.

the credibility of their own literary and practical approaches to asceticism.[67] The Pachomian traditions featuring Antony do more than simply recognize that an ascetic collective could surpass the level of excellence achieved by a solitary monk. They also sanction the continuity of the Pachomian project under the new leadership whom Pachomius chose and, eventually, under the stewardship of Theodore as well. Antony affirmed that Pachomius had led his followers along a spiritual path defined by Scripture, he indicated that the spirit of Pachomius's endeavor lived on in Pachomius's chosen successors, and he gave both explicit sanction to Horsiesios and implicit approval of Theodore.[68] This story clearly conveyed the message that, in the *Koinonia*, Pachomius had succeeded in creating an ascetic life governed by Scripture that his successors would continue without interruption. The figure of Antony, then, sanctioned both the community built by Pachomius and also the direct connection its new leadership claimed to have with the Pachomian legacy.[69]

At this point, it is perhaps best to consider again why Theodore's first address to the superiors of the Pachomian monasteries would have had a particularly powerful effect. Pachomian monks were taught to think of their community as a divinely sanctioned enterprise in which men could live in complete accordance with Scripture. The social environment within the *Koinonia* pushed individual monks to learn the scriptural foundations of the community. It also encouraged them to absorb oral traditions about Pachomius that emphasized how, in a practical way, one could organize his life around these biblical teachings. A speech that used Scripture and Pachomian examples would show clearly to the eight monastic leaders who had deposed Horsiesios that their behavior violated the standards of conduct appropriate for members of the *Koinonia*. It also emphasized to them that, without realizing their error, they had strayed from the Pachomian (and scriptural) path.[70] If this behavior remained uncorrected, the community that emerged would be fundamentally different from that which Pachomius had envisioned. It should then come as no surprise that our text describes the fathers quickly accept-

---

67. Note, for example, Jerome's introduction of Antony in the *Life of Paul* (ch. 7–16). For Athanasius's skillful use of Antony see Brakke, *Athanasius and Asceticism*, 245–65. On the circle of Didymus and its reliance upon Antony to validate Didymus's urban, intellectualized asceticism, see Socrates, *HE* 4.25; Sozomen, *HE* 3.15; Jerome, *Ep.* 68.2; and Rufinus, *HE* 11.7; as well as the discussions of R. Layton, *Didymus the Blind and His Circle in Late-Antique Alexandria: Virtue and Narrative in Biblical Scholarship* (Urbana, 2004), 19–26; and E. Watts, *City and School in Late Antique Athens and Alexandria* (Berkeley, 2006), 182–84.

68. G¹ 120 records Antony describing Horsiesios as "the Israelite" and urging Athanasius to care for his monks.

69. Athanasius is used for a similar purpose in Pachomian tradition (e.g *Bo.* 200–2; G¹ 140).

70. For the rhetorical effect of similar Pachomian material dating from roughly the period of Theodore's life, see the discussion of *Paralipomena* 23 by Wipszycka, "Économie de la congregation Pachômienne," 193–96.

ing Theodore's recommendation that they moderate their behavior and return to their Pachomian roots. They had long been conditioned to see such a course as most appealing.

THE HISTORIA MONACHORUM AND VISITORS' EXPOSURE TO ASCETIC ORAL TRADITIONS

This discussion of the Pachomian *Koinonia* reveals how monastic groups used their collective past to communicate standards of behavior to current members. In a Pachomian context, one can clearly see a distinct set of communal attributes celebrated in the traditions that circulated in the second and third generations after the *Koinonia*'s founding. Each Pachomian monk, it seems, came to appreciate the unique project that Pachomius undertook. The daily routines and social relationships that ordered Pachomian ascetic life contributed greatly to the power that the historical figure of the founder exerted over the behaviors of monks. At the same time, because they were explicitly based upon a scriptural foundation, the values that Pachomius, Theodore, and other Pachomian leaders embodied resonated beyond the confines of the Pachomian monasteries. Pachomian brothers often hosted visitors from other monastic groups and members of the general Christian public. By the time of Horsiesios (and perhaps even under Pachomius himself), rules had been established governing the interactions between visitors and monks. While these regulations excluded visitors from some elements of the daily routine, outsiders were permitted to share in a surprisingly large part of the day's activities.

When visiting monks and clerics presented themselves at the gatehouse, their feet were washed and they were given "everything suitable to monks."[71] When Pachomius's community was young, these visitors stayed with the monks within the monastery proper. As the monastery grew and life within it became more complicated, this policy changed and visitors were instead housed in a separate guesthouse.[72] Outside monks and clerics were still permitted to join the brothers in prayer and take part in the daily *synaxis*. Secular visitors too seem to have been regularly accommodated at the monastery, although female visitors were segregated from males and each group was apparently set apart from the monks.[73] It is unclear what involvement male laymen could have in the daily Pachomian routine but, even if they were unable to participate in the *synaxis*, it must be assumed that they had informal conversations with members of the community.[74]

71. *Pr.* 51.
72. Note *Pr.* 51. The change in this rule evidently caused some controversy outside of the community. Note, for example, *Bo.* 40.
73. *Pr.* 52.
74. This is suggested, albeit somewhat imperfectly, by the interactions that Pachomian monks are known to have had with secular outsiders (e.g., *Bo.* 39, 56).

Even this limited experience of Pachomian life left an impression upon visitors. Many people who stopped at a Pachomian monastery evidently carried away with them an appreciation for the power of Pachomian teachings and a basic knowledge of the accomplishments of the monastery's leadership. The fruits of their experiences did not remain with the visitors alone, however. As early as the middle of the fourth century, knowledge of Pachomius's deeds and his teaching had spread throughout Egypt.[75] These reports exercised such power on the imaginations of Christians that at least two monks decided to join the *Koinonia* after hearing reports about Pachomius's teachings and practices.[76] There was a downside to the spread of these oral reports. Late in his life, Pachomius was called to face a synod of bishops at Latopolis because "some of those who spoke about him ... exaggerated his achievements beyond measure" and an argument erupted about whether he had transgressed the limits of acceptable behavior.[77] At least ostensibly, Pachomius was brought before the synod because of reports in circulation about him.[78] Notably, this controversy was resolved when Pachomius made reference to these same testimonies and the Christian foundation upon which they were based. In his defense, Pachomius recalled an exorcism he performed that had been witnessed by some of the bishops who were to pass judgment on him. As was his custom, Pachomius then drew upon biblical passages to describe how this action was not an act of vanity but a sign of divine grace.[79] This defense suggests a great confidence on the part of Pachomius that the synod knew both his deeds and the underlying scriptural basis upon which he claimed to be able to perform them.

The spread of Pachomian historical traditions beyond the controlled confines of the *Koinonia* is far from unique among Egyptian ascetic groups. In fact, there is abundant evidence that, as the fourth century progressed, Egyptian ascetics hosted visitors with ever greater frequency.[80] Some of these were local laity, like the people from neighboring villages who came to hear sermons at Shenoute's

---

75. G^1 112 and *Bo.* 89 both suggest the widespread circulation of traditions about Pachomius in Egypt as early as the 330s and 340s.

76. For the two monks who joined on the basis of this testimony see *Bo.* 29–30 and 89–91 as well as G^1 34–36 and 94–95.

77. G^1 112.

78. The real situation was more complicated and involved a regional power struggle. On this context, note the discussion of Rousseau, *Pachomius*, 73, 171–72; and Brakke, *Athanasius and Asceticism*, 115–16.

79. E.g., G^1 112, trans. Veilleux.

80. On this larger pattern see, for example, Georgia Frank, "Miracles, Monks and Monuments: The *Historia Monachorum in Aegypto* as Pilgrims' Tales," in *Pilgrimage and Holy Space in Late Antique Egypt*, ed. D. Frankfurter (Leiden, 1998), 483–505; B. Kötting, "Wallfahrten zu lebenden Personen in Altertum," in *Wallfahrt kennt keine Grenzen*, ed. L. Kriss-Rettenbeck and G. Mohler (Munich/Zurich, 1984), 226–34; and H. Behlmer, "Visitors to Shenoute's Monastery," in *Pilgrimage and Holy Space in Late Antique Egypt*, ed. D. Frankfurter (Leiden, 1998), 341–71.

White Monastery.⁸¹ Others traveled within Egypt to seek the assistance of holy men and listen to their teachings. Their ranks included refugees, government officials and, if the title of a lost Shenoutan work is to be believed, even barbarians.⁸² A smaller but better known selection of travelers, like Rufinus, came from great distances in order to "visit the companies of monks and pay a round of visits to the heavenly family on earth."⁸³

When these visitors departed, they carried with them an awareness of the traditions that distinguished their hosts' ascetic community. Regular visitors to Shenoute's monastery, for example, evidently came to appreciate the inspired actions of the abbot against his nemesis, the pagan Gesius.⁸⁴ Indeed, this event became something of a defining moment for the abbot and Shenoute himself repeatedly referred to it in sermons before monks and visitors alike.⁸⁵ The experiences of travelers like Rufinus and Palladius show that even visitors who stopped briefly at many different monasteries became familiar with the traditions that illustrated Egyptian monastic practice.⁸⁶

One late-fourth-century text, the *Historia Monachorum in Aegypto*, does a particularly good job of both recapturing the internal historical testimony that

---

81. On this, note Behlmer, "Visitors to Shenoute's Monastery," 341–42. For Shenoute's use of these discourses to paint a portrait of himself as an exemplar see M. Foat, "Shenute: Discourse in the Presence of Eraklammon," *Orientalia Lovaniensia Periodica* 24 (1994), 113–32, esp. 115–16, 119–20.

82. For refugees, see the oration "God is Blessed" (trans. D. Brakke, "Shenoute: On Cleaving to Profitable Things," *OLP* 20 [1989], 115–41). S. Emmel, "The Historical Circumstances of Shenoute's Sermon 'God is Blessed'," in θεμελια: *Spätantike und koptologische Studien Peter Grossmann zum 65 Geburtstag*, ed. M. Krause and S. Schaten (Wiesbaden, 1998), 81–96. On other sorts of visitors, see Behlmer, "Visitors to Shenoute's Monastery," 369–71.

83. Jerome, *Ep.* 3.1.

84. On the conflict with Gesius, note S. Emmel, "From the Other Side of the Nile: Shenute and Panopolis," in *Perspectives on Panopolis: An Egyptian Town from Alexander the Great to the Arab Conquest*, ed. A. Egberts, B. Muhs, and J. van der Vliet (Leiden, 2002), 95–113. See as well, D. Brakke, *Demons and the Making of the Monk: Spiritual Combat in Early Christianity* (Cambridge, MA, 2006), 97–99, 103–4.

85. This becomes clear from the many references to Gesius in Besa's *Life of Shenoute* (e.g., ch. 88, 125–27), the lost work of Shenoute ⲅⲉⲥⲓⲟⲥ ⲡⲉⲧⲥ2ⲁⲓ ⲛⲛⲉϥⲡⲣⲟ (on this note Emmel, "Shenute and Panopolis," 99–100), and even as obscure a thing as his exegesis of Job 41 ("A Beloved Asked Me Years Ago;" note on this the discussion of Brakke, *Demons*, 112–13). Gesius appears as late as 440 in Shenoute's sermon "God is Blessed," a sermon preached to a crowd of refugees.

86. The *Apophthegmata Patrum* is, of course, the best example of the diversity of traditions that made their way from the internal discourse of individual monasteries into wider circulation. While a great testimony to the most memorable sayings and anecdotes that defined Egyptian ascetic practices, these materials have come down to us at great remove from the social contexts from which they first emerged. The longer traditions like these circulate in a wider world, the more likely it is that their defining features are smoothed over by a process of oral transmission that privileges broader ascetic themes over specific details. On this phenomenon in general see the comments of J. Vansina, *Oral Tradition as History* (Madison, 1985), 19–21.

circulated within a variety of Egyptian ascetic communities and the circumstances under which visitors learned about this information. It records a trip to Egypt made in 394 by a group of seven Palestinian monks. On this journey, the monks visited a number of monastic sites, watched the distinctive practices of individual monastic leaders, and had extensive anecdote-filled conversations with their hosts. When they returned home, they produced a record of "the practices of the Egyptian monks which (they) witnessed."[87] The remarkable document that resulted describes what these visitors saw and heard during their time in Egypt. Although on one level the text represents a travelogue, it had a much more profound purpose.[88] All of the author's experiences of Egyptian ascetic life "provide a paradigm and a testimony for the perfect, to edify and benefit those who are beginners in the ascetic life" in much the same way that the author himself benefited from them.[89] These Palestinian travelers saw a universal significance and general applicability in the practices they observed in Egypt. In fact, the author of the *Historia Monachorum* even claims that it is solely by Jesus' "teaching that the Egyptian monks regulate their lives."[90]

While the *Historia Monachorum* definitively asserts that all of the diverse practices of Egyptian monks drew a common inspiration from Jesus' teaching, it also highlights the distinctive elements of practice that defined the monasteries that the monks visited. Indeed, many of the accounts focus upon a specific, notable practice that distinguishes a particular holy man and his circle of followers. So, for example, the travelers spoke about the ability of the priest Eulogius to discern the spiritual state of every monk who approached his altar, and they celebrated the devotion that the monastic superior Sarapion showed to the poor.[91] The description of Apa Theon is even more thematically driven.[92] Theon "had practiced silence" for thirty years and, when they visited him, the travelers learned a number of stories that highlighted remarkable ways in which Theon made his influence felt despite his vow. Although he seldom left his cell, Theon routinely cured sick visitors by laying his hands on them through the window.[93] Theon taught in Greek, Latin, and Coptic by writing words of wisdom on a slate and once even converted a band of robbers to the monastic life through his silent prayers.[94] Other portraits within the *Historia Monachorum* center upon even more peculiar ascetic themes.

87. *HM* Prologue 2 (trans. Russell).
88. On the *HM* as an example of travel writing, see G. Frank, "Miracles, Monks and Monuments," 483–505.
89. *HM* Prologue 12 (trans. Russell).
90. *HM* Prologue 4 (trans. Russell).
91. *HM* 16; 18.
92. *HM* 6.
93. *HM* 6.1.
94. *HM* 6.3; 6.2.

Allusions to metal-working pervade the short description of the former blacksmith Apa Apelles[95] and Apa Amoun's profile centers upon his ability to control large and particularly fearsome snakes.[96]

Many of the shorter portraits in the *Historia Monachorum* focus upon the eccentric practices of individual ascetics, but the text also highlights some elements of ascetic practice that distinguished larger monastic communities. Often these were illustrated by a cluster of narratives the travelers collected in the course of conversations with members of these communities. One of the most developed such portraits concerns John of Lycopolis and the large community of monks that he administered.[97] The stories about John collected in the *Historia Monachorum* highlight two distinctive attributes. The first centers upon his clairvoyance. During their visit to John's community, the travelers heard many accounts of John's gift of discernment. They learned that he had predicted the political and military successes of the emperor Theodosius,[98] he had foreseen the repulse of a military attack,[99] and he even knew that the Palestinian travelers were lying when they said that no cleric was in their party.[100]

John's clairvoyance resulted from one of the defining elements of John's ascetic discipline. John himself was said to have remarked to the authors, "Everyone who has not renounced the world fully and completely . . . his preoccupations, being bodily and earthly, distract his mind."[101] If, however, one can distance oneself from worldly concerns, John suggests that he will be "granted partial knowledge of God . . . and also gain the knowledge of other things. He sees mysteries, for God shows him them."[102] The stories illustrating John's gift of foresight validate his emphasis upon the full and pure contemplative renunciation of worldly concerns.

Neither John's clairvoyance nor his emphasis upon the purity of the ascetic's mind is completely new to the late fourth century ascetic environment.[103] Perhaps

---

95. *HM* 13.1–2.
96. *HM* 9.
97. *HM* 1.
98. *HM* 1.1, 1.64.
99. *HM* 1.2.
100. *HM* 1.14–15.
101. *HM* 1.26.
102. HM 1.28 (all trans. Russell).
103. For clairvoyance as an almost universal marker of the prestige of late antique holy men see most notably P. Brown, *The Making of Late Antiquity* (Cambridge, MA., 1978), 96. The teaching of John's contemporary Evagrius Ponticus parallels John's own emphasis upon the purity of an ascetic's contemplation. On the concept of *apatheia* in Evagrius, see *Praktikos* 1.2. On this idea, see S. Rappe, "Pagan Elements in Christian Education," in *Education in Greek and Roman Antiquity*, ed. Y. L. Too (Leiden, 2001), 425–26; and E. Clark, *The Origenist Controversy: The Cultural Construction of an Early Christian Debate* (Princeton, 1992), 67–69. For John's connection to this Evagrian idea, note D. Brakke, *Demons*, 132–33.

more unique to John's circle was the peculiar emphasis that he placed upon avoiding all contact with women.[104] John provided the travelers with an explanation of this teaching. He told them the story of an accomplished monk who failed to recognize that his achievements came not through his own practices but through divine grace. One evening, Satan sent to him the image of a beautiful woman who was lost in the desert. The monk took her in to his enclosure and eventually became filled with lust for her. When he tried to act on his impulses, she promptly disappeared. In despair, he gave up his ascetic practices and returned to the secular world.[105] For John, this story had a clear lesson: "It is not in our interest to have our dwellings near inhabited places or to associate with women. For meetings of this kind give rise to an unexpungeable memory, which we draw from what we have seen."[106] When considering the appropriate level of interaction that an ascetic ought to have with a woman, John's broader concern for the intellectual purity of ascetic contemplation led to an awareness of the way that experiences of others created distracting thoughts. The absolute isolation from women that he practiced and pushed his followers to adopt represented a strategy to avoid this potential pitfall. It also became a peculiar attribute of his asceticism that was simultaneously explained in his teaching and illustrated by stories told by John and his associates.

The stories that the travelers collected from other communities also highlighted distinctive ascetic practices and spiritual achievements. In its accounts of the achievements of Apa Apollo and his numerous followers, for example, the *Historia Monachorum* details their great successes in combating paganism in Egypt.[107] Similarly, the anecdotes collected about Apa Paul emphasize the degree to which his ascetic training stressed unquestioning obedience to Antony, his ascetic master.[108] Although less well illustrated by anecdotes, the result of this training was clear to the travelers: "The disciple acquired such absolute obedience that God gave him the grace to drive out demons. Indeed, those demons which Antony was unable to exorcise he sent to Paul."[109]

The profiles of John of Lycopolis, Apollo, and Paul describe particular features of the fathers' ascetic practice in a way that gives them a universal Christian resonance. John's segregation from women, for example, is explained by his teaching and validated by his clairvoyance, the rare gift of an untroubled mind. The extreme obedience that Paul showed to Antony receives similar, though less specific, validation in his ability to drive out demons. Apollo's vigorous anti-pagan activities receive a different, though equally resounding, Christian sanction. This notable

104. E.g., *HM* 1.5–9.
105. The story is recorded in *HM* 1.32–36.
106. HM 1.36 (trans. Russell).
107. *HM* 8.20–37.
108. *HM* 24.2, 3, 6–7, 8.
109. *HM* 24.10 (trans. Russell).

feature of Apollo's asceticism fulfills "one of the Apostle's sayings" and the "powers manifested in [Apollo's] works" are thus legitimated by their place in a broader, biblically demarcated, Christian narrative.[110]

The larger Christian context within which the *Historia Monachorum* places these exotic Egyptian ascetic practices suggests one reason why the visiting Palestinian ascetics found the stories they heard from their Egyptian hosts so useful, but the social environment in which the stories were shared seems to have been at least as influential. The travelers picked up most of the illustrative stories that found their way into the text from conversations with Egyptian monks and priests, as the portrait of John of Lycopolis shows. Although John spoke at some length with the visitors, they collected many of their stories about him from other monks living in the vicinity. Their stories were reliable because their "way of life is held in high esteem by all the people of that region. Whatever they said about [John] was not in the least embellished to enhance his reputation but, on the contrary, tended to be understated."[111] Similar conversations with monks informed the portrait of Apollo[112] and time spent with the priest and renowned ascetic Apelles helped to shape the text's picture of a less famous Apa John.[113] In every case, the power of this oral testimony derived from the inherent spiritual authority of its source.

Many of the contextual details of these exchanges are lost to us, but one conversation that the visitors had with the cleric Copres suggests the social setting in which these conversations took place. Copres was himself an accomplished ascetic who headed a community of fifty monks.[114] After meeting the visitors outside of his enclosure and washing their feet, Copres shared the orally transmitted historical traditions that illustrated teachings particular to the community that he headed.[115] He explained the "rule of life" his ascetic ancestors followed and proceeded to regale the travelers with tales of saints who walked through fire, strode calmly across the Nile, flew through the air, grew magical figs, and even turned the desert sand into fertile soil for peasants.[116] Copres told these magnificent and often improbable tales in a way that displayed a particular gift for long-winded exaggeration. After three days of these stories, it seems that some in the party of travelers grew tired of Copres. In spite of his claims that the visitors could verify his accounts by going to view the magnificent fig, his visitors began to suspect the veracity of his accounts. It is then that *Historia Monachorum* records something stunning:

110. *HM* 8.20.
111. *HM* 1.3.
112. *HM* 8.43, 60–62.
113. For Apelles, see *HM* 13.2.
114. *HM* 10.1 (trans. Russell).
115. *HM* 10.2.
116. *HM* 10.30–32; 10.20–22; 10.26.9.

While Father Copres was telling us these stories, one of our party, overcome with incredulity at what was being said, dozed off. And he saw a wonderful book lying in the father's hands, which was inscribed in letters of gold. And beside the father stood a white-haired man who said to him, in a threatening manner, "Are you dozing instead of listening attentively to the reading?" He immediately woke up and told the rest of us who were listening to Copres, in Latin, what he had seen.[117]

According to this vision, the incredulity of the listener was misplaced and was due to a misunderstanding of the nature of Copres' testimony. The stories that Copres told were not, in fact, oral traditions conveyed by a verbose and rather unreliable narrator. They were instead divinely inscribed writings read out by a holy man.

On first glance, this dream seems to be a slightly peculiar way of arguing for the reliability of one of the author's more problematic oral sources. This dream does more than simply defend the credibility of an uncomfortably exaggerated source, however. When authors offer simple defenses of the credibility of oral reports, they frequently resort to arguments designed to illustrate the truth of the information according to a logical standard.[118] Copres' dream was not such a logical proof. In fact, the nature of the text in which it is found very much determined its shape. The *Historia Monachorum* is a communal document, designed to communicate the possibilities of Christian ascetic accomplishment and provide its Palestinian audience with examples of successful practice. The pilgrim's dream, then, addresses a different, and more complicated, question. It does not simply confirm the reliability of Copres' story. It definitively establishes that Copres' stories belonged within the travelers' universal narrative of Christian ascetic practice.[119]

SOCIAL RELATIONS AND THE POWER OF THE MASTER: BARSANUPHIUS AND JOHN

The *Historia Monachorum* illustrates how a common Christian textual and symbolic language translated the idiosyncratic rules of individual ascetic groups into practices with a universal relevance. Nevertheless, the text grew out of a number of one-time meetings between traveling monks and Egyptian ascetics. While the travelers evidently both enjoyed their visits and respected their hosts, no long-standing personal relationships tied these monks to the sources of the oral traditions they brought back to Palestine. By all indications, one-time visits like these

---

117. *HM* 10.25.

118. B. Stock, *The Implications of Literacy: Written Language and Models of Interpretation in the Eleventh and Twelfth Centuries* (Princeton, 1983), 65–72.

119. The specific identity of the scolding, supernatural, gray-haired figure and his golden-lettered book is never directly established, but he clearly represents a divine figure. Compare, for example, the Greek text of the *Passio Perpetuae et Felicitatis* 4.23 and 12.6; Theodoret, RH 21.22.

seem to have been somewhat exceptional. Many of the outsiders who came to ascetic communities came again, often regularly. In some cases, these visitors even established close spiritual relationships with individual monks. Although they usually continued to live outside of the monastery, these regular visitors and spiritual disciples shared the personal connections that helped monks become attached to the traditions of their community. These repeat visitors, then, occupied a midway point between the monk and the outsider.

Very few sources provide detailed profiles of these men but, even with such limited material, it remains possible to get a sense of who they were. In some respects they probably strongly resembled *philoponoi* or *spoudaioi*, groups of laymen who assisted urban clergy in certain liturgical and ceremonial contexts beginning perhaps in the fifth century.[120] In Alexandria, the actions of these men extended beyond simply helping bishops. As we move later in time, their roles and activities become clearer. An early seventh-century text shows *philoponoi* actively assisting visitors to the healing shrine of saints Cyrus and John in the Alexandrian suburb of Menouthis.[121] Some groups of *philoponoi* also enjoyed close relationships with particular ascetic communities, which perhaps explains the tendency for *philoponia* to become attached to monasteries.[122]

These individuals agreed to live a "life of humility and great chastity" that could include a clear commitment to charity, frugal eating habits, frequent fasting, and only occasional use of the baths (or even complete abstention from them). Chastity too represented an ideal that could be achieved either through lifetime celibacy or through an end to sexual activity after children were born.[123] Although these men approximated the lifestyle of a monk, personal obligations prevented them from joining monasteries. One particularly telling text describes the friends of a *philoponos* named Paul asking him, "Why do you not become a monk? You do not

---

120. On their duties see Haas, *Alexandria in Late Antiquity: Topography and Social Conflict* (Baltimore, 1997), 238–40, and E. Wipszycka, "Les confréries dans la vie religieuse de l'Egypte chrétienne," in *Proceedings of the Twelfth International Congress of Papyrology*, ed. R. Samuel (Toronto, 1970), 514–15. The best evidence for their increasing influence in the course of the fifth century comes in two related accounts of a lunch that Athanasius held in which he predicted that a shrine to Elisha and John the Baptist would be constructed on the site of the Serapeum. The earlier version of this, which dates from the episcopate of Theophilus, speaks only of clerics attending (T. Orlandi, "Un frammento copto di Teofilo di Alessandria," *Rivista degli Studi Orientali* 44 [1970], 23–26). When this text is later included in a church history in the later fifth or early sixth century, *philoponoi* are added to the lunch as, evidently, an expected part of the gathering (*Storia della Chiesa*, vol. 1, 46.15–48.2). It is clear that at some point between these two texts *philoponoi* had developed into influential figures whose presence around the bishop could simply be assumed.

121. Sophronius, *SS Cyri et Joannis Miracula* 35 = PG 87 Col. 3544.

122. For the *philoponia* and their connection to monasteries, see Wipszycka, "Les confréries," 519–20.

123. For this description see Zacharias, *Vit. Sev.* 12, and Wipszycka, "Les confréries," 513.

have [living] parents and you have no intention to marry."[124] Paul's decision to serve as a *philoponos* puzzled his friends because he lacked any significant personal obligations. Other similarly devoted and socially unconstrained men would simply have joined a monastery.[125]

Even if they were not *philoponoi* or *spoudaioi* themselves, lay associates of monastic circles were similarly pious and socially engaged figures. Perhaps no source better details the balance such men struck between their spiritual devotion and personal obligations than the extraordinary collection of letters associated with the Gazan hermits Barsanuphius and John. Although almost completely secluded from the world, these two elders governed an ascetic community at Tawatha, just outside of the city of Gaza, through letters mostly dictated to and carried back by the abbot of the monastery.[126] These letters reveal a fascinating collection of lay associates who, in the composite, seem to behave in ways that are very much like Egyptian *philoponoi* and *spoudaioi*.[127] They were extremely devoted supporters of the community who could not sufficiently disentangle themselves from business and personal obligations to become monks.[128] One such correspon-

---

124. L. Clugnet, "Vies et récits d'anachorètes, II: Texts grecs inédits du Ms. Grec de Paris 1596," *Revue de l'orient Chrétien* 1 (1905), 47–48, quoted in Wipszycka, "Les confréries," 513.

125. It is interesting to compare the Egyptian *philoponoi* with the Syrian Sons and Daughters of the Covenant. Both are groups of lay Christians who assisted in services but the Sons and Daughters of the Covenant are evidently an older institution with greater restriction placed upon their membership than the Egyptian *philoponoi*. On the Covenanters, see G. Nedungatt, "The Covenanters of the Early Syriac-Speaking Church," *Orientalia Christiana Periodica* 39 (1973), 191–215; and A. Vööbus, "The Institution of the *Benai Qeiama* and *Benat Qeiama* in the Ancient Syrian Church," *Church History* 30 (1961), 19–27. One of the earliest descriptions of them occurs in Aphrahat's *Sixth Demonstration* (primarily 6.8). They are best known from the *Rabbula Canons* (on which see A. Vööbus, *Syriac and Arabic Documents Regarding Legislation Relative to Syrian Asceticism* [Stockholm, 1960], 34–50).

126. For these letters, see the editions of F. Neyt, P. de Angelis-Noah, and L. Regnault, *Barsanuphe et Jean de Gaza: Correspondence*, vol. 1, t. 1–2; vol. 2, t. 1–2; vol. 3, *Sources Chrétiennes*, nos. 426, 427, 450, 451, 468, (Paris, 1997, 1998, 2000, 2001, 2002). Note as well the important studies of J. Hevelone-Harper, *Disciples of the Desert: Monks, Laity, and Spiritual Authority in Sixth-Century Gaza* (Baltimore, 2005); and B. Bitton-Ashkelony and A. Kofsky, *The Monastic School of Gaza* (Leiden, 2006), 82–106. The nature of instruction in this community is also distinctive. On it, see L. Perrone, "The Necessity of Advice: Spiritual Direction as a School of Christianity in the Correspondence of Barsanuphius and John of Gaza," in *Christian Gaza in Late Antiquity*, ed. B. Bitton-Ashkelony and A. Kofsky (Leiden, 2004), 131–49.

127. On the appearance of laity in this letter collection, see the general overview of L. Regnault, "Moines et laïcs dans la region de Gaza au VIe Siècle," in *Christian Gaza in Late Antiquity*, 165–72. Also consider the discussion of monastic and lay relationships in Bitton-Ashkelony and Kofsky, *Monastic School of Gaza*, 205–10.

128. Two exchanges between Aelianus, an important lay associate of the community, and Barsanuphius and John show how complicated it could be for such men to remove themselves from their worldly responsibilities. Even though Aelianus wanted to become a monk, he had to find a way to dispose of his property while ensuring the continued support of his γραίας (perhaps his mother) and other dependants (*Letters* 571, 572). For discussion see Hevelone-Harper, *Disciples of the Desert*, 122–23.

dent, described simply as "a Christ-loving layman," twice asked John about what he ought to do when necessity compelled him to bathe.[129] He also solicited advice repeatedly about how to handle household affairs, manage a sick slave, and deal with his insufficiently pious father.[130] Another man, the brother of a monk in the monastery, who is called a "lover of monks," paid for the construction of an infirmary at Tawatha.[131] In fact, many of these secular associates ranked among the local elite and represented the business interests of the community, a task that often required a substantial commitment of time.[132]

Perhaps the most interesting example of the conflict between worldly and ascetic demands involves a "pious layman, a lawyer and friend of the monastery of the Fathers."[133] He was asked to do some important task because he usually "did for God with haste that which was asked of him." On this occasion, "at the instigation of the Devil," he failed to act expeditiously. Barsanuphius then wrote to him: "We know that we are a cause of distress to you . . . with complete liberty, tell us if we are oppressing you and we will no longer oppress you."[134] Barsanuphius's words had a clear effect. "When this man heard these things, it was as if a fire was in his heart. He vigorously undertook this matter . . . then, coming [to the monastery] he prostrated himself and begged for forgiveness."[135] Although Barsanuphius had measured his words, the lawyer clearly understood their meaning—his affiliation with the monastery required him to place its needs before his other concerns. By failing to do so, the man had disappointed Barsanuphius and endangered his close relationship with the monk.

Elsewhere in the collection of letters one finds more explicit statements about the deep affection that lay associates felt for Barsanuphius and John. Perhaps the most powerful statement comes from Aelianus, a wealthy man who would one day head the Tawatha monastery.[136] In one letter Aelianus appeals to Barsanuphius to "Apply your grace to your servant, and pray to the Lord God for the salvation of my soul . . . and that under your protection I leave from the body and simply that I become your servant for eternity."[137]

Barsanuphius then responded that God "has persuaded me to treat you as a true spiritual son. I confide in you the secrets that I do not confide to many, this

129. *Letters* 770, 771.
130. *Letters* 764, 765, 767. For discussion of this man and his interaction with John see Hevelone-Harper, *Disciples of the Desert*, 101–2.
131. *Life of Dositheus*, 1; cf. Hevelone-Harper, *Disciples of the Desert*, 65.
132. E.g., *Letter* 723, 740.
133. *Letter* 745.
134. *Letter* 745.
135. *Letter* 745.
136. On Aelianus and his accession see Hevelone-Harper, *Disciples of the Desert*, 119–24 as well as *Letters* 571–75.
137. *Letter* 573.

is a proof of my filial adoption." God also "has seen how your image is engraved in my heart and I trust that it will not be effaced."[138] Despite the close spiritual relationship that the two men enjoyed, Barsanuphius also warned Aelianus to remain vigilant and "take care that you do not again forget to preserve continually the memory of what I have said and do not become careless."[139]

This powerful letter explicitly lays out the nature of the spiritual discipleship that bound the monk Barsanuphius and the civilian Aelianus. By adopting the layman Aelianus as his spiritual son, Barsanuphius agreed to serve as his temporal teacher and spiritual guardian. Barsanuphius shared great and secret wisdom with his charge and, in return, he expected that Aelianus would remain completely committed to his memory and his teachings.[140] Although Aelianus remained outside of the monastery, Barsanuphius felt it perfectly appropriate both to refer to him as a spiritual son and to expect the man to live according to the guidelines that he laid out.

As Aelianus's case shows, spiritual discipleships like this blurred the line between monk and layman by binding an individual who lived outside of the monastery to the personal authority and teachings of a monastic superior. In another letter, Barsanuphius's colleague, John, makes explicit the degree of obedience expected of such a monastic associate. "A pious layman who is earnest and concerned for his soul wrote asking the same Elder (John) 'What is appropriate to do? Whatever seems good to one or through the asking of the fathers?'"[141] John responded: "If someone is motivated to do something good by himself and not through the asking of the fathers, this is illegal and he does it without sanction. But if someone does something through their request, this is full of the law and the Prophets. For it is a sign of humility to ask."[142] Although a man might live in the world, his spiritual masters asserted full authority over his life and expected him to acknowledge this through his conduct.[143]

The laity who associated themselves with Barsanuphius and John willingly traded their personal autonomy for the spiritual guidance and protection that the two holy men offered. When they visited the monastery at Tawatha, one must imagine that the associates of Barsanuphius and John eagerly soaked up all of the stories and lessons that the monks living under their rules had to offer. In fact, it seems that the two reclusive monks encouraged such an environment within the monastery. In one letter, John even describes what the conversations with visitors

---

138. *Letter* 573.
139. *Letter* 573.
140. For Barsanuphius's notion of complete commitment to the guidance of a master see Perrone, "Necessity of Advice," 137–44.
141. *Letter* 693.
142. *Letter* 693.
143. On this exchange, see Perrone, "Necessity of Advice," 144–45.

were supposed to be like. "As far as is possible, do not give to those passing through conversation about profane subjects ... discuss with them material from the *Lives of the Fathers,* from the Gospel, from the Apostle, or from the Prophets."[144] This particular injunction underlines the universality of Barsanuphius and John's teaching. Despite the peculiar nature of the ascetic group that they headed, it rested upon a scriptural foundation that all Christians shared and through which they could access its teaching.

Some stories illustrating the teaching and celebrating the achievements of Barsanuphius and John also seem to have circulated among the monks and their lay visitors. The *Discourses* of Dorotheus of Gaza (who once served as the secretary for John) occasionally allude to incidents from his own time in Tawatha and speak about his interactions with senior monks in the community.[145] However, the most impressive of the surviving historical traditions associated with this community appears in the *Ecclesiastical History* of Evagrius Scholasticus. Writing in the early 590s, Evagrius recalls the seclusion and miraculous deeds of Barsanuphius. Evagrius then notes that "he is believed still to be alive, confined in a little room" even though no one has seen or heard from him in fifty years. "Eustochius, the prelate of Jerusalem,[146] did not believe this, but when he decided to dig through into the little room where the man of God was confined, fire blazed forth."[147]

In some ways, the story that Evagrius tells bears many of the hallmarks of the distinguishing anecdotes preserved by the *Historia Monachorum* travelers and alluded to in the *Instructions* of Pachomian monks. It describes Barsanuphius's peculiar practice of ascetic leadership by seclusion, easily the most recognizable feature of the ascetic community that he founded. It also mentions the failed excavation of the bishop of Jerusalem to highlight divine approval of Barsanuphius's particular style of ascetic leadership. It does this in particularly resonant fashion. The fire-bolts that issued from Barsanuphius's cell appear often in late antique Christian literature when someone threatens a holy figure or object. They usually signify divine disapproval of the effort.[148] The audience for this tale would understand that this miracle illustrated divine sanction of Barsanuphius's method of

---

144. *Letter* 584.

145. See, for example, Dorotheus, *Discourse* 6. Dorotheus's own ultimate position in the monastery of Barsanuphius and John remains something of a question. For discussion see Hevelone-Harper, *Disciples of the Desert,* 61–77 (esp. 74–77), and E. Wheeler, "Introduction," in *Dorotheus of Gaza: Discourses and Sayings,* trans. Wheeler (Kalamazoo, MI, 1977), 55–67.

146. From 552–562; Barsanuphius's last datable correspondence refers to the plague of 542 (*Letter* 569).

147. Evagrius, *HE* 4.33 (trans. Whitby).

148. For a list of parallels note the helpful discussion of M. Whitby, *The Ecclesiastical History of Evagrius Scholasticus* (Liverpool, 2000), 237–38n105 as well as the comments of A. J. Festugière, *Antioche païenne et chrétienne* (Paris, 1959), 396n82.

leadership and served as a warning to those who sought to dislodge the holy man from his enclosure.

Evagrius's account does not allow one to say with complete conviction that this story circulated first in Tawatha, but it likely originated from a source close to the monastery of Barsanuphius. This story highlights a tension between the unquestioning loyalty of the Tawatha monks to a silent, secluded ascetic master and bishop Eustochius's (reasonable) expectation that the leader of a monastery be living and interactive. The divine fire that issued from Barsanuphius's cell resolved this conflict in favor of the monastic community. Indeed, this story reinforces a theme that played an integral role in shaping Barsanuphius's community. Barsanuphius worked hard to fashion a monastic culture that did not permit monks to doubt the divinely-inspired methods he used to govern Tawatha. At one point, however, a disagreement between a monk and the superior of the monastery led to an open revolt in which a group of monks began to question whether Barsanuphius actually existed. When he learned of this, Barsanuphius left his enclosure, came to the monastery, and washed the feet of all of the monks. Those who doubted him immediately sought forgiveness. Barsanuphius responded with a forceful letter urging his followers to follow biblical injunctions by focusing on spiritual matters and avoiding distracting questions. Barsanuphius framed this message in intimately personal terms. He exhorted the leader of the revolt to "work as a good and obedient worker and not seek this from me who yearns to see you . . . For in due time, if God inspires me, on my own, I will come forth and kiss the feet of all of you."[149] By carefully invoking the ties of personal discipleship that bound these monks to him, Barsanuphius transformed a dangerous challenge to the peculiar administrative structure of his community into a solemn refusal to acknowledge the master's love for his disciples. In so doing, Barsanuphius established the absolute impropriety of the monk's demand and described in clear terms the divine sanction of his withdrawal. He had succinctly justified the communal structure that he created.

By the middle of the sixth century, the unquestioning loyalty to an absent master that Barsanuphius so dramatically affirmed on that day had become a defining feature of the community. It would be unsurprising to learn that many more stories justifying this blind loyalty circulated among the monks and their visitors. Such anecdotes both confirmed divine approval of the community's structure and helped to perpetuate the personal relationship that Barsanuphius's spiritual disciples continued to feel with their silent spiritual father.

The historical traditions that circulated in late antique ascetic groups played many of the same roles as those that developed within intellectual circles. These stories

---

149. *Letter* 125.50–54 (ed. Neyt, Noah, Regnault).

described the extraordinary discipline of accomplished masters and they celebrated the miracles that God performed through these supremely restrained men. Perhaps most importantly, these pieces of communal history showed how one could successfully follow the divinely-inspired ascetic path set by a monastery's founder. Two elements contributed to the power that this discourse had over both members of an ascetic community and Christians living in the wider world. First, these stories drew upon universally recognizable passages of Scripture and other powerful Christian *topoi* to advertise the degree to which the particular ideas of a monastic leader grew out of mainstream Christian teaching. This meant that John of Lycopolis could make his idea that a monk ought not to speak with a woman seem to be an admirable ascetic technique instead of an odd quirk by tying it specifically to Scripture. Second, Christians often initially learned of these nuggets of communal history from respected and accomplished ascetics, many of whom served as their spiritual mentors. Christian hierarchy then encouraged these listeners, some of whom did not belong to the monastery, to attach significance to the specific practices of the community.

The Pachomian *Koinonia* serves as a good example of how well-ordered social relationships combined with careful interpretation of Scripture to create an environment in which the historical traditions of a community could serve to regulate the conduct of its members. With a stated goal of monastic mutual improvement, the Pachomian monks fashioned daily routines and personal relationships that reinforced an individual monk's acceptance of the stories illustrating the distinctive practices of his master. However, because they were often closely tied to Scripture and emanated from men of recognizable holiness, these illustrative anecdotes resonated beyond the *Koinonia's* carefully constructed social settings. The same is true of other, non-Pachomian ascetic communities. Travelers often accepted the universal applicability of the stories they heard about ascetic masters because they arose from a scriptural foundation. As the *Historia Monachorum* shows, visitors proved willing to accept even implausible testimony when they could be convinced that their hosts' peculiar teaching and practices derived from a Christian source of recognized authority.

In the same way that some outsiders could identify with the historical traditions of ascetic circles because of their biblical foundations, others accepted their importance because of the social connections that they developed with ascetic leaders. This proved to be true of both ascetics and lay visitors. The surviving correspondence that the ascetics Barsanuphius and John sent to their disciples shows the great personal affection that monks and monastic affiliates had for their spiritual fathers. Their intimate relationships grew out of a specifically Christian understanding of the immediate and eternal benefits that came from the complete subordination of one's life to a holy man. The promise of these rewards caused many followers to try to order their lives according to the models of ascetic practice put forth by their spiritual fathers.

Ascetic circles represent some of the most restrictive and controlled late Roman social environments. One would consequently expect the historical traditions that circulated within their walls to be both profoundly powerful in shaping the behavior of monks and largely irrelevant to those who lived beyond the monastery's borders. However, much of what made these stories appealing to monks also made them relevant to large numbers of Christian outsiders. By using communal history to show how closely ascetic practices adhered to biblical teachings, monastic leaders presented their ideas in terms with which many Christians could identify. As the reputations of these holy men grew so too did their circles of disciples. Many of these disciples continued living as pious laymen, striving each day to emulate the ascetic model set by their spiritual fathers. Because of such men, the history of monastic circles had the potential to shape the behavior of even those who lived beyond the confines of a monastery.

5

Anti-Chalcedonian Ascetics and their Student Associates

This section began by discussing the relationship between the Christian students who intervened to stop Paralius's beating and the Enaton monastery. While familiar with the monks and their leadership, these students also stood apart from the ascetics who lived in this monastery; they were simultaneously monastic associates and lay outsiders. The preceding chapter has examined how personal relationships between monks helped ascetics to live according to the teachings of their spiritual fathers. These teachings and the illustrative stories that showed their practical application resonated with monks and laymen. In some cases, individual laymen became the spiritual disciples of important ascetics. Attracted by tales of a monk's great intercessory power and trusting in the promise of his personal spiritual guidance, these men often tried to live according to monastic ideals in the world.

A range of fifth- and sixth-century sources suggest that Paralius's rescuers fit into the category of secular ascetic affiliates. This was especially true of Zacharias Scholasticus, evidently the most vocal of their members. Zacharias had strong personal ties to prominent anti-Chalcedonian ascetics in Gaza and the important anti-Chalcedonian ascetic community housed at the Enaton monastery outside of Alexandria. In some of his own writings, he employs the language of spiritual discipleship used to describe the relationship of Barsanuphius and his lay affiliates. Nevertheless, Zacharias and his associates also make it clear that, despite the great respect that they had for their spiritual fathers, they also found themselves bound by a worldly code of behavior. These young men faced the difficult task of fulfilling the intellectual and social demands of student life while still following the spiritual path charted by anti-Chalcedonian ascetic leaders. Zacharias and his friends often succeeded in bridging the gap between these two, quite distinct, sets of ideas and behaviors. Sometimes, however, the gulf between the teachings of monks and the ideas presented in classrooms proved unbridgeable. In these cases, the young men had to choose between the values that defined their religious life and those promoted by their teachers and fellow students. These proved to be difficult choices that Zacharias and his friends had to make, but these decisions also shaped their everyday behavior—including their reaction to Paralius's beating.

THE LIMITS OF ASCETIC INFLUENCE

The rules, daily regimens, and strict hierarchies that organized life within many late antique monasteries shaped the outlook of the monks who lived within their walls. Nevertheless, the discipline of individual monks often failed to measure up to the unforgiving standards laid out by their superiors. The *Canons* of Shenoute's White Monastery, for example, emphasize that the restriction of one's food intake is a great ascetic virtue.[1] In order to further the sense of a shared monastic enterprise, all healthy monks received the same modest serving of food at meals.[2] They were permitted only small portions of additional food throughout the day (not more than three loaves of bread at a time) and were further expected to accept unappetizing food without complaint.[3] Above all, Shenoute's monks were encouraged to fast frequently as one of their most basic spiritual exercises. Two days a week were marked as fast days, a Lenten fast was expected of all monks, and Shenoute encouraged the monks to fast on their own "for the sake of God" for up to a week at a time.[4]

These themes appear often in Shenoute's *Canons* and form an important part of the discipline that he encouraged his followers to adopt.[5] However, despite the commitment that Shenoute's followers demonstrated to his larger ascetic project, they found it very difficult to live according to the strict dietary regimen that Shenoute laid out. The realities of life within the monastery forced monks to dis-

---

1. On this, note particularly the discussion of B. Layton, "Social Structure and Food Consumption in an Early Christian Monastery: The Evidence of Shenoute's Canons and the White Monastery Federation A.D. 385–465," *Le Muséon* 115 (2002), 25–55; and B. Layton, "Rules, Patterns, and the Exercise of Power in Shenoute's Monastery: The Problem of World Replacement and Identity Maintenance," *JECS* 15 (2007), 72.

2. Layton, "Social Structure," 37, on the basis of Canon 5 XS325 = L.IV:55. Note as well Can. 6 XV63 = Amél. 2.313 (trans. Layton, ibid., 37n61).

3. On additional food during the day, see Layton, "Social Structure," 47, on the basis of Can. 5 XL184 and XS = L.IV:56–57. For the restrictions on complaints, see Layton, "Social Structure," 46n93.

4. Layton, "Social Structure," 47–48.

5. For the frequency with which such ideas appear in the *Canons*, see Layton, "Social Structure," 48, table 4.

regard some of the more impractical elements of Shenoute's ascetic teaching. Monks seem to have often complained about the quality of the food and the perception that food service workers doled out unequal portion sizes.[6] The theft of food by hungry monks presented a more significant threat to monastic discipline. Shenoute seems to have chastised his charges for stealing food almost as often as he celebrated the virtues of fasting and austerity.[7] Indeed, Shenoute thought the problem significant enough to remind the monks that such behavior risked undoing all the benefits they had acquired through their ascetic labor.[8] Shenoute evidently thought that the small concessions these monks made to their metabolism represented deliberate decisions to choose a path other than that laid out in the *Canons* of the monastery. While a relatively minor matter by itself, such selective regard for the rules of the community could (and, at one point, did) lead to more significant disobedience among the monks.[9]

Pachomian sources suggest that a similar gap existed between the ideals of the community and the actual practices of individual monks within the *Koinonia*. For outsiders, the silence of the monks preparing food in the kitchen and eating meals in the refectory stood out as one of the most striking features of Pachomian monasticism.[10] The *Rules* of the community made this explicit, with particular emphasis placed upon silence among the workers within the bakery unless an urgent question needed to be asked of a neighbor.[11] Indeed, the leaders of the community absolutely forbade "chatting" as "the way of the idle and those who are heedless of their souls' fervor."[12] A further, unexpressed goal may have been to prevent the emergence of a communal sensibility based upon shared duties instead of a common ascetic purpose.[13]

Pachomius's effort to restrict the natural social inclinations of his monks proved just as unenforceable as Shenoute's attempt to regularize the diet of his

6. On these complaints, see Layton, "Social Structure," 37–38.
7. For stealing food or "eating by theft," see the detailed discussion of Layton, "Social Structure," 49–50.
8. Layton, "Social Structure," 50.
9. Layton, "Social Structure," 50. See as well Brakke, *Demons and the Making of the Monk: Spiritual Combat in Early Christianity* (Cambridge, MA, 2006), 3–5, and the important discussion of C. Schroeder, "Purity and Pollution in the Asceticism of Shenute of Atripe," *Studia Patristica* 35 (2001), 145–46.
10. Note, for example, *Historia Monachorum* 3.2 and Palladius, *Lausaic History* 32.6. See too the discussion of Rousseau, *Pachomius: The Making of a Community in Fourth-Century Egypt*, 2nd ed. (Berkeley, 1999), 84.
11. E.g., *Hors. Reg.* 40; *Bo.* 77.
12. *Hors. Reg.* 15, trans. Veilleux.
13. The grouping of particular Pachomian houses according to the tasks they performed is ably examined by E. Wipszycka, "Contribution à l'étude de l'économie de la congrégation Pachômienne," *JJP* 26 (1996), 167–210. I thank Peter Brown for this suggestion about the possible reason for these restrictions.

four thousand charges. Pachomian sources themselves describe moments when this particular element of the communal discipline broke down. The most notorious case occurred after Pachomius placed Theodore in charge of the monastery at Tabennesi and, with it, the monastery's bakery. At one point Pachomius received word that five of the bakers had broken the rule of silence and he summoned Theodore.[14] Then, not long after, he received word that this had happened again, this time with eighteen bakers involved.[15] Though seemingly insignificant, this second breach of monastic rules resulted in Theodore's resigning his leadership position at the monastery. Pachomian sources also take pains to emphasize the larger significance of this seemingly slight (and understandable) misstep. The *Bohairic Life*, for example, records Pachomius as saying in response to this situation "I assure you that, if a commandment is given even about a slight matter, it is nonetheless important . . . if this commandment had not been profitable to their souls, I would not have arranged the matter thus."[16] Like Shenoute, the leadership of the Pachomian *Koinonia* seems to have fought a long and frequently ineffective campaign to compel its monks to adhere completely to the rules of the community.

The problems that these otherwise extremely effective monastic leaders had in regulating the conduct of monks living within the highly regimented and tightly controlled monastic environment were magnified greatly when an ascetic's spiritual disciple lived in the world. In that environment, an individual's needs, desires, and personal responsibilities competed fiercely with his commitment to the ascetic teachings of his spiritual father. The secular followers of Barsanuphius and John stand out as particularly good examples. None expresses the tension between the needs of his spiritual discipleship and his worldly obligations better than Aelianus.[17] In one letter Aelianus addresses a direct question to John. He writes, "I wish, by the grace of God, to retire to a monastic life, but I hesitate. For is it necessary for me to renounce all of my things and retire now or should I first arrange my affairs and then leave the world?"[18] Aelianus particularly fretted about an old woman and a group of slaves for whom he was responsible and worried that their care might disturb his retreat from the world. John, and later Barsanuphius himself, both counseled Aelianus that an ascetic life within the monastery would be good for him, but only if he could separate himself entirely from worldly affairs. If he truly wished to lead an ascetic life, he would have to make permanent arrangements for those under his care. Barsanuphius said this most explicitly. "The

14. *Bo.* 74; G^1 89, 91.
15. *Bo.* 77.
16. *Bo.* 74, trans. Veilleux.
17. For Aelianus, see *Letters* 571–98. Note Hevelone-Harper, *Disciples of the Desert: Monks, Laity, and Spiritual Authority in Sixth-Century Gaza* (Baltimore, 2005), 119–24 as well as the discussion above.
18. *Letter* 571.

inhabitants of the world entirely work against you. For those who are enlaced in worldly things become worldly, but those who stand away from the things of the world ascend."[19] The true follower of the ascetic path laid out by these two monks needed to step away completely from all of the things that bound him to the world. If he failed to do so, he would find himself repeatedly dragged back to his worldly concerns.

Barsanuphius understood the challenge that worldly affairs presented to his spiritual disciples, but he still expected these men to place their obligations to him before any other duties they needed to perform. Barsanuphius's anger at the unnamed lawyer who forgot to do legal work on behalf of the monastery is perhaps typical of his refusal to accept the excuse that other, worldly demands simply proved more pressing.[20] And Barsanuphius's attempt to get one of his followers to stop discussing theology seems not to have persuaded the man to stop associating with amateur theologians.[21] Even Aelianus, a man who sincerely desired to live an ascetic life, did not manage to disentangle himself from worldly affairs until John asked him to step into a leadership position in the monastery.[22] At times, even the most committed spiritual disciples of Barsanuphius and John privileged the social and economic demands of a busy life above the requests and teaching of their ascetic mentors.

Although the monastic settings differ, the experiences of the lay disciples of Barsanuphius and John closely resembled those of the Alexandrian students who involved themselves in Paralius's beating. Zacharias Scholasticus's *Life of Severus*, a text written by one of Paralius's rescuers, describes the great religious commitment of these young men. One of their classmates, a young man named Menas, actually was a *philoponos* and played an active role assisting in church services.[23] Zacharias and other students showed no less enthusiasm than Menas, but they did not have the same formally defined ecclesiastical duties as real *philoponoi*. Instead they seem to have thought of themselves as near-*philoponoi*. Zacharias describes his group like this: "We constantly were found in the holy churches in the city with those whom one calls the *philoponoi*."[24] These students imitated the temperate lifestyle and strict schedule of the *philoponoi*, but they stood apart from the institutional structures that bound Menas and other *philoponoi* to the church of Alexandria. They were, in a sense, *philoponoi* wannabes.

Instead of affiliating themselves with the bishop, it seems that this group of pious Alexandrian students attached themselves to a group of intellectually trained

19. *Letter* 572.
20. *Letter* 745.
21. *Letters* 693–96; cf. Hevelone-Harper, *Disciples of the Desert*, 26.
22. *Letter* 575; cf. Hevelone-Harper, *Disciples of the Desert*, 123.
23. *Vit. Sev.* 32.
24. *Vit. Sev.* 24.

monks who lived nine miles outside of the city in the important anti-Chalcedonian monastery of the Enaton. The main point of contact seems to have been a monk named Stephen, a former sophist, who belonged to one of the many smaller subgroups (*koinobia*) of which the Enaton was comprised.[25] Stephen took particular interest in addressing and refuting doctrinal arguments framed by pagan intellectuals[26] and he paired these argumentative skills with a keen sense for the appropriate way to encourage pagans to take the first tentative steps towards Christianity.[27]

The Enaton had a history of reaching out to Alexandrian students,[28] but the *koinobion* to which Stephen belonged nurtured especially strong ties to the city's schools. Salomon, Stephen's superior, seems to have been able to summon a small army of Christian students from the classroom of the teacher Aphthonius whenever they were needed.[29] Stephen himself seems to have been acquainted with Zacharias and his fellow students.[30] The *Life of Severus* describes this connection even more explicitly after Paralius's baptism. Paralius then joined the Enaton and "he approached divine philosophy so eagerly that many young students who were called became like him and chose monastic life in the convent of the worthy Stephen, who held them all in the net of Apostolic [i.e., Anti-Chalcedonian] doctrine."[31] Elsewhere Zacharias describes Stephen as "a teacher to us all" and indicates that Stephen's outreach also drew into the monastery a man "schooled in the art of medicine and profane philosophy."[32] It then becomes clear that Stephen (and probably Salomon too) sought to build personal relationships with Alexandrian students in order to attract them to a rigorous, ascetically modeled sort of Christianity.

The *Life of Severus* suggests that Zacharias and his associates understood themselves to be spiritual disciples of Enaton, but it does not provide enough detail to allow one to reconstruct the ties that bound these Alexandrian students to the *koinobion* of Salomon. However, a later section of the text, describing Zacharias's

25. *Vit. Sev.* 14. As both the *Life of Severus* and the *Life of Longinus* (13) suggest, the Enaton in the fifth century was a collection of *koinobia* headed by individual *koinobiarchs*. They must be distinguished, however, from Pachomian communities to which they bear no direct connection. On the Enaton generally, see P. van Cauwenbergh, *Étude sur les moines d'Égypte: depuis le Concile de Chalcédoine, jusqu'à l'invasion arabe* (Paris-Louvain, 1914), 64–72. See also J. Gascou, "The Enaton," *Coptic Encyclopedia* 954–57.

26. *Vit. Sev.* 16.

27. It was Stephen, for example, who taught Paralius to pray to the "Creator of all things" (*Vit. Sev.* 21), an appropriately vague first Christian prayer.

28. E.g., John Rufus, *Plerophories* 13.

29. *Vit. Sev.* 25.

30. *Vit. Sev.* 27. It is possible, however, that they did not meet until after Paralius's rescue.

31. *Vit. Sev.* 43.

32. *Vit. Sev.* 43.

efforts to organize a similar *philoponoi*-like student association among law students in Berytus, shows how these personal connections may have developed. During the week, the students spent their time studying law. On Saturdays, they used half of the day to review their class assignments and the other half to study Christian theological texts. Sundays were wholly devoted to religious study.[33] They chose Evagrius, an austere Antiochene student with a reputation for "persuading many young men to exchange the vanity of forensic oratory for the divine philosophy," to serve as their president.[34] The group was not wholly a student organization, however. These law students had a consultative relationship with the priest Kosmas and his assistant, a Palestinian named John, that enabled them to ask for assistance when it was needed.[35] Perhaps more importantly, they also saw their group as spiritually connected to the monastery of Peter the Iberian in Maiuma, the place to which a number of them ultimately retired after completing their studies.[36] Nor was this sort of relationship with law students in Berytus a new thing for Peter and his monks. Two of the monastery's highest-ranking monks had earlier joined the monastery after completing their legal studies in Berytus.[37]

Despite the strong influence that Peter the Iberian exercised on this student group, Evagrius provided them with a more powerful and immediate ascetic model to follow. He set a high bar. He attended church each night and "fasted every day and, as it is said, destroyed the bloom of his youth through divine philosophy. He tormented his body with vigils and never washed himself except on a single day, the day before Easter."[38] As the students became more familiar with each other they all strove to emulate Evagrius's discipline. It became their custom to "offer evening prayers to God together in the holy churches . . . [after] having completed the assignments of legal study and the work that went along with it."[39] Over time, their enthusiasm grew and one member of the group, Severus, the

33. *Vit. Sev.* 53–54.
34. *Vit. Sev.* 54, 56.
35. E.g., *Vit. Sev.* 64; cf. *Vit. Sev.* 80.
36. Two members of the group saw Peter appear to them in dreams, another received a letter from Peter "exhorting the group to the observance of the divine laws" (*Vit. Sev.* 87), and a fourth, the Gazan Zacharias, visited with Peter himself (*Vit. Sev.* 89). Severus of Antioch also writes of his personal connection to Peter the Iberian in *Select Letters* 5.11 (ed. Brooks, p. 328). The relationship is further discussed in *Vit. Sev.* 83, 87–89, 93. Note, however, *Vit. Sev.* 86, which suggests that at least one of these students may not ever have spoken personally with Peter the Iberian.
37. These were John Rufus and a man named Theodore (*Vit. Sev.* 86). For Peter's role in reaching out to students enrolled in the law schools of Berytus, see C. Horn, *Asceticism and Christological Controversy in Fifth-Century Palestine: The Career of Peter the Iberian* (Oxford, 2006), 224–25; B. Bitton-Ashkelony and A. Kofsky, *The Monastic School of Gaza* (Leiden, 2006), 28. Note too *Vit. Pet. Ib.* 152; *Plerophories* 71.
38. *Vit. Sev.* 56. When considering the Berytus example of Evagrius, we should keep in mind his similarity to the Alexandrian Menas, another important figure in Zacharias's composite text.
39. *Vit. Sev.* 55.

future bishop of Antioch, went so far as to follow the example of his spiritual father Evagrius. "He fasted each day, he never took baths, and not only participated in the evening services in the church of God, but mostly stayed the night [in it]."[40]

These students still remained dedicated to their studies, however. According to Zacharias, Severus came to possess in the law "the knowledge of a professor" and had once expressed his misgivings about joining the group because he feared that Zacharias would "make a monk of me . . . I am a student of law and I love law very much."[41] Family obligations also compelled the students to finish their training. One man had a wife and children, while others feared disappointing their fathers.[42] Even Evagrius had been dissuaded from entering a monastery by a father who "forced him to go to Phoenicia to study law."[43] This group of law students, then, demonstrates the particular challenges faced by young men who sought to balance their studies, their family obligations, the expectations of their friends, and the personal dedication they had to a quasi-ascetic lifestyle. By joining together, these young men fashioned a network of peers which, in loose collaboration with neighboring monks and clergy, helped them meet their personal, intellectual, and spiritual needs.

FINDING THE ASCETIC AND INTELLECTUAL BALANCE

In both Alexandria and Berytus, students enjoyed fewer practical responsibilities than, say, a practicing lawyer, but they also faced a different set of challenges. Their classes and conversations with fellow students forced these young men to consider new ideas that conflicted with some of the basic teaching upon which their faith rested. This presented a particular challenge to students enrolled in schools headed by pagan teachers like Isidore, Ammonius, and Asclepiodotus. We are consequently fortunate that Zacharias Scholasticus devoted many of his writings to the process of carving out intellectually sophisticated anti-Chalcedonian responses to many of the ideas that circulated in the Alexandrian schools. His writings, many of which began circulating not long after he left Alexandria, provide the unique opportunity to understand how students worked to make sense of the competing influences of their teachers and ascetic mentors.

Zacharias himself was born in Maiuma, the port of Gaza, probably in 465 or

---

40. *Vit. Sev.* 82. It is worth noting here that some of these practices among the lay law students of Berytus echo those of the lay spiritual disciples of Barsanuphius and John (cf. chapter 4, above).
41. *Vit. Sev.* 52.
42. *Vit. Sev.* 87, 89.
43. *Vit. Sev.* 55.

466.⁴⁴ Gaza at the time enjoyed close intellectual ties to Alexandria and in the later fifth century a good number of Gazans made a trip there to complete their educations. Consistent with this, in the 480s, Zacharias began rhetorical and rudimentary philosophical study in Alexandria. In 487, he moved to Berytus to pursue legal study, and in the early 490s, he moved to Constantinople to begin practicing law. It appears that he continued to do so through the 510s before eventually becoming the bishop of Mytilene sometime before 536.⁴⁵ However, he seems to have retained ties to the Gazan and Alexandrian cultural world well into adulthood.⁴⁶

Zacharias's early religious experiences resemble his peripatetic intellectual training. He writes that he grew up in the shadow of the monastery of Peter the Iberian and seems to have developed strong feelings of attachment to Peter during his childhood.⁴⁷ This connection endured even after Zacharias went off to study in Alexandria. In fact, Zacharias tells of one time when he returned home on a break from school and brought one of his Alexandrian friends with him. Both students visited Peter's community, ate with his monks, and journeyed to Ashkelon to speak with the master (who was, at the time, living a life of retreat).⁴⁸ Zacharias spoke about Peter as a modern-day apostle and collected enough information about him to compose a biography.⁴⁹ In addition, sources written later by leaders of Peter's monastery confirm that Zacharias was a frequent visitor and conversation partner in the late 480s and early 490s.⁵⁰

---

44. On the basic details of Zacharias's life, see P. Allen, "Zachariah Scholasticus and the *Historia Ecclesiastica* of Evagrius Scholasticus," *JTS*, n.s., 31 (1980), 471–72; M. Minniti Colonna, *Zacaria Scolastico, Ammonio: Introduzione, testo critico, traduzione, commentario* (Naples, 1973), 15–20; E. Honigmann, *Patristic Studies*, ST 173 (Vatican City, 1953), 194–204.

45. Allen, "Zachariah Scholasticus," 471; Honigmann, *Patristic Studies*, 195.

46. His relationship with Aeneas of Gaza is particularly notable here. In addition to serving as a source for the arguments presented in Zacharias's *Ammonius*, Aeneas appears in Zacharias's *Life of Isaiah* (12–13 [Syr.]; 8 [Lat.]) and his *Life of Severus* (90).

47. Zacharias states that he felt that he could not join the monastery because his father lived close by and would prevent him from doing so (*Vit. Sev.* 88). On his relationship with Peter, see Horn, *Asceticism and Christological Controversy*, 44–46 and Bitton-Ashkelony and Kofsky, *Monastic School of Gaza*, 29–33.

48. *Vit. Sev.* 89. Although Peter spent his last years living outside of Ashkelon, the Maiuma community he founded grew prominent again when, following his death in 491, Peter's disciples returned with his body and expanded the facilities (*Vit. Pet.* 191). On this see Horn, *Asceticism and Christological Controversy*, 101–6 and 210–11. Note too the discussion of Bitton-Ashkelony and Kofsky, *Monastic School of Gaza*, 27–36, 61.

49. On Peter as an apostle see *Vit. Sev.* 78. For the biography, see the fragment published by E. W. Brooks, *Fragmentum Vitae Petri Iberi*, in *Vitae virorum apud monophysitas celeberrimorum*, CSCO 7–8, (Paris, 1907), 7.18 (Syr.) and 8.12 (Lat.). This text and its Georgian adaptation are discussed further below.

50. John Rufus, *Plerophories* 73.

Zacharias also claimed a second spiritual mentor, a solitary ascetic and sometime associate of Peter the Iberian named Isaiah. Like Peter, Zacharias included Isaiah among the "prophets of our time" and he composed a short biography of the monk to illustrate his holiness.[51] Zacharias seems to have been a frequent visitor to Isaiah's enclosure and he looked at the old ascetic with deep reverence.[52] Nevertheless, Isaiah had a more ambiguous influence on Zacharias than did Peter the Iberian. A native Egyptian, Isaiah had come to the area around Gaza to separate himself from disruptive visitors[53] and communicated with the outside world only through an Egyptian associate named Peter (who is distinct from Peter the Iberian).[54] He eventually found himself at the head of a large community of monks and spent much of the rest of his career concerned with organizing these men and enhancing their spiritual lives.[55] While his holiness was unquestioned, the specific concerns to which Isaiah devoted himself made his instruction less practically applicable to Zacharias.

The spiritual discipleships that Zacharias developed with Peter the Iberian, Isaiah, and their followers rooted him in the ascetic life of Gaza. The influence of these men reached beyond Gaza into Egypt, however, and Zacharias was able to find like-minded ascetic communities during his time in Alexandria. Isaiah, of course, came from Egypt and continued to enjoy a strong reputation in the region. Peter the Iberian, however, had a much greater influence on Egyptian ascetic and ecclesiastical life, particularly in and around the city of Alexandria. Peter had begun life as an Iberian prince who, at the age of twelve, was sent to Constantinople.[56] After some years in the capital, he snuck off to Jerusalem and, ultimately, to the Gazan port of Maiuma in order to live an undisturbed ascetic life.[57] Peter

---

51. Zacharias, *Vita Isaiae monachi*, in Brooks, *Vitae virorum* (text) 7:1–16, (trans.) 8:1–10. Subsequent references to this text will be to *Vit. Isaiae*, with page references to both the Syriac edition and Brooks's Latin translation. On Isaiah, see Bitton-Ashkelony and Kofsky, *Monastic School of Gaza*, 20–23.

52. This is suggested by John Rufus, *Pler*. 73.

53. Zacharias, *Vit. Isaiae*, 5–7 (Syr.); 4–5 (Lat.).

54. Zacharias, *Vit. Isaiae* 13 (Syr.), 9 (Lat.); John Rufus, *Vit. Pet*. 138.

55. This focus of his teaching is, at any rate, suggested by his surviving work, the *Ascetic Discourses* and the sayings attributed to him in the *Apophthegmata Patrum*. This seems to be confirmed by Zacharias in *Vit. Isaiae* 8 (Syr.), 8–9 (Lat.). Note here as well the discussions of D. Chitty, "Abba Isaiah," *JTS* 22 (1971), 47–72, as well as the important parallels between Isaiah and Barsanuphius described by Hevelone-Harper, *Disciples of the Desert*, 16–17.

56. The most detailed source describing Peter's life and career is the anonymous *Life of Peter*. For this see the edition and translation of R. Raabe, *Petrus der Iberer, ein Charakterbild zur Kirchen und Sittengeschichte des fünften Jahrhunderts* (Liepzig, 1895), as well as the recent English translation of C. Horn and R. Phenix (*John Rufus: The Lives of Peter the Iberian, Theodosius of Jerusalem, and the Monk Romanus* [Atlanta, 2008]). All references to this text refer to the chapter numbers of this more recent edition. On Peter's biography see Horn, *Asceticism and Christological Controversy*, 50–106.

57. For his decision to retreat from Jerusalem to Maiuma, see the interesting discussion of *Vit. Pet*. 71–72; and Horn, *Asceticism and Christological Controversy*, 74.

rose to greater prominence in the aftermath of the Council of Chalcedon in 451 when he joined an alternative, anti-Chalcedonian ecclesiastical hierarchy created by the Palestinian monk Theodosius.[58] As the most notable ascetic in the region around Maiuma, Peter was tapped to serve as bishop of that city in August of 452.[59] In 453, however, Juvenal, the pro-Chalcedonian patriarch of Jerusalem, returned with imperial troops at his back. He forced Theodosius and many other anti-Chalcedonian monk-bishops into exile.[60] Peter the Iberian fled to Alexandria.

In Alexandria, Peter led furtive worship services for congregations opposed to Chalcedon and even cooperated with Longinus, the head of the Enaton, in his efforts to install the Enaton monk Timothy Aelurus as the patriarch of Alexandria.[61] When Timothy was sent into exile in 460, Peter seems to have taken it upon himself to encourage the resistance of anti-Chalcedonian ascetics.[62] He spent much of the next two decades traveling around Egypt, but he paid particular attention to the monasteries in and around the city of Alexandria.[63] When Peter returned to Palestine in c. 475, he maintained these close ties to Timothy Aelurus and, apparently, to the anti-Chalcedonian Alexandrian ascetics who supported the patriarch as well.[64]

The extensive interactions between Peter the Iberian and the anti-Chalcedonian ascetic communities around Alexandria caused their theological interests to converge. This meant that Zacharias and other Gazans pursuing their studies in Alexandria found much that was familiar in the ascetic environment of the city. For the spiritual disciples of Peter the Iberian, the Enaton seems to have represented a natural surrogate ascetic community to which they could gravitate. Not only did Peter himself have clear ties with Timothy Aelurus, the Enaton's most famous alumnus, but he seems also to have enjoyed a connection to the monastery's leadership.

Zacharias evidently did not find the transition between these two ascetic environments extremely difficult, probably because the two communities shared com-

---

58. John Rufus, *Plerophories* 20; *Vit. Pet.* 52. On Juvenal of Jerusalem's actions at the Council of Chalcedon and the anti-Chalcedonian response, note Zacharias, *HE* 3.3 and Horn, *Asceticism and Christological Controversy*, 77–90.

59. *Vit. Pet.* 78–79.

60. *Vit. Pet.* 81.

61. *Vit. Pet.* 91. For this section note as well the fragmentary Coptic (Bohairic) *Life of Timothy Aelurus* (published in Evelyn White, *New Texts from the Monastery of Saint Macarius: The Monasteries of Wadi 'n Natrûn*, Vol. 1 [New York, 1926], 164–67). See as well the similar account of Zacharias, *HE* 4.1.

62. On Timothy's exile, see Evagrius, *HE* 2.11; Zacharias, *HE* 4.9; *Vit. Pet.* 70–71. See too Horn, *Asceticism and Christological Controversy*, 95.

63. *Vit. Pet.* 71.

64. For Peter's ties to Timothy Aelurus, see Bitton-Ashkelony and Kofsky, *Monastic School of Gaza*, 26–27.

mon ascetic and political concerns. This connection becomes clear from the communal historical traditions preserved in works written by John Rufus, Peter the Iberian's successor as the head of the Maiuma community. John composed a biography of Peter the Iberian, but his *Plerophories* stand out as his most notable composition.[65] These are, the manuscript claims, "the witnesses and revelations that God has made to the saints, on the subject of the heresy of the two natures and the prevarications that came about at Chalcedon."[66] In all, the work describes the context and preserves the content of eighty-nine visions and other forms of divine witness in which God communicated with leading Egyptian and Palestinian ascetics as well as some selected lay associates. Though probably written down in the 510s, much of this material derives from the testimony of Peter the Iberian and was likely communicated to John following his arrival in Maiuma in the early 480s.[67]

While John Rufus quotes a diverse group of sources, the way in which he presents his material shows the deep intertwining of Gazan and Alexandrian anti-Chalcedonian ideas. John's master, Peter the Iberian, and the Alexandrian patriarch Timothy Aelurus stand out as the two most authoritative voices in the work and each one serves to define its most prominent themes. As one would expect, Peter often serves to introduce particular themes around which a number of subsequent accounts will coalesce. So, for example, when John Rufus introduces a section of the work describing the perfidy of Juvenal of Jerusalem at Chalcedon, he does so by first using stories told to him by Peter.[68] With Peter's authority placed behind this idea, John then includes two other memorable incidents witnessed by less famous Christian figures that also suggest God's anger at Juvenal.[69]

John Rufus relies differently upon the authoritative figure of Timothy Aelurus. Whereas John knew Peter personally and interacted with him repeatedly, he knew Timothy Aelurus primarily through his writings and the reports of men who had visited with Timothy in exile. Nevertheless, the statements of Timothy often served the same introductory function as the recollections of Peter the Iberian. So, for example, visions of Timothy introduced a set of divine communications that strongly disapproved of Proterius, the controversial bishop who became the

---

65. For discussion of John Rufus's literary output see E. Schwartz, *Johannes Rufus, ein monophysitischer Schriftsteller* (Heidelberg, 1912); J. E. Steppa, *John Rufus and the World Vision of Anti-Chalcedonian Culture* (Piscataway, NJ, 2002); and Horn, *Asceticism and Christological Controversy*, 18–43.

66. *Plerophories* (henceforth *Plero.*) heading, p. 11 (Nau). Subsequent references to the text will refer to the individual chapter numbers within the compilation.

67. Steppa, *John Rufus*, 57. For the 510s as the date of composition for the *Plerophories*, see Steppa, *John Rufus*, 60–61. For the orality of the text see Horn, *Asceticism and Christological Controversy*, 17, 27, 38. The identity of John's sources suggests that much of the original oral material dates from the 470s and 480s.

68. *Plero.* 16–20.

69. *Plero.* 19–20.

Alexandrian patriarch in the aftermath of Chalcedon.[70] By marking Proterius as a figure of evil, Timothy's authoritative visions lay the framework for a dramatic concluding revelation in which Proterius mentions to a lay woman in Alexandria that the successor of Dioscorus will be the Antichrist.[71]

This rhetorical strategy proved particularly effective in presenting one of the more controversial themes that resonated within these Egyptian and Palestinian ascetic communities. For some anti-Chalcedonian ascetics in Gaza and Egypt, the ecclesiastical divisions caused by the council marked the beginning of the end of time. These monks knew of many different divine communications that proved this idea. Some marked Juvenal of Jerusalem as the Antichrist and others spoke about the imminent end of the world.[72] This was a timely theological approach—the impending arrival of the year 500 had generated considerable collective unease among Chalcedonians and anti-Chalcedonians alike that the end of the world was approaching—but it was one that some anti-Chalcedonian leaders exploited in a particularly skillful way.[73]

Peter the Iberian occasionally introduced these ideas to his followers,[74] but the ascetics of Gaza and Maiuma saw Timothy Aelurus as the most forceful voice behind this theology of catastrophe. John Rufus shows this most clearly by concluding the *Plerophories* with a rambling theological discussion in which he communicates Timothy's view that Chalcedon has opened a divine breach. According to John, Timothy held that the council had "unjustly called the anger of God upon all the earth."[75] He continues: "It is with this repudiation that the statement of the Apostle is brought about; and now the sovereignty of the Roman Empire reaches its end . . . she has opened the door to the impiety that is called the Tome of Leo so that now we see and understand its effect."[76] Timothy then states, "The Council

---

70. *Plero.* 66, 68.
71. *Plero.* 69.
72. E.g., *Plero.* 88. Among the other examples of this type of testimony are *Plero.* 17 (Peter the Iberian's story about a monk barring his cell to Juvenal); *Plero.* 20 (the vision of a priest named Paul equating Juvenal with a servant of the Antichrist); and *Plero.* 89 (a composite tradition describing the connection between the city of Rome's falling under barbarian control and the Tome of Leo). The last tradition probably alludes to Odoacer's coup and is the earliest surviving classification of this event as Rome's fall. On this theme see as well Bitton-Ashkelony and Kofsky, *Monastic School of Gaza*, 56–57.
73. For the significance of the approach of 500, see P. Magdalino, "The History of the Future and Its Uses: Prophecy, Policy, and Propaganda," in *The Making of Byzantine History*, ed. R. Beaton and C. Roueché (Aldershot, 1993), 3–34; and M. Meier, *Das andere Zeitalter Justinians, Kontingenzerfahrung und Kontingenzbewältigung im 6. Jht. N. Chr.* (Göttingen, 2003), 16–21. For Chalcedonian use of similar rhetoric see Cyril of Scythopolis, *Vita Euthymii* 27 and the *Oracle of Baalbek* (on which see P. J. Alexander, *The Oracle of Baalbek: The Tiburtine Sibyl in Greek Dress*. Dumbarton Oaks Studies 10 [Washington, D.C., 1967]).
74. *Plero.* 12, cf. *Plero.* 13.
75. *Plero.* 89 (150.9).
76. *Plero.* 89 (150.11–151.1).

of Chalcedon, with its perverse faith and innovative decrees, is an impure sign of the end, the anathema, the precursor of the Antichrist."[77] Nor is this an isolated idea within Timothy's corpus. In a short narration of recent church history, which he composed in the early 460s, Timothy makes similar arguments that one can see the impiety of the Chalcedonian creed by looking at contemporary political catastrophes.[78] These in turn anticipate the end of the created world.

These eschatological ideas seem to have originated from texts and anecdotes carefully constructed by Timothy Aelurus and Peter the Iberian, but they resonated far beyond Peter's circle of Gazan ascetics. Even within the *Plerophories*, one sees Phoenician, Syrian, and other Palestinian ascetics contributing material that supported this anti-Chalcedonian eschatology. Egyptians too identified with these themes.[79] In fact, a surviving letter of Timothy Aelurus suggests that he intended for his eschatological interpretation of Chalcedon not only to circulate among Alexandrian Christians but also to serve as a primary means of influencing their behaviors. The ascetics who lived around Alexandria (and especially those housed in Timothy Aelurus's old monastery of the Enaton) seem to have been particularly fond of these ideas. Not only did the Enaton and other monasteries create their own strongly anti-Chalcedonian historical traditions that emphasized the impiety of Chalcedon and the glory of ascetic resistance,[80] but these Egyptian communities also drew upon Palestinian traditions of resistance.[81]

The ascetic environment described in the *Plerophories* shaped the religious worldview of Zacharias Scholasticus both as a young man in Gaza and as a student in Alexandria. As an adolescent who identified with Peter the Iberian's monastery, Zacharias readily accepted many of the anti-Chalcedonian themes emphasized in the oral traditions of the community. To give just one example, Zacharias refused to enter any church or shrine presided over by Chalcedonians—a practice ideal-

77. *Plero.* 89 (154.12–155.2).
78. The Syriac text is found in *Textes Syriaques Édites et Traduits*, ed. F. Nau, PO 13.2, 202–17.
79. Timothy Aelurus, *Letter 6*, in R. Y. Ebied and L. R. Wickham, "Collection of Unpublished Syriac Letters of Timothy Aelurus," *JTS*, n.s., 21.2 (1970), 321–69.
80. Anti-Chalcedonian resistance plays a vital role in framing the persona of Longinus, the head of the Enaton following the council. Note particularly the *Life of Longinus* 29–39 and the discussion of T. Vivian, "Humility and Resistance in Late Antique Egypt: The *Life of Longinus*," *Coptic Church Review* 20 (1999), 4–9.
81. In fact, both the *Plerophories* and the *Life of Peter the Iberian* circulated in Egypt. For Coptic manuscripts of the *Plerophories* see W. E. Crum, *Coptic Ostraca from the Collection of the Egypt Exploration Fund, the Cairo Museum, and Others* (London, 1902), 42, ostracon no. 459; Crum, ed., *Theological Texts from Coptic Papyri* (Oxford, 1913), 62–64; T. Orlandi, "Giovanni Rufo di Maiuma, Pleroforie (K 2502a–b; [appendice] K 7343; K 2502c–e)," in *Koptische Papyri theologischen Inhalts, Mitteilungen aus der Papyrussammlung der Österreichischen Nationalbibliothek* (Vienna, 1974), 110–20; and Orlandi, "Un frammento delle Pleroforie in Copto," *Studi e Ricerche sull'Oriente Cristiano* 2 (1979), 3–12. The *Life of Peter the Iberian* evidently was later incorporated into a hagiography of Timothy Aelurus. On this, note Evelyn White, *New Texts from the Monastery of Saint Macarius*, 164.

ized by both the writings of Timothy and tales told by Peter.⁸² Zacharias also revered the monk Isaiah, Peter the Iberian, and Timothy Aelurus. Zacharias once termed Peter and Isaiah "two of three among our generation of prophets"⁸³ and called Timothy "one who showed that he was really what a priest should be."⁸⁴ These were important figures whose prominence in Zacharias's ascetic community underlined the reliability of what they said. Indeed, the *Plerophories* makes this idea explicit. John Rufus writes about his ascetic sources: "The facts that will be reported may seem incredible or prodigious to some, but they come from men who are pure, aged, and respected in their faith."⁸⁵ This faith in the authority of one's ascetic spiritual fathers formed a necessary first step for the sort of personal relationship that Zacharias developed with these men. If an ideal priest and contemporary prophets all agreed that Chalcedon represented the beginning of the end of the world, we must understand the power this idea would have had over Zacharias. Its truth was affirmed by every authority structure within the anti-Chalcedonian communities to which he belonged.

Zacharias never admits to questioning his commitment to anti-Chalcedonian spiritual mentors or to the anti-Chalcedonian ideas that they advanced, but Alexandria's scholastic environment posed distinct challenges to him. The most prominent schools of rhetoric and philosophy were headed by pagans, many of whom were disciples of the Athenian philosopher Proclus, and they were infused with an enthusiasm for a hybridized paganism that mixed Neoplatonic philosophy with an interest in traditional Egyptian practices.⁸⁶ Within these intellectual circles, two significant trends evidently troubled Zacharias and his fellow Christian students. First, these influential teachers demanded (and commanded) the respect and loyalty of students while making no effort to hide their paganism. In so doing, they seem to have encouraged students to think about paganism in a positive light.⁸⁷ In addition, they were inflexible about particular philosophical

---

82. For Timothy see *Letter* 4 in Ebied and Wickham, "Letters of Timothy Aelurus," esp. 362–63. For Peter see, most notably, *Plero.* 76.

83. *Vit. Isaiae* 3.5.

84. Zacharias, *HE* 4.3.

85. *Plero.* 10.

86. The Proclan disciples included Ammonius, Heliodorus, Isidore, and Asclepiodotus. For more on this collection of scholars see chapter 3 as well as E. Watts, *City and School in Late Antique Athens and Alexandria* (Berkeley, 2006), 208–12. Their hybridized religious practices were described by Damascius as "adapting Greek notions [of philosophical/religious practice] to conform with Egyptian ones" (*Vit. Is. Ath.* 4A; Z. fr. 3). On these religious practices, see D. Frankfurter, "The Consequences of Hellenism in Late Antique Egypt: Religious Worlds and Actors," *Archiv für Religionsgeschichte* 2 (2000), 185–92; as well as P. Athanassiadi, *Damascius: The Philosophical History* (Athens, 1999), 20–31; and G. Bowersock, *Hellenism in Late Antiquity* (Ann Arbor, 1990), 60–61.

87. E. Watts, "The Student Self in Late Antiquity," in *Religion and the Self in Antiquity*, ed. D. Brakke, M. Satlow, and S. Weitzman (Bloomington, 2005), 234–51.

doctrines that later fifth-century Christians found disagreeable. The most notable of these was the Aristotelian notion of the eternity of the world, an idea that was particularly problematic when juxtaposed with the great emphasis placed upon eschatology in the anti-Chalcedonian discourse of Peter the Iberian, Timothy Aelurus, and their followers.

THE ASCETIC AND SOPHISTIC MÉLANGE OF ZACHARIAS SCHOLASTICUS

Zacharias's student experiences are particularly interesting because, alone among his compatriots, he wrote a number of works that reflect some of the tensions between his literary studies and his ascetically influenced anti-Chalcedonianism.[88] These include biographies of Peter the Iberian and Isaiah as well as a philosophical dialog, the *Ammonius*. As they currently exist, the lives of Peter the Iberian and Isaiah are not in a great state. The full text of Peter's biography survives in a significantly altered Georgian translation that manages to transform its subject into a partisan of Chalcedon; the text is otherwise known only from one possible Syriac fragment.[89] That of Isaiah is preserved separately in a Syriac translation.[90] The Isaiah text, however, is sufficiently intact to reflect Zacharias's particular interests at the time of its composition.

Zacharias evidently intended this work to establish Isaiah as an ascetic exemplar to the anti-Chalcedonian community.[91] In pursuing this goal, he includes a set of miracles, prophecies, and visions of the future that both confirm Isaiah's spiritual achievements and, to a lesser degree, define his anti-Chalcedonian convictions. At the same time, there are two elements of Zacharias's portrait that are

---

88. Elements of this discussion have been previously published as "Creating the Ascetic and Sophistic Mélange," *ARAM* 17/18 (2006–7), 153–64.

89. Note, however, the doubts expressed by Horn, *Asceticism and Christological Controversy*, 45.

90. The *Lives* of Peter the Iberian and Isaiah were evidently first published during Zacharias's time in Berytus. At a later point, they were revised and republished as part of a larger collection of anti-Chalcedonian hagiography. On the text of Peter the Iberian's life, see D. M. Lang, "Peter the Iberian and his Biographers," *Journal of Ecclesiastical History* 2.2 (1951), 158–68. On the apparent republication of the texts, see M. A. Kugener, "Observations sur la Vie de l'ascète Isaïe et sur les Vies de Pierre l'Ibérien et de Théodore d'Antinoé par Zacharie le Scholastique," *BZ* 9 (1909), 464–70.

91. In this context, it is important to note that Zacharias and the monks living under Peter the Iberian both took great pains to associate Isaiah with Peter's aggressive resistance to the Council of Chalcedon. They spoke about Peter and Isaiah both refusing to meet with the emperor Zeno in order to discuss his Henotikon (ch. 53 of the Georgian *Life of Peter the Iberian* and *Vit. Isaiae* 14–15 [Syr.] 10 [Latin]; cf. Rufus, *Vit. Pet.* 140; D. M. Lang, "Peter the Iberian and his Biographers," 162). This portrait seems inconsistent with the theologically disengaged Isaiah who wrote the *Ascetic Discourses*. Evidently, Peter's associates used stories like this to claim Isaiah for their own anti-Chalcedonian cause.

rather peculiar inclusions. The first of these concerns the insurrection of Illus in 484, a revolt notable for the efforts made by its leaders to reach out to both pagan intellectuals and disenchanted Chalcedonians. Because of the activities of Pamprepius, this endeavor was well known to Christian students like Zacharias and evidently concerned them a great deal.[92] At the same time, Calandion of Antioch, John Talaias, and other Chalcedonian leaders also supported the rebellion of Illus as a way to uphold the Council of Chalcedon more strongly.[93]

Because of Calandion of Antioch and John Talaias in Alexandria, the revolt of Illus had an undeniable place in the history of the anti-Chalcedonian movement. So it is not unreasonable to find mention of it in Zacharias's life of Isaiah. Nevertheless, it is notable how Zacharias describes the uprising. Zacharias would later emphasize the ties Illus established with Calandion and John in his *Ecclesiastical History*,[94] but the *Life of Isaiah* does not present Illus's revolt as a threat because of the Chalcedonian connections of its leadership. Instead, in the *Life of Isaiah*, Zacharias evokes notions of religious struggle and describes Isaiah calming Christian anxieties about a situation in which "Illus had become deranged, for it is said that he was deceived by the magus Pamprepius and led into paganism."[95] In the 480s and 490s, Zacharias and other Christians studying under Pamprepius's associates in Alexandria saw the revolt's failure as a Christian victory over devious and deceitful pagans. This incident in the *Life of Isaiah*, then, must be understood as a part of an anti-pagan discourse with particular meaning in late fifth-century Egyptian and Palestinian intellectual environments. In these contexts, Illus's actions against Zeno signified the failings of intellectual pagan leaders. Zacharias could then position Isaiah as a figure who provided leadership to Christian students concerned about pagan influences in the intellectual environment.

Another segment of the *Life of Isaiah* works to establish a new sort of relationship between Christian wisdom and pagan learning. This is based upon the testimony of Aeneas of Gaza. Aeneas, who is described as "a most learned and Christian man (who is) known all over for his wisdom," is quoted as saying, "Often, when I was in doubt about a passage from the writings of Plato, Aristotle, or Plotinus, and could not find a solution in their commentaries or interpret them

---

92. Zacharias's concern about the rebellion is apparent in both the *Life of Isaiah* and his *Life of Severus* (*Vit. Sev.* 40).

93. Evagrius Scholasticus, *HE* 3.16, and Zacharias, *HE* 5.9, describe Calandion's support for Illus and Leontius. John Talaias is mentioned by Zacharias, *HE* 5.6–7, and Liberatus, *Breviarium* 16. For a discussion of Chalcedonian support of this revolt, see H. Elton, "Illus and the Imperial Aristocracy Under Zeno," *Byzantion* 70 (2000), 402 and W. H. C. Frend, *The Rise of the Monophysite Movement* (Cambridge, 1972), 177–81.

94. On the nature of Zacharias's *Ecclesiastical History* see chapter 1, note 69, above.

95. *Vita Isaiae* 10. This story is not original; it parallels a similar story told by Rufinus about Athanasius and the emperor Julian (Rufinus, *HE* 1.34).

by myself, I asked (Isaiah) and he enlightened me . . . In this way, he also refuted their falsehoods and strengthened the truth of Christian doctrine."⁹⁶ Isaiah here serves as a true philosopher-monk, an ascetic who is better versed in philosophical argumentation than even the best-trained intellectuals. This inverts the standard literary image of a Christian ascetic who shuns classical philosophy for the practical wisdom of Christian asceticism,⁹⁷ but this inversion is deliberate.⁹⁸ It shapes Isaiah into an exemplary figure who personifies the ascetic and sophistic cultural fusion idealized by students like Zacharias. In Zacharias's portrait, Isaiah is both an uncompromising anti-Chalcedonian ascetic and a leader who can respond to the intellectual concerns of Christians involved in the schools. This is a peculiar mixture of attributes, but it is also one that a student like Zacharias would have seen as ideal.

Zacharias's anti-eternalist philosophical dialog *Ammonius* is a very different sort of work, but one that ought equally to be seen as a product of the interaction of his ascetic and sophistic environments. The *Ammonius* begins with a short conversation between law students in Berytus who had once studied in Alexandria under the influential Neoplatonist Ammonius. One of the students then offers to recount a series of discussions he had with Ammonius that reflect upon the unreliability of his teachings about the eternity of the world. The arguments in the work itself are not original—many of them are copied directly from Aeneas of Gaza's *Theophrastus*.⁹⁹ On the whole, they use philosophical concepts to defend the idea that the world is not co-eternal with God and to illustrate that God will not be diminished by its destruction. This was the same basic aim as that of Aeneas's text.

Nevertheless, there is an important distinction in tone between the earlier argument framed by Aeneas and that put forth by Zacharias. While Aeneas is understated about his Christianity and chooses to emphasize the philosophical implications of his arguments, Zacharias makes it clear how his arguments support Christian doctrine. So, for example, after Zacharias refutes Ammonius's argument that the dissolution of the cosmos would diminish God, he states, "many of those present in the class at that time . . . were placed among us and leaned towards our arguments, or more correctly, they leaned towards Christianity out of faith and love of truth."¹⁰⁰ Following another discussion with Ammonius, Zacharias states that Ammonius asked his students to leave the auditorium "so

---

96. *Vita Isaiae* 8.

97. Note, for example, *Life of Antony* 78. Relevant as well is the discussion of S. Rubenson, "Philosophy and Simplicity: The Problem of Classical Education in Early Christian Biography," in *Greek Biography and Panegyric in Late Antiquity*, ed. T. Hägg and P. Rousseau (Berkeley, 2000), 118.

98. It may also reflect the realities of Isaiah's career. See Bitton-Ashkelony and Kofsky, *Monastic School of Gaza*, 22.

99. For an assessment of their similarities, see Colonna, *Zacaria Scolastico*, 53–55.

100. *Amm.* 357–60.

that they would not be persuaded by the argument and convinced to live as Christians again."[101]

The *Ammonius* derives from Aeneas's *Theophrastus*, but the explicit emphasis that Zacharias puts upon the Christian significance of its argument distinguishes his dialog from its model. Still, it is reasonable to wonder why Zacharias thought this adaptation was necessary, especially when it classifies belief in the eventual destruction of the world as a primary marker of confessional affiliation.[102] It seems that the answer to this question lies in the particular intellectual needs of a group of students who, like Zacharias, had experience of both the philosophical schools of Alexandria and the anti-Chalcedonian monasteries of Palestine. The oral traditions circulating in the 480s in these anti-Chalcedonian monasteries were filled with visions, portents, and other divine communications either suggesting that the council of Chalcedon was a sign of the end of the world or equating pro-Chalcedonian leaders like Juvenal of Jerusalem with the Antichrist. Much of this material came from the disciples of Peter the Iberian, a group to which Zacharias had close ties. Furthermore, it was preserved by John Rufus, one of Zacharias's friends at about the same time that he composed the *Ammonius*.[103] No doubt some of this apocalyptic thinking was influenced by the general Christian unease associated with the approach of the year 500, but we should not disregard the importance that these stories had in demonstrating God's extreme distaste for Chalcedonian leadership and in defining the necessity of anti-Chalcedonian resistance.

If we understand Zacharias's defense of the destructibility of the world in this intellectual context, its significance becomes clearer. This was a philosophical defense of a point that mattered particularly to students with an interest in both philosophy and anti-Chalcedonian ascetic culture. Notions of the world that were consistent with the doctrines of great thinkers were important to students of philosophy who, after all, spent a great deal of time considering such notions. These were young men who particularly valued truth and, perhaps for this reason, found themselves uncomfortable overlooking the cultural ambiguities that often allowed Christians to cull from pagan learning "whatever was useful while smiling at the myths."[104]

This concern for truth had added import because, as associates of ascetics like Peter the Iberian, these students had a conviction that the doctrines of the council of Chalcedon were wrong. On the question of the world's eternity, the teaching of philosophers and the ideas of their ascetic mentors clashed. If their philosophical teacher was correct and the world could not be destroyed, then the eschatological

101. *Amm.* 1001–4.
102. This is doubly curious when one considers that the *Theophrastus* had appeared in the late 480s and, according to the *Life of Severus* 90, Aeneas was well known to Zacharias's peers.
103. On their communication, see *Vit. Sev.* 86.
104. Choricius of Gaza, *Laud. Marc.* 1.2.6.1–4.

visions that underpinned this student belief that Chalcedon was the height of apostasy would be suspect. Aeneas had previously addressed these objections from a philosophical standpoint, but he did not make plain the Christian significance of his argument. By reworking the philosophical arguments of Aeneas's *Theophrastus* into the explicitly Christian exchanges of the *Ammonius,* Zacharias refashioned them in a way that resonated for individuals who participated in both ascetic and sophistic cultural circles.

The *Ammonius* and the *Life of Isaiah* are documents that highlight the particular impact that Zacharias's ascetic and sophistic interactions had on his intellectual conceptions of the world. Though they are different types of texts that deal with seemingly disconnected themes, it is essential that we appreciate them as the products of one mind. The *Ammonius,* while primarily a philosophical dialog, also must be appreciated as a document supporting beliefs that were important to anti-Chalcedonians. The *Life of Isaiah* was a hagiography that also contained references important to Christian students of pagan intellectuals. Zacharias's compositions, then, provide us with a unique opportunity to see how he created a particular discourse from the diverse cultural ideas circulating in the Palestinian and Egyptian intellectual world of the later fifth century. This was his own discourse, neither fully sophistic nor fully ascetic, but completely comprehensible to those whose minds were shaped in these two intellectual environments.

A STUDENT RIOT AND ITS COMMEMORATION: THE "LIFE OF PARALIUS"

Over time, the personal and intellectual challenges that Zacharias and his fellow anti-Chalcedonian student-*philoponoi* faced while studying in an environment dominated by pagan Neoplatonists generated great hostility towards some of their teachers. It also contributed to a general suspicion of the religious motivations of their professors and fellow students. Zacharias and his friends did not face these social and intellectual challenges alone, however. Under the guidance of the monks of the Enaton, some of whom were alumni of the city's sophistic and philosophical schools, Zacharias and his student-*philoponoi* friends evidently came to see all of their scholastic interactions through a confessional prism. This extended far beyond their particular concern for the theological implications of Neoplatonic philosophy. In fact, Zacharias proudly explains how he would try to influence the literary tastes of fellow students so that they turned away from pagan authors like Libanius and embraced Christian writers like Basil.[105] For these young men, every element of the scholastic environment had a specific religious meaning, and pagan influences, real or imagined, always threatened proper anti-Chalcedonian belief.

105. *Vit. Sev.* 13.

This charged backdrop helps to explain the aggressive reaction that Zacharias and his fellow students had to the beating of Paralius. As described above, Paralius's fellow students beat him up because he publicly attacked the integrity of their teacher Horapollon and a number of the philosophers with whom their teacher associated.[106] His beating was less a defense of pagan practices than a corrective action designed to defend Horapollon's honor and teach Paralius to mind his place in the school's scholastic hierarchy. Zacharias and his two friends understood these circumstances but, when they came upon this scene, they still immediately joined Paralius in screaming that "one who wished to be a Christian should not suffer in this way."[107] Although Horapollon's students protested that the beating was motivated not by a general dislike of Christians but by a specific hostility towards Paralius, this failed to sway the student-*philoponoi*. To them, Paralius's beating, like Ammonius's argument for the eternity of the world and Pamprepius's support for Illus, had only a religious significance. But unlike these other points of tension within the Alexandrian scholastic environment, this violence represented a direct physical threat to pious anti-Chalcedonian students. It could then serve as a spectacle that focused public attention upon the extremely inhospitable religious environment created in Alexandria's schools by the city's pagan teachers.

Although this student hostility grew out of roots set deeply within certain segments of the Alexandrian anti-Chalcedonian ascetic community, these complaints did not resonate with everyone. When Zacharias and his friends turned up with Paralius at the Enaton, the leadership of the monastery had to be made to understand that Paralius "had suffered unjustly for having abused the error of pagans" and had "offered Christ these sufferings for his sake."[108] Indeed, while some monks immediately appreciated the religious significance of the situation, the Enaton leadership became interested in intervening only after it had heard Zacharias's argument that the beating grew out of a broader climate that encouraged paganism, disadvantaged anti-Chalcedonian Christianity, and punished criticism. With Zacharias and his friends providing the narrative context, the bruised and battered Paralius could illustrate graphically the worst elements of a broader student-*philoponoi* narrative of religious conflict in the Alexandrian schools.

Once Salomon and the other Enaton monks became convinced that there had been a religious motivation behind Paralius's beating, the student-*philoponoi* version of events swept through the city. Zacharias and his friends had successfully defined the meaning of this event, but they quickly lost all control over the actions taken in response to it. Salomon led a group of monks on the nine-mile journey into Alexandria. He used his connections in the city to "stir up many of the leaders

---

106. *Vit. Sev.* 22–23. For discussion of these events, see chapter 3, above.
107. *Vit. Sev.* 23–24.
108. *Vit. Sev.* 24.

of the city" against the pagans and used his influence to bring the beating to the attention of the patriarch.[109] He also summoned Aphthonius, a Christian teacher of rhetoric, and his cohort of students. This assemblage then presented itself before the prefect of the city in order to demand the punishment of Horapollon and his students. Fearing the worst, Horapollon fled the city on Friday evening. This set the stage for the Saturday raid on the Menouthis shrine of Isis, the Sunday liturgy during which acclamations were chanted against Horapollon, and the parade of idols from Menouthis that afternoon.[110]

By the end of the weekend, Zacharias and his associates could celebrate these events as a complete triumph over the teachers and students who they felt had challenged their anti-Chalcedonian worldview. These four students had managed to turn the attention of the Enaton monks and the Alexandrian public to the city's schools and, because of their words, the public had seen in these classrooms exactly the sort of inhospitable environment that the young anti-Chalcedonian students described. The same hostility towards pagan teachers that later flowed through Zacharias's written work inspired this stage of the riot.

Paralius's beating and its aftermath had a profound transformative effect on the Alexandrian schools. Pagan teachers like Horapollon, Asclepiodotus, Isidore, and their associates found themselves objects of public scrutiny. As the student-*philoponoi* portrait of life in the schools of these Neoplatonic teachers entered the Alexandrian imagination, the pressure on these professors increased. The next year saw the imperially sponsored investigation of Nicomedes, an inquiry that led to the arrest and torture of Horapollon, the flight of Isidore, Damascius, and Asclepiodotus, and the infamous doctrinal compromise made by Ammonius.[111] This chain of events dramatically changed the face of Alexandrian teaching. The men who figured most prominently in the oral traditions celebrating pagan activity among the city's teachers had either been beaten into silence or forced to leave the city.[112] Others, like Ammonius and, ultimately, Horapollon, remained in the city, but at great cost to their reputations.[113] The failure of these intellectual leaders to respond "philosophically" to this investigation set off a crisis of confidence within the community of pagan Neoplatonists. By convincing Alexandrian Christian authorities of the spiritual dangers posed by these pagan teachers, the student *philoponoi* had succeeded in neutralizing some of the most dangerous influences from the schools.

---

109. *Vit. Sev.* 25.
110. *Vit. Sev.* 27–35. These events are described more fully in chapter 1, above, and chapter 8, below.
111. For discussion of these events, see chapter 3, above.
112. For these men, see chapter 3, above.
113. Note the comments of Damascius, *Vit. Is.* 118 (Ammonius) and 120B (Horapollon).

Their victory remained incomplete, however. While the riot and subsequent investigation removed the most uncompromising teachers and the most explicit pagan influences from the Alexandrian scholastic environment, they failed to affect the content of the classroom instruction. Because Paralius's beating had done nothing to interest a wider public in, say, the anti-Chalcedonian implications of Aristotelian ideas about the eternity of the world, eternalist teaching continued without interruption in the schools of the city.[114] In the 490s, it seems that the student-*philoponoi* decided to fight directly against the influence of pagan teachers.[115] Zacharias's *Ammonius* stands out as a clear product of this historical moment. The audacity of Zacharias's direct attack upon the character and intellectual credibility of his teacher Ammonius far exceeded the bounds of respectful philosophical debate. Absent the blows Ammonius's reputation had received from the riot and Nicomedes' subsequent investigation, it is unlikely that Zacharias would have dared to launch this sort of brazen assault. Circumstances, however, left him emboldened at the same moment that his teacher appeared greatly weakened.

Zacharias acted with similar audacity against his pagan fellow students. He writes that, following the death of his friend Menas, he delivered a funeral oration before an assembled crowd of students.[116] Menas was widely liked and this speech was given before a mixed audience of pagans and Christians who had gathered to honor the memory of a deceased intellectual brother. Zacharias's provocative speech deliberately exceeded the bounds of propriety within an intellectual context. Zacharias "made mention of the destruction of the pagan idols . . . The pagans, who we had invited to come and hear, and who came without knowing what I would say, cried over their misfortune and one of them called out in anger 'If you had the intention of speaking about the gods, why did you bring us to the tomb of your friend?'"[117]

This oration, while extremely inappropriate, also had great symbolic importance. Like Zacharias, Menas had a conflicted identity within the scholastic environment. He was both a friend to pagan classmates and a dedicated member of the anti-Chalcedonian student-*philoponoi*. His funeral, then, represented an opportunity to commemorate his person and to define his memory for those with whom he had studied. Zacharias's speech was so offensive because it offered a definition of Menas that was very much at odds with the one that much of his audience expected. Many of the students in the audience evidently expected to celebrate Menas as a conciliatory figure who had maintained good relations with

114. On this note Watts, *City and School*, 222–31 as well as chapter 3, above.

115. Once begun by the generation of Zacharias Scholasticus, this task was evidently continued by subsequent Alexandrian *philoponoi* like John Philoponus. On this see Watts, *City and School*, 237–55. Note too the discussion of Philoponus in L. MacCoull, "Philosophy in its Social Context," in *Egypt in the Byzantine World, 300–700*, ed. R. Bagnall (Cambridge, 2007), 67–82.

116. *Vit. Sev.* 45–46.

117. *Vit. Sev.* 45–46.

both pagan and Christian fellow students. A speech emphasizing this part of Menas's life would have provided a welcome opportunity for Alexandrian students to move beyond the religious divisions that Paralius's beating had opened in their community. It would have reaffirmed the values of brotherhood and collegiality that late antique schools worked to build and, perhaps, given these students a model to follow as they worked towards reconciliation.

Zacharias chose instead to use this occasion to memorialize Menas's role as an anti-Chalcedonian partisan. He turned his audience's attention away from Menas's friendly relationships with his colleagues and instead emphasized the vigor with which Menas combated paganism. By giving such a speech at Menas's tomb, Zacharias had robbed the larger scholastic community of a symbolic figure of reconciliation in order to celebrate the recent victory of the student-*philoponoi*. He wanted to embrace, not abandon, these events.

Zacharias's funeral oration suggests the degree to which the riot had become a central moment in the history of this group of anti-Chalcedonian students. Menas's funeral only began the process through which Zacharias and his friends crafted a more confident historical narrative in which anti-Chalcedonian students challenged and prevailed over their pagan teachers. At the center of this effort to frame a new, communal, historical narrative was a text that would later become a part of Zacharias's *Life of Severus*.[118] Although, like the *Ammonius,* Zacharias probably published this text when he was living in Constantinople, the themes it advances and the powerful use it makes of contemporary Alexandrian personalities suggests either a primary or a secondary audience of current and former anti-Chalcedonian students of the Alexandrian schools.[119]

The *Life of Severus* is the modern name for the work that Zacharias entitled "A History of the Deeds of Severus." While the text bears some striking formal resemblances to fifth- and sixth-century biographies, it is far from clear that Zacharias intended for the work to be received as a biography.[120] Instead, he frames it as

---

118. For this argument, see E. Watts, "Winning the Intracommunal Dialogues: Zacharias Scholasticus' *Life of Severus*," *JECS* 13 (2005), 437–64. Elements of this discussion first appeared in that article.

119. The bold rhetorical move of attacking living pagan teachers by name would resonate much less in Constantinople than in an Alexandrian cultural environment. The same is true of Zacharias's concern with the particular force of Alexandrian pagan teaching and anecdotes. A cultivated audience in Constantinople may have appreciated these things abstractly, but they lacked personal experience of them. These texts would not have had the same appeal for them as they did for men who shared Zacharias's experiences studying in Alexandria. In fact, we have good evidence that much of Zacharias's work that now survives in Syriac circulated in Alexandria. His *Ecclesiastical History,* for example, was sent back to Amida as part of a collection of books collected by bishop Marē during his exile in Alexandria in the 520s. On this, see Allen, "Zachariah Scholasticus and the *Historia Ecclesiastica* of Evagrius Scholasticus," 471–88.

120. See, for example, the comments of R. A. Darling Young, "Zacharias: *The Life of Severus*," in *Ascetic Behavior in Greco-Roman Antiquity*, ed. V. Wimbush (Minneapolis, 1990), 312–13.

a defense of Severus's character against a recently published pamphlet. This alleged that Severus had conducted pagan sacrifices while a student in Berytus.[121] The work itself is made up of four sections. It begins with a brief fictitious conversation between Zacharias and an unnamed associate in which Zacharias learns about the pamphlet and the slanders it contains. The next section turns to Severus's early life, family background, and rhetorical education in Alexandria. It describes how Menas predicted that Severus would become a great bishop, and then recounts the series of events involving Paralius.[122] Menas's funeral concludes the section. Zacharias then shifts settings to Berytus, the location of Severus's legal study. Here too, Zacharias focuses upon a group of students with close ties to anti-Chalcedonian Palestinian monasteries, a group Severus joined part of the way through law school. The final section of the text outlines the fate of these students after graduation, with particular emphasis placed upon Severus's own decision to forego his law career and join a Palestinian monastery. Zacharias then concludes by describing Severus's role in arguing against the actions of Elias, the Chalcedonian patriarch of Jerusalem, and Severus's ultimate selection as patriarch of Antioch.[123]

From this basic outline, one can see that Zacharias structured his defense of Severus around the notion that the future bishop participated in anti-pagan actions throughout his scholastic career. Zacharias is trying to convince his readers that Severus could not ever have been a pagan because he manifested the same basic character attributes when he was a student, a Palestinian ascetic, an anti-Chalcedonian advocate, and a powerful candidate for bishop. In Zacharias's telling Severus underwent an ascetic and spiritual progression, but his basic Christian piety remained unchanged throughout his life.

The Alexandrian section of the text fits badly within this larger composition. Instead of Severus, it focuses upon Paralius and the riot his beating touched off. In fact, the discussion of Paralius's life fills thirty pages of text—and Severus does not receive even a single mention. One can contrast this, for example, with the description of anti-pagan activity in the law schools of Berytus. As in Alexandria, Severus played only a small part in these actions.[124] Zacharias, however, carefully contrived a role for him as an all-important advisor who approved each step of the proceedings.[125] Unlike the Alexandrian section, Zacharias's retelling of events in Berytus advances the goal of establishing Severus's anti-pagan credentials.

121. "The slanderer attacked him not only on the basis of his way of life and conduct, but also because formerly he worshipped evil demons and idols" (*Vit. Sev.* 9).
122. *Vit. Sev.* 24.
123. *Vit. Sev.* 100–105. On this, see Steppa, *John Rufus*, 13; and R. A. Darling, "The patriarchate of Severus of Antioch, 512–518" (PhD diss. University of Chicago, 1982), 27–30.
124. R. A. Darling Young, "Zacharias: *Life of Severus*," 323, comments that "Severus seems to have played an ambiguous role at best" in these events.
125. E.g., *Vit. Sev.* 65; 70.

The Paralius material differs from the rest of the *Life of Severus* in an even more striking way. It has its own sophisticated internal structure and is organized like a biography of Paralius. It begins with an account of his family and early education, moves to his conversion and proper education as a Christian, describes the monastery he founded and the conversions he brought about, and then concludes with his premature death.[126] In its story of Paralius's spiritual progression from a pagan to an anti-Chalcedonian ascetic, the text provides a positive illustration of the benefits that come to students from a productive engagement with ascetic culture. At the same time, except in quite general terms, this narration appears to contribute little to the overall thematic goal of framing the career of Severus. Severus had no known involvement with either Paralius or the particular teachers who are singled out in the text. Furthermore, Paralius's spiritual progression is somewhat at odds with Zacharias's implied statement that Severus could not have experimented with paganism because his later ascetic affiliations are prefigured in his earlier student activity. Consequently, in both its structure and its content, this part of the text seems to stand alone as an independent composition—possibly as the remnants of a previously-published and self-contained *Life of Paralius*.

The themes upon which Zacharias focuses in this text also suggest that the material was once published in a different form. These themes mirror those found in the *Life of Isaiah* and the *Ammonius*. As in the *Life of Isaiah*, his Paralius biography describes ascetic leaders who possessed an intelligence that was manifestly superior to that of pagan philosophers.[127] Like the *Ammonius*, Zacharias's discussion of Paralius's life also indicts the credibility and judgment of the Alexandrian pagan intellectual leadership. The city's pagan philosophers not only proved themselves unable to answer Paralius's theological questions, but they also displayed an unphilosophical cowardice by fleeing Alexandria following Paralius's accusations.[128] Finally, later in the narration, Zacharias introduced Illus's revolt to show both the poor judgment of pagan intellectuals and the inefficacy of their prayers.[129]

---

126. On the biographic structure, see P. Cox, *Biography in Late Antiquity: A Quest for the Holy Man* (Berkeley, 1983), 3–17. The Paralius section seems to work within this structure, but it does not perfectly conform to the model described by Cox. Notable in Zacharias's text is the focus upon a chronological account of Paralius's life; there is much discussion of *praxeis* (deeds) and little of *ēthos* (character). This may in part be due to the short period of time between Paralius's conversion and his death. He joined the Enaton monastery not long after his baptism (*Vit. Sev.* 39). After the death of Stephen, his mentor at Enaton, he returned home, founded a Christian ascetic community, and died not long after. As his conversion likely dates to 486 or 487, his death probably occurred in the 490s. Not coincidentally, no material in the Paralius section of the text postdates Paralius's death.

127. So, for example, the monk Stephen is one who "had received from God the grace to vanquish totally (pagans), in discussions." (*Vit. Sev.* 16).

128. *Vit. Sev.* 27. Compare their behavior with Damascius's discussion of the necessity for a philosopher to stand firm when faced with danger (*Vit. Is.* 146B).

129. *Vit. Sev.* 40.

But the significance of the Paralius text goes beyond simply a reiteration of the points found in the *Ammonius* and the *Life of Isaiah*. Broadly speaking, this putative *Life of Paralius* contains another type of attack that is less doctrinal than it is cultural. It looks to neutralize the orally transmitted accounts of pagan miracles that were circulating within the Alexandrian intellectual community. A great deal of this oral testimony circulated in the Alexandrian schools of the 480s and, as we have seen, influenced student religious conviction. Indeed, Paralius himself continued to hold to his pagan beliefs long after his brother began to raise difficult theological questions because he had heard the account of the miraculous conception of Asclepiodotus's child.

Zacharias's attack on these oral testimonies centered upon the story of Asclepiodotus's child and was carefully designed to render these testimonies collectively unbelievable.[130] Asclepiodotus is introduced as a man who attracted the admiration of pagans through his magical skill[131] and who stumbled through ever more elaborate pagan infertility treatments (including sexual unification with an idol) before lying about the birth of his child. In fact, Zacharias's discussion of this anecdote has a similar dynamic to the philosophical discussions in the *Ammonius*. In both cases, there is a systematic disproof of a notion that pagan teachers held to be authoritative. This takes place within the Alexandrian scholastic environment and focuses upon a student's demonstration of the duplicity of that community's intellectual leadership. The other long narrative in the text, the discussion of the Christian attack on the Menouthis Isis shrine, should similarly be understood as a part of this pagan-Christian dialog within the schools. Instead of attacking a prominent leader of the pagan intellectual community, this account seeks to discredit a locus of pagan religious activity.

Zacharias's description of the Menouthis Isis shrine and the raid in which it was plundered works as both a traditional description of violence directed against a pagan temple and a narration that highlights the event as a triumph for the student-*philoponoi*.[132] Zacharias vividly describes the public mockery of pagan

---

130. Although Zacharias just focuses upon the Asclepiodotus story, his retelling of it unfolds much like the accounts preserved in Damascius's *Life of Isidore*. Both the Asclepiodotus story and some of the tales told by Damascius emphasize the particular divine privileges given to a philosophical initiate. They also sanction the activities described with a divinely inspired dream. In one case among many, Damascius tells of a cave near a shrine in Phrygia that emitted deadly fumes. Because he was an initiate, Damascius was able to enter the cave, descend to its end, and emerge unhurt. He then had a dream in which the Mother of the gods insisted that he celebrate a feast symbolizing his salvation from death. (*Vit. Is.* 87A).

131. This appears to be an accurate description of the opinion contemporaries held of Asclepiodotus (cf. Damascius, *Vit. Is.* 85A).

132. On the formulaic elements, see Brakke, *Demons*, 213–39. Despite these formulaic elements, it seems reasonable to accept the basic course of events that Zacharias describes. His text aims to assert student-*philoponoi* ownership for these events and most of his energy is exerted in inserting

images, the pagan use of demonic language to describe gods, and the night that he spent alongside the impotent Menouthan idols. Numerous contemporary Christian texts parallel these descriptions in order to simultaneously attack paganism and positively define the Christian achievements of the text's subject.[133] At the same time, one cannot discount the roles played by Paralius, Zacharias, and the student-*philoponoi* in these events. In Zacharias's retelling, all of these anti-pagan actions are theirs. The discrediting and sacking of the shrine resulted from actions taken by Paralius. He and the student-*philoponoi* together disproved the power of the pagan gods by spending the night with their idols. Even the public procession, which represents the culmination of communal anti-pagan feeling, is partially situated within this Christian and pagan intellectual dialog by the chanted condemnation of Horapollon.[134] Zacharias's description of the Menouthis raid paints this as a triumph of Christianity, but also as a triumph that reflects particularly upon the student-*philoponoi* and the religious situation in the schools.[135]

In the aftermath of this riot the rhetoric and expectations of the student-*philoponoi* changed. They began to demonstrate a startling degree of self-confidence. Before the riot, the activity of these young men consisted mainly in trying to engage their fellow students in theological conversations about Christianity.[136] They disliked the influence of their pagan teachers but did not directly confront them. After Paralius's beating, however, they began to attack the ideas and character of their teachers. In their minds, this event had transformed them from impotent bystanders to engaged reformers. Zacharias (and, presumably, his friends) came to believe that these events had presented them with both the op-

---

people like Menas and Paralius into his narration. This case becomes infinitely more difficult to make if the reader thinks that he fabricated events that occurred quite recently. This issue will be revisited at greater length below.

133. For the demonic language, see Brakke, *Demons*, 216–26. On the mocking procession of idols, see Socrates *HE* 5.16–17 and Rufinus *HE* 11.22. For staying or sleeping beside pagan gods, see Athanasius's *Vit. Ant.* 12–14 and, much later, *Life of Daniel the Stylite*, 14–15. On iconoclastic anti-pagan violence in Egypt, see D. Frankfurter, "'Things Unbefitting Christians:' Violence and Christianization in 5th century Panopolis," *JECS* 8.2 (2000), 282–84.

134. On processions in the Alexandrian environment, see Haas, *Alexandria in Late Antiquity: Topography and Social Conflict* (Baltimore, 1997), 82–90. John of Nikiu, *Chron.* 84.103 shows how popular chants tended to mark such occasions as communal triumphs. See as well *Historia Acephala* 5.13 for chants against bishop Lucius.

135. D. Frankfurter's idea of the "regional activity" of the shrine ("The Consequences of Hellenism," 189–192) is a good one—but this is not all that Zacharias is describing. His interest in the Menouthis shrine comes only because of the role it played in intellectual communities.

136. Unfortunately, our only indication of their pre-riot activities comes from *Vit. Sev.* 12–13, a segment of the text composed thirty years after the violence.

portunity and the means to remake the Alexandrian schools into spaces that supported instead of challenged their anti-Chalcedonian worldview. The beating of Paralius was celebrated as a great communal achievement, first in speeches given by the students and later in texts like the biography of Paralius. The optimism that flowed out from it also led to the publication of other texts that challenged pagan philosophical teachings that conflicted with the anti-Chalcedonian worldview of Peter the Iberian and the monks at the Enaton. These, presumably, echoed more direct personal challenges.

Perhaps most striking is how long anti-Chalcedonians with ties to the Alexandrian Neoplatonic environment continued these challenges to the authority of Alexandrian teachers. In addition to Zacharias's *Ammonius*, two other extant Christian philosophical refutations of eternalist writings appeared in the decades following the riot. One of these was written by Procopius of Gaza and the other by the Alexandrian John Philoponus—we have no other contemporary texts of this sort from other parts of the Roman world.[137] In fact, John Philoponus had personal ties to the same Gazan and Alexandrian anti-Chalcedonian environment that inspired Zacharias, and he seems to have drawn upon these to support a bid to overturn eternalist dominance in the Alexandrian philosophical schools. This proliferation of texts suggests that Zacharias was not alone in sensing both the need and the opportunity to respond to the tension between local anti-Chalcedonian eschatological discourse and Neoplatonic philosophical teaching.

The events surrounding Paralius's beating show both the power of communal discourse and its malleability. The escalation of violence caused by Zacharias and his student-*philoponoi* friends was a direct result of the way in which they had come to construct their community. They had carved a precariously balanced mixture of sophistic and anti-Chalcedonian ascetic cultural values out of what they felt to be a pagan-dominated intellectual environment. The stories that these students told and the intellectual discussions that they had with one another reinforced their view that leading Alexandrian teachers sought to pull them away from the religious ideas of their ascetic mentors. Such notions pushed these young men to act aggressively in response to Paralius's beating. At the same time, the events following the beating seem to have catalyzed an aggressive textual response among the student-*philoponoi*. Celebrations of communal triumph now figured prominently in the writing and historical memory of the community. In addition, a general optimism for continued change seems to have pervaded its membership. Their challenges to Neoplatonic teachers and their teaching became more brazen as their expectation for success increased. This course of events shows plainly the

---

137. For John Philoponus, see Watts, *City and School*, 237–55.

dynamic interplay between the ideas that circulated within a group and the actions that the community took.

Late antique monasteries often strike observers as highly structured environments in which individual monks followed well-defined routines, adopted rigorous ascetic practices, and endeavored to live according to the teachings of revered spiritual fathers. Indeed, communal ascetic life often depended upon a social environment in which ascetic progression was tied tightly to conformity with a uniform set of standards. Pachomius, for example, created a strict and relatively inflexible hierarchy within the *Koinonia* that allotted specific duties to individual monks. Ordinary monks lived in smaller houses of up to twenty men in which affairs were managed by a housemaster and social interactions between brothers helped to regulate the rhythms of daily life.

The personal and social bonds that joined these monks in a common ascetic project also encouraged them to adopt a set of communal values. All of these had at least an ostensible scriptural basis, which the Pachomian community reinforced in morning prayers and in the more intimate devotional discussions that filled the evening hours. It was through these and other, more informal conversations that monks learned about the history of their community, the impressive deeds of its founders, and the community's own ideas about how the lessons of Scripture could be applied practically in an individual monk's life. This social setting enabled monks to inform one another about the teachings and events that shaped the Pachomian community's history. Pachomius's project succeeded precisely because the friendships and quasi-familial relationships that individual monks developed with one another reinforced their commitment to the ideals of the larger group.

The distinctive routines of life within the Pachomian *Koinonia* facilitated the transmission of historical traditions and other stories that illustrated the practical application of the more esoteric teachings that monks heard from their elders. Non-Pachomian communities organized themselves and their days differently, but many seem to have encouraged similarly strong bonds to develop among their members. Indeed, the intense emotional ties encouraged by this sort of environment created a "totalizing discourse" designed to overwhelm and ultimately replace the values, ideals, and behaviors that once permitted monks to function in the wider world with the specific patterns of behavior that enabled them to succeed in a monastery.[138]

Monastery walls could not contain the power of this teaching nor could they prevent the spread of historical traditions and anecdotes that illustrated its practi-

---

138. Note on this the important discussion of Layton, "Rules, Patterns, and Power," 45–73, esp. 58–69.

cal application. As these ideas and stories began to circulate freely in surrounding cities and towns, monastic leaders began receiving outside visitors eager for instruction. Some visitors even established regular relationships with a monastic leader, in which they recognized him as a spiritual father and agreed to live according to his teaching.

There were limits to the practical effects that this teaching could have, however. This was true not just of secular monastic affiliates but of ascetics living within monasteries as well. While daily biblical exegesis could explain God's word and informal conversations could show how to apply this teaching to the realities of daily life, many monks still found it impossible to live according to the strict codes of conduct that the monastic leaders set for them. The challenges proved even greater for secular affiliates of these monasteries. While monks devoted all of their time to the struggle to discipline their bodies and minds, secular disciples balanced their ascetic commitments with other responsibilities. These men showed great devotion to ascetic communities and their heads, but they also found themselves occasionally forced to choose between the demands of their spiritual father and the obligations of their secular lives. Each of these men found himself bound by two distinct and very different sets of social expectations. Each consequently had to work hard to balance his spiritual and secular ambitions.

Perhaps no group of lay ascetic affiliates shows the tension between worldly and monastic ideals better than Christian Alexandrian students like Zacharias Scholasticus. Zacharias came to the city's schools with a strong attachment to the community of monks headed by the anti-Chalcedonian ascetic Peter the Iberian. The stories and ideas that circulated among Peter's ascetic followers in the 480s greatly reinforced his hostility to Chalcedon by championing the principled resistance of men like Timothy Aelurus and attacking proponents of Chalcedon like Juvenal of Jerusalem. Both Peter the Iberian and Timothy Aelurus drew upon eschatological ideas in their attacks on Chalcedonian leaders, and these notions permeated the theological discussions, illustrative stories, and historical traditions retold by their admirers. As a result, the secular affiliates of Peter the Iberian's monastery came away with a strongly held set of beliefs about the Council of Chalcedon.

When Zacharias left Gaza, he found a similar ascetic environment in the monastery of the Enaton, nine miles outside Alexandria. Not only did the monks of the Enaton advocate many of the same ideas as Zacharias's Gazan mentors, but they also seem to have held some of the same anti-Chalcedonian leaders in high regard. The Enaton proved particularly hospitable for another reason, however. Among its various *koinobia* was one made up in part by monks who had once been students in Alexandria's schools of rhetoric. These monks proved an invaluable resource for students like Zacharias and his friends because the scholastic environment in which they spent most of them time set strict and well-developed standards of conduct for its members. Perhaps egged on by the Enaton monks, these young men developed a profound distrust of their teachers, which caused them to see religious provocation in some unlikely places. A perfect example of this is Zacharias's reaction to the Aristotelian teaching that the world was eternal, an idea, he strongly asserted, that pulled people away from Christianity. It did, at least if one followed Zacharias in defining as proper Christians only those who accepted the anti-Chalcedonian eschatology of Peter the Iberian and Timothy Aelurus. It is, however, extremely unlikely that Ammonius or any of the other Alexandrian Neoplatonists anticipated (or even understood) Zacharias's peculiar reaction to an eight-hundred-year-old idea. The vigor of Zacharias's reaction, then, was fed by the tension that he felt between ideas presented in his classroom and the beliefs sustained by his personal relationships with anti-Chalcedonian ascetics.

This same sort of over-reaction characterized the response of Zacharias and his friends to Paralius's beating. They understood the conventions of student life and even appreciated the importance of rituals such as the hazing of new students.[139] Their experiences within the Alexandrian schools, however, led these young men to understand Paralius's beating not as the corrective action of scholastic older brothers but as a religious provocation. Furthermore, because Zacharias and his friends saw the hand of pagan professors behind every action taken in the schools, they immediately put the blame for this violence upon Paralius's teacher, Horapollon.

Zacharias's (inaccurate) description of the cause of these events reflected the specific experiences and frustrations of Alexandrian students who had affiliated themselves with anti-Chalcedonian monasteries. The particular circumstances of Paralius's beating made this explanation seem compelling to other Alexandrian Christians as well. Persuaded by Zacharias and his friends that Paralius's beating had been caused by a religiously inhospitable environment, the Alexandrian anti-Chalcedonian community acted against both the students who had attacked Paralius and the teachers who had corrupted their souls. The riot, then, represented a triumph for the worldview of the student-*philoponoi*.

The enthusiasm generated by this riot altered both the rhetoric and the behavior of the student-*philoponoi*. Judging by the tone and content of Zacharias's writings, he and his peers saw this as a transformative event that enabled them to seize control of the intellectual and theological agenda within the Alexandrian schools. In this way, a riot that saw its course shaped by the particular insecurities of a group of anti-Chalcedonian students became the centerpiece of a new communal history in which young men self-confidently proclaimed their success in exposing the personal and spiritual failings of their teachers.

---

139. E.g., *Vit. Sev.* 47.

PART THREE

Defining the Alexandrian Bishop

In his sermon, the patriarch of God (Peter Mongus) read the description we had sent of the idols, in which he indicated the material they were made from and the number of idols we had found. After that, the people eagerly brought all the graven images of the pagan gods, from the baths as well as from the houses, and placed them in the center and set them on fire. . . . (Peter) immediately summoned, before the Tychaion, the prefect of Egypt, the dux, and all who had any authority, such as those in the senate, the great men of the city, and the wealthy. When he was seated with them, he led in the pagan priest (34) and ordered him to stand up in a high place . . . (35) The people were shouting many similar things [i.e., insults] to the pagans, and praised Zeno, who ended in fear of God, who held the scepter of the empire at that moment, and Peter, the great patriarch, as well as the leaders of the city who were seated with him.

VIT. SEV. 33–34

ON SUNDAY, THE NARROW CONFLICT sparked by the beating of Paralius exploded into a broader disturbance that allowed Peter Mongus to display the awesome organizing powers available to the Alexandrian patriarch. Although it unfolded quickly, Peter Mongus precisely choreographed the final stage of this violence. The day began as a normal Sunday would, with crowds of congregants processing to the city's churches. Many already had learned of the affair involving Paralius and Horapollon; some perhaps knew that their bishop had sent a group of monks and student-*philoponoi* to the eastern suburb of Menouthis to sack an Isaic shrine. None of them, however, understood precisely why this had been done and all looked to their bishop to interpret the weekend's events for them.

By the time Peter began the service at the church of St. Michael on the site of the old Caesareum, a congregation of a few thousand people had probably assembled.[1] The bishop's opinion-makers then began preparing the gathered crowd for the subject of the day's ceremony. The *philoponoi* started leading the congregation in chants against the pagan teacher Horapollon. The crowd happily participated in this and the chants evidently continued until Peter began his sermon. The list that his agents had sent back served as the centerpiece of his presentation

---

1. The Caesareum precinct is described by Philo as "huge and conspicuous ... embellished with porticoes, libraries, chambers, groves, gateways, broadwalks, and courts." (Philo, *Leg. Ad Gaium* 151; given its context this description is probably somewhat exaggerated). It was converted into a church in the fourth century. No estimates survive for the capacity of the converted Caesareum, but three thousand people is not an unreasonable number for the size of a congregation that could be held in a large urban basilica. For this number see R. Krautheimer, *Three Christian Capitals: Topography and Politics* (Berkeley, 1983), 76.

and, as he read it out, the energy of the crowd built. The Eucharist followed the sermon and, after symbolically and collectively affirming their membership in the community of Christians, the energized thousands filed out of the church. The more excitable members of Peter's congregation rampaged through the city, pulling down whatever pagan statuary they could find in public spaces and private homes, and piling the *spolia* up to be burned.[2]

Peter then summoned all of the city's Christians to join him at an assembly outside of the city's Tychaion, a decommissioned pagan temple in the center of the city that may have bordered the city's scholastic quarter. As they gathered, Peter's flock would have looked up to see their bishop enthroned and flanked by the imperial officials and local notables who governed the city. None could have missed the symbolism. Whereas Peter used the morning service to teach his flock about the significance of the weekend's events, the afternoon assembly illustrated how the bishop now guided the entire city's response to them. And Peter guided the city along a familiar path. He sat and watched as twenty camels carried loads of religious objects before the crowd, with commentary provided by a terrified priest of Isis who had been abducted from Menouthis. Peter's *philoponoi* and other helpers led the crowd as it chanted insults against the priest and his gods. When the last object passed by and the show was over, the crowd chanted again—this time in a way that affirmed its loyalty to the emperor Zeno, its confidence in the Alexandrian city council, and, most importantly, its admiration for the patriarch. While one may think such acclamations a relatively unremarkable conclusion to a late antique public gathering, they were hard won.[3] For most of the 480s many anti-Chalcedonians in Alexandria had come to distrust (and occasionally denounce) Peter for his close theological cooperation with the emperor Zeno. On this Sunday, however, Peter had organized a spectacle that united the city behind him. With these concluding acclamations, he had brought about exactly the unifying effect he had sought.

This section of the book considers two essential elements that enabled Peter to achieve such a dramatic triumph. It first examines the unique mechanisms for shaping popular opinion that were available to bishops in major cities like Alexandria. The privileges and prerogatives of their office provided bishops with a set of tools that enabled them to build strong bonds with large numbers of followers. Bishops served as the spiritual guides of their congregations and the mediators through whom the teachings of Christ were communicated. They controlled con-

---

2. C. Haas has suggested that the baths in Kom el-Dikka may have been one of the areas that this mob plundered. On this see Haas, "Kôm el-Dikka in Context: The Auditoria and the History of Late Antique Alexandria," in *Alexandria: Auditoria of Kom el-Dikka and Late Antique Education*, ed. T. Derda, T. Markiewicz, and E. Wipszycka (Warsaw, 2007), 94.

3. Compare, for example, the failed attempt by supporters of the emperor Justinian to generate public acclamations of support for the emperor during the Nika Riot (*Chron. Pasch.* 623–24).

siderable resources that had been granted to the church to support the poorest members of their congregation.[4] Bishops also took upon themselves certain civic functions and sat in judgment of lawsuits brought by individual Christians.

A bishop needed to convince his congregation that he could provide effective spiritual and practical leadership. This could prove to be a most difficult task because Christian communities had particularly well-developed techniques for preserving and communicating their history, which taught congregations to expect their bishop to behave in particular ways. While this tendency affected all churches, it had particular implications for the Alexandrian see in the fifth century. In the fourth and early fifth centuries, Alexandria produced three paradigmatic bishops (Athanasius, Theophilus, and Cyril) who enjoyed unparalleled success in marshaling the spiritual, human, and financial resources available to them. They also showed themselves to be adept at convincing Alexandrian Christians of the justice and necessity of their actions, often by drawing explicitly upon the historical legacies of their predecessors. Theophilus, for example, frequently looked back to Athanasius during the early years of his episcopate. Cyril, for his part, used the historical precedents of both Theophilus and Athanasius to frame his actions. While this rhetoric often proved persuasive, a bishop who could not live up to these models had to fight the perception that he was ineffective. Peter Mongus unfortunately fit into this category for much of his career.

The tangible and rhetorical aspects of a bishop's authority will be explored in a chronologically organized survey of Alexandrian episcopal self-presentation in the fourth and fifth centuries. Unlike the first two sections of the book, this narrative will spread across three, thematically distinct chapters that all bear directly upon the Alexandrian environment. There are two reasons for this. First, whereas pagan and Christian student reactions to communal histories and value structures dominated the first two days of the riot, Peter Mongus used his authority to generate a particular set of responses on the third day. This requires us to be more aware of the options available to him as he encouraged Alexandrian Christians to think and behave in particular ways under these circumstances. In addition, our evidence demands this sort of specific, tripartite treatment. Alexandrian bishops positioned themselves in three distinct ways between the episcopate of Athanasius and the beginning of Peter Mongus's tenure. Upon ordination, Peter then had available to him three recent idioms that he could (and did) draw upon to define the nature of his position.[5] Each of these must be examined in order to properly understand the actions Peter took and the symbolism he used to explain them.

---

4. P. Brown, *Poverty and Leadership in the Later Roman Empire* (Hanover, 2002), 14–18; 49, 57–60.

5. Fifth-century Alexandrian bishops did recall earlier Alexandrian episcopal exemplars like Dionysius and Peter I, but they did so with less frequency. A notable fifth-century exception to this

The section's first chapter begins by looking at Athanasius and the efforts that he made to tie the authority of the bishop of Alexandria to his strong and unwavering advocacy of orthodoxy. Athanasius took advantage of a number of unique features of the early fourth-century church to shape popular perceptions about his own actions and those of his opponents. Although Athanasius had a mixed record in establishing the propriety of his actions during his lifetime, later historical traditions were less equivocal about his legacy. This owes much to formal Christian ceremonies. In the same way that religious services allowed living bishops to shape thinking about current affairs, so too did the liturgical commemoration of past bishops shape a congregation's understanding of its own history. This commemoration often smoothed over the rough edges of an individual's career to create a thematically consistent and easily apprehended historical profile.

The section's second chapter examines a different sort of historical profile. Just as Athanasius served as a model for episcopal defense of orthodoxy, bishop Theophilus's attack on the Alexandrian Serapeum and the complex of temples at Canopus marked him as an exemplar of anti-pagan leadership. Theophilus drew upon the personal ties he cultivated with both lay and ascetic followers to build support for his actions and used his position at the head of the church to fashion elaborate public spectacles that celebrated his victories. He then cemented these victories with extensive building projects that filled in the old pagan civic landscape with new Christian churches, martyria, and urban monasteries. The chapter concludes by showing how Theophilus's successor Cyril drew upon the legacies of both Athanasius and Theophilus. Early in his episcopate, Cyril choreographed a number of actions designed to evoke Theophilus. While Cyril never abandoned the Theophilan paradigm, his later actions show a more careful leader who drew upon different historical models to redefine himself as both an anti-pagan champion and a fighter for doctrinal orthodoxy.

The section's third chapter explores how the Council of Chalcedon limited the power of Cyril's successors, the Alexandrian bishops Dioscorus (444-451) and Timothy Aelurus (457-77), by setting their teachings outside of imperially sanctioned orthodoxy. Not only did this development deny these bishops access to imperial funds and render them less effective patrons, but it also forced each man into a lengthy exile. Fittingly, these two men looked to Athanasius for a historical model that explained their unwillingness to compromise in the face of imperial pressure. Despite the loss of financial and political patronage, the evocation of historical exemplars like Athanasius gave anti-Chalcedonian bishops a way to encourage their congregations to remain loyal.

---

is Peter the Iberian who, while not an Alexandrian, identified quite strongly with Peter I (*Vit. Pet. Ib.* 180–82). The apostle Mark was evoked often, but (for obvious reasons) he provides a less replicable model of leadership.

This course was closed to Peter Mongus, an opponent of Chalcedon who, later in his episcopate, entered into theological cooperation with the emperor Zeno. Peter's political circumstances prevented him from aggressively championing the anti-Chalcedonian ideas that had defined the careers of Dioscorus and Timothy Aelurus. At times, this made him appear to be a weak and ineffectual leader. Peter Mongus's decisive intervention against scholastic paganism in 486 defined him according to a different set of standards. Both Theophilus and Cyril had tried and failed to eliminate paganism in Menouthis; Peter used this moment as an occasion to succeed where his illustrious predecessors could not. Peter then took advantage of the power of his pulpit to define publicly, in the clearest terms, the larger meaning of the actions he ordered. In so doing, he sought to brand himself as an effective leader before a large and often skeptical public.

6

Creating the Legend of the Alexandrian Bishop

On May 5, 365 an order from the praetorian prefect of the East was posted in Alexandria in the name of the emperor Valens. It expelled from their cities all of the bishops who had been exiled by the emperor Constantius and returned to their sees under Julian.[1] The law cleverly left enforcement of this up to the city council of each city. If an affected bishop did not leave, the council that governed his city was to pay a fine of three hundred pounds of gold. Additional financial penalties fell upon provincial and military officials who acquiesced in this civic disobedience.[2] By the terms of this letter, it seemed that Athanasius, the Nicene bishop of Alexandria, was to be forced into exile for the fifth time in his long career at the head of the Alexandrian church.

Although Athanasius was a formidable figure in the city, Valens's letter had its desired effect on the anxious civic and provincial leaders who governed Alexandria. "Because the curiales were not numerous, with the aid of the prefect Flavian and his administration, they undertook to force the bishop from the city, as much to obey the imperial order as because of the great deal of gold."[3] The population

---

1. Socrates Scholasticus, *HE* 4.13; Sozomen, *HE* 6.12.5. Sozomen indicates that this letter was sent directly to the provincial governors, bypassing the prefects. The procedure described by Socrates seems more consistent with late Roman norms. For discussion of this episode, see T. D. Barnes, *Athanasius and Constantius: Theology and Politics in the Constantinian Empire* (Cambridge, MA, 1993), 162–63, and N. Lenski, *Failure of Empire: Valens and the Roman State in the Fourth Century* A.D. (Berkeley, 2002), 247.

2. For the penalty on the *curia*, see *Historia Acephala* 5.1. Sozomen, *HE* 6.12.5 notes the additional penalties on provincial and military officials.

3. *Historia Acephala* 5.2.

of Alexandria responded in outrage. "Many Christians resisted this and spoke out against it before the civic leaders and judges. They affirmed that Athanasius was not subject to this definition and this imperial order because Constantius did not persecute him but in fact restored him and Julian had persecuted him."[4] Technically, this argument was true, but it was also deceptive—the bishop had been banished and restored by both Constantius and Julian—and the prefect Flavian remained unconvinced. The crowd responded angrily. "The people [ran] together from every quarter; there was much commotion and perturbation throughout the city; an insurrection was expected."[5] This slow-boiling anger continued for over a month and prompted the prefect to write to the emperor for further instructions. Until such time as he got a response, Athanasius could remain in the city.

In October, Athanasius finally chose to go into hiding, fleeing his church the night before a military detachment turned up to arrest him. He spent his short exile in and around Alexandria.[6] When he returned to the city in February of 366, he was met by the imperial *notarius* Brasidas who stood at the head of a delegation of "city councilors and a multitude from among the Christian population" gathered to lead the bishop to his church.[7] Athanasius's return had become a civic celebration sanctioned by imperial and civic officials and energized by a huge crowd of enthusiastic supporters. The remarkable support that the prelate received from his congregation enabled him to triumph over a hostile emperor and a nervous local political establishment.[8]

Although 366 offers the most dramatic such scene, Athanasius had enjoyed similar processions in the past. Upon his return from a seven-year exile in 346, for example, "crowds of people and all of the authorities" of the city of Alexandria greeted him "with a triumphal procession at the one hundredth mile marker" leading to the city.[9] And, in August of 355, the raucous calls of Athanasius's supporters nearly prevented the execution of another order pushing Athanasius into exile.[10]

---

4. *Historia Acephala* 5.2.

5. Sozomen, *HE* 6.12. For the duration of the rioting, see *Historia Acephala* 5.3. Though Sozomen seems to compress the events of this month into a very short time span, his description of the rioting is more informative than that of the *HA*. On these events, note as well the testimony of Socrates, 4.13; Epiphanius, *Adv. Haers.* 68.11; Theophanes 5861.

6. For his night flight, see the *Historia Acephala* 5.4. Both Socrates and Sozomen record that he hid in an ancestral tomb, presumably in or near to the city of Alexandria itself. On this see Barnes, *Athanasius*, 163, 291n66.

7. *Historia Acephala* 5.7.

8. The revolt of Procopius had given Athanasius an inadvertent assist in turning this trick. For the revolt of Procopius and its effect on the religious policies of Valens, see Lenski, *Failure of Empire*, 246–49 and Barnes, *Athanasius*, 163.

9. *Festal Index* 18; cf. *Historia Acephala* 1.1–2. Note as well Barnes, *Athanasius*, 92.

10. Barnes, *Athanasius* 118–19. On the initial efforts of the notarius Diogenes to push Athanasius out, see Athanasius, *Ap. ad Const.* 22; *Historia Acephala* 1.9. For the eventual success of these efforts

Throughout his episcopate, Athanasius gradually developed a distinctive personal identity that emphasized a particular sort of spiritual authority and promised his followers divinely inspired leadership. His efforts generated such a large and passionate following among Alexandrian Nicene Christians that even imperial authorities found themselves grudgingly backing away from open confrontation with the bishop.

MECHANISMS OF EPISCOPAL POWER

Athanasius's career shows how potent a weapon popularity could prove for a late antique bishop. Athanasius used many different tools to develop so ardent a following but, early in his episcopate, Athanasius relied heavily upon the financial and material resources given to the Alexandrian church by the emperor. Beginning with the emperor Constantine, large sums of money were made available to the church for construction projects and general support of its activities.[11] Lucrative grants in kind supplemented these monetary gifts. In Alexandria, the bishop received a portion of the grain shipments that passed through the city to give to widows in his own congregation.[12] Some of this he also sent along to his subordinate bishops throughout Egypt and Libya for distribution in their territories. The emperor also occasionally granted the church other items, like a batch of linen tunics once given to Athanasius.[13] Private giving far surpassed these imperial grants.[14] Some of these gifts came from bishops themselves,[15] but most wealth

---

the following February see Athanasius, *Ap. ad Const.* 25; *Defense of his Flight* 6.1; *Historia Acephala* 1.10; *Festal Index* 28.

11. Note, for example, Eusebius, *Vit. Con.* 2.46. For discussion of this trend, see Barnes, *Athanasius*, 176–78; P. Brown, *Power and Persuasion: Towards a Christian Empire* (Madison, WI, 1992), 90, and *Poverty and Leadership in the Later Roman Empire* (Hanover, 2002), 26–32. The level of imperial support for construction varied between cities but, in Alexandria, direct imperial support for construction continued into at least the fifth century. On this see J. Thomas, *Private Religious Foundations in the Byzatnine Empire* (Washington, 1987), 60–61; and L. Antonini, "La chiese cristiane nell'Egitto dal IV a IX secolo secondi i documenti dei papyri greci," *Aegyptus* 20 (1940), 129–208, at 161 no. 2 and 163 no. 18.

12. Athanasius, *Defense against the Arians*, 18.2.

13. Athanasius, *Defense against the Arians*, 60.2. For interpretation of this grant see Barnes, *Athanasius*, 178–79.

14. C. Rapp, *Holy Bishops in Late Antiquity: The Nature of Christian Leadership in an Age of Transition* (Berkeley, 2005), 215–19; Brown, *Poverty*, 32.

15. Rapp, *Holy Bishops*, 199–200. For the sale of property see Rapp, 212–15 as well as L. W. Countryman, *The Rich Christian in the Church of the Early Empire: Contradictions and Accommodations* (New York, 1980), 114–18. Many bishops did not fit this category, with Athanasius a prime example (suggested by Rufinus, *HE* 10.15, Soc. *HE* 1.15, Soz. *HE* 2.17.5–31, Gelasius of Cyzicus 3.13.10–14). Bishops in smaller cities tended to be of much humbler status. On this, note Brown, *Poverty*, 48.

entered church coffers from the pockets of the congregation. The tradition of such charitable giving reached back into earliest Christianity and, by the later fourth century, had become a central part of a Christian's religious obligation.[16] Like the wealth that entered the church from imperial coffers, this private wealth too often came under the direct control of the bishop.[17]

Beyond administering the church's resources, bishops served as public advocates and political patrons for their followers. Many of the prominent local citizens who became bishops were so chosen because of their connections to the powerful and their ability to speak effectively on behalf of their city.[18] In times of emergency, bishops of this caliber could be counted upon to lead embassies to imperial officials to plead for the interest of their communities.[19] The patronage activities of bishops extended to more mundane matters as well. Bishops could write letters of support and recommendation for individuals or groups of people who needed the intervention of a powerful patron.[20] Bishops also could hear civil cases and mediate between disputants in an ecclesiastical court,[21] a

---

16. Brown, *Poverty*, 18–24, 96.

17. This was not always true, however. Alexandrian Christians also gave directly to the poor and to support monks and virgins (e.g., Palladius, *Hist. Laus.* 21.2–4 [money directly to the poor], *Hist. Laus.* 14.1–3 [support for monks]; *Apo. Pat. Anon. Coll.* 47 [support for monks]). For private religious foundations in Egypt generally see Thomas, *Private Religious Foundations*, 59–110. Even so, the financial resources of the Alexandrian bishop grew steadily throughout the fourth century (C. Haas, *Alexandria in Late Antiquity: Topography and Social Conflict* [Baltimore, 1997], 224–26).

18. Examples of such figures abound, though Synesius is perhaps the figure most often discussed in this context. See, for example, Rapp, *Holy Bishops*, 156–60; Brown, *Power and Persuasion*, 137–40; Alan Cameron and J. Long, *Barbarians and Politics at the Court of Arcadius* (Berkeley, 1993), 71–102; J. H. W. G. Liebeschuetz, "Why Did Synesius Become Bishop of Ptolemais?" *Byzantion* 56 (1986), 180–95, and *Barbarians and Bishops: Army, Church, and State in the Age of Arcadius and Chrysostom* (Oxford, 1990), 105–38, 228–35.

19. Perhaps the best known such incident involved bishop Flavian of Antioch and his trip to Constantinople following the Riot of the Statues. On this, see the vivid description of Brown, *Power and Persuasion*, 104–108. For a less successful embassy note Ambrose, *Ep.* 51.2, a description of the unfortunate bishop of Thessalonica in 388.

20. For this sort of intervention see, for example, *Life of Theodore of Sykeon*, 115; *Pap. Abinn.* 19, *The Abinnaeus Archive*, ed. H. I. Bell (Oxford, 1962), 65. Also important are the discussion of R. Rémondon, "L'Église dans la société égyptienne à l'époque Byzantine," *Chronique d'Égypte* 47 (1972), 254–77, and the examples described by Brown, *Poverty*, 89–90.

21. For relevant laws see *CTh* 1.27.1 and 2; *Sirmondian Constitution* 1. On *Episcopalis Audientia* see Rapp, *Holy Bishops*, 242–44; Brown, *Poverty*, 68; and the more extensive discussion of J. C. Lamoreaux, "Episcopal Courts in Late Antiquity," *JECS* 3 (1995), 143–67. Note as well, H. A. Drake, *Constantine and the Bishops: The Politics of Intolerance* (Baltimore, 2000), 322–25. It is worth mentioning that the specific scope and authority of these courts evolved over time. Succeeding emperors amended the privileges Constantine had initially established.

prerogative they used to defuse conflicts and encourage the disputants to reconcile with one another.[22]

While all Christians seem to have valued the tangible benefits effective bishops brought to them, urban Christians living in large cities like Alexandria particularly depended upon the financial resources that bishops controlled and the patronage that they offered. This had much to do with the nature of urban life in late antiquity. Cities in the later Roman world contained large numbers of poor people. One often-cited estimate suggests that perhaps 10 percent of the population of a large city could have been classified as poor.[23] These large numbers obscure a more complicated reality. A range of people living in a variety of difficult situations could be categorized as poor. Some of the urban poor were citizens who had long lived in the city and, as a result, could take advantage of the resources granted to the city administration by the imperial government.[24] While far from desirable, the condition of the urban citizen poor was far better than that of the migrants who had come to the city to escape the greater poverty of rural areas.[25] This second category of poor found themselves without even the meager resources available to poor citizens. They likely made up a large portion of the masses described as huddling outside the doors of Egyptian churches on Saturday nights so as to receive the next day's grant of food.[26] While not poor themselves, another, far larger, category of people in the later Roman world understood that an earner's illness, injury, or premature death could push them into poverty at any time.[27]

The tangible resources controlled by bishops of large cities helped to alleviate the needs of the poor and allay the fears of the potential poor. The imperial government provided money and food for a bishop to use to support needy Christians in his city. This built upon the long-articulated view that a bishop should serve as

---

22. For the view that these courts primarily worked to mediate disputes, see J. Harries, *Law and Empire in Late Antiquity* (Cambridge, 1999), 191–211; a point discussed also by Rapp, *Holy Bishops*, 243–52.

23. John Chrysostom, *Homily 66 on Matthew 3*, PG 58.630.6–11. Note on this passage the discussions of Brown, *Power and Persuasion*, 94; and *Poverty*, 14.

24. Brown, *Poverty*, 3–5. On the size and distribution methods of these municipal grants of food see, for example, C. Virlouvet, *Tessera frumentaria: Les procédures de la distribution du blé public à Rome à la fin de la République et au début de l'Empire* (Rome, 1995). For the necessity of such distributions see the vital study of P. Garnsey, *Famine and Food Supply in the Greco-Roman World: Responses to Risk and Crisis* (Cambridge, 1988).

25. Brown, *Power and Persuasion*, 93; *Poverty*, 7.

26. E.g., F. Nau, "Histoire des solitaires égyptiens," no. 214, *Revue de l'Orient chrétien* 13 (1908), 282.

27. See Brown, *Poverty*, 15, 57–60. John Chrysostom estimated that perhaps four-fifths of the city of Antioch fit into this "middling" category and felt all of the anxieties that came along with a life in which descent into poverty remained a real possibility (*Homily 66 on Matthew 3* = PG 58.630.10–11).

the physical protector of his flock,[28] but these imperial efforts formalized the social obligation that a bishop had to assist fellow Christians within his city.[29] At the same time, this system trained large numbers of Christians to think of their bishop as a personal benefactor. Indeed, the church worked to ensure that its regular distribution of money, food, and goods to the needy involved face-to-face encounters that reinforced the personal relationship behind the exchange.[30]

These distributions benefited people across a wide social and economic spectrum. The truly poor, of course, received support and, over time, the poor rolls of a church came to represent something of a registry of the impoverished in each city.[31] However, bishops also sought to support many of those who teetered on the edge of poverty. In a sense, their needs were greater because, in addition to their financial challenges, these families also struggled to maintain a reputable social position and the personal protections it afforded.[32] The so-called poor dole of a bishop actually distributed dramatically different sums of money depending upon the needs and social status of the recipients. This was particularly true of widows. Some received enough simply to keep their families alive, while others were granted funds to allow them to live in the comfort to which they had become accustomed.[33] For middling families still headed by a husband, the bishop could also provide work, though seldom in positions that enhanced one's status.[34]

Bishops also used their influence to protect families who found their social position at risk. Both Augustine and Basil of Caesarea wrote to imperial officials in attempts to limit financial demands that threatened to pull members of their flocks down to lower social and economic levels.[35] Their efforts primarily centered upon guildsmen who were adversely affected by high tax demands, but, at least in Augustine's case, the bishop's concern also extended to middling members of local town

28. Rapp, *Holy Bishops*, 200, 223–26; Brown, *Power and Persuasion*, 91; Brown, *Poverty*, 45. For some examples of this idea see Eusebius, *HE* 8.9.7–10.1 and Ps.-Athanasius, *Canon 14* in *The Canons of Athanasius*, ed. and trans. W. Riedel and W. E. Crum (Amsterdam, 1973), 25–26.

29. Brown, *Poverty*, 32.

30. Brown, *Power and Persuasion*, 97.

31. Brown, *Power and Persuasion*, 98. On poor rolls in general see M. Rouche, "Le matricule des pauvres. Evolution d'une institution de charité du Bas-Empire jusqu'à la fin du Haut Moyen Age," in *Études sur l'histoire de la pauvreté*, ed. M. Mollat (Paris, 1974), 83–110, as well as ancient sources as diverse as Augustine, *Ep.* 20*.2 and *Canon 11 of the Council of Chalcedon*.

32. Brown, *Poverty*, 49.

33. On these differences, note Brown, *Poverty*, 60. For the larger outlays see Gregory the Great, *Ep.* 1.39, a text that describes a gift of 40 *solidi* to his aunt for "shoe money for her boys" (*offeras ad calciarium puerorum solidos quadraginta*) and 20 *solidi* to two other matrons. In addition, each woman received a sizeable food allotment. The amount Gregory set aside for others on the poor dole could be as little as one half a *solidus* a year.

34. Note here, for example, the discussion of the *parabalani* in Haas, *Alexandria in Late Antiquity*, 235–38; 314–16.

35. Augustine, *Ep.* 22*.2; Basil, *Ep.* 110. For discussion see Brown, *Poverty*, 57.

councils.³⁶ These efforts often succeeded in building strong connections between the bishop and his flock but, unlike grants to the truly poor, this sort of generosity helped people who, while insecure, were far from powerless. They could (and often did) reciprocate. Indeed, Basil's guildsmen repaid his efforts by demonstrating outside the office of a hostile governor who had summoned their bishop. When the governor saw the gathered crowd, he meekly dismissed Basil.³⁷

In this way, the experiences of Basil mirrored the procession that kept Athanasius in Alexandria in May of 365. Both events show that a bishop who came to be viewed as an effective patron by caring for the vulnerable in his congregation could generate a powerful following. The power of a bishop to mobilize large crowds of congregants, however, came from more than simply the material goods and patronage he could provide. Many late antique bishops who honestly distributed the wealth of their churches and labored to protect the interests of their congregants failed to generate even a fraction of the popular support that Athanasius and Basil could call out into the streets. During Athanasius's episcopate, for example, he faced challenges from bishops like Gregory, George of Cappadocia, and Lucius. Emperors put each of these men in charge of the financial and material resources that the government provided the Alexandrian church and, as officially recognized bishops, they also enjoyed access to provincial and imperial officials.³⁸ Nevertheless, each man failed to generate the popular enthusiasm that the deposed Athanasius continued to command. This is especially true of George, who was lynched in December 361, and Lucius who, upon entering the city for the second time in September 367, was forced to hide in his mother's house until a detachment of soldiers could escort him through a hostile crowd.³⁹ A successful and influential

---

36. For Augustine's request note the study of F. Jacques, "Le défenseur de la cité d'après la Lettre 22* de Saint Augustin," *Revue des études augustinienne* 32 (1986), 56–73.

37. Gregory Nazianzus, *Or.* 43.57; cf. the discussion of Brown, *Poverty*, 57.

38. For discussion of the process by which emperors shifted resources away from bishops who had fallen out of favor, see Brown, *Power and Persuasion*, 90; Barnes, *Athanasius*, 116, 178. Athanasius states clearly that grain was taken from his control and given to George following the Council of Arles in 356 (*History of the Arians* 31.2, a description that suggests such action was expected under the circumstances) and suggests that the same may have been done in 338 (*Defense against the Arians* 18.2). A similar substitution may have been made to help Lucius establish himself, but given Lucius's rather pathetic regime, it is unlikely to have been more than a technical substitution.

39. For George's death, see *Historia Acephala* 2.8–10; Socrates, *HE* 3.2; Sozomen, *HE* 5.7. The emperor Julian blamed the lynching on Alexandrian pagans (*Ep.* 60, cf. Socrates, *HE* 3.3), perhaps with reason. George was also previously pushed out of the city by a mob of Athanasian partisans. For this, see *Historia Acephala* 2.3–4; *Storia della Chiesa di Alessandria* 32.20–24. On George's fate, see Barnes, *Athanasius*, 155. On Lucius, see *Historia Acephala* 5.11–14; *Festal Index* 39. Barnes (*Athanasius*, 163) suggests that Lucius returned in 367 without official support. This may be true but, given the military evacuation he eventually received, one cannot imagine that he returned to Alexandria without at least tacit support from imperial officials

bishop needed to do more for his congregants than simply protect their rights and preserve their material well-being.

While material resources gave a bishop the means with which to improve the lives of his congregation, his ability to convince his flock of his worthiness to serve as their spiritual father forged a deeper connection.[40] The bishop brought newcomers into the Christian community and taught them what membership in it entailed. He presided over the baptism that simultaneously welcomed them formally into the church and cleansed them of their sins. He took responsibility for instructing them how to avoid sin, praising them when they succeeded and admonishing them when they failed. He administered the Eucharist, the regular moment that reaffirmed both a Christian's particular relationship with God and his place in the church. And, finally, the bishop preached weekly sermons that examined Scripture, explained Christian doctrine, and instructed his congregation how these teachings ought to be applied to their lives.[41] In Alexandria, at least, these sermons seem to have reached a diverse audience of elite and non-elite Christians.[42]

The bishop provided powerful teaching that, under the best of circumstances, shaped the ways in which his flock lived, and promised them release from their sins. Only bishops of a particular character could truly convince the congregation of their ability to provide such important guidance. The authority of a bishop derived from the belief that the Holy Spirit inspired his words, a spiritual connection that ensured the divine origin of his teaching.[43] If the bishop truly enjoyed such a connection, his personal conduct would reflect a similar divine inspiration. Like a respectable teacher of philosophy, an effective and persuasive bishop needed to live in a way consistent with his teaching.[44] This idea has Pauline roots and

---

40. *Didascalia*, ch. 7, p. 75, ll. 10–15. References to the *Didascalia*, a third-century Syrian document laying out the structure of a congregation, come from *The Didascalia Apostolorum*, ed. and trans. A. Vööbus, CSCO vol. 401/2, 407/8 (Louvain, 1979).

41. These sermons and the effect that they had on audiences have been a subject of much recent discussion, most of it concerned with John Chrysostom. The most important such study is that of W. Mayer, "John Chrysostom: Extraordinary Preacher, Ordinary Audience," in *Preacher and Audience: Studies in Early Christian and Byzantine Homiletics*, ed. M. Cunningham and P. Allen (Leiden, 1998), 105–38. See as well the work of J. Maxwell, *Christianization and Communication in Late Antiquity: John Chrysostom and his Congregation in Antioch* (Cambridge, 2006) and A. Hartney, *John Chrysostom and the Transformation of the City* (London, 2004), 33–65.

42. On the nature of the Alexandrian churchgoing crowd see Leontius, *Life of John the Almsgiver*, 42. Other Alexandrian evidence suggests that elite and non-elite Christians paid careful attention to the services given by the patriarch. Timothy Salofacialos ran afoul of his congregation for tampering with the diptychs (Zacharias, *HE* 5.5) and even the sainted bishop Peter I earned their displeasure for his actions when conducting a mass (*M. Petr. Al* 17). For discussion see Haas, *Alexandria in Late Antiquity*, 243.

43. Rapp, *Holy Bishops*, 57–58.

44. This idea is well expressed by Jerome when he states that "the leader of the church should possess an eloquence that is intimately linked with integrity of conduct, so his actions are not silenced

influenced the thinking of, among others, Clement of Alexandria, Origen, Theodore of Mopsuestia, and John Chrysostom.⁴⁵ The *Didascalia* provides one of the more exhaustive lists of the personal attributes that an effective bishop must demonstrate. He should be "chaste, humble, not anxious, watchful, not loving of money, without reproach, not quarrelsome, compassionate, not excessively talkative, a lover of good things, a lover of the poor . . . and perfect in all things as one to whom the order and place of God is entrusted."⁴⁶ Beyond this, he was to be a peacemaker within the community who was untouched by injustice and evil.⁴⁷ Perhaps most importantly, an effective bishop was inspired by the Holy Spirit and, in his conduct, refrained from violence and showed no desire to accumulate wealth.⁴⁸ Mindful of these limits, a good bishop also fought hard to combat any heresy that he found threatening his congregation.⁴⁹

Many bishops understood the need to demonstrate this connection to the Holy Spirit early in their careers. Basil of Caesarea, for example, worked hard to establish his credentials as a charitable and generous individual during a famine that gripped Cappadocia during his rise to the episcopate.⁵⁰ In an effort to help alleviate the suffering, Basil used his own money to provide housing and food for starving migrants from the countryside and forcefully upbraided the wealthy in the region who hesitated to follow his example. Basil's personal sacrifices and his inspired call for others to follow his lead helped to mark him as an ecclesiastical leader truly inspired by the Holy Spirit. The context is important, however. As Peter Brown has argued, Basil's actions must be seen against a wider backdrop in which Eustathians, a competing Christian group, were attracting attention through their charitable efforts.⁵¹ As Basil understood, this competitive environment demanded that bishops demonstrate publicly the degree to which the Holy Spirit animated both their actions and their teaching. Basil succeeded in convincing people of his spiritual inspiration. Less skilled bishops risked losing their congregations.

---

by his preaching or his words an embarrassment because his deeds are deficient" (*Commentary on the Letter to Titus*, 1).

45. Paul, I Timothy 3; Clement of Alexandria, *On Virginity*, 1.13.5; Origen, *Commentary on Letter to Romans* 8.10; *Commentary on Matthew* 15.21–28; *Homily on Leviticus* 6.3; Theodore of Mopsuestia, *Commentary on I Timothy* 3.1; John Chrysostom, *Homily on I Timothy* 3.10.2. For discussion, see Rapp, *Holy Bishops*, 32–41.

46. *Didascalia*, ch. 3.1; p. 27, ll. 17–24.

47. *Didascalia*, ch. 4; p. 43.20ff.

48. *Didascalia*, ch. 4; p. 45.10.

49. Ignatius of Antioch, *Letter to Polycarp* 1.3. Note as well the discussion of Ignatius's ideas in Rapp, *Holy Bishops*, 26–28.

50. For a new perspective on these events see Brown, *Poverty*, 35–41.

51. Brown, *Poverty*, 36–37.

ATHANASIUS AND THE POLITICS OF SELF-DEFINITION

In the same way that a powerful demonstration of the qualities that marked an ideal bishop could convince a city to support him enthusiastically, a bishop who clearly did not possess these qualities could be seen as illegitimate and unworthy of support. Indeed, when bishops from different Christian groups competed for popular support, they would often fling charges against one another that, if true, would show how a rival did not live according to a divinely inspired standard. While this rhetoric appeared frequently in late antiquity, perhaps no situation better shows these techniques in action than the three-way conflict between Melitians, Arians, and followers of Athanasius in Alexandria.

Though the Melitian-Athanasian and Arian-Athanasian conflicts concerned two different subjects, the basic standards used to evaluate the legitimacy of a bishop and his teaching lay at their hearts. The Melitian schism emerged out of the Great Persecution and concerned the fundamental question of when the conduct of a bishop negated his divinely bestowed authority over the church.[52] The Arian controversy, by contrast, centered instead upon the degree to which the divine inspiration of a bishop should control the content and direction of Christian teaching. At its root was the teaching of Arius, an Alexandrian presbyter in charge of the church in the Alexandrian parish of Baucalis,[53] and his contention that he possessed a spiritual inspiration that put him beyond the traditional doctrinal authority of his bishop.[54]

The Alexandrian bishop Alexander and his successor Athanasius understood that the Melitian schism and the Arian controversy each presented significant challenges to their leadership. Both bishops also realized that their response to these challenges needed to be swift and decisive, even if this forced them to challenge the boundaries of episcopal propriety. After Constantine assumed control of the east in 324, both Alexander and Athanasius used the power of their position

---

52. On the Melitian schism, see the discussion of T. Vivian, *St. Peter of Alexandria: Bishop and Martyr* (Philadelphia, 1988), 15–50; S. Davis, *The Early Coptic Papacy: The Egyptian Church and Its Leadership in Late Antiquity* (Cairo, 2004), 36–40; and Barnes, *Athanasius*, 14. For a somewhat polemical account of its origins, see Athanasius, *Defense against the Arians*, 59.1. Melitius took a much harder line about the length of penance required for the readmission of a Christian who lapsed during the persecution. For an anecdote illustrating these differences see Epiphanius, *Panarion* 68.1–3.

53. Epiphanius, *Panarion*, 3.153.16.

54. For a detailed reconstruction of the early conflict, see R. Williams, *Arius: Heresy and Tradition* (London, 1987) 48–81, and C. R. Galvão-Sobrinho, "The Rise of the Christian Bishop; Doctrine and Power in the Later Roman Empire, AD 318–80," (PhD diss. Yale University, 1999), 91–107. On the association of Arius and his opponent, Alexander of Alexandria, with different sources of authority, see Arius, *Thalia* in Athanasius, *Orationes tres contra Arianos*, 26.20.44–21.3. For interpretation, see R. Williams, *Arius*, 85–86 and Rapp, *Holy Bishops*, 29.

as the imperially recognized bishop to build support for their views. Alexander received an especially welcome vote of official backing when, under the direction of the emperor, the Council of Nicaea upheld his doctrinal authority in the Arian controversy (though it encouraged reconciliation with the Melitians). This imperial support had more tangible effects as well. After Alexander passed from the scene in 326, Athanasius took advantage of an imperial grant of grain to reward those loyal to him[55] and seems to have selectively distributed a levy of linen tunics taken in part from Melitians.[56]

Nevertheless, the followers of Arius and Melitius continued to make significant inroads into the support that the bishop enjoyed. Arius, for example, composed songs and organized meetings so that his ideas could be spread and remembered by laborers in Alexandria.[57] For their part, the Melitians seem to have done an excellent job attracting support among the native Coptic population.[58] The situation demanded more forceful action and Athanasius seems to have sanctioned its use. By the end of 331, complaints started reaching the imperial court about Athanasius's use of violence and intimidation, initially against his Melitian opponents.[59] Most dramatically, Athanasius was charged with ordering his associate Macarius to smash the sacral chalice and overturn the altar used by Ischyras, a Melitian priest working in the Mareotis district near to Athanasius's Alexandrian home base.[60]

Although Athanasius was able to defend himself against these accusations before the emperor in 332, charges of ordering the murder of Arsenius, the Melitian bishop of Hypsele were soon added to what came to be a standing indictment of the bishop.[61] When this charge too failed to stick, Athanasius's Arian and Melitian opponents framed an even broader complaint, accusing the bishop of the systematic use of violence and intimidation. Two Melitian bishops charged that Athanasius had convinced the prefect to jail them, another spoke about how he had been deposed for failing to maintain communion with Athanasius, and five more spoke about being assaulted on his orders.[62] Eventually, Athanasius was forced to defend

---

55. This seems to be suggested by his complaint that his supporters were removed from the list of grain recipients following one of his depositions (*Defense Against the Arians*, 18.2).

56. These Melitians subsequently accused him of extorting the tunics (*Defense Against the Arians*, 60.1–4; *Festal Letter* 4.5).

57. See C. Galvão-Sobrinho, forthcoming.

58. For the Coptic character of the Melitian movement, see W. H. C. Frend, *The Rise of the Monophysite Movement* (Cambridge, 1972), 81; H. I. Bell, *Jews and Christians in Egypt: The Jewish Troubles in Alexandria and the Athanasian Controversy Illustrated by Texts from Greek Papyri in the British Museum* (London, 1924), 44.

59. *Festal Letter* 4.5; *Defense against the Arians*, 60.4; *Festal Index* 3. For discussion, see Barnes, *Athanasius*, 21.

60. *Defense against the Arians*, 63.

61. Ibid.

62. Sozomen, *HE* 2.25; for discussion see Barnes, *Athanasius*, 22.

himself against these charges at a synod in Tyre in 335.[63] This synod ruled that Athanasius's conduct merited his deposition, a finding that the Alexandrian bishop appealed before the emperor.[64] Athanasius seemed on the verge of getting a reprieve until representatives of the council turned up and added the new charge that Athanasius had threatened to withhold grain from Constantinople. Athanasius's angry response to this finally provoked Constantine to order him into exile on November 7, 335.[65]

These incidents early in Athanasius's episcopate bring to light a number of important trends that would continue to influence his actions for the rest of his career. The first concerned the use of imperial power and patronage against opponents. As a member of the first generation of bishops to find these resources available, Athanasius thought that he understood how to use imperial support to put pressure on other Christian groups. Athanasius initially deployed these resources to attack the Melitians. As a native Egyptian group with a parallel ecclesiastical hierarchy and the explicit recognition of the Council of Nicaea, they presented a particular sort of danger to Athanasius. In his confrontation with the followers of Arius in and around Alexandria, Athanasius needed to be able to count upon the support of a vast Egyptian Christian heartland. While Arius had failed to penetrate Upper Egypt to any significant degree in the 320s, the Melitians had both a sizable Egyptian following and Nicene sanction to continue ministering. Athanasius also understood the Melitian limitations. As an Egyptian group, they appeared to have no champions outside of the region and no real access to imperial power.[66] A move against them seemed both prudent and likely to succeed.

Athanasius had miscalculated, however. He had used the blunt instrument of imperial power to perform an extremely delicate task, and his opponents quickly capitalized on his clumsiness. Supporters of Arius led by Eusebius, the powerful bishop of Nicomedia, quickly took up the Melitian cause and broadcast their complaints to an imperial audience. They did so shrewdly, using language that resonated in a particularly damning way among ordinary Christians. The charges against Athanasius fit into the very categories that Christians considered when they evaluated the moral conduct of bishops. His embezzlement of linen tunics taken from Melitians suggested an inappropriate love of money.[67] His intimidation

---

63. On the context of these events see Drake, *Constantine and the Bishops*, 261–68, as well as the different reconstruction of Barnes, *Athanasius*, 21–23.

64. *Festal Index* 8; *Defense against the Arians* 86.2–87.2.

65. *Festal Index* 8.

66. This problem seems clear enough from the difficulty the Melitian delegation had in securing an imperial audience before their alliance with Eusebius of Nicomedia. For description of this context, see Drake, *Constantine and the Bishops*, 262.

67. Cf. *Didascalia*, ch. 3.1; p. 27, ll. 17–24.

of Melitian clergy suggested a similarly disqualifying tendency to violent action, the polar opposite of the peaceful character a bishop was supposed to exhibit.[68] From time to time, his opponents also advanced a further charge that Athanasius had been improperly ordained.[69] This suggested that the Holy Spirit had never infused Athanasius with divine authority.[70] If these charges could be substantiated, they threatened to undermine the confidence of Athanasius's congregation that the Holy Spirit acted through their bishop.

Athanasius evidently understood the power of these charges. Although the accusation that Athanasius threatened Constantinople's grain supply forced him into exile, he would subsequently spend little time defending himself against it. Instead, both Athanasius and his opponents vigorously contested whether he had been legitimately consecrated and if his behavior as bishop marked him as unfit to lead the church. The nature of the dispute changed, however, with Athanasius's exile in 335. Instead of a bishop who used his position and access to imperial patronage to repress his opponents, Athanasius could now present himself as a victim of unscrupulous enemies who had turned the state against him. This was important because the strategy that Athanasius had adopted through the early part of the 330s had plainly failed.[71] Stripped of the patronage powers he had counted upon to build popular support, Athanasius needed to find a new way to define himself and his actions for an Egyptian audience.

ATHANASIUS'S RESTORATION AND REDEFINITION

The death of Constantine in 337 released Athanasius from his exile, but his return to Alexandria provided no real security. The opponents who had forced Athanasius out in 335 began working immediately to have him sent away again and they found Constantine's son Constantius receptive to their complaints. At a council that met only months after Constantine's death, Athanasian opponents revived the old charges of Athanasius's improper ordination and conduct as bishop.[72] They

68. Cf. *Didascalia*, ch. 4; 45.10. For the rhetoric of violence as used against Athanasius, see M. Gaddis, *There Is No Crime for Those Who Have Christ: Religious Violence in the Christian Roman Empire* (Berkeley, 2005), 276–78.

69. For Athanasius's ordination see Sozomen, *HE* 2.17, 25 and, more problematically, Athanasius, *Apology against the Arians* 6.

70. E.g., *Apostolic Tradition* iii.3 (in G. Dix and rev. H. Chadwick, *The Treatise of the Apostolic Tradition of St. Hippolytus of Rome* [London, 1968]).

71. This seems largely to have consisted of attempts (usually successful) to deflect the charges of his critics and produce countercharges against them. Perhaps no better example of this survives than his *Fourth Festal Letter* (of 332) in which he celebrates "our enemies having been put to shame and reproved by the Church, because they persecuted us without a cause." (*Ep. Fest.* 4.1).

72. Barnes, *Athanasius*, 36–37.

ordered him deposed on these grounds and selected a replacement.[73] The emperor Constantius then endorsed their findings.

Athanasius responded by calling a council of Egyptian bishops. Predictably, it vindicated him completely and signed off on a letter that explained in detail the reasons for its finding.[74] Athanasius's agents distributed this letter and some supporting documents to metropolitans and other important bishops throughout the empire.[75] While the synod's letter may have reassured Athanasius's Egyptian followers, there is no evidence that he sought to distribute it widely in his home region. Instead, Athanasius intended for it to be a political defense that would help him to marshal allies from around the empire. Within Egypt, Athanasius capitalized upon his episcopal duty to organize Christian religious life so as to build support among his congregation. Like his predecessors, Athanasius wrote an annual *Festal Letter* to the leaders and membership of the Egyptian church. This stated the correct date for Easter and then provided some brief teaching that related the festival to contemporary circumstances.[76] Because of their role in setting the Christian calendar, these letters circulated widely.

Athanasius's tenth *Festal Letter* shows him using this formidable tool to influence his congregation's view of the controversy surrounding him. In it the bishop employed a new, highly charged rhetoric in which he obliquely equated his current situation and that of his followers with the challenges endured by just men living through persecution. Written at about the time of Constantius's endorsement of his deposition, the letter describes an atmosphere of fear in which Athanasius's enemies constantly move against him.[77] Amidst references to the Assyrians and Nebuchadnezzar,[78] Athanasius reminds his congregation that God ensures the salvation of the faithful even "when enemies have persecuted us and have sought to seize us."[79] One generation removed from the Great Persecution, Athanasius reintroduced his Egyptian congregation to the once-familiar world of the unjustly oppressed and promised them that any suffering they might endure on his behalf would be rewarded by God.[80]

---

73. Athanasius, *Encyclical Letter* 6.1.

74. The letter of this synod comprises chapters 3–19 of Athanasius's *Defense against the Arians*.

75. Barnes, *Athanasius*, 40; cf. *Apol. c. Ar.* 20.

76. On the Athanasian *Festal Letters*, see A. Camplani, *Le Lettre festali di Atanasio di Alessandria* (Rome, 1989).

77. *Ep. Fest.* 10.1, dated to 338.

78. *Ep. Fest.* 10.3.

79. *Ep. Fest.* 10.4, an allusion to Romans 8.35 which Athanasius previously introduced. The translation is that of the NPNF volume. For the context of this letter, see Barnes, *Athanasius* 43–44.

80. For the residual power of the memory of state persecution among fourth-century Christians, see Gaddis, *There is no Crime*, 79. Note as well the important discussion of the commemoration of martyrdom in E. Castelli, *Martyrdom and Memory: Early Christian Culture Making* (New York, 2004).

As 338 progressed, Athanasius again raised the rhetorical bar in Egypt. From the early stages of his episcopate, Athanasius had cultivated a relationship with leading members of Egypt's growing ascetic movement in which he advocated for their interests and instructed them in their affairs.[81] His delicate combination of regulation and toleration of ascetic independence made Athanasius a beloved figure in many monastic circles.[82] As imperial opposition increasingly threatened his grip on the Alexandrian patriarchate, Athanasius came to appreciate the broader symbolic power of his ascetic associates.[83] In the summer of that year, Athanasius arranged for Antony, the ascetic seen as the father of the movement, to visit Alexandria.[84] Amidst vast crowds of people, Antony spoke out against the followers of Arius and performed miracles before being escorted by Athanasius and a crowd of followers to the gate of the city.[85]

Antony's visit communicated God's sanction of Athanasius and his convictions, but it did not relieve the pressure being put on him by imperial authorities. This only increased during the winter of 338/9. By the time that Athanasius sent out his *Festal Letter* of 339, his political position looked extremely precarious. The letter, however, suggests that Athanasius felt confident that the very public messages he had sent in 338 had proven his orthodoxy and legitimacy. Taking up his duty as interpreter of Scripture for his congregation, Athanasius explained what a number of Pauline and Gospel passages teach about the importance of virtue and outlined how his congregation should apply these ideas during the upcoming Easter. The final third of the letter, however, spoke specifically about what this teaching meant in the current situation. Athanasius called upon his parishioners

81. Athanasius's first two *Festal Letters* (329 and 330) show some familiarity with asceticism as well as a desire to advertise his connection to ascetics. The best analysis of this feature of Athanasius's career remains that of D. Brakke, *Athanasius and Asceticism*, 2nd ed. (Baltimore, 1998). On this, note as well, S. Elm, *Virgins of God: The Making of Asceticism in Late Antiquity* (Oxford, 1994), 331–72. On Letter 2 in particular note Brakke, *Athanasius and Asceticism*, 320–23; Barnes, *Athanasius*, 188–91; Camplani, *Lettere Festali*, 201.

82. The best example, of course, concerns his relationship with the Pachomian community. If Pachomian sources are to be believed, this began with a defense of Pachomian independence during a tour of Upper Egypt in 329/30 (*Life of Pachomius*, Bo. 28; G¹ 30). For discussion of this encounter, see Brakke, *Athanasius*, 111–28 (esp. 113–20 on this first encounter); Barnes, *Athanasius*, 121; Rousseau, *Pachomius: The Making of a Community in Fourth-Century Egypt* 2nd ed. (Berkeley, 1999), 72.

83. Early in his episcopate, Athanasius's efforts at controlling ascetic life may have been motivated by a concern about the growth of Melitian asceticism in Egypt. On Melitian monks, see J. Goehring, "Monastic Diversity and Ideological Boundaries in Fourth-Century Christian Egypt," *JECS* 5 (1997), 64–72. Monastic sources make clear that competition existed from Melitian groups (e.g., *Apo. Pat. Sisoes* 48 = PG 65.405), to the degree that Pachomian monasteries screened visitors for Melitian affiliations (e.g., Bo. 128–29).

84. *Vit. Ant.* 69–70.

85. The first person plural verbs in *Vit. Ant.* 71 suggest that Athanasius accompanied the monk and his adoring crowd to the gate.

to "let no one of us fail in his duty in these things; counting as nothing the affliction or the trials which, especially at this time, have been enviously directed against us by the party of Eusebius."[86] While quite real, the threats that his enemies posed to Athanasius's own life and the physical well-being of his followers were to be welcomed because resisting them would be an act of virtue for which a reward awaited in heaven.[87] Athanasius concluded by marking that year's Easter feast as an act of resistance to be celebrated "not at all as an occasion of distress and mourning" but as a way for his followers to remain unified despite the "temporal trials brought upon us by godliness."[88]

Athanasius's call to resistance shows how the ideas about virtue present in Scripture could be applied in a specific way during this particular Easter season. Athanasius's eleventh Festal Letter probably gives us a good sense of the topics the bishop focused upon in his preaching in February and March of 339. His audience would soon have the opportunity to follow their prelate's instructions. On March 18, Athanasius "was pursued during the night . . . and on the following day fled from the church of Theonas after having baptized many."[89] He then went into hiding. On Thursday, March 22 the Arian bishop Gregory arrived in the city, supported by the prefect of Egypt and imperial troops.[90] Athanasius remained in Alexandria for nearly a month, leaving for the West only after he furtively performed the Easter service on April 15.[91]

Athanasius could not have staged his deposition any better. He had spent most of the past year preparing his followers for this moment and, by forcing him from his church, Philagrius, the governor, had given Athanasius the very scene he wanted. As the victim of unjustly applied state power, Athanasius could readily associate his struggles with those of the confessor-bishops whose legacies had been seared into the Christian collective memory by centuries of government persecution.[92]

Not long after leaving Alexandria, Athanasius wrote a letter, intended for general circulation, which used these powerful images to describe the suffering that his followers endured during his last month in the city.[93] Athanasius wrote that the "treatment we have undergone surpasses the bitterness of any persecution . . . (because) now the whole Church is injured, the priesthood insulted, and

86. *Festal Letter* 11.12.
87. *Festal Letter* 11.12.
88. *Festal Letter* 11.13.
89. *Festal Index* 11.
90. *Festal Index* 11; Athanasius, *Ep. enc.* 1.
91. The date of his departure (April 16) and his involvement in Easter festivities are suggested by his *Encyclical Letter* (*Ep. enc.* 5).
92. For the important role played by law and the use of state power in early Christian martyrdoms see Castelli, *Martyrdom and Memory*, 33–68.
93. On the *Encyclical Letter*, see Barnes, *Athanasius*, 47–50.

worst of all, piety is persecuted by impiety."⁹⁴ He described for his audience the posting of Philagrius's letter deposing Athanasius in terms that echoed the opening of the Great Persecution 37 years earlier.⁹⁵ To underline the improper use of power that this represented, Athanasius also recorded the response of his congregation. Athanasius had, of course, been preparing them for this day for nearly a year and, when it came, his flock responded with "just indignation and exclaimed against... this novel and iniquitous attempt against the Church."⁹⁶ When the Arian bishop Gregory arrived in the city, people apparently continued to resist in the way that Athanasius had taught. They "assembled in the churches, in order to prevent the impiety of the Arians from mingling itself with the faith of the Church" by taking control of the sanctuaries.⁹⁷ The prefect met their resistance with violence and sent a mob of "the heathen multitude, with the Jews and disorderly persons" to attack this assembly.⁹⁸ According to Athanasius, this non-Christian mob burned a church and baptistery,⁹⁹ consumed holy wine, and, most strikingly, attacked monks and sexually assaulted female ascetics.¹⁰⁰ These outrages continued even during holy week. Athanasius describes the prefect entering a Good Friday service and finding a hostile crowd. He responded by arresting and scourging thirty-four women, among them holy virgins, who had spoken out against him. On Easter, after Athanasius had fled from the church in which he was hiding, the governor arrested the assembled congregation.¹⁰¹

Athanasius's rhetoric resonated because of the ways in which Christian communities celebrated the deeds of previous martyrs.¹⁰² This was helped too by Athanasius's own efforts to prepare a fertile intellectual ground in which to implant a new understanding of the familiar narrative of persecution. With Christianity now supported by the emperor, Athanasius had taught his followers to expect persecution to take a different, but no less destructive, form. This new persecution would attack their ascetic symbols and their bishops, the new standard-bearers of an assertive Christianity. It would turn state patronage away from these holy men and use state-sponsored violence to try to divide the faithful and push Christians towards heresy.

This rhetoric also marked Athanasius as the perfect figure to lead the resis-

94. *Ep. enc.* 1.
95. *Ep. enc.* 2; cf. Eusebius, *HE* 8.2.4, Lactantius, *de Mor.* 13.
96. *Ep. enc.* 2.
97. *Ep. enc.* 3.
98. *Ep. enc.* 3–4.
99. The *Encyclical Letter* is unclear about which church was attacked, though it is reasonable to guess that this would have been the church of Theonas.
100. *Ep. enc.* 3–4. On the destruction of churches in the Great Persecution, cf. Eusebius, *HE* 8.2; Lactantius, *de Mor.* 12.
101. *Ep. enc.* 5.
102. For Athanasius's use of the rhetoric of persecution, see Gaddis, *There Is No Crime*, 77–87.

tance to this new form of persecution. In the months leading up to its onset, he had emphasized to his congregation the divine rewards that would come to those who remained united in orthodoxy. He championed and supported the ascetics who now suffered at the hands of the state. And, in spite of grave threats, he continued to offer orthodox leadership that explained the nature of salvation by affirming the true nature of Christ.[103] Perhaps just as importantly, this rhetoric also allowed Athanasius to dismiss the real blows that his exile inflicted upon his ability to provide support to his congregation. Philagrius's decree robbed him of control over grain distributions to the poor and the financial disbursements that could give employment to the needy. It removed him from the episcopal courts. No longer could he provide legally sanctioned mediation and adjudication to his flock. Nevertheless, Athanasius managed to classify even this patronage as a black mark by showing how it was used by Gregory to fight against Christ and his devotees.[104]

In the short years between his return from exile in 337 and his second exile in 339, Athanasius transformed himself from a bishop who used imperial support to enhance his position into one whose spiritual authority encouraged followers to resist even direct state opposition. Athanasius brought about this rhetorical transformation in Egypt, before an Egyptian audience, but, as his *Encyclical Letter* suggests, he understood that this rhetoric had a larger appeal across the empire. Hence, when he set out from Alexandria in April of 339, Athanasius decided to fight against his Arian replacement not in the streets and churches of Egypt but in the larger, better-lit imperial political arena.[105] He succeeded in this enterprise largely because of the explicit backing that the Western emperor Constans gave him.[106] Despite this, Athanasius's influence in Alexandria remained so strong that, when he returned to the city in 346, a huge crowd met him one hundred miles from Alexandria and escorted him in triumph into the city.[107] Indeed, during his exile, Athanasius continued to increase the number of bishops and churches in communion with him.[108]

Even as the overthrow of Constans in 350 thrust Athanasius into another difficult political position, his following in Egypt continued to grow as he deftly deployed his particular, personally specific, rhetoric of contemporary persecu-

---

103. *Festal Letter* 11.12–13.
104. E.g., *Ep. enc.* 5.3.4–6.
105. Perhaps the best summary of this complicated stage of Athanasius's career is that of Barnes, *Athanasius*, 47–91.
106. Constans evidently threatened civil war if Athanasius was not restored. See Socrates, *HE* 2.22; cf. Rufinus, *HE* 10.20; Philostorgius *HE* 3.12; Theodoret, *HE* 2.8. Note as well the discussion of Barnes, *Athanasius*, 89–91.
107. *Festal Index* 18; cf. *Historia Acephala* 1.1–2.
108. Barnes, *Athanasius*, 95.

tion. The late 340s and early 350s saw a series of publications addressed to a range of Egyptian and non-Egyptian audiences, which further developed the same general points he had expressed so potently in 338 and 339.[109] The events leading up to Athanasius's third exile in 356 pushed this rhetoric to a new level. Now Athanasius could not flee to the West to gather political support for his position, as he had in the exiles of 335 and 339. Western bishops had begun to lose the freedom to intervene in his case[110] and, with the overthrow of Constans and Constantius's defeat of the usurper Magnentius, no alternative political power remained there. As pressure mounted on Athanasius in the mid-350s, he refashioned his defense to draw even more upon his Egyptian supporters. In 355, a display of popular anger helped Athanasius fight off an attempt to send him into exile. Then, in February of 356, another attempt to arrest the bishop prompted great popular outcry. The resulting violence saw soldiers storming a church in which Athanasius was presiding over a marathon midnight service. Athanasius and his supporters could again point to "naked swords and javelins and instruments of war" displayed in the church, as well as stripped virgins, plundered sacred vessels, and random killings.[111]

Athanasius fled Alexandria after his followers' display of resistance, but his flock had already been trained to see this situation as another instance of imperial persecution. They marked the holy virgins who had been killed as "martyrs," placed their bodies outside the church, and displayed the arrows and other military equipment that had been used in the assault.[112] Athanasius eventually found sanctuary among Egyptian monks, with whom he spent the duration of his exile. The work that he wrote during this period (which included his influential biography of Antony) further enhanced his reputation as a champion of ascetics.[113] In other texts, Athanasius elaborated upon the reasons for his flight from imperial persecutors in Alexandria[114] and narrated the violent actions of officials who supported his Arian opponents.[115] In so doing, Athanasius created a similar popular mood to that which prevailed in 339. But Athanasius's presence in Egypt, first among his devotees in Alexandria and later among the monks of the countryside, significantly enhanced its effect. With his spiritual inspiration now beyond doubt,

109. The most notable of these is his *Defense Against the Arians*, probably written in 349.

110. Barnes, *Athanasius*, 109–19.

111. Athanasius, *Arian History* 81, quoting a petition of protest sent by his congregation after these events. For discussion, see Gaddis, *There Is No Crime*, 79–80; Barnes, *Athanasius*, 119.

112. *Arian History* 81; cf. Gaddis, *There Is No Crime*, 81–83.

113. For the idea that Athanasius intended for the *Life of Antony* to first reach an Egyptian audience see W. C. Gruen, "The compilation and dissemination of 'The Life of Antony' (Saint Athanasius, Patriarch of Alexandria)," (PhD diss., University of Pennsylvania, 2005).

114. *Defense of his Flight* (*De fuga*), probably composed in 357.

115. Most notably his *Arian History* (*Historia Arianorum*), also likely composed in 357. On this text, note the discussion of Barnes, *Athanasius*, 126–32.

the acts of violence against Athanasius and his followers looked ever more like true persecution.

This brings us back to where we began, with Valens's failed attempt to depose Athanasius in 365. Valens's threatened financial penalty had frightened the Alexandrian council, but the vigorous response of other Christians more than compensated for their hesitancy. In fact, every effort to depose Athanasius met with greater resistance from his followers, many of whom saw their bishop's claim to be a principled defender of orthodoxy further validated by each imposition of force. Although Athanasius had been in exile for nearly fifteen of the preceding thirty years, a generation of Egyptian Christians had literally grown up with Athanasius's rhetoric of contemporary persecution. Indeed, with the Christian community now two generations removed from the horrors of the early fourth century, few were left who had seen anything other than this Athanasian version of persecution. They had come to accept the idea that their bishop was a defender of orthodoxy who braved violence and intimidation to protect the unity of the Egyptian church.

The events of 365 reveal an Athanasius who had prevailed in a long and difficult battle to craft a distinctive personal identity. He had beaten back the early charges of misuse of power and had managed to present himself in a new way, as an orthodox Christian champion persecuted by heretics and a misguided state. More than any tangible gifts of patronage, Athanasius's success in defining himself generated enthusiastic support from his congregation and inspired their spirited resistance to imperial pressure. It would be this victory that would keep the bishop secure in his position, despite an anti-Nicene emperor, from 365 until his death in 373.

THE ATHANASIAN HISTORICAL LEGACY

Athanasius's Alexandrian successors and Nicene supporters worked to ensure that the bishop's death did little to diminish the power and appeal of his well-crafted persona. A day celebrating Athanasius soon entered the liturgical calendar of the Nicene church across the empire.[116] Other days of celebration also found their way into local liturgical calendars, including days specific to both the Egyptian and Constantinopolitan churches.[117] Through the regular celebration of Athanasius's achievements, these festal days ensured widespread popular recognition of the spiritual leadership that the bishop had claimed. These celebrations also served a

116. Athanasius's death was commemorated on January 18, a commemoration that evidently began in the 370s.

117. *Coptic Synaxary,* Pashons 7; Constantinople also commemorated Athanasius on May 2, the date when his relics came to Constantinople. See B. Croke, "Reinventing Constantinople: Theodosius I's Imprint on the Imperial City," in *From the Tetrarchs to the Theodosians,* ed. S. McGill, C. Sogno, and E. Watts (Cambridge, 2010).

more important and less obvious purpose. In the same way that the preservation of a carefully tended Platonic historical legacy enabled leaders of the Old Academy to justify contemporary actions by evoking historical precedents, Christian leaders could draw upon the historical legacy of Athanasius to inspire support for their current policies. This proved to be especially important when those policies demanded that congregants resist imperial power.

The process that transformed Athanasius from a living Christian leader into a historical exemplar unfolded extremely quickly. Not even a decade after Athanasius's death, Gregory Nazianzen could convincingly begin his oration *On the Great Athanasius*[118] with the powerful statement: " When praising Athanasius, I will be praising virtue. For it is the same thing, to speak about him and to praise virtue, because he had, or, to speak more truly, he has gathered all virtue into himself."[119] For Gregory, Athanasius could already be compared with "men like Enoch, Noah, Abraham, Isaac, Jacob, the Twelve Patriarchs, Moses" and a long list of other Old and New Testament figures whose individual virtues he assembled in himself.[120] Gregory, however, quickly moved beyond this unobjectionable but rather uninspiring rhetorical template. The rest of the oration grafts Athanasius's life and career on to this family tree of Christian exemplars in a way that shows clearly the biblical prototypes on which Athanasius modeled his behavior. Athanasius's early life revealed the intelligence, moderation, and devotion to the study and understanding of Christian Scripture that one would expect of a future church leader.[121] As bishop, Athanasius showed moderate character and embodied the episcopal ideals described by Paul "in perfect exactness."[122] He lived a life of prayer with frequent fasting and meditation. He helped the poor, stood up to the powerful, and defended the weak. He protected virgins and widows, regulated the affairs of ascetics, and effectively taught his flock.[123]

Unfortunately, Gregory continues, arguments about theology made it difficult for the church to get the full benefit of Athanasius's skills. These arguments affected Athanasius profoundly when the "acts of insolence" of the Arian George of Cappadocia forced him into exile.[124] For Gregory, these moments of crisis made clear the degree to which Athanasius had based his behaviors on biblical exemplars. He persevered under persecution like Job[125] and, when he finally fled Alexandria, he "arranged his exile most excellently, for he betook himself to the holy

---

118. Gregory Nazianzen, *Or.* 21. This oration likely dates to the late 370s or early 380s.
119. *Or.* 21.1 = *In laudem Athanasii* 35.1081.39–42.
120. On the importance of the figure of Moses see Rapp, *Holy Bishops*, 125–33.
121. *Or.* 21.6–9.
122. *Or.* 21.10.
123. *Or.* 21.10.
124. *Or.* 21.12–17.
125. *Or.* 21.17–18.

and divine homes of contemplation in Egypt."[126] Among the monks, Athanasius served as a mediator of disputes and a lawgiver. The former role, Gregory suggests, reprised the actions of David and the latter showed him to be a new Moses.[127] Despite the challenges that George posed to the Nicene churches, Athanasius remained a "pillar of the Church" whose legacy inspired the people of Alexandria to resist the Arian pretender.[128] Under Julian, Athanasius earned another exile because of his indomitable resistance to imperial pressure and his ability to continue to inspire the faithful.[129] Throughout all of this, Athanasius maintained the unity of his congregation.[130] This achievement, Gregory claims, stands above Athanasius's vigils, his ascetic labors, and even his exiles.[131] Athanasius's commitment to it meant that "his life and habits formed the ideal of a bishop" and ensured that he earned for himself a spot within the ranks of martyrs and apostles.[132]

Gregory's portrait of Athanasius bears strong similarities to Athanasius's own efforts to define himself, but his oration differs in the way that it marks the significance of his actions. Gregory has shifted the rhetorical setting by explicitly placing Athanasius among the apostles and other biblical figures. This transformed Athanasius from a figure tied to the specific circumstances of the mid-fourth century into a timeless Christian exemplar whose actions illustrate general ideals of Christian conduct. In this way, Gregory's encomium of Athanasius resembles Speusippus's funeral oration for Plato and Xenocrates' biography of his teacher. Like these Academic texts, Gregory's encomium of Athanasius renders the evolving character of a living person into an individual with a static, thematically coherent, historical legacy.[133] In fact, the annual celebrations of the bishop's memory ensured that Christians would hear many of the same things about Athanasius in much the same way each year. However, like that of the Academic Plato, the Athanasian historical legacy opened itself to an infinite number of interpretations. While the man had died, his apostolic legacy remained a powerful tool that could explain contemporary circumstances and suggest appropriate behaviors for pious Christians.

Two *encomia* delivered in the early seventh century by Constantine of Siout on

---

126. *Or.* 21.19.

127. *Or.* 21.20.

128. *Or.* 21.26.

129. *Or.* 21.32.

130. *Or.* 21.35. For unity as a theme that Athanasius himself frequently advocated, see *Festal Letter* 11.11.

131. *Or.* 21.36.

132. *Or.* 21.37.

133. As time passed, the basic register of Athanasius's achievements did grow. Miracle accounts and other illustrative anecdotes gradually found their way into presentations of Athanasius's life throughout late antiquity, but the general themes that these texts emphasized continued to be much the same.

Athanasius's festival days show how the bishop's historical legacy could be reinterpreted and made relevant to contemporary circumstances.[134] The first of these starts from much the same premise as Gregory's earlier encomium. It celebrates "the memory of the Apostolic man who lived after the Apostles."[135] Athanasius earned this title, Constantine continues, "as if a reward on account of his contests and successes for the faith, just as those who receive high rank from a king" because of their struggles for his regime.[136] The greatest of his contests was that which prevented the "herd of Arian wolves" from dragging the faithful away from orthodoxy.[137]

After comparing Athanasius and Moses,[138] Constantine then lays out the tangible results of Athanasius's robust defense of God and orthodoxy. The first and most interesting incident he describes relates to a tsunami that struck Alexandria in 365.[139] Constantine speaks about the sea rising up into a wall of water and rushing into the city of Alexandria. "When they saw the height and the force of the waves, (the people of Alexandria) thought that it would submerge the entire earth and rivers and the mountains and the hills."[140] The people despaired but Athanasius, "the mediator between man and God,"[141] "came into this spiritual tempest so that he could speak with God."[142] Holding the book of Genesis in his hands, Athanasius reminded God of his promise to Noah to never again submerge the world. Respecting this pledge and the messenger who spoke of it to him, God told Athanasius not to fear. "Immediately the sea flowed back, its waves quieted upon its surface, its anger quieted, its height reduced, and its elevation went back down to the bottom."[143] Athanasius then led all of the people of the city in a mass in which he spoke about this event and encouraged them to give thanks to God. This ability to encourage God to control the sea, Constantine concludes, shows how Athanasius was indeed a second Moses.[144]

Constantine's celebration of Athanasius's role in pushing back the sea draws

---

134. Athanasius's memory was celebrated on the 7th of Pashons (May 2 in the Julian calendar). Constantine's orations have been edited and translated by T. Orlandi, *Constantini Episcopi Urbis Siout: Encomia in Athanasium Duo*, 2 vols., CSCO 349–50, (Louvain, 1974).

135. Constantine of Siout, *Enc. in Athan.* I, 1.1.12–13.

136. *Enc. in Athan.* I, 1.10.19–24. I take ΟΥΚΛΗΡΟC here to suggest the lots of land given to members of a victorious army.

137. *Enc. in Athan.* I, 1.11.3.

138. *Enc. in Athan.* I, 1.12–20.

139. *Enc. in Athan.* I, 2.21–28. This tsunami and the earthquake that caused it are well documented in other sources (e.g., Sozomen, 6.2; Ammianus, 26.19; Jerome, *Life of Hilarion* 40; idem, *Commentary on Isaiah* 15.5; Themistius, *Or* 7.86b and 11.150c–d; Socrates 4.3). For discussion, see G. Kelly, "Ammianus and the Great Tsunami," *JRS* 94 (2004), 141–51.

140. *Enc. in Athan.* I, 2.22.18–20.

141. ΠΜΕϹΙΤΗϹ ΜΠΝΟΥΤΕ ΜΝ ΝΡⲰΜΕ (*Enc. in Athan.* I, 2.23.22–23).

142. *Enc. in Athan.* I, 2.23.1–3.

143. *Enc. in Athan.* I, 2.25.8–11.

144. *Enc. in Athan.* I, 2.28.

upon the well-established idea of the bishop as a mediator between God and man, but it also emphasizes that Athanasius earned this privileged position in large part because of the many "persecutions which he endured on behalf of the orthodox faith."[145] These included expulsions from the city, exiles to the mountains,[146] and a great many other afflictions set up by his opponents. Nevertheless, Athanasius persevered because he knew that God was with him and, when it was necessary, God would work to preserve him from danger.[147] God's willingness to listen to Athanasius's appeals shows his approval of the way Athanasius lived.

Constantine also wanted his readers to see a deeper and more profound meaning in Athanasius's life. Though Constantine acknowledges that some listeners may think that their circumstances will never allow them to duplicate the achievements of Athanasius,[148] they must consider that "his memory is for us a profit for the soul and a sort of corrector."[149] The historical figure of Athanasius matters because he exemplifies the virtues that made one an effective Christian. Even if his example could not be duplicated exactly, Athanasius's principled resistance to heresy in general and Arianism in particular suggested a pattern of behavior that had value regardless of the historical moment. Constantine hoped his audience would see this and, to the degree that it was possible, model their behavior on Athanasius's example.

The second of Constantine's encomia of Athanasius makes an even clearer statement about how the lessons of Athanasius's life ought to affect the actions of both the bishop and his congregation. As in his first sermon, Constantine spends a great deal of time celebrating the ways in which Athanasius fought for orthodoxy against extreme and often fearsome Arian persecution. He explains that Athanasius received the cognomen "Apostolic" because "truly and justly did he share in it since he was afflicted with contests and persecutions like the Apostles, when they expelled him from his throne, plotting against him, accusing him, slandering him."[150] Despite this, Athanasius "persevered each day" and continued fighting for his faith. This put Athanasius in a unique position. His fight for the Trinity enabled him to intercede on behalf of those who followed his example in order to ensure that they joined him in heaven.[151] But Athanasius did not just provide a path that orthodox Christians could follow. He gave them the raw materials that would enable their defense of orthodoxy to succeed.

145. *Enc. in Athan.* I, 3.29.22–23.
146. An alternative is, perhaps, monastic communities. The Coptic reads ⲚⲦⲞⲨⲈⲒⲎ, perhaps a deliberate ambiguity on the part of Constantine.
147. *Enc. in Athan.* I, 3.29–32; this section contains a remarkable story about God hiding Athanasius from an ambush that was set for him.
148. E.g., *Enc. in Athan.* 1, 1.7; 3.34.
149. *Enc. in Athan.* I, 6.45.24–25.
150. *Enc. in Athan.* II, 1.6.7–12.
151. *Enc. in Athan.* II, 4.30–31.

When Constantine reaches this point, the real significance of the sermon becomes apparent. He appeals directly to Athanasius and says to him:

> Not just the Arians will be shut down with your words, but others who will come and transgress the faith, I speak about the ones who assemble at the synod of Chalcedon, the ones who dissolved the unity of the entire empire by daring to divide the indivisible, God the Word who took on flesh for our salvation, having two natures in one. And they who descend from the line of Mani and Valentinus and Marcion and Apollinaris and Eutyches until Julian the old wretch, these are Manichean fantasists.[152]

Constantine's reference to Chalcedonianism as a transgression of the faith shows why Athanasius's words and the model of his behavior remained directly relevant to Constantine's congregation. Like Athanasius, they too lived in a time when orthodoxy needed champions to defend it against a hostile state. In the early seventh century, this state championed Chalcedonianism instead of Arianism. Constantine certainly invoked the example of Athanasius to galvanize anti-Chalcedonian resistance but, if a passage from the *Synaxary* of the Coptic Church is to be trusted,[153] another target may well have been a less glamorous but more intractable enemy. In a puzzling reference, the *Synaxary* states that "(Constantine) strove with all of his might to extirpate the roots of the Arians who were in the neighborhood of his town and in the mountains[154] which surrounded it."[155] It has been argued, plausibly, that this refers to Melitian communities in the area around Siout.[156] Whatever the nature of the group to which this term refers, it does seem that the very fight against Arianism that Constantine sees as defining the career of Athanasius also helped to define his own episcopate. In a way, Constantine's celebration of Athanasius justifies his own anti-Chalcedonian and anti-Melitian activities. His interpretation of Athanasius both provides a model for his audience and serves to reinforce his own spiritual authority.

The Athanasian *encomia* of Gregory Nazianzen and Constantine of Siout are

---

152. *Enc. in Athan.* II, 4.31.21–30.

153. A full summary of Constantine's life is preserved in the Sahidic recension of the Arabic *Synaxarion*. For discussion of this see R-G. Coquin, "Constantine of Siout," *Coptic Encyclopedia*, 2.591. On Constantine in general, note as well the longer studies, R-G. Coquin, "Saint Constantin, évêque d'Asyūt," *Studia Orientalia Christiana Collectanea* 16 (1981), 151–70; and G. Garitte, "Constantin, évêque d' Assiout," in *Coptic Studies in Honor of W. E. Crum, Bulletin of the Byzantine Institute* 2 (1950), 287–304.

154. As Coquin points out, the Arabic *jabal* in this passage is a possible mistranslation of ⲦⲞⲞⲨ and may obscure a reference to monasteries.

155. This quotation is taken from Coquin, "Constantine of Siout," 591, col. 2.

156. As noted above, there is evidence for the survival of Melitian communities (and particularly Melitian monasteries) into the eighth century (e.g., W. E. Crum, "Some Further Melitian Documents," *JEA* 13 [1927], 19–26). Because Athanasius conflated Melitians and Arians, it is certainly plausible that this conflation would have persisted in the writings of those who claimed to follow his path.

examples of perhaps the most important tool available to teach Christian congregations about Athanasius's life. Sermons like these communicated details of Athanasius's career, defined his legacy for their audience, and, because they were repeated many times, served to periodically reinforce their own lessons. Indeed, Athanasius is mentioned on no less than fourteen different days in the *Synaxary*. Most of these mentions highlight either his anti-Arian activities or his connection to prominent ascetics.[157] A Christian who attended liturgy regularly could not avoid learning about the bishop and his importance.[158] As Constantine's second *encomium* shows, however, these celebrations did more than simply inform their listeners about Athanasius. The sermons given on these days could also interpret the examples provided by men like Athanasius and use these historical figures to encourage Christians to adopt certain behaviors or attitudes.

Late antique bishops influenced the lives of their congregations through the tangible benefits that they delivered and through their instruction in how to interpret and apply the teachings of Scripture. People came to them for this instruction because they believed that the bishop, and the bishop alone, could lead them away from a life of sin and towards salvation. These duties mattered, however, only if a bishop could convince his congregation that the Holy Spirit inspired his teachings and his actions. Informed by Pauline instruction and biblical exemplars, Christians expected that effective bishops would display attributes suggesting that they enjoyed an intimate connection to the divine. This sort of bishop lived chastely, looked to help the poor, showed no love of money, and fought heresy, while demonstrating no propensity to violence.[159] Regardless of the tangible benefits he could bring them, a bishop who did not display this rare mixture of characteristics ran the risk of losing the confidence of his congregation. Bishops who showed too much of a propensity to violence or tendency to self-aggrandizement could even earn the label, "tyrant-bishop."[160]

Athanasius of Alexandria was a unique figure who, at various times, inspired

---

157. In addition to Athanasius's own feast day (Pashons 7), he is mentioned on Thout 16 and 30, Paopi 4 and 18, Tobi 22, Meshir 2 and 20, Paremoude 11, Pashons 14, Paoni 2 and 6, Mesori 18, and Nasi 4. His opposition to Arianism and the persecutions he endured because of it are the focus of accounts on Thout 30, Paopi 4, Meshir 20, Mesori 18, and Nasi 4. His support for ascetics is featured on Tobi 22, Meshir 2, Paremoude 11, Pashons 14, and Paoni 6. Thout 16 celebrates the consecration of sanctuaries in Jerusalem at which Athanasius was an attendee. Paopi 18 commemorates Theophilus, Athanasius's protégé. Paoni 2 commemorates the transfer of the relics of John the Baptist and Elijah.

158. It is clear that the audience in individual churches varied from year to year and even from week to week. On this, note especially the comments of Mayer, "John Chrysostom," 114–22.

159. *Didascalia*, ch. 3.1; p. 27, l. 24.

160. On this concept, note the discussion of Gaddis, *There is no Crime*, 268–81.

charges of tyrant-like behavior and earned a reputation for piously resisting the violence of imperial officials. Early in his career, Athanasius aggressively used the political tools available to a late antique bishop to undermine his opponents. These actions prompted charges that he had abused his position as bishop. Although Athanasius vigorously fought these accusations and convinced many Egyptian Christians that they were untrue, his own political missteps and a change in imperial administration forced him into exile. In the end, Athanasius would endure five different exiles between 335 and 366, which prevented him from delivering the reliable access to money and patronage that imperial recognition conveyed to bishops. Nevertheless, over this time Athanasius succeeded in increasing both the number of his followers and the fervor of their support.

Athanasius accomplished this because he defined himself as a bishop who championed orthodoxy, fought for the needs of virgins and ascetics, and resisted the threats and intimidation tactics of his opponents. Athanasius masterfully arranged public events that reinforced this self-definition, a skill perhaps best displayed during the year and a half between his first and second exiles. As the threat of imperial intervention increased, Athanasius used his role as the city's foremost Christian teacher to define the coming showdown as one that would pit the orthodox against violent heretics. Virtue, he argued, demanded that he and his followers resist the violence that his opponents would use to dislodge him. Athanasius later repeated this line of argument, with even greater effect, in the 350s and 360s. By 365, Athanasius had transformed himself into a symbol of principled Christian resistance to political pressure whose example could inspire others to act in a similar fashion. What began as a defense of Athanasius's spiritual authority now resonated as a powerful call to action.

Athanasius remained an important figure even after his death. In Egypt and elsewhere, the church calendar frequently commemorated Athanasius in ways that highlighted his exiles and his support for ascetics. These celebrations of Athanasius smoothed away the controversial aspects of his career in order to create a sort of two-dimensional historical character who matched the apostles and prophets in his commitment to charity, peacefulness, and orthodoxy. The many references to the bishop's career during the year ensured that Christians who attended church would be familiar with Athanasius. On occasion, they would even hear their bishop deliver a sermon explaining what Athanasius did and how his example could be imitated in contemporary situations. These commemorations ensured that the call to action that Athanasius repeatedly issued to his followers remained meaningful for subsequent Christian generations.

7

Theophilus and Cyril

The Alexandrian Bishop Triumphant

Athanasius succeeded in establishing an effective Nicene presence in Alexandria that could survive the most aggressive attacks of both ecclesiastical opponents and imperial officials. The accession of Theodosius I brought a dramatic shift in the position of Nicene bishops throughout the empire. Imperial authorities became much more attentive to the needs and requests of Nicene bishops. The model of episcopal resistance to Christian emperors created by Athanasius and celebrated by Nicene Christians throughout the Eastern empire remained inspirational, but it no longer offered a practical set of behaviors through which a bishop could demonstrate authoritative spiritual leadership.

The Theodosian age was, by contrast, an age of opportunity, in which Nicene emperors offered imperial cooperation to encourage the growth and development of the Alexandrian Nicene church. Beginning with Theophilus, Alexandrian Nicene bishops cultivated this imperial support and used it to assert themselves within their city and its surroundings. Early in his career, Theophilus drew upon the same episcopal and ascetic coalition that Athanasius had used to sustain himself and his followers during his later exiles.[1] He mobilized them for a far different purpose, however. Instead of defending the church against impious attacks, they led an offensive that spread the faith by destroying Alexandria's pagan religious infrastructure. With imperial help, they then refashioned the city's sacred space through the construction of urban monasteries and martyria.

---

1. Theophilus's difficulties with ascetics like the Tall Brothers manifested themselves later in the 390s, after the initial and most active stages of his anti-pagan campaigns. Theophilus's relations with Egyptian ascetics are explored in more detail below.

Theophilus's grand project forced his followers, both ascetic and lay, to accept a new kind of episcopal leadership that seemed to sanction behaviors and value institutions that Athanasius had not. For this to happen, Theophilus needed to articulate his authority according to different standards than those used by Athanasius. In doing so, Theophilus realized something important. In the same way that the historical example of Athanasius could be used to prescribe conduct, it could also be deployed as a tool to justify actions that might otherwise bring the spiritual authority of a bishop into question. With this Athanasian sanction established, Theophilus's anti-pagan activities enabled him to claim a new form of exemplary episcopal leadership.

Although he occasionally challenged imperial officials, Theophilus's successor Cyril operated within this same general political climate. Like Theophilus, Cyril understood clearly how the twin tools of patronage and Christian ceremonial could be used to influence popular perceptions of contemporary events. Early in his regime, Cyril choreographed a number of actions designed to evoke Theophilus. Cyril's later actions, however, show a more nuanced self-presentation. While Cyril continued to echo Theophilus by taking periodic swipes at paganism, he also used the figure of Athanasius to present himself as a fighter for doctrinal orthodoxy. In the end, Theophilus and Cyril represent two figures who articulated a set of evolving rationales to justify imperial and episcopal cooperation as well as the new activities this close relationship permitted.

THEOPHILUS AND THE HISTORICAL CHARACTER OF ATHANASIUS

After his death in 373, Athanasius was succeeded as patriarch by two somewhat nondescript brothers, Peter II and Timothy. When Timothy died in July 385, the (relatively) young and dynamic Theophilus stepped into his place. Theophilus, a native of Memphis,[2] had served under Athanasius and his immediate successors.[3] He broke with the Athanasian episcopal model by developing a close relationship

2. John of Nikiu, 79.1.
3. For overviews of the career of Theophilus, see C. Haas, *Alexandria in Late Antiquity: Topography and Social Conflict* (Baltimore, 1997), 160–68; N. Russell, *Theophilus of Alexandria* (London, 2007), 3–45; S. Davis, *The Early Coptic Papacy: The Egyptian Church and Its Leadership in Late Antiquity* (Cairo, 2004), 63–70. On the specific questions of Theophilus's involvement in the destruction of Alexandrian pagan temples, see the important discussion of J. Hahn, *Gewalt und religiöser Konflikt: Studien zu den Auseinandersetzungen zwischen Christen, Heiden, und Juden im Osten des Römischen Reiches (von Konstantin bis Theodosius II)* (Berlin, 2004), 81–105; and idem, "The Conversion of the Cult Statues: The Destruction of the Serapeum 392 A.D. and the Transformation of Alexandria into the 'Christ-Loving' City," in *From Temple to Church: Destruction and Renewal of Local Cultic Topography in Late Antiquity*, ed. J. Hahn, S. Emmel, and U. Gotter (Leiden, 2008), 335–63.

with the imperial court in Constantinople as well as the civil and military officials sent by it to govern Egypt.[4] Theophilus then drew upon both Egyptian ascetics and imperial officials to replace the city's pagan infrastructure with something that better served the needs of its growing Christian population.

Theophilus's program impacted the city and its suburbs in many different places, but no part of it attracted more attention than his successful effort in the early 390s to refashion the Alexandrian Serapeum and its surrounding precincts.[5] The imperfect nature of our sources makes it impossible to reconstruct precisely the process through which this occurred, but a basic outline of events can be recovered from the earliest surviving account, that of Rufinus of Aquileia.[6]

Rufinus describes a series of disturbances that began when Theophilus requested and received imperial permission to restore a decrepit basilica that had been donated to Alexandria's Arian bishops by Constantius.[7] When renovation began, the workmen found an underground pagan shrine (probably a Mith-

---

4. Theophilus's simultaneously obsequious and forceful letter to the emperor Theodosius, which accompanied his Easter Tables (in B. Krusch, ed., *Studien zur christlich-mittelalterlichen Chronologie. Der 84 jährige Ostercyclus und seine Quellen* [Leipzig, 1880], 20–21; cf. Russell, *Theophilus*, 79–82) shows the careful balance the patriarch tried to strike between flattery of the sovereign and assertion of patriarchal spiritual authority.

5. Scholars have proposed a range of dates for the destruction of the Serapeum. For 391 see, among others, Haas, *Alexandria in Late Antiquity*, 161; J. McKenzie, S. Gibson, and A. T. Reyes, "Reconstructing the Serapeum in Alexandria from the Archaeological Evidence," *JRS* 94 (2004), 107. For 391/2 see, again among others, G. Bowersock, *Hellenism in Late Antiquity* (Ann Arbor, 1990), 22. For 392, see Hahn, *Gewalt und religiöser Konflikt*, 82–84; idem, "Conversion of Cult Statues," 340–45. Much of this discussion hinges upon the dating and interpretation of *CTh* 16.10.11, a law of 391 restricting pagan access to cultic sites. As Hahn reasonably argues (*Gewalt und religiöser Konflikt*, 82–84; "Conversion of Cult Statues," 340), this law does not sanction the destruction of temples. However, edicts neither set off the violence that led pagans to occupy the Serapeum nor mediated between these pagan defenders and angry Christians. These functions were performed by imperial rescripts or other communications (Rufinus [*HE* 11.22], for example, indicates that a rescript resolved the standoff). Communications like this would not have been included in the *Theodosian Code*. *CTh* 16.10.11 may, however, have precipitated Theophilus's initial actions by signaling an imperial climate in which Theodosius would be willing to sanction anti-pagan activity. If so, this suggests that the events began in 391 but may have climaxed later.

6. The challenges of reconstructing these events have been analyzed repeatedly in the past decade. See, for example, Haas, *Alexandria in Late Antiquity*, 161; Russell, *Theophilus*, 7–10; Davis, *Early Coptic Papacy*, 64–65. The most comprehensive recent treatment of the sources for this event is that of Hahn, *Gewalt und religiöser Konflikt*, 85–97. Rufinus's treatment (*HE* 11.22–30) was assembled from two earlier sources in the first years of the fifth century. His account of the riot and destruction of the cult statue drew upon a Palestinian account written by a Sophronius and his description of the transfer of relics to the site derives from a Theophilan source. This second, Theophilan source will be discussed in more detail below.

7. *HE* 11.22. Sozomen suggests that this may have been a ruined temple of Dionysus (*HE* 7.15).

raeum), which still contained images.[8] Theophilus seems to have "led in public procession the tokens of its bloody mysteries."[9] The pagans then "began to behave violently and to give vent to their fury in public ... they used weapons, battling up and down the streets so that the two sides (pagan and Christian) were at open war."[10] Led by a cadre of intellectuals, the pagan rioters retreated to the Serapeum hill, a fortified complex that could be likened to the Acropolis of Alexandria, and began to transform it into a base for guerilla operations.[11] They led a group of Christian prisoners with them, a captive population whose numbers grew as the pagan rioters launched sorties into the city and brought back prisoners.[12] Although imperial officials in Alexandria tried to mediate, the situation was resolved only when the emperor Theodosius intervened. In his "great clemency," Theodosius marked as martyrs the Christians who had been killed, granted amnesty to the pagan rioters, and ordered that the pagan cults in the city "be done away with (so that) the reason for the conflict would disappear."[13] When this imperial letter was read out, the pagan defenders melted away into the cheering crowd that had assembled.

The aftermath of this settlement shows that, regardless of the apparent compromise Theodosius had ordered, Theophilus and his church had prevailed. Theodosius had effected a settlement that subtly but undeniably gave Theophilus the freedom to act as he wished against Alexandria's pagans. Theodosius's law had no enforcement mechanisms, but it needed none to change the city. With the legal restraints that protected pagan cults now loosened, Theophilus could pursue a religious realignment of his own design. Alexandria's pagans clearly sensed this shift. Although absolved of legal accountability, many of the pagan intellectuals who led the defense of the temple fled Alexandria.[14] Other teachers, even those who did not participate in the violence, found themselves removed from public teaching positions. An epigram by Palladas suggests that Theophilus may have

8. Such, at any rate, is the information provided by Socrates Scholasticus (*HE* 5.16). This supplementary detail may well be correct because Socrates reconstructed these events based upon the oral traditions of two pagan teachers who participated in the subsequent riot.

9. Socrates, *HE* 5.16.

10. Rufinus, *HE* 11.22 (trans. Amidon).

11. For the intellectual leadership of this group see Watts, *City and School in Late Antique Athens and Alexandria* (Berkeley, 2006), 190–91; Hahn, *Gewalt und religiöser Konflikt*, 92–93. On the nature of the Serapeum site see McKenzie, Gibson, and Reyes, "Reconstructing the Serapeum," 73–121.

12. Rufinus, *HE* 11.22. The Christian rhetorician Gessius seems to have been one of these prisoners and, after the rioters vacated the temple, he was found brutally murdered on its grounds (on which see Palladas, *Anth. Pal.* 7.686.1–6; cf. Haas, *Alexandria*, 163).

13. Rufinus, *HE* 11.22 (trans. Amidon). J. Hahn (*Gewalt und religiöser Konflikt*, 87–88) thinks it improbable that these were the real terms on which the hill was evacuated.

14. Hahn, *Gewalt und religiöser Konflikt*, 99.

FIGURE 4. Serapeum site, Alexandria. Photo by Manasi Watts.

been involved in this process of scholastic cleansing.[15] Their troubles, however, were minor when compared to the fate of the Serapeum complex itself.

After Serapis's defenders had dispersed from the hill, a crowd made up of curious Christians and a troop of soldiers wandered cautiously around the abandoned temple compound. Suddenly, one of the soldiers "seized a double-headed axe, drew himself up, and struck" the famous chryselephantine statue of Serapis housed on the site.[16] The soldier continued to hit it until the statue collapsed.

> After this, the head was wrenched off of the neck ... and dragged off; then the feet and other members were chopped off with axes and dragged apart with ropes attached, and piece by piece, each in a different place, the decrepit dotard was burned to ashes before the eyes of the Alexandria which had worshipped him. Last of all, the torso which was left was put to the torch in the amphitheater, and that was the end of the vain superstition and ancient error of Serapis.[17]

While the actions of the soldier may well have been spontaneous, the distribution and ritual immolation of the pieces of the Serapis statue across the different

---

15. Hahn, *Gewalt und religiöser Konflikt*, 100, suggests this on the basis in part of *Anth. Gr.* 9.175. Cf. Alan Cameron, "Palladas and Christian Polemic," *JRS* 55 (1965), 27.

16. Rufinus, *HE* 11.23 (trans. Amidon).

17. Rufinus, *HE* 11.23 (trans. Amidon).

quarters of the city suggests a degree of organization one would not expect to find in a mob. Indeed, these events evoke the well-established Alexandrian custom of killing, dismembering, and burning the bodies of criminals or members of disruptive communities as a ritualized purification of the city.[18] Christian martyrs (including, it was said, St. Mark) had suffered this fate and, given this communal history, the ritualized desecration and destruction of Serapis would seem appropriate.[19] However, these processions did not simply symbolize the fall of Serapis. They also celebrated the emergence of a new arrangement within Alexandria through which Theophilus and agents of imperial authority now cooperated with one another to exercise power over the religious affairs of the city.

Perhaps emboldened by an additional imperial edict,[20] Theophilus's reach quickly extended beyond the hill of the Serapeum. Within the city of Alexandria, "the busts of Serapis, which had been in every house in the walls, the entrances, the doorposts, and even the windows, were so cut and filed away that not even a trace or mention of him or any other demon remained."[21] Other temples were also struck. Much to the chagrin of Palladas, the Alexandrian Tychaion was transformed by Theophilus into a wine shop.[22] Perhaps because of this extreme profanation, its statues remained standing at least until the seventh century.[23] Those associated with other cults were less fortunate. Theophilus's associates melted many

---

18. On this ritual, see Haas, *Alexandria*, 87–89. Theophilus, however, seems to have created a new idiom in which the ritual purification takes place entirely within city walls and the desecrated objects remain in public view. For discussion of this see D. Frankfurter, "Iconoclasm and Christianization in Late Antique Egypt: Christian Treatments of Space and Image," in *From Temple to Church: Destruction and Renewal of Local Cultic Topography in Late Antiquity*, ed. J. Hahn, S. Emmel, and U. Gotter (Leiden, 2008), 146–47.

19. Most famously, the Arian bishop George of Cappadocia experienced this (e.g., Socrates, *HE* 3.3), but previous generations of Christian martyrs had been similarly sentenced (e.g., the Alexandrian martyrs described in Eusebius, *HE* 6.41; cf. the Jewish victims of the pogrom of 38 described in Philo, *In Flacc.* 65). For Saint Mark, see his fictionalized life in the *History of the Patriarchs of Alexandria*, 1.1.

20. *CTh* 16.10.12. For the ambiguous connections between this edict, an earlier anti-pagan edict (*CTh* 16.10.11), the imperial letter resolving the Serapeum standoff, and the action that precipitated the violence, see, most notably, Hahn, *Gewalt und religiöser Konflikt*, 81–84. Note as well the comparable situation in Constantinople with *CTh* 16.1.2 and 16.5.6, edicts that provide legal cover for anti-Arian activities (N. McLynn, "Moments of Truth: Gregory Nazianzen and Theodosius I," in *From the Tetrarchs to the Theodosians*, edited by S. McGill, C. Sogno, and E. Watts (Cambridge, 2010).

21. Rufinus, *HE* 11.29.

22. Palladas, *Anth. Pal.* 9.180–83. On this see Haas, *Alexandria*, 167; Hahn, *Gewalt und religiöser Konflikt*, 95. On the Tychaion more generally see the important studies of C. Gibson, "Alexander in the Tychaion: Ps.-Libanius on the Statues," *GRBS* 47 (2007), 431–54; and "The Alexandrian Tychaion and the date of Ps.-Nicolaus *Progymnasmata*," *CQ*, (forthcoming). J. McKenzie, *The Architecture of Alexandria and Egypt, 300 B.C.–A.D. 700* (New Haven, 2007), 245–46, suggests that Palladas may be speaking metaphorically.

23. Gibson, "The Alexandrian Tychaion," forthcoming.

statues down and leveled "all deserted shrines in Alexandria . . . almost column by column."[24] Theophilus's interests extended beyond Alexandria as well. Assisted by a cohort of monks, Theophilus's associates attacked and destroyed the Serapeum and other major temples of the Alexandrian suburb of Canopus at this time.[25] While smaller than their Alexandrian brethren, the Canopic shrines "were revered . . . to such an extent that their popularity was far greater than that of Alexandria."[26] Although some suburban shrines (like the temple of Isis in Menouthis) continued to function secretly, the destruction of these temples represented a major Christian triumph.

In order to secure the territory he and his allies had just conquered, Theophilus embarked upon a building and resettlement program designed to garrison these formerly pagan sites with strong Christian fighters. The Alexandrian Serapeum became the site of a church, a shrine housing the remains of John the Baptist and the prophet Elisha, and perhaps a monastery as well.[27] The martyrium attached to the church was a particularly impressive building, later described as "massive, its dimensions lofty and it was very much decorated."[28] Intriguingly, these were not conversions of whatever remained of the pagan buildings on the site[29] but were instead new structures constructed to the west of the old colonnaded court.[30] In Canopus, Theophilus pursued a similar strategy. The pagan Eunapius indicates that he installed martyria containing the "bones and heads of those condemned for

---

24. For the melting down and destruction of cult statues see Socrates, *HE* 5.15; *Anth. Pal.* 9.441.1–6. The temple destruction is best described in Rufinus, *HE* 11.28.

25. Both Rufinus (*HE* 11.26) and Eunapius (*VS* 472–73) speak about the destruction of the Canopic Serapeum and multiple other temples. Eunapius suggests that monks may have been involved, a point perhaps reinforced by an account in the Coptic *Storia della Chiesa di Alessandria* (vol. II, 12.19–24). On ascetic involvement in the assault on Canopus, see Hahn, *Gewalt und religiöser Konflikt*, 102. For the Canopic shrines in general, see F. Kayser, "Oreilles et couronnes: à propos des cultes de Canope," *BIFAO* 91 (1991), 207–17.

26. Rufinus, *HE* 11.26; cf. Eunapius, *VS* 471.

27. Rufinus, *HE* 11.27–28; *Storia della Chiesa*, II.14.10–16.2; Sozomen, *HE* 7.15. On the martyrium and church note the important discussion of the archeological evidence by McKenzie, Gibson, and Reyes, "Reconstructing the Serapeum," 107–10, and the treatment of McKenzie, *Architecture of Alexandria*, 246. In his discussion of the aftermath of the Serapeum destruction, Eunapius describes Theophilus "importing so-called monks into the sacred places" (*VS* 472) and mentions that he did this at Canopus too.

28. John of Nikiu, 78.46 (trans. Charles). Sozomen (*HE* 7.15.10) states that the church was named after Arcadius, suggesting perhaps that the structure may have been completed after 395 (though Arcadius had been proclaimed Augustus in 383 and could be so honored before his father's death). On the custom of associating such Alexandrian structures with the imperial family, note McKenzie, *Architecture of Alexandria*, 246–47.

29. Rufinus (*HE* 11.27) and Eunapius (*VS* 472) indicate that the temple and its associated buildings were completely leveled, but both Evagrius Scholasticus (*HE* 2.5) and the *Life of Peter the Iberian* 72 suggest that the Serapeum could still be used in the mid-fifth century.

30. On this, note McKenzie, Gibson, and Reyes, "Reconstructing the Serapeum," 109.

many crimes" (i.e., Christian martyrs) near the site of the old Canopic Serapeum and settled monks there as well.[31] Theophilus apparently first tried to populate this monastery with Palestinian monks but, when these proved insufficiently hearty to confront the remaining pagans, he then sent for some Pachomians. "These men, through the power of their *askesis* and their continuous prayers, expelled the demons and caused Canopus to become a place open to any monk who wished."[32] In the more remote Eastern suburb of Menouthis, Theophilus constructed a church dedicated to the Holy Evangelists to which Cyril, his nephew and successor, would eventually add martyria dedicated to the saints Cyrus and John.[33]

This construction played an important role in Theophilus's efforts to "Christianize" the Alexandrian sacred environment. The relics provided spiritual power that could overcome that of traditional Egyptian deities. Speaking about the Menouthis shrine to the martyrs Cyrus and John, Sophronius describes relics pushing Isis "into flight from earth to Tartarus."[34] Theophilus apparently thought that the relics of apostles and prophets had even more power over the old gods than Alexandrian martyrs. When he had the chance, Theophilus seems to have made use of them to clear important pagan cultic centers like the Alexandrian Serapeum.[35] The monasteries that he sponsored had a more concrete effect on the environment. While the relics of saints patrolled the spiritual periphery and prevented pagan gods from returning to their old haunts, the physical presence of monks similarly deterred the gods' devotees from trying to reclaim this space.[36] Like a squad of police, these resident monks guarded the old temple space, observed the actions of all visitors, and reported those who behaved with suspicious reverence.[37]

These projects proved effective in building and maintaining a new Alexandrian religious landscape, but the methods that Theophilus used put him very much at

31. Eunapius, VS 472.
32. *Storia della Chiesa*, II.12.21–24. On the Pachomian monastery Theophilus founded and its activities see J.-L. Fournet and J. Gascou, "Moines pachômiens et batellerie," *Alexandrie médiévale* 2, *Études alexandrines* 8 (2002), 23–45. Despite the urban setting, this monastery still remained a closed ascetic environment in which only monks were ever completely welcome.
33. Sophronius, *Laudes in ss. Cyrum et Joannem* 27 (PG 87.3, 3412–13).
34. Sophronius, *Laudes in ss. Cyrum et Joannem*, 29 (PG 87.3.3416–17). Sophronius refers to this goddess indirectly but the formal functions he attributes to her (e.g., *Laudes* 24 = PG 87.3.3409) match those of the Menouthan Isis described by Zacharias in the *Life of Severus*. On this, note J. A. McGuckin, "The Influence of the Isis Cult on St. Cyril of Alexandria's Christology," *Studia Patristica* 24 (1993), 291–99.
35. For this idea, note Russell, *Theophilus*, 11.
36. Of course, monks could, and did, combat the presence of demons as well (cf. D. Brakke, *Demons and the Making of the Monk: Spiritual Combat in Early Christianity* [Cambridge, MA, 2006], 213–26).
37. Gesius's conflict with Shenoute evidently began when one of Shenoute's monks observed Gesius pouring a libation to the gods on the site of a recently demolished temple. On this incident, note Brakke, *Demons*, 97–98.

odds with the model of episcopal behavior that Athanasius had helped to define for Alexandrians. Perhaps dissuaded by the continued vigor of the Alexandrian pagan community during his lifetime,[38] Athanasius did not work aggressively to transform pagan temples into Christian spaces. Although his early career saw him attempt to use imperial power to enhance his position in the city, he became known for arguing passionately against the use of force in religious matters and for resisting when violence was improperly applied. Athanasius also did not place particular emphasis upon relics, arguing instead that holiness resided with people who were "within the truth."[39]

Theophilus's apparent break with the Athanasian model of ecclesiastical leadership proved contentious within the Egyptian church. His building activities aroused suspicion that he had redirected money intended for the poor to construct churches and martyria.[40] Even celebrated actions like the storming of the Serapeum and the Canopic shrines generated a mixed reaction. Some of the traditions preserved in the *Apophthegmata Patrum* provide a possible cross section of popular responses to Theophilus's efforts. One of the traditions preserved under the heading of Epiphanius mentions a charioteer, the son of a woman named Mary, who fell, got up, and won his race. "At this point, the crowd cried out 'The son of Mary has fallen, risen again and is the victor.' When this cry was still being spoken, a report about the temple of Serapis reached the crowd, saying that the great Theophilus had gone and thrown down the image of Serapis, and become master of the temple."[41]

A more ambiguous report appears under Theophilus's own heading. It describes a time when Theophilus summoned monks to go to Alexandria to pray and destroy pagan temples. When they sat down to eat with him, they were brought veal. They ate, pretending not to realize what it was. Then Theophilus asked them if they wanted any more meat. Now forced to acknowledge that their obligation to accept hospitality would cause them to violate dietary laws, they stopped eating.[42] Far from serving as their champion, Theophilus here appears as a character who introduces monks into a struggle without consideration for or understanding of the particular contours of ascetic life.[43]

---

38. Note the suggestion of Haas, *Alexandria*, 159, that the lynching of George of Cappadocia may have encouraged Alexandrian bishops to refrain from provoking the city's pagan communities.

39. Athanasius's view of relics is laid out in *Festal Letter* 41 and analyzed in D. Brakke, "'Outside the Places, Within the Truth': Athanasius of Alexandria and the Localization of the Holy," in *Pilgrimage and Holy Space*, 445–81.

40. Palladius, *Dialog* 6.22. For this complaint, note M. Gaddis, *There is no Crime for Those Who Have Christ: Religious Violence in the Christian Roman Empire* (Berkeley, 2005), 275; and P. Brown, *Power and Persuasion: Towards a Christian Empire* (Madison, WI, 1992), 118–20.

41. Epiphanius 2 = *Apo. Pat.* 164.15–21.

42. Theophilus 3 = *Apo. Pat.* 200.1–10.

43. Brakke, *Demons*, 219–20.

Another passage in the Alphabetic collection of *Apophthegmata* expresses more covert disapproval of Theophilus's use of monks in urban anti-pagan campaigns.

> On another day, when I [Doulas] came to his cell, I found him [Bessarion] standing at prayer with his hands raised towards heaven. For fourteen days, he remained like this. Then he called me and said to me, "Follow me." We went into the desert . . . walking on, we came to a cave where, on entering, we found a brother seated, engaged in plaiting a rope . . . We continued our journey toward Lycopolis, till we reached Abba John's cell . . . Abba Bessarion said that a decree (ἀπόφασις) had gone forth that the temples should be destroyed. That is what happened: they were destroyed. On our return, we came again to the cave where we had seen the brother. . . . When we entered, we found him dead . . . When we took the body to bury it, we discovered that it was a woman by nature. The old man marveled and said, "See how women triumph over Satan and we behave shamefully in the cities."[44]

This long passage contrasts the quiet, contemplative behavior of the female ascetic and the shameful actions of monks who responded to a summons to destroy temples in the city.[45] While the text does not name Theophilus as the source of this summons, his involvement in calling the monks from their carefully regulated lives in the desert would have been understood. Like the picture of the patriarch who served veal to his ascetic visitors, this anecdote reveals a Theophilus who is concerned with worldly matters and either ignorant of the true purpose of ascetic discipline or unconcerned about the negative effect that his request would have on monks.[46]

Beginning with Athanasius, Alexandrian Nicene patriarchs had used their close relationship to ascetics to demonstrate their spiritual authority to their followers. The existence of an undercurrent of criticism suggesting that Theophilus either failed to understand ascetics or actively undermined their practice could prove extremely dangerous, especially if the doubts that monks harbored about his leadership spread to the general population. Indeed, in 399, Theophilus penned an ill-advised Paschal Letter in which he defended the incorporeality of God. Many monks responded violently and marched to Alexandria "where they incited unrest against the bishop, judging him impious, and threatening to put him to death."[47] Understanding both the physical threat that these monks posed and the danger that their charges of impiety would undermine his spiritual authority, Theophilus quickly beat a theological retreat.

---

44. Bessarion 4 = *Apo. Pat.* 140.15–141.8 (trans. Brakke, *Demons*, 220).

45. For an interpretation of this passage, see Brakke, *Demons*, 221. The order to destroy temples must be linked to the shameful conduct in the cities, unless the latter comment is to be understood as a *non sequitur*.

46. Brakke, *Demons*, 221

47. Socrates, *HE* 6.7. On the larger controversy that this incited, see E. Clark, *The Origenist Controversy: The Cultural Construction of an Early Christian Debate* (Princeton, 1992).

Theophilus showed similar skill in managing the ascetic reaction to his anti-pagan activities. There exist different versions of the damning Apophthegmatic tradition describing Bessarion, the female ascetic, and the "shamefulness" of monks participating in Theophilus's campaign, alternative accounts that blunt the charge that the bishop had drawn the monks into a shameful enterprise. Both the Latin and Greek systematic collections cleave the temple destructions from the description of the female brother in the cave and mark them not as shameful acts but as the fulfillment of a divine command.[48] This shift transforms a tradition implicitly hostile to Theophilus into one that celebrates his anti-pagan activity, a transformation enhanced by the introduction of two ascetic witnesses who attest to the divine sanction of his actions.[49] This suggests that Theophilus had managed to convince others that his attempt to remake the Alexandrian religious landscape did not conflict with but derived from his spiritual authority as Alexandrian bishop.[50]

Coptic texts show that Theophilus accomplished this transformation in part by drawing explicitly upon the historical legacy of Athanasius. The best evidence for this comes from a tradition preserved in the late antique Coptic church history known to scholars as the *Storia della Chiesa di Alessandria*.[51] This text attributes an Athanasian inspiration to Theophilus's construction of the martyria of John the Baptist and Elisha on the Serapeum site. The narration begins with the reign of the emperor Julian and describes how, when Julian set out on his Persian campaign, Palestinian Jews tried to burn tombs that contained the remains of saints, including those of John the Baptist and Elisha.[52] When those two tombs failed to burn, some of the monks in the area "went in the night, took the bones, fled with them . . . [they] easily reached Alexandria, and handed the bones over to Athanasius."[53]

The text then leaps forward to a later date when Athanasius was having what

---

48. E.g., *Verba sen.* 12.3.

49. Some of this certainly reflects the change in attitudes towards Theophilus as the Origenist controversy cooled, but that does not explain why a negative feature of his career was transformed into a positive element. If the goal was to suppress a negative view of Theophilus's actions, hostile traditions would simply have been dropped from the narrative.

50. Hahn ("The Conversion of the Cult Statues," 350) suggests that Theophilus may have tried to distance himself from the destruction of the Serapeum, though he admits that no trace of this effort is to be found in Alexandrian sources.

51. This text, which probably dates to the late fifth or early sixth century, charts the history of the Alexandrian church from Peter I to Timothy Aelurus. On this see T. Orlandi, *Storia della Chiesa di Alessandria*, vol. I (Milan, 1968), vol. II (Milan, 1970). For a discussion of its dating see Orlandi, *Storia della Chiesa*, 2.125–30.

52. *Storia della Chiesa*, 1.42.2–44.10.

53. *Storia della Chiesa*, 1.44.11–46.5.

seems to have been a regularly scheduled lunch with clerics and *philoponoi*. The lunch took place in "the garden on the street which they called Hermes on the south side of the city. This opened to some dung and some deserted open spaces. Athanasius said, 'If I find the time I will purify this dung and in this place build the martyrium of John the Baptist.'"⁵⁴ Theophilus, the story continues, was eating at this lunch with Athanasius and "heard the statement that the Spirit spoke to Athanasius and held it in his heart."⁵⁵

The story picks up again when the author reaches the time of Theophilus's episcopate.⁵⁶ It speaks of Athanasius's last days when, consumed by fever, he spoke about Serapis and said, "If I find any freedom of speech before the divine Christ, I will not cease to prostrate myself before the feet of the Savior until he shuts the door of Serapis."⁵⁷ It then comments, anachronistically, that the emperor Jovian issued such an order seven days after Athanasius's death. The importance of this strange story becomes clear when, five lines later, the text begins its treatment of Theophilus's career. After some perfunctory comments about his fine character,⁵⁸ the author launches into a narration of his use of monks in clearing out pagan sanctuaries.⁵⁹ He explains that Theophilus gave Athanasius's garden in the southern part of the city to the monks and they built a church on the site.⁶⁰

> Then Theophilus remembered the statement which his father had made regarding the place of John the Baptist. For the Lord had produced great wealth. The emperor had ordered the closure of the temples and he assembled a lot of money. And according to the word of God and the wish of his servant Athanasius, he [Theophilus] built a martyrium opposite the garden of Athanasius and adorned it with many ornaments, which the emperors gave to him.⁶¹

When it was completed, the remains of John the Baptist were placed within the martyrium. They immediately began to perform great wonders, some of which the text briefly describes.⁶²

---

54. *Storia della Chiesa*, 1.46.15–48.2.
55. ⲀϤⲤⲰⲦⲘ ⲈⲠϢⲀϪⲈ ⲚⲦⲀϤϪⲞⲞϤ ⲚϬⲒ ⲠⲠⲈⲨⲘⲀ ⲈⲐⲀⲚⲀⲤⲒⲞⲤ, ⲀϤⲔⲀⲀϤ 2Ⲙ ⲠⲈϤϨⲎⲦ (*Storia della Chiesa*, 1.48.5–6). The spirit speaking in this way to Athanasius represents an explicit statement that Theophilus's action enjoyed both divine inspiration and Athanasian sanction.
56. This section of the *Storia della Chiesa* is only partially preserved. Following Orlandi (*Storia della Chiesa*, 2.61), I draw upon the *History of the Patriarchs* of Severus of Al-Ashmunein, an apparently faithful paraphrase of some elements missing from our Coptic text.
57. The Coptic text resumes at this point. *Storia della Chiesa*, 2.12.1–4.
58. *Storia della Chiesa*, 2.12.9–12.
59. *Storia della Chiesa*, 2.12.13–24.
60. *Storia della Chiesa*, 2.12.25–14.9.
61. *Storia della Chiesa*, 2.14.10–18.
62. *Storia della Chiesa*, 2.14.24ff.

In these stories, the spiritual authority of Athanasius has been introduced to sanction two of the most controversial elements of Theophilus's refashioning of the Serapeum site. The text first claims that the destruction of the temple occurred because "the Holy Spirit spoke to Athanasius" and, after his death, Athanasius continually petitioned Jesus that the Serapeum be shut.[63] It then demonstrates Athanasius's approval of the two martyria that Theophilus constructed adjacent to the Serapeum by describing how the bishop secured the relics, chose the locations, and died while waiting for the site to become purified. Indeed, Theophilus only decided to build the shrines after remembering that their construction would fulfill the "word of God" and the "wish of Athanasius."[64] In many ways, the existence of such a text is not surprising. Coptic tradition celebrated Theophilus as a builder of churches and martyria even more than it highlighted his successes in combating pagans. Medieval sources suggest that this identification was celebrated liturgically on five different occasions throughout the year.[65] His building projects even generated a cycle of pseudonymous homilies describing the construction of three other churches, that of St. Raphael, the church of the Holy Family, and the church of the Three Children.[66] These texts, all later forgeries,[67] follow the same general pattern as the narration of the John the Baptist shrine. The John the Baptist narrative appears to be something different, however. It first appeared less than a decade after the temple's destruction.[68] As early as 402, Rufinus knew a version of this account that described the transfer of relics to Athanasius, Athanasius's decision to hide them in the baptistery, and his idea that when "the remnants of idolatry had been thrown down flat, golden roofs might rise for them on temples once unholy."[69] This suggests that a narrative

---

63. While the *Storia della Chiesa* contains some anachronistic material, this sort of wild chronological inaccuracy is atypical. This suggests that the Jovian reference may be a later interpolation. The present arrangement evidently baffled Severus of Al-Ashmunein because he excised this anecdote and inserted it into the middle of his biography of Athanasius.

64. Also notable here is the comment that the building of the church was paid for by funds seized from pagan temples by the emperor. This blunts the charge that Theophilus misused church funds intended for support of the poor.

65. The *Synaxary* of the Coptic church commemorates Theophilus's building projects on five different occasions: Paopi 18, Paopi 20, Pashons 10, Paoni 2, and Nasi 3.

66. For discussion of this literary cycle, see T. Orlandi, "Theophilus of Alexandria in Coptic Literature," *Studia Patristica* 16 (1985), 100–104. On the homily connected to St. Raphael, note as well the more recent findings of R. Coquin, "Discours attribué au patriarche Cyrille, sur la dédicace de l'Église de Raphaël, rapportant les propos de son oncle, le patriarche Théophile," *Bulletin de la Société d'archéologie Copte* 33 (1994), 25–56.

67. Orlandi, "Theophilus of Alexandria," 103.

68. For this important argument, see T. Orlandi, "Uno scritto di Teofilo di Alessandria sulla distruzione del Serapeum," *La Parola del Passato* 23 (1968), 295–304.

69. Rufinus, *HE* 11.28.

drawing upon the historical figure of Athanasius to justify both the "purification" of the Serapeum site and the construction of the martyria began circulating at the turn of the fifth century.

A short Coptic fragment of a sermon suggests that this idea originated with Theophilus himself.[70] This text, which has been identified as a part of Theophilus's otherwise lost homily *de aedificatione Martyrii Iohannis Baptistae,* records the scene in which "my father Athanasius" received the remains of John the Baptist and Elisha.[71] It then describes, in language nearly identical to that of the *Storia della Chiesa,* Athanasius's lunch in the garden and his comment to his guests that "If I should have the occasion, I will purify that place and build the martyrium of the saints John the Baptist and Elisha."[72] The narrator then says that he heard the words of "my father" because "I was an attendant" and "I placed what was said in heart."[73]

These are clearly the words of Theophilus and, while they differ slightly from what Rufinus and the *Storia della Chiesa* record, they correspond quite closely to the information found in those texts.[74] This suggests that, not long after the Serapeum fell, Theophilus had already begun to use the power of his pulpit to establish an Athanasian origin for the notion that the Serapeum site needed to be "purified" and that a shrine for John and Elisha was to be built on the site. Theophilus's appropriation of the historical legacy of Athanasius enabled him to demonstrate that his controversial actions were perfectly consistent with the spiritual authority inherent in his position. Furthermore, if this homily was delivered as written, this act of historical justification would have occurred in a liturgical context.

Other sources suggest that this line of argument may have been developed even more in anecdotes told by Theophilus and his supporters. The seventh-century historian John of Nikiu preserves perhaps the most interesting such account. In a section of the text ostensibly devoted to Athanasius, John describes the destruction of the Serapeum and the construction of the church of John the Baptist on its site.[75] John then begins a short digression on Theophilus's childhood. He describes his birth in Memphis, the death of his parents, and the Ethiopian slave who raised Theophilus and his sister. "One night," John writes, "about the time of dawn, this

---

70. This was first published as T. Orlandi, "Un frammento copto di Teofilo di Alessandria," *Rivista degli Studi Orientali* 44 (1970), 23–26.

71. The existence of such a text is suggested by *Storia della Chiesa,* 2.16.9–12.

72. The Coptic text is that of Orlandi, "Un frammento," 25 recto, col. 2 ln. 29–verso, col. 1, ln. 11.

73. Orlandi, "Un frammento," 25, verso, col. 1, ll. 11–22.

74. Two notable additions to the account when it appears in the *Storia* are 1) the presence of the *philoponoi* in the garden with Athanasius and 2) the comments about ⲍⲉⲛⲕⲟⲡⲣⲓⲁ being purified from the space on which the martyria were to be constructed. The first addition may perhaps have been made to correspond better to sixth-century realities. The second addition is more mysterious.

75. John of Nikiu, 78.42–47.

slave took the children by the hand and brought them to a temple of abominable gods, namely of Artemis and Apollo, in order to pray there . . . when the children entered, the gods fell to earth and were broken."[76] Fearing the popular response, the slave took the children first to Nikiu and later to Alexandria. In Alexandria, they came into the church when Athanasius was preaching. "At that time, God revealed to the Father Athanasius, the patriarch of Alexandria, the circumstances of the children"[77] and what they had done in the temple. Athanasius arranged for them to be baptized. Theophilus became a reader in the church and his sister, whom John celebrates as the mother of "the holy Cyril," was entrusted to a convent of virgins until her marriage to Cyril's father.[78]

John's narration likely preserves a mixture of traditions. Some of his information came from the local traditions of Nikiu, other pieces probably derived from family traditions that took form during the time of Cyril.[79] Although nothing that John preserves can be proven to derive from the time of Theophilus, his short digression reveals another way in which the legacy of Athanasius was used to sanction Theophilus's anti-pagan actions. Within this anecdote, Theophilus's mere presence shatters pagan statues. It is this power that God reveals to Athanasius and it is this attribute, and no other, that causes Athanasius to enroll him into the church hierarchy. To John, there was no question that both Athanasius and the Holy Spirit supported Theophilus's later efforts to destroy paganism.

Texts with a more dubious connection to Theophilus even show a move to ascribe this power to smash idols to Athanasius himself. Perhaps the most notable is a sermon celebrating Athanasius that may have been delivered by Theophilus's nephew Cyril.[80] After speaking at length about the ways in which Constantius tried and failed to intimidate Athanasius, the sermon describes an occasion when Athanasius, who had been exiled to Isauria, intervened to prevent local Christians from attending a festival at a rock-hewn temple of Apollo.[81] On the day of the festival, the temple caved in, smashing the statue of Apollo and those devotees who were near it.[82] All of the people in the city then proclaimed their devotion

---

76. John of Nikiu, 79.3–4, trans. Charles.
77. John of Nikiu, 79.7, trans. Charles.
78. John of Nikiu, 79.9–14.
79. The peculiar suggestion that the group fled first to Nikiu clearly derives from local tradition. The fact that Cyril's mother is featured as prominently as Theophilus in this story suggests that this anecdote is designed to reflect on Cyril as much as Theophilus.
80. The text is the *Encomio di Atanasio*, edited by T. Orlandi, *Testi Copti: 1. Encomio di Atanasio, 2. Vita di Atanasio; Testi e Documenti per lo Studio dell'Antichita* 21 (Milan, 1969), 9–83. For the attribution of the text to Cyril, note the comments of Orlandi, 7–8. Evidence for this attribution is, however, inconclusive.
81. This section of the text is Orlandi, *Enc. di At.*, 28.3–31.12. The Isaurian exile is a fiction.
82. *Enc. di At.* 29.22–30.8.

to the Christian God. With this, the speaker claims, "Christ won, the devil was shamed. The Gods of the Hellenes fell to earth, they came to pieces. Christ too with his cross received victory."[83]

Nothing suggests that this particular narrative reaches back to Theophilus, but its mere existence speaks to the important way in which Theophilus's efforts transformed the historical character of Athanasius. By detailing and celebrating Athanasius's inspired resistance to imperial persecution, this sermon follows the pattern established in the Athanasian encomia of Gregory and Constantine of Siout. However, the Athanasius presented here also has the ability to anticipate the destruction of pagan temples and the skill to use his foresight to convert pagans and bring lapsed Christians into the church. These additional attributes suggest that, at the time that this sermon was delivered, Athanasius's historical persona had evolved so that one could now plausibly speak of him as an effective anti-pagan crusader. Perhaps better than anything else, this shows the great success of Theophilus's efforts to convince Egyptian Christians that Athanasius, working as God's agent, had inspired his remaking of the Alexandrian religious landscape.

THE LEGACY OF THEOPHILUS

During his early episcopate Theophilus appears to have been interested in generating an Athanasian sanction for his actions. Shortly after his death, however, it seems that Theophilus emerged as a distinct historical character with his own identity as a powerful opponent of paganism. Perhaps the clearest indication of this comes from one of the fragments of an illustrated early-fifth-century Alexandrian chronicle.[84] The sixth surviving page covers the years between 383 and 392. It describes the accession of Theophilus to the patriarchal throne[85] and then, in its final lines, seems to describe the replacement of Hellenic temples with Christian structures.[86] Perhaps more interesting is the survival of marginal illustrations that show each event. On the lower right hand corner of the recto of the page is a drawing of a mummy labeled Timotheos and below it an illustration of a bearded man holding a book of the gospel who is identified as Saint Theophilus.[87] On the

---

83. ⲀⲠⲈⲬⲢⲒⲤⲦⲞⲤ ⲬⲢⲞ, ⲀⲠⲆⲒⲀⲂⲞⲖⲞⲤ ⲬⲒ ϢⲒⲠⲈ. ⲀⲚⲚⲞⲨⲦⲈ ⲚⲚ2ⲈⲖⲖⲎⲚ 2ⲈⲈⲠⲈⲤⲎⲦ, ⲀⲨⲢ ⲖⲀⲔⲘ ⲖⲀⲔⲘ. ⲀⲠⲈⲬⲢⲒⲤⲦⲞⲤ 2ⲰⲰϤ ⲘⲚ ⲠⲈϤⲤⲦⲀⲨⲢⲞⲤ ⲬⲒ ⲚⲦⲚⲒⲔⲎ (*Enc. di At.* 30.12–16).

84. The *Chronicle* was published as A. Bauer and J. Strzygowski, *Eine alexandrinische Weltchronik: Text und Miniaturen eines griechischen Papyrus des Sammlung W. Goleniscev*, Denkschriften der kaiserlichen Akademie der Wissenschaften in Wien, Phil.-hist., Klasse, Bd. 51, Abh. 2 (Vienna, 1905).

85. Bauer and Strzygowski, *Eine alexandrinische Weltchronik*, Tafel VI, recto ll. 17–22. This event, which actually took place in 385, is misdated to 387.

86. Bauer and Strzygowski, *Eine alexandrinische Weltchronik*, Tafel VI, verso, ll. 23–26. The text is extremely fragmentary here but the words Ἑλλήνων and Χριστιανῶν are both legible.

87. Bauer and Strzygowski, *Eine alexandrinische Weltchronik*, Tafel VI, fr. B.

FIGURE 5. Theophilus standing atop bust of Serapis. Marginal illustration from an early fifth- century Alexandrian Chronicle. From Bauer and Strzygowski, *Eine Alexandrinische Weltchronik*, (Vienna, 1905), fig. VI verso.

reverse of the page, Theophilus appears for a second time. He is again holding a book of the Bible, but this time he stands atop a pedestal, beneath which is a bust of Serapis.[88]

A recent study has argued convincingly that these images should be understood as visual parallels to the portraits of biblical prophets that appear in one of the text's earlier fragments.[89] This suggests that the illustrator saw fit to compare, at least implicitly, Theophilus's anti-pagan campaign with the efforts of prophets to

88. Bauer and Strzygowski, *Eine alexandrinische Weltchronik*, Tafel VI, B (verso).
89. Davis, *Early Coptic Papacy*, 64.

combat idolatry.⁹⁰ Theophilus's involvement in anti-pagan violence, which had once threatened to undermine his spiritual legitimacy, became the feature that defined him as a modern heir of the prophets.

This memory of Theophilus seems to have greatly influenced the behavior and the public profile of his nephew and successor Cyril. Outside of Egypt, the memory of Theophilus was tainted by his battle against the beloved Constantinopolitan bishop John Chrysostom.⁹¹ To John's partisans, Theophilus was a vindictive man who used his episcopal powers to pursue personal feuds.⁹² Within Egypt, however, Theophilus's conflict with Chrysostom receives almost no later historical attention.⁹³ Instead, popular perceptions of Theophilus were defined by his anti-pagan activity and, as a result, Cyril's connection to him remained largely a positive attribute.⁹⁴ As we have already seen, an Egyptian tradition developed that extended Theophilus's innate anti-pagan powers to his sister, the mother of Cyril.⁹⁵ Theophilus's example influenced more than just the rhetoric used by Cyril and his supporters, however. Although he had been groomed by his uncle to take power upon his death, Cyril had not yet been officially named when Theophilus died (apparently unexpectedly) in 412.⁹⁶ Instead of assuming power peacefully, Cyril

---

90. Davis, *Early Coptic Papacy*, 64; 206n93. Davis finds further support for this in Theophilus's claim to have cut down his opponents with "a prophet's sickle" (Jerome, *Ep.* 87).

91. For a succinct discussion of this conflict see S. Wessel, *Cyril of Alexandria and the Nestorian Controversy: The Making of a Saint and of a Heretic* (Oxford, 2004), 23–31.

92. This is the basic thrust of the accounts of Socrates (*HE* 6.7–15); Sozomen (*HE* 8.9–19); and Palladius (*Dialogus de vita Iohannis Chrysostomi*). For discussion and analysis see Wessel, *Cyril of Alexandria*, 23–30.

93. John of Nikiu, for example, attributes Chrysostom's exile not to Theophilus but to the empress Eudoxia (84.38–43).

94. Wessel has argued that Cyril "earnestly tried to distance himself from his uncle's episcopacy in every way" by even "going so far as to reinstall John Chrysostom in the diptychs" (*Cyril of Alexandria*, 49). This is a difficult interpretation to maintain for a number of reasons. First, any effort Cyril made to move away from his uncle would have caused political problems for him with Theophilus's partisans, the group upon which he could count for the most ardent support during the early years of his episcopacy. In addition, as will be seen below, the Egyptian evidence provides no support for this notion. Beyond this, even the evidence Wessel advances is inconclusive. As she admits (49n113), Cyril resisted reinstalling Chrysostom in the diptychs until Western pressure compelled him to do so. She also mentions the call for unity made in Cyril's first *Festal Letter* and characterizes it as a "departure from his uncle's contentious theological discourse" (*Cyril of Alexandria*, 31). This text, however, never disavows Theophilus or says anything with which Theophilus would have disagreed. It is perhaps more natural to see this as a call for reconciliation within a church divided by the recent, violent struggle to determine Theophilus's successor (this is discussed further below). In this context, the recall to the church of those who had behaved immorally (*Festal Letter* 1, SC 372, pp. 156, 158) has particular resonance.

95. John of Nikiu (79.2–12) maintains that both Theophilus and his sister were responsible for the crumbling of the statues of Apollo and Artemis in Memphis.

96. Theophilus's mentoring of Cyril is suggested by John of Nikiu 79.12 and by Cyril himself in his *Letter to Acacius of Beroea* (*Ep.* 33.7; see the translation of J. A. McGuckin, *St. Cyril of Alexandria:*

was forced to battle a rival for the patriarchal throne.[97] For three days partisans of the two sides contested with one another in the streets of Alexandria before Cyril finally took control of the city's churches.[98] He then began a series of actions that resembled those through which Theophilus remade Alexandrian religious life. As soon as he took power, Cyril punished the Novatians (a Christian sect that had supported his rival) by confiscating their property and churches.[99] Then, in 414, he took action against the large population of Alexandrian Jews.[100] After a series of small but increasingly violent disputes, Cyril ordered his supporters to seize synagogues in the city and drive Jews from their homes. This brought Cyril into conflict with Orestes, the prefect of Egypt, who sent a report of the event to the emperor.[101] His report fueled more explosive anger among Cyril's supporters and resulted in a riot in which Orestes was nearly killed.[102] In response, Orestes arrested Ammonius, a monastic supporter of Cyril, who died under questioning. Cyril promptly had Ammonius declared a martyr, before backing down in the face of opposition from Alexandria's Christian elite.[103] After a brief détente, the anger of Cyril's supporters turned against the philosopher Hypatia, a prominent member of the Alexandrian elite who had been working with Orestes to manage the conflict. Seizing Hypatia, Cyril's supporters murdered and dismembered her before incinerating her remains.[104]

To outsiders, these acts looked like compelling evidence that Cyril had "assumed power to regulate affairs beyond his sacerdotal function"[105] and condoned violence of an unchristian character.[106] Many Egyptians, however, thought that these events reflected differently upon the character of the new bishop. This happened in large part because of the way that Cyril presented his actions. No surviv-

---

The Christological Controversy [Leiden, 1994], 336–42). It is stated explicitly in the *Synaxarion* of the Coptic church (Abib 3).

97. On this event see, Haas, *Alexandria in Late Antiquity*, 296.

98. Socrates, *HE* 7.7.

99. Socrates, *HE* 7.7.

100. On this event, see the discussion of Haas, *Alexandria in Late Antiquity*, 298–301, as well as the detailed analysis of Wessel, *Cyril of Alexandria*, 33–45.

101. Socrates, *HE* 7.13.

102. For the anti-Jewish actions, the reaction of Orestes, and the subsequent riot, see Socrates, *HE* 7.13, and Haas, *Alexandria in Late Antiquity*, 299–304.

103. Socrates, *HE* 7.13.

104. Among the many recent studies of the events leading up to Hypatia's death and the implications of her murder are Watts, *City and School*, 187–203; Wessel, *Cyril of Alexandria*, 46–57; Haas, *Alexandria in Late Antiquity*, 295–316; and M. Dzielska, *Hypatia of Alexandria*, trans. F. Lyra (Cambridge, MA, 1995), 88–93.

105. *HE* 7.7.

106. *HE* 7.15.

ing Egyptian source discusses Cyril's actions against the Novatians, but John of Nikiu preserves what appear to be Egyptian narratives describing the Alexandrian pogrom and the murder of Hypatia.[107] His account begins by explaining that Hypatia appeared in Alexandria during the reign of Theodosius II. She was "a female philosopher, a pagan . . . and she was devoted at all times to magic, astrolabes, and instruments of music and she beguiled many people through her Satanic wiles."[108] Among her victims was the governor of the city who, under her influence, stopped going to church and stood by while a group of Jews stationed armed men around the city in order to "wickedly massacre the Christians."[109]

The surviving Alexandrian Christians then went to Cyril and organized a raid in which they "marched in wrath to the synagogues of the Jews and took possession of them, and purified them and turned them into churches. And one of them they named after the name of St. George."[110] After the Jewish "assassins" were expelled from the city, the crowd "proceeded to seek for the pagan woman who had beguiled the people of the city and the prefect through her enchantments."[111] They found Hypatia, brought her to the cathedral, tore off her clothing, and "dragged her through the streets of the city until she died. And they carried her to a place named Cinaron and they burned her body."[112] All the people then "surrounded the patriarch Cyril and named him 'the new Theophilus;' for he had destroyed the last remains of idolatry in the city."[113]

John's account does a number of remarkable things. Not only does it conflate the Jewish pogrom of 414 and the murder of Hypatia in the spring of 415, but it establishes the sorcery of Hypatia as a cause for both events.[114] Perhaps its most striking feature is the assertion that these twin acts of violence marked Cyril as "the new Theophilus." As surprising as this claim seems, John's narrative has done

107. For John's biography, see A. Carile, "Giovanni di Nikius, cronista bizantino-copto del VII secolo," *Felix Ravenna* 121-122 (1981), 107-109, and M. H. Zotenberg, *La Chronique de Jean, Évêque de Nikiou* (Paris, 1879), 2-6. Until it reaches the seventh century, this text is largely derivative and is heavily dependant upon the texts of John Malalas, John of Antioch, and, for the Theodosian dynasty, Socrates (Carile, 113-14 and Zotenberg, 11-15). When John diverges from these Greek texts, he seems to have relied heavily upon Egyptian materials. Among the most notable are the chronicle's account of Cambyses' invasion of Egypt (*Chron.* 51.18), which draws upon the fanciful Coptic description of the event edited by H. L. Jansen (*The Coptic Story of Cambyses' Invasion of Egypt* [Oslo, 1950]), and a series of statements about the glory of Severus of Antioch (*Chron.* 89.37-57), which parallels the comments about Severus's time in Egypt found in the *History of the Alexandrian Patrirachs*.
108. John of Nikiu, 84.87, trans. Charles.
109. John of Nikiu, 84.97, trans. Charles.
110. John of Nikiu, 84.98, trans. Charles.
111. John of Nikiu, 84.100, trans. Charles.
112. John of Nikiu, 84.101-2, trans. Charles.
113. John of Nikiu, 84.103, trans. Charles.
114. This charge of sorcery laid out in John of Nikiu probably represents the διαβολή that Socrates Scholasticus describes as leading to her death (*HE* 7.15). On this point, cf. Dzielska, *Hypatia*, 91.

a great deal to support it. In fact, the actions that John ascribes to Cyril's partisans mirror the course of events that led to Theophilus's transformation of the Serapeum. John, of course, begins not with a Christian procession that provoked pagan anger but with the "magician" Hypatia who incited Jewish violence against Christians. The anti-Christian violence that these two events incited looks much the same, however. In both cases, non-Christian mobs resorted to guerilla tactics to seize and kill innocent Christians. Both Cyril and Theophilus then catalyze a response that leads to the seizure of non-Christian sacred buildings, their "purification" and replacement with churches or shrines dedicated to Christian martyrs, and the expulsion from Alexandria of the pagans and Jews who led the violence. John's description of the murder of Hypatia also parallels the ritual purification of the city that accompanied the destruction of the cultic statue of Serapis. Like the Serapis statue, Hypatia was seized, dismembered, and paraded through the streets of the city before her remains were burned within the city limits.

John's narrative should in no way be taken as an authoritative reconstruction of what actually happened during this time, but it does reveal to us the rhetorical possibility of recasting these events so that they reflected favorably upon Cyril. While it is probably correct to suggest that Cyril lost control of his followers as these events unfolded,[115] Socrates Scholasticus shows that some contemporaries blamed the bishop for creating the political climate that led people to commit these outrages. Socrates' idea that Cyril encouraged a climate of violence echoes the unease felt by some contemporary Alexandrian Christians. This threatened Cyril's spiritual authority in much the same way that monastic suspicions had posed a challenge to Theophilus a generation before. Like his uncle, Cyril responded to this challenge by evoking the memory of a respected predecessor. Just as Athanasius posthumously sanctioned Theophilus's apparent excesses, so too could the historical memory of Theophilus transform these acts of violence from evidence of Cyril's failings into demonstrations of his impressive anti-pagan credentials.

These events could perhaps be excused as necessary evils required of a new bishop taking power after a disputed election but, even after Cyril's position was secure, the anti-pagan legacy of Theophilus seems to have guided some of his conduct.[116] Two incidents particularly stand out. The most notable concerned his efforts in Menouthis, probably in the 420s.[117] Theophilus's Christianization pro-

---

115. E.g., Davis, *Early Coptic Papacy*, 71–73.
116. Davis, *Early Coptic Papacy*, 73–74.
117. For the 420s, see J. A. McGuckin, "Influence of the Isis Cult," 191–99. McGuckin argues that this process began before the conflict with Nestorius erupted in 429. Note as well the arguments for this date presented by D. Montserrat, "Pilgrimage to the Shrine of SS Cyrus and John at Menouthis in Late Antiquity," in *Pilgrimage and Holy Space*, 262–64. On the Christian shrine and its nature

gram had implanted a church of the Holy Evangelists in Menouthis but had otherwise trodden lightly on the town's sacred terrain.[118] Theophilus's limited reach enabled the survival of an Isaic temple in Menouthis that became an important center for pagan religious activity following his destruction of the temples of Canopus.[119] The temple itself functioned as an incubation shrine that provided healing and oracles to those who visited it.[120] Its potency apparently attracted Christians as well as pagan visitors.[121] According to a later source that claims to paraphrase a Cyrillian sermon,[122] Cyril, seeing "the deception of the demon and the harm done to the faithful, became a supplicant to the Savior and prayed that the evil cease."[123] That night he received a vision in which an angel showed him the remains of the Diocletianic martyrs Cyrus and John and commanded them to be moved to Menouthis.[124] They were then put under the care of a detachment of Pachomian monks drawn from the monastery in Canopus that Theophilus had founded.[125] This process parallels that used by Theophilus to remake the sacred space of Alexandria and Canopus.[126]

Cyril began his career by strongly associating himself with the anti-pagan legacy of his uncle Theophilus. As his episcopate proceeded, the nature of Cyril's

---

note N. Fernandez Marcos, *Los Thaumata de Sofronio. Contribucion al estudio de la incubatio cristana* (Madrid, 1975). It is important to note as well the questions raised in the recent study of J. Gascou, "Les origines du culte des saints Cyr et Jean," *Analecta Bollandiana* 125 (2007), 1–35. The shrine must have been in operation by the late fifth or early sixth century for the iatrosophist Gessius to be plausibly associated with it.

118. Sophronius, *Enc.* 27 = PG 87.3 3413. Gascou ("Les origins du culte des saints Cyr et Jean," 26–29) has expressed doubts about the existence of the Theophilan church of the Holy Evangelists.

119. On the network of pagan shrines that survived Theophilus in and around Alexandria see D. Frankfurter, "The Consequences of Hellenism in Late Antique Egypt: Religious Worlds and Actors," *Archiv für Religionsgeschichte* 2 (2000), 184–89.

120. For these functions of the Isaic temple see Sophronius, *Encomium of Ss. Cyrus and John*, 24–25 = PG 87.3 3409–10. This temple is the functional predecessor of the one to which Paralius would travel in the 480s.

121. Sophronius writes: "This demon [Isis] swept away many with its false images and persuaded them to call upon its altar with hope of healing or a prophecy; it called not only unbelievers…but even the faithful and those who bore the signs of Christ." (*Enc.* 25 = PG 87.3 3410).

122. The sermons that Cyril delivered in Menouthis have been lost but were read and paraphrased by Sophronius of Jerusalem. Fragments of these sermons (drawn from Sophronius) are found in Cyril, *Homiliae Diversae* 18 = PG 77.1101. Gascou ("Les origins du culte des saints Cyr et Jean") argues that these sermons are not genuine products of Cyril but later fabrications.

123. Sophronius, *Enc.* 26 = PG 87.3 3412.

124. Sophronius, *Enc.* 27 = PG 87.3 3413. On the church that resulted, see McKenzie, *Architecture of Alexandria*, 247, 249.

125. Davis, *Early Coptic Papacy*, 74.

126. In both cases the bishops sought to guard the physical space of the new complex with a colony of ascetics while installing relics of martyrs to destroy the power of the old gods. For this latter idea in relation to the Menouthan complex note Sophronius, *Enc.* 29 = PG 87.3 3416.

leadership developed in a more nuanced fashion. Cyril began invoking Athanasius with greater frequency and, like Athanasius, he worked to fashion strong bonds with ascetic communities while struggling to preserve the theological purity and primacy of the Alexandrian see.[127] Indeed, under Cyril's astute leadership, these agendas often complemented one another. Cyril, for example, peppered his delegation to the first Council of Ephesus with Egyptian ascetics so he could simultaneously reinforce his following and advertise his role in championing their concerns.

Cyril's decision to involve Egyptian ascetics in Christological warfare influenced the way that monastic traditions represented the bishop and the Council of Ephesus. Besa's *Life of Shenoute,* for example, describes Shenoute's trip to Ephesus "together with the holy Cyril."[128] When Nestorius arrived, he came to a chair on which those organizing the synod had placed the four Gospels. Nestorius removed the gospels from the chair and sat upon it. Shenoute picked up the gospels, hit Nestorius with them, and cried: "Do you want the Son of God to sit on the ground while you sit on the chair?"[129] Nestorius responded by pointing out that Shenoute had no standing as either a bishop or an archimandrite and, as such, had no business being present. Shenoute chastised Nestorius for not seeing that God sought to rebuke him. Nestorius then fell off of the chair and was possessed by the devil. The story ends with Cyril kissing Shenoute, placing his stole around his neck, and making him an archimandrite. This anecdote concerns Shenoute, but Cyril plays an important role in sanctioning the extraordinary behavior of the old monk. Cyril provided the invitation that enabled Shenoute to leave his monastery for Ephesus. Cyril's embrace of Shenoute after the monk had struck Nestorius also indicates approval of the ascetic's violent behavior. Cyril had become a character whose actions show the appropriate blend of concern for orthodoxy and attention to ascetic propriety.

Nevertheless, Egyptian sources emphasize that Cyril's anti-pagan activism complemented his support for ascetics and vigorous defense of orthodoxy. While Cyril's battle with Nestorius helped to define his legacy, his fidelity to the anti-pagan model established by Theophilus was not forgotten.[130] The *Storia della Chiesa* makes this equation most memorably. It speaks about two marvels which showed Cyril's great wisdom.[131] The first of these centered upon Cyril's refutation of the arguments in the emperor Julian's *Contra Galilaeos,* a project that he un-

127. For Athanasius as a model used by Cyril see Wessel, *Cyril of Alexandria,* 112–37.
128. This anecdote appears in Besa, *Life of Shenoute,* 128–30 (trans. Bell); cf. Ps.-Dioscorus, *Panegyric on Macarius of Tkow,* 4.1. Note as well the discussion of Gaddis, *There is No Crime,* 252–53, 296–97.
129. Besa, *Life of Shenoute,* 129.
130. E.g., *Storia della Chiesa,* 2.38.2–46.20; Severus, *History of the Patriarchs,* XII (Cyril).
131. *Storia della Chiesa,* 2.36.29–37.5.

dertook in order to prevent people from being seduced by the wisdom and authority of the former emperor.[132] Not long after Cyril published his works against Julian, the historian continues, Cyril learned of Nestorius's teaching. Alarmed that such ideas had appeared so soon after he had made the ideas of Julian pass away, Cyril sent a series of letters and ascetic messengers that asked Nestorius to return to orthodoxy.[133] When Nestorius refused these appeals, Cyril "sought the weapons of his fathers, Athanasius and Alexander,[134] he clothed himself in the armor of their army, he received the breastplate of the faith ... [and] he went out to war, as David did."[135] Popular imagination held that Cyril, armed in the uniquely Alexandrian weaponry of Athanasius and Alexander, then battled Nestorius with an army of ascetic supporters.[136]

Although the chronology of this narrative is impossible,[137] the connections that it makes between Cyril's anti-pagan writings, his theological conflict with Nestorius, and his reliance upon monastic emissaries reveal a historical identity woven from three distinct threads. While such a description of the bishop does not exist before the late fifth century, the complicated historical character of Cyril present in the *Storia della Chiesa* reflects popular understanding of the bishop's legacy. Cyril himself ensured this. Even after the eruption of his conflict with Nestorius, the bishop continued to work steadily to combat paganism. Indeed, the appearance of the *Contra Julianum* in 438 shows how seriously Cyril continued to take this struggle. This resulted in a public view of the bishop that highlighted his strong support for ascetics and vigorous opposition to Nestorianism as much as his fidelity to the crusading example of Theophilus.

Perhaps no bishop made a more skillful or more surprising use of Athanasius's historical legacy than his former secretary Theophilus. Although a younger contemporary of Athanasius, Theophilus assumed control of the Alexandrian episcopate in a very different political climate. Instead of maneuvering around hostile

---

132. *Storia della Chiesa*, 2.38.6–42.14.

133. The connection between Cyril's *Contra Julianum* and Nestorius's ideas does not survive in the existing fragments of the *Storia* but can be restored based upon the text of Severus.

134. This Alexander must be Athanasius's patriarchal predecessor, not the Macedonian founder of the city.

135. *Storia della Chiesa*, 2.46.20–27.

136. This is a picture that finds echoes throughout both Coptic and Syriac anti-Chalcedonian literature. See, for example, ps-Theopistus, *History of Dioscorus*, ed. and trans. F. Nau, "Histoire de Dioscore, patriarche d'Alexandrie," *Journal Asiatique* 10 (1903), 5–108 (text), 241–310 (trans), chs. 1, 4, 6, 7, 9, 12–17, 19.

137. The deposition of Nestorius at the first Council of Ephesus preceded the publication of the *Contra Julianum* by seven years.

emperors like Constantius and Valens, Theophilus forged a strong working relationship with the emperor Theodosius, which opened up significant imperial resources for his use. In the 390s, Theophilus drew upon this imperial support to remake the Alexandrian sacred landscape. The process began with the renovation of an abandoned basilica but accelerated greatly with the occupation of the Alexandrian Serapeum and the subsequent destruction of its brother-shrine in Canopus. Theophilus then "purified" each site by establishing monasteries and building shrines containing important Christian relics. Although he received substantial imperial support, Theophilus's efforts required the active participation of Egyptian Christians and, in particular, the area's monks. His methods made some ascetics uneasy, however. They worried about the vast sums of money Theophilus's construction projects required, the violence that he directed against pagan temples, and the time he asked them to spend outside of their ascetic environment.

Theophilus responded by refashioning the historical character of Athanasius. In his construction, Athanasius remained an orthodox champion who sustained the faith in the face of imperial pressure.[138] Theophilus, however, added another dimension to this Athanasius. Athanasius not only thought about how to preserve orthodoxy, he also had carefully planned the shape of its eventual triumph. He prayed constantly for the purification of Alexandria from the "filth" of Serapis and, knowing that this would eventually come, he took custody of relics that could be installed in place of the old god. Guided by Athanasius's example and by the prayers that he continued to make after his death, Theophilus could claim to have completed a process that Athanasius began. These actions, then, represented ways in which the Holy Spirit acted through him to fulfill plans first articulated to Athanasius.

From the earliest stages of his episcopate, Theophilus's successor Cyril understood the twin powers of the legacies of Athanasius and Theophilus. During the first years of his career, Cyril seems to have adhered closely to the rhetorical model established by his uncle. This included, most infamously, the lynching of Hypatia, an action his supporters claimed marked Cyril as "a new Theophilus." Cyril's later actions, however, show a more careful leader who drew upon different historical models to redefine himself as a fighter for doctrinal orthodoxy. As he matured and solidified his position, Cyril remained committed to the occasional public anti-pagan display. The outbreak of his conflict with Nestorius also allowed Cyril to avail himself of the model of episcopal behavior presented by Athanasius. In his opposition to Nestorianism, Cyril skillfully framed himself as the heir to a long tradition of Alexandrian theological generalship that had produced resounding victories against Arianism. He could then don the armor of Athanasius without shedding the anti-pagan mantle of Theophilus.

138. This is suggested most strongly in the odd details regarding the transfer of Palestinian relics to his care during the reign of Julian.

Despite the backing of the imperial court and a large number of Alexandrian Christians, both Theophilus and Cyril found it necessary to explain how their actions were consistent with the behavior of an inspired Christian teacher. This suggests something important about late antique Alexandrian bishops. They had great power to influence the lives and behaviors of large numbers of people, but this power could only be effectively exercised when those people believed that the directions their bishop gave came from God. The most effective Alexandrian bishops understood this dynamic and appreciated the importance of reassuring their congregations that, regardless of the political climate, their bishop remained a true and effective guide to spiritual salvation.

8

Peter Mongus Struggles with the Past

This section began by reconstructing the procession of Menouthan spolia that Peter Mongus organized on the last day of the riot. The preceding two chapters have outlined the delicate balance that bishops maintained between the firm exercise of authority their positions demanded and the piety, humility, and peacefulness that Christians customarily expected them to display. In fourth-century Alexandria, bishops like Athanasius and Peter II defended their conduct by emphasizing their defense of orthodoxy and support for ascetics and virgins against violence.[1] The later years of the fourth century saw the imperial court turn from an adversary of the Alexandrian Nicene bishop into one of his most important supporters. This shift empowered Theophilus to remake the sacred topography of his city. Despite the Christian triumph that he orchestrated, Theophilus found himself drawing upon the familiar ecclesiastical narrative of Athanasius to illustrate the propriety of his conduct.

On first glance, the fourth century experience of Theophilus would seem to suggest that Peter Mongus's involvement in Paralius's beating would, if anything, complicate the delicate political situation in which he found himself. However, the early fifth century saw popular expectations of the Alexandrian bishop evolve in ways that opened significant new avenues for defining his authority. Theophilus found it necessary to create an Athanasian sanction for his anti-pagan activities in the 390s, but by the time of his death, his battles against paganism had come to mark him as a genuine champion of the faith. For the next generation, the Alexandrian church would become accustomed to strong bishops who, evoking the legacy of Theophilus, worked with the imperial court to fight for orthodox Christianity.

1. For Peter II, see Theodoret, *HE* 4.19.

The Council of Chalcedon changed this by dividing the Alexandrian church from the source of its imperial patronage. Alexandrian bishops now found themselves unable to draw effectively upon this powerful Theophilan legacy. Instead of the Theophilan model, the anti-Chalcedonian bishop Dioscorus and his successor Timothy Aelurus found themselves harkening back to the resistance paradigm first established by Athanasius. Timothy in particular evoked Athanasius as a Christian beacon who could lead the community to orthodoxy and borrowed Athanasian language to frame the historical moments after Chalcedon as a repeat of the state-sponsored anti-Arian violence of the 350s. From all indications, Timothy's rhetorical emulation of Athanasius generated strong and enduring support for him in monasteries and among lay Egyptian Christians.

As Timothy's successor, Peter Mongus found himself in a very difficult position. The tone of imperial policy shifted in the early 480s and, in the interest of ending the dispute over Chalcedon, the emperor Zeno framed a vague theological compromise. While he remained opposed to Chalcedon, Peter found Zeno's compromise flexible enough to be acceptable. Peter, then, came into communion with the emperor. The ardently anti-Chalcedonian ascetic supporters of Timothy Aelurus, however, found Peter's acceptance of this compromise unpalatable. They quickly turned against him, and growing numbers of ascetics strongly opposed Peter for much of his episcopate. When the Enaton monks brought the beaten Paralius and his promise to reveal a hidden pagan shrine to Peter Mongus, however, they offered Peter a new way to demonstrate his authority to an unconvinced public. His cooperation with Zeno meant that Peter could not emulate Athanasius and Timothy Aelurus, but Paralius offered him the chance to show that he was an anti-pagan champion like Theophilus. Peter then choreographed a raid on Menouthis that echoed the actions of Theophilus a century before. In so doing, he hoped to establish himself as a legitimate link in an important spiritual chain.

CHALCEDON AND THE REDEFINITION OF THE ALEXANDRIAN BISHOP

The death of Cyril in 444 led to a shift in the way that Alexandrian bishops presented themselves to their supporters. While Cyril's successor Dioscorus continued to pursue many of the same policies as his predecessor, he also moved quickly to distance himself from Cyril's family. Dioscorus removed them from church offices, eliminated stipends that Cyril had previously paid them, and may even have used violence against those who resisted.[2] Prudently, Dioscorus also seems to have stopped explicitly drawing upon the historical legacy of Theophilus to

---

2. M. Gaddis, *There Is No Crime for Those Who Have Christ: Religious Violence in the Christian Roman Empire* (Berkeley, 2005), 319.

frame his spiritual authority. Dioscorus does not seem to have played an important role in any anti-pagan actions, although a Coptic source does present him as approving of one attack on a pagan temple.[3] Even if such actions had once been Dioscorus's priority, the rapidly changing imperial political and religious climate of the 440s compelled Dioscorus to focus much more on Christian doctrinal disputes than on combat with pagans.

The complicated events of the early years of Dioscorus's career centered upon the theological and political conflict between the Alexandrian and Constantinopolitan sees, which Nestorius had reopened in the 420s.[4] Although Cyril's victory at Ephesus and Nestorius's subsequent deposition had ostensibly settled the dispute, tension between the two centers remained high throughout the 430s and early 440s. This simmering conflict exploded when a Constantinopolitan monk named Eutyches stumbled into theological conflict with his bishop Flavian by stripping away some of the nuance from the theology Cyril had used to vanquish Nestorius.[5] A synod called by Flavian in 448 condemned Eutyches for misrepresenting Cyril, a verdict also sanctioned by Pope Leo I. Dioscorus, however, jumped to the defense of Eutyches. He lined up the support of the emperor Theodosius II, and convinced the emperor to call a second council at Ephesus to address the matter. When the council assembled in 449, Dioscorus used a combination of imperial guards and Egyptian monks to force his agenda forward.[6] He arranged for the exoneration of Eutyches, the deposition of Flavian, and the proclamation of a set of findings that did not take into account the ideas of Flavian or those contained in a letter sent to the council by Pope Leo. This letter, the famous Tome of Leo, would remain a focus of controversy long after the council disbanded. Outraged that his Tome had not been read, and disgusted at Dioscorus's use of force, Leo dismissed the second council of Ephesus as a "Robber Council."[7]

---

3. *Panegyric of Macarius of Tkow*, 5. Although attributed to Dioscorus, this panegyric most certainly dates to the sixth century or later. See *Panegyric of Macarius, Bishop of Tkow, Attributed to Dioscorus of Alexandria*, trans. D. W. Johnson (Louvain, 1980), 9–11.

4. Conflict between the sees of Constantinople and Alexandria dated back into the fourth century. Before Nestorius, the biggest explosion had been the contest between John Chrysostom and Theophilus. For background on this particular controversy, see E. Clark, *The Origenist Controversy: The Cultural Construction of an Early Christian Debate* (Princeton, 1992), 37–8; 45–7. For a detailed analysis of conditions in the mid-fifth century see P. Blaudeau, *Alexandrie et Constantinople (451-491): de l'Histoire à la Géo-Ecclésiologie* (Rome, 2006).

5. For more on the context of this formulation see Davis, *Early Coptic Papacy* 80–81.

6. On Ephesus II, note the recent discussions of Davis, *Early Coptic Papacy*, 82–83; and the more extensive treatment of Gaddis, *There Is No Crime*, 299–309. For the controversial use of military force (a charge that Dioscorus would vigorously deny) see *Acta Conciliorum Oecumenicorum*, ed. E. Schwartz (Berlin, 1927), vol. 2.1.1.858–62.

7. Leo first characterized it as such in July of 451 (Leo, *Ep.* 95). For similar characterizations, see Cyril of Scythopolis, *Euthymius* 27 and *Sabas* 56. For discussion, see Gaddis, *There Is No Crime*, 309.

Unfortunately for Dioscorus, Theodosius II, his imperial patron, died in a riding accident in 450. He was succeeded by Marcian, a former military official who married Theodosius's sister Pulcheria and then was crowned emperor by his new bride. Driven by a combination of political and theological concerns,[8] Marcian joined forces with Pope Leo to overturn the actions taken at the second council of Ephesus. The emperor recalled the bishops exiled at Ephesus and, in 451, convened a new council in Chalcedon that was charged with returning order to the church.[9] When the bishops assembled, they undertook the significant project of progressively dismantling the findings of Ephesus II. The bishops rehabilitated Flavian of Constantinople, read and approved the Tome of Leo, and then tried Dioscorus for misconduct. Sensing the tone of the meeting, Dioscorus refused to appear for his trial. The council summoned a host of witnesses to complain about the bishop's tyrannical behavior and then deposed him for his failure to answer the charges.[10] As Dioscorus sailed into exile, the council tried and failed to get a group of Egyptian bishops to sign on to the Tome of Leo.[11] Despite this failure, the next session of the council still adopted central elements of Leo's Tome as the basis for its confession of faith.

While some supporters of Dioscorus steadfastly refused to endorse the Tome or the findings of Chalcedon more generally, the pressure tactics employed by the emperor and the bishop of Rome did produce some significant defections.[12] The most important of these was Juvenal of Jerusalem, a stalwart supporter of both Cyril and Dioscorus at the two Ephesian councils. In one of Chalcedon's most dramatic early moments, Juvenal abandoned Dioscorus and agreed to the orthodoxy of Flavian's confession of faith, which had been condemned at Ephesus. He later took a place on the committee that drew up the final Chalcedonian confession of faith, a document that followed the general outlines of Leo's Tome.[13]

Although the Council of Chalcedon largely succeeded in forcing a consensus upon its participants, the popular reaction to it was often far from friendly. Asia

---

8. One can perhaps assume that some of the championing of Leo arose from a desire by Marcian to secure Western imperial political support. Anti-Chalcedonian sources, however, say that Marcian was motivated by Nestorian beliefs (e.g., *History of Dioscorus*, 3).

9. For Chalcedon, see the important and concise reconstruction of Gaddis, *There Is No Crime*, 310–22.

10. Gaddis, *There Is No Crime*, 321.

11. Throughout the council a small group of Egyptian bishops remained loyal to Dioscorus, although a remark at the council suggested that they eventually numbered as few as six (*Acta Conciliorum Oecumenicorum* 2.1.1.179).

12. Thalassius of Caesarea, Eusebius of Ancyra, and Basil of Seleucia were among the chief supporters of Dioscorus at Ephesus who turned against him at Chalcedon. See E. Honigmann, "Juvenal of Jerusalem," *DOP* 5 (1950), 241–42 and J. E. Steppa, *John Rufus and the World Vision of Anti-Chalcedonian Culture* (Piscataway, NJ, 2002), 3–4.

13. *Acta Conciliorum Oecumenicorum* 2.1.2.125. See, as well, Honigmann, "Juvenal," 244–45.

Minor, Syria, and Phoenicia all saw isolated opposition to Chalcedon emerge among clergy and monks, but the Chalcedonian results proved particularly hard for Egyptians and Palestinians to accept.[14] The ascetic communities of Palestine erupted in anger when they learned of Juvenal's political retreat at Chalcedon. Enraged crowds of anti-Chalcedonian monks met Juvenal upon his return to Palestine and forced him to flee.[15] They then established their own, anti-Chalcedonian hierarchy in the province, which was dismantled only when Juvenal came back with imperial troops in 453. Juvenal's reappearance provoked violent acts of resistance which resulted most significantly in a massacre of anti-Chalcedonian monks by imperial troops in Nablus.[16]

Although events in Egypt played out differently, the area around Alexandria saw especially determined resistance to Chalcedon. After the council, imperial authorities seem to have ordered officials to compel leading Egyptian clergy and archimandrites to indicate their acceptance of the Tome of Leo.[17] Coptic texts describe a series of incidents in which anti-Chalcedonian leaders heroically resisted this imperial pressure. The *Life of Longinus*, for example, describes how Longinus, the archimandrite of the Enaton, stood down an imperial army before persuading the general and his soldiers to renounce Leo's Tome.[18] Remarkably, the conversion of the army was said to cause the people of Alexandria to seize and burn the Chalcedonian prefect of the city.[19] Another Coptic tradition commemorates the resistance shown by Macarius of Tkow to these imperial commissioners.[20] It describes how Macarius chastised the Chalcedonian patriarch Proterius for accepting the Tome and challenged the orthodoxy of the document in front of the

14. On the general reaction to the synod see W. H. C. Frend, *The Rise of the Monophysite Movement* (Cambridge, 1972), 143–56. For negative reaction in Asia Minor see John Rufus, *Plerophories* 21–22. In Phoenicia, Eustathius of Berytus claimed to have signed the canons of the council "under duress" (Zacharias, *HE* 3.1).

15. Among the ascetic leaders was Theodosius, the monk who would soon be proclaimed patriarch of Jerusalem (Zacharias, *HE* 3.3–5; Evagrius *HE* 2.5; John Rufus, *Plerophories* 56). For discussion of this situation see Steppa, *John Rufus*, 5–12; Honigmann, "Juvenal," 247–56; and C. Horn, *Asceticism and Christological Controversy in Fifth-Century Palestine: The Career of Peter the Iberian* (Oxford, 2006), 77–91.

16. Zacharias Scholasticus, *HE* 3.5; John Rufus, *Plerophories*, 10. These incidents are also preserved in Coptic traditions (e.g., *Panegyric of Macarius of Tkow*, 7–8).

17. This is suggested by *Life of Longinus*, 29–32. The official conveying the initial letter is ΟΥΜΑΓΙⲤⲦⲢⲒⲀⲚⲞⲤ. When military support is deployed to help convince recalcitrant monks, it is commanded by ⲠⲀⲞΥΧ. The *Panegyric on Macarius of Tkow*, 9.1 speaks of a decurion (ⲠⲀⲒⲔⲞΥⲢⲒⲞⲚ) commanding soldiers who delivered the messages to Longinus. It was, however, only a courier (ⲠⲂⲈⲖⲈⲦⲀⲢⲒⲞⲤ) who brought the Tome to the Alexandrian clergy (cf. *History of Dioscorus*, 19).

18. *Life of Longinus*, 29–36.

19. *Life of Longinus*, 37. This event is unattested elsewhere and certainly fictional.

20. *Panegyric of Macarius of Tkow*, 15; cf. *Synaxarion* of the Coptic church, Baba 27.

imperial courier sent to secure its acceptance by the Alexandrian clergy.[21] The enraged courier kicked Macarius in the genitals and Macarius fell dead on the spot.[22] The people of Alexandria then took up the body, wrapped it in fine clothes, and took it to the martyrium of John the Baptist and Elisha.[23] When the body of Macarius was placed in the shrine, a blind twelve-year old child saw a vision of John and Elisha in which they embraced Macarius like a long-lost brother. Macarius's position of honor was confirmed when a bolt of lightening struck dead a scoffing Chalcedonian.[24]

The decision to place Macarius's remains in the prominent Alexandrian martyrium of Elisha and John shows the determination with which anti-Chalcedonian leaders moved to define resistance to the Tome of Leo as a central feature of Alexandrian Christian identity. While Egyptian exemplars like Macarius and Longinus and Palestinian leaders like Peter the Iberian and Theodosius highlighted the importance of opposition to Chalcedon, Dioscorus represented the symbolic heart of the Egyptian anti-Chalcedonian movement. Following Chalcedon, Dioscorus passed three miserable years in exile in Gangra[25] before dying in 454. Almost immediately, anti-Chalcedonian leaders in Alexandria used Dioscorus's death to transform him into the most significant martyr created by the emperor's violent imposition of the Tome of Leo upon his subjects.[26] They quickly worked to integrate Dioscorus's refusal to accept the Tome into a broader narrative of Egyptian Christian ecclesiastical history and to show how his actions drew upon the well-known examples of his predecessors.

In the late 450s or early 460s Dioscorus's successor, Timothy Aelurus, authored the first surviving attempt to cast Dioscorus's spiritual authority in this fashion. This work, a short history of events from the first council of Ephesus to the death of Marcian, formed a part of Timothy's larger theological refutation of Chalcedon and Leo's Tome.[27] In concise and clear terms, Timothy explains how Dioscorus's

21. *Panegyric of Macarius of Tkow*, 15.5–8.
22. *Panegyric of Macarius of Tkow*, 15.8; cf. *History of Dioscorus*, 19; *Synaxarion* of the Coptic church, Baba 27.
23. *Panegyric of Macarius of Tkow*, 16.1.
24. *Panegyric of Macarius*, 16.2–3 (vision of the blind child); 15.8 (lightening strike).
25. The *History of Dioscorus* 13–15 describes Dioscorus enduring a scarcity of food and supplies as well as the hostility of the local bishop. Cf. *Panegyric of Macarius of Tkow*, 14.1
26. The *History of the Patriarchs*, for example, describes him as being persecuted "at the hands of the prince Marcian and his wife." This reflects a rhetorical tradition that dates back to the 450s and the writings of Dioscorus's successor, Timothy Aelurus. Davis (*Early Coptic Papacy*, 85–88) frames Dioscorus's "martyrdom" and its aftermath in terms of "ecclesiastical colonialism."
27. This Syriac text (which takes up folios 1–29 of British Museum 12156, a sixth-century compilation) appears to be a shorter, reorganized version of the Armenian text published by K. Ter-Mekertsschian and E. Ter-Minassiantz, *Timotheus Älurus, des Patriarchen von Alexandrien, Widerlegung*

refusal to accept Leo's Tome was inspired by the Holy Spirit and evoked illustrious Alexandrian predecessors like Cyril and Athanasius.[28] Timothy emphasizes that, because of his defense of the faith at both Ephesus and Chalcedon, other bishops recognized Dioscorus as a "guardian of the faith and ... his words came from the Holy Spirit."[29] At Chalcedon, Dioscorus had remained true to this message of the Holy Spirit and the legacy of Cyril by refusing to sign the Tome.[30] His deposition, exile, and death in Gangra led him to be awarded "the crown of justice from the director of combat, from Christ, the just judge, with all the saints."[31] In the same way that Athanasius had once positioned himself as the heir to Alexander and the spiritual tradition to which he belonged, Timothy looked to present Dioscorus as the inheritor of the orthodox mantle of Cyril and his predecessors.

In Timothy's narrative one can already begin to see the outlines of a strategy that reaffirmed Dioscorus's spiritual authority despite his censure by the largest church council to date. The *History of Dioscorus,* a pseudonymous later treatment of the patriarch's exile and martyrdom, provides a much more developed example of this approach. Best preserved in a sixth-century Syriac redaction,[32] this (originally Egyptian) text integrates Dioscorus's refusal to accept the Tome of Leo into a broader narrative of Egyptian Christian history. It then illustrates how the great ecclesiastical and ascetic exemplars of the past inspired and approved of Dioscorus's actions. Both Cyril and Athanasius make frequent appearances. In the fourth chapter, for example, Dioscorus responds to news about the theological inclinations of the emperor Marcian by saying that Cyril had told

---

der auf der Synode zu Chalcedon festgesetzten Lehre (Leipzig, 1908). The *History* is found on folios 11a–13b. For the Syriac manuscript see W. Wright, *Catalogue of the Syriac Manuscripts in the British Museum*, vol. 2 (London, 1871), no. DCCXXXIX, pp. 639–48, and the text of Nau (*Textes Syriaques Édites et Traduits,* ed. F. Nau, PO 13.2, 209–10). On the relationship between the Armenian and Syriac texts, see J. Lebon, "Version arménienne et version syriaque de Timothée Élure," in *Handes Amsorya, Monatsschrift für Armenische Philologie* 41 (1927), 713–22; as well as J. Lebon, *Le Monophysitisme Sévérien* (Louvain, 1909), 100–8.

28. It is particularly notable that, while previous Alexandrian exemplars like Peter I were available, they go unmentioned in the text. For Timothy Aelurus and most other early anti-Chalcedonian figures, principled theological resistance to imperial power began with Alexander, Athanasius, and the Christian emperors of the fourth century. Other anti-Chalcedonian sources would, on occasion, mention the examples of pre-Constantinian bishops (e.g., the *History of Dioscorus,* discussed below) but comparisons to Athanasius and Cyril are much more common. A notable (Palestinian) exception is the *Life of Peter the Iberian,* in which Peter I is offered as the dominant model (*Vit. Pet.* 180–82).

29. Timothy Aelurus, *History,* 209.

30. Timothy Aelurus, *History,* 210.

31. Timothy Aelurus, *History,* 210; cf. II Timothy 4.8.

32. The Syriac version of the text has several small but significant additions designed to join Egyptian anti-Chalcedonian communal history with that of Syrian anti-Chalcedonians. On this see E. Watts, "Dioscorus as a Paradigm of Resistance in Syriac and Coptic Anti-Chalcedonian Literature," forthcoming.

him to conserve energy during the reign of Theodosius II because he would later have to fight for orthodoxy, be sent into exile, and accept death. This did not worry Dioscorus, the text continues, because he knew that Athanasius had been sent into exile repeatedly.

The sixth chapter of the *History* integrates Dioscorus's refusal to endorse the Tome of Leo more fully into the history of Alexandrian episcopal resistance. The chapter begins with Dioscorus receiving the summons to attend Chalcedon. The entire populace of Alexandria sees him off and, as the ship departs, Dioscorus prays that God will allow him to follow the examples of his illustrious predecessors. He invokes the martyrdom of St. Mark, the theological combat of Dionysius against Paul of Samosata, the battle of Theonas against Origenism, the martyrdom of Peter of Alexandria, the anti-Arianism of Alexander, the multiple exiles of Athanasius (which, according to Dioscorus, marked him a martyr a thousand times over), and the battles that Cyril fought against Nestorius.[33] The sixteenth chapter then recounts a set of miracles that showed Dioscorus to be like Alexander and Athanasius, including one in which Dioscorus restrained an angel from attacking a bishop who insulted the legacy of Cyril. The seventeenth chapter describes a meeting between Dioscorus and the Pachomian *koinobiarch* Paphnutius, in which Dioscorus reverently discussed the examples set by his predecessors as bishops while Paphnutius ruminated on the great deeds of Pachomius, Petronius, Theodore, and Shenoute. The nineteenth chapter then describes a vision in which Cyril introduced Dioscorus to a crowd of bishops including Alexander, Athanasius, and Ignatius of Antioch. Cyril then told Dioscorus that he would join their ranks in two months.

The *History of Dioscorus* defines the extent of Dioscorus's spiritual authority by placing him within the company of revered Egyptian bishops, martyrs, and leaders of spiritual resistance whose contributions to the Christian community were presented in church each week.[34] The most interesting figures to be included in this list were the ascetic leaders who, on first blush, would seem to offer only a superfluous blessing to the bishop. Nevertheless, the complex of overlapping narratives that shaped later popular perceptions of Dioscorus frequently drew upon the legacies of men like Paphnutius and Shenoute.[35] Their presence in Dioscoran hagiography, of course, parallels the way in which the figures of Antony and Pachomius were used to demonstrate the spiritual authority of Athanasius. These

---

33. *History of Dioscorus* 6.

34. Indeed, Cyril and Athanasius are mentioned when Dioscorus's life and deeds are commemorated in the Synaxary (e.g., Thout 7; Hathor 2, 30).

35. The *Panegryic of Macarius of Tkow*, for example, describes an encounter between Paphnutius and Shenoute. Paphnutius, who suffered from gout, asked Shenoute if he could help cure the ailment. Shenoute responded by saying that only Dioscorus could do this (*Panegyric of Macarius*, 15.3).

narratives, then, recreate the same rhetorical ascetic-episcopal alliance that underpinned Athanasius's Christological resistance.

While echoes of Athanasius and Cyril strongly shaped the legacy of Dioscorus, anti-Chalcedonian authors make no effort to tie Dioscorus to Theophilus. Particularly striking is the absence of Theophilus from the list of patriarchs whose example Dioscorus follows in the *History of Dioscorus*. In addition to the martyrs Mark and Dionysius, every Alexandrian patriarch who held the throne from the 280s until the time of Dioscorus merited inclusion, with the exception of the short-lived Achillas and the unremarkable brothers Peter II and Timothy. Theophilus, then, represents a significant (and clearly deliberate) exclusion from the list, a situation made all the more remarkable by the prominent role that he had played in defining the career of Cyril. Nevertheless, the position of Dioscorus after Chalcedon made any evocation of Theophilus unlikely.[36] He had neither the opportunity nor the resources to energetically oppose paganism. Alexandrian Christians continued to commemorate Theophilus's accomplishments in these areas, but the first generation of anti-Chalcedonians seem to have pushed him aside as an exemplar whose career could not be emulated under current conditions.

This same general pattern continued under Dioscorus's successor Timothy Aelurus. After Dioscorus's exile to Gangra, imperial officials chose Proterius, a former associate of the exiled bishop, as his replacement.[37] Proterius spent much of his time under armed guard and, by 457, his unpopularity led a group in the city (including Peter the Iberian, the exiled bishop of Maiuma) to proclaim Timothy Aelurus as a rival patriarch.[38] Not even a month later, Proterius was attacked and murdered, with his remains scattered throughout the city and desecrated.[39] The murder of Proterius caused Chalcedonians both in Alexandria and outside of Egypt to call for the punishment of Timothy.[40] In 460, the emperor Leo I ordered

---

36. Theophilus's role as an opponent of John Chrysostom may be a factor here. It is, however, worth noting that later Coptic tradition simply celebrated Theophilus's other achievements and ignored his conflict with John Chrysostom (e.g., John of Nikiu, 84.38–43; note too the discussion in chapter 7, above).

37. The *Panegyric of Macarius of Tkow* (15.5) claims that Dioscorus had warned Proterius that he would succumb to this temptation.

38. *Life of Peter the Iberian*, 91; Zacharias, *HE* 4.1; Evagrius Scholasticus, 2.8. For more discussion see chapter 5, above.

39. Evagrius, 2.8; Zacharias, *HE* 4.1–2; *Vit. Pet. Ib.*, 92; Theophanes 111.2–3. For discussion, see C. Haas, *Alexandria in Late Antiquity: Topography and Social Conflict* (Baltimore, 1997), 317–18; Davis, *Early Coptic Papacy*, 88–89. Note as well the unsympathetic ending of Proterius's life described in the London manuscript of the *History of Dioscorus*.

40. The letter from the Egyptian clergy is preserved in Evagrius, 2.8. Pope Leo also wrote a letter in which he speaks about Timothy's tyrannical rule over the church (*Ep.* 156). For discussion of Leo's intervention, see Evagrius, 2.9–10; Davis, *Early Coptic Papacy*, 89.

Timothy exiled to Gangra, just as Dioscorus had been.⁴¹ His place was taken by the Chalcedonian Timothy Salofacialos. Timothy Aelurus would later be moved even farther away from his flock, to Chersonesus in the Crimea.⁴² He remained in exile until 475 before returning to Alexandria for the final two years of his life.

Given the questionable circumstances surrounding his ordination and the suspicion of his involvement in the death of Proterius, Timothy Aelurus shrewdly presented himself as the dutiful successor of Dioscorus as well as the defender of the spiritual and personal legacy of Discorus's revered predecessors. Timothy most vividly demonstrated this when he returned from exile carrying the remains of Dioscorus in a silver casket. Timothy entered Alexandria and immediately arranged for Dioscorus to be "buried with great state, laying him in the place of the bishops, and honoring him as a confessor."⁴³ While certainly less dramatic than Dioscorus's funeral, Timothy's writings similarly positioned him as Dioscorus's heir. While Timothy's brief narrative description of Chalcedon and its consequences preserves his most intense defense of Dioscorus's legacy, his theological pamphlets similarly emphasize Timothy's connection to Dioscorus and previous generations of Alexandrian ecclesiastical leaders. These pamphlets consisted almost entirely of a series of *florilegia* in which Timothy assembled passages from Athanasius, Cyril, and other Alexandrian bishops in order to attack the ideas presented by Leo and his supporters at Chalcedon.⁴⁴ Remarkably, Timothy seems to have written these texts specifically so that they would be equally devoid of original theological interpretations and any distinctive authorial voice. Their clear and complete reliance upon arguments made by revered church fathers emphasized both the "innovations" of Chalcedon and Timothy's fidelity to the church's intellectual and spiritual legacy.⁴⁵

Later traditions show how successfully Timothy linked his own experiences to those of Dioscorus. Timothy features prominently in the *History of Dioscorus*, which marks him as Dioscorus's spiritual and ecclesiastical successor. It describes Dioscorus exhorting his congregation to let no one but Timothy run the church as he sailed off to the Council of Chalcedon.⁴⁶ It then recounts a vision in which

---

41. Theophanes, *Chron.*, AM 5951–52; Zacharias, *HE* 4.7, 11. Note, as well, C. Haas, "Patriarch and People: Peter Mongus of Alexandria and Episcopal Leadership in the Late Fifth Century," *JECS* 1 (1993), 299–300.

42. Zacharias, *HE* 4.11.

43. Zacharias, *HE* 5.4. For discussion of this adventus, see P. Blaudeau, *Alexandrie et Constantinople*, 342, 351–52.

44. R. Y. Ebied and L. R. Wickham, "Timothy Aelurus: Against the Definition of the Council of Chalcedon," in *After Chalcedon: Studies in Theology and Church History Offered to Professor Albert van Roey for his Seventieth Birthday* (Leuven, 1985), 116. For another example of Timothy's writing style, see the letter reproduced in Zacharias, *HE* 4.12.

45. Ebied and Wickham, "Timothy Aelurus," 116–17.

46. *History of Dioscorus*, 6.

Dioscorus spoke with Elisha and John the Baptist and was warned that Jesus would remove the saints from the house which was built for them in Alexandria after the death of Timothy Aelurus because, at that point, He would initiate a great chastisement of sinners.[47] Finally, in a vision before the end of his life, Cyril instructed Dioscorus to write to Timothy, declare Timothy his successor, and give him final instructions.[48]

Like the sixth-century *History of Dioscorus*, both Severus of Al'Ashmunein's tenth-century *History of the Patriarchs of Alexandria* and the fifteenth-century *Synaxary* of the Coptic Church[49] similarly elide the anti-Chalcedonian leadership roles of Dioscorus and Timothy. The *History of the Patriarchs* uses the historical figure of Dioscorus to frame Timothy's entire career. The extremely brief biography introduces Timothy as the successor of the "militant Father Dioscorus" and alludes to the hardships he suffered for his faith including "banishment to the island of Gangra, like Dioscorus, for seven full years."[50] Timothy's banishment, of course, lasted far longer than seven years and included time in the Crimea as well but, like Timothy himself, later Egyptian sources evidently privileged the Dioscoran parallel above a more factual account of his career.[51] The *Synaxary* similarly focuses upon the difficulties that Timothy endured. It highlights his exile[52] and the political opposition he faced[53] as well as his position as the theological and spiritual heir of Dioscorus.[54] These presentations show that, once Timothy Aelurus made his case persuasively, the notion that he had inherited and faithfully upheld the positions of Dioscorus shaped popular opinion of him for centuries.

The first generation of Alexandrian anti-Chalcedonians won a significant propaganda victory when they successfully incorporated Dioscorus into the traditional Alexandrian narrative of principled episcopal resistance to imperial power. These efforts had some interesting side effects, most notably the historical transformation of the heroic Timothy Aelurus into a one-dimensional keeper of the Dioscoran legacy,[55] but a revitalization of the old Athanasian model of episcopal behavior proved essential in defining the continued spiritual authority of

---

47. *History of Dioscorus*, 7. It is possible to read this as an indictment of Peter Mongus as well as a positive statement about Timothy Aelurus.

48. *History of Dioscorus*, 19.

49. The surviving Arabic version of the *Synaxary* is a fifteenth-century translation of Michael, bishop of Athrib and Malig.

50. Severus, *History of the Patriarchs*, Timothy II = Ch. 13.445 (trans. Evetts).

51. Note as well *Synaxary*, Mesori 7; 23. Dioscorus was in Gangra only three years before he died.

52. E.g., Mesori 7.

53. E.g., Mesori 23.

54. Mesori 7; cf. Hathor 2, 30.

55. Perhaps more representative of the key role that Timothy played is the reverence that anti-Chalcedonians like John Rufus had for the bishop.

Alexandrian anti-Chalcedonian bishops. For most of the quarter century following Chalcedon, the anti-Chalcedonian bishops Dioscorus and Timothy Aelurus competed directly with the Chalcedonian bishops Proterius and Timothy Salofacialos for the allegiance of Alexandrian Christians. Proterius and Salofacialos usually enjoyed imperial backing as well as the abundant material resources, patronage ties, and military support that went along with such recognition.[56] Dioscorus and Timothy Aelurus could no longer provide these tangible benefits. Indeed, the *History of Dioscorus* preserves a curious episode in which an Alexandrian merchant stopping in Gangra gives Dioscorus the gold and silver he has earned on his voyage. Dioscorus's decision to distribute this money as alms prompted an imperial investigation into whether he stole church funds before he left Egypt.[57]

Loyalty to Dioscorus and Timothy Aelurus promised no tangible benefits and carried with it personal risk, but a large majority of the Alexandrian and Egyptian population remained strongly anti-Chalcedonian. Indeed, when Timothy Aelurus returned to Alexandria from exile, a great crowd of supporters greeted him "with torches and also songs of praise by the various people and languages there."[58] While the anti-Chalcedonians had been stripped of all temporal authority over the church, their appropriation of the well-known Athanasian model of episcopal resistance greatly enhanced their spiritual authority. Like Athanasius before them, these leaders promised their followers abundant spiritual rewards for their endurance. Perhaps nothing shows this better than the surviving letters written by Timothy Aelurus during his exile. In his sixth letter, for example, Timothy writes, "I am convinced because of the piety which is yours in our Lord, that you are running with us the same noble course in the cause of the orthodox faith, enduring, suffering persecution and afflictions."[59] As Athanasius had done in his tenth Festal Letter, Timothy promised his flock salvation as a reward for their suffering and contrasted this with the punishment that awaited those who accepted Chalcedon. These, the promises of an exile who claimed only the spiritual authority of a successor of Dioscorus and Athanasius, proved more attractive and more power-

---

56. It is worth noting, however, that Timothy Aelurus seems to have been extremely generous in granting money to the poor, widows, and Alexandria's pilgrim hostels. On this, note Haas, "Peter Mongus," 301 as well as Zacharias, *HE* 4.3. After his restoration in 475, Timothy apparently presented a set of honorific grants of grain to the "great men and rulers of the city" and resumed giving money to the poor (Zacharias, *HE* 5.4).

57. *History of Dioscorus* 14 (gift of money and use for alms); 20 (imperial investigation). Cf. Zacharias, *HE* 4.3, for similar charges leveled against Timothy Aelurus.

58. Zacharias, *HE* 5.4.

59. This is Letter Six in the collection of R. Y. Ebied and L. R. Wickham, "Collection of Unpublished Syriac Letters of Timothy Aelurus," *JTS*, n.s., 21.2 (1970), 321–69. The translation that follows is theirs.

ful to his audience than the resources that the emperor made available to his Chalcedonian opponents.

Practical considerations may be added to these less tangible arguments. While its rhetoric (and its bishops) could change quickly, the clerics and bureaucrats of the Alexandrian church turned with the abruptness and precision of a hobbled battleship. The bishop had the highest pulpit in the city, but his priests, deacons, and presbyters, as well as lay Christians like the *philoponoi,* set the cadence of Egyptian Christian life. The aftermath of Chalcedon seems not to have done much to change the composition or personal loyalties of these groups. Following the council, one source indicates that a few clergy were forced to live in exile,[60] and a second claims that some clerics "severed themselves from Proterius's communion."[61] Most clergy, however, seem to have continued their regular routine without interruption.[62] One must imagine that many priests ordained by Cyril and Disocorus remained in place, conducting services, reading the diptychs and teaching their congregations while Dioscorus, Proterius, Timothy Aelurus, and Timothy Salofacialos pushed one another from the episcopal seat. These clergymen, laymen, and the institutions they represented changed slowly and had been trained to look back into the deep past that Timothy Aelurus wisely evoked. The vocal support for Timothy both in the 450s and upon his return in 475 suggests that, in Timothy's evocation of Athanasius, Cyril, and Dioscorus, many saw the church of the patriarchs.[63]

One should not overestimate the significance of Timothy Aelurus's rhetorical victories, however. Popular support was not always particularly potent, and it came with a real price. In the naked calculations that bishops invariably performed, the vast majority of Christians mattered less than the small, devoted, and active minority upon whose actions a bishop's effectiveness often depended. Timothy's rhetoric had earned the support of the quiescent majority and engaged minority, but his long exile effectively forced him to trade great local ecclesiastical autonomy for this Egyptian devotion to his symbolic leadership. For most of a generation, the Egyptian church became accustomed to theologically pure but

60. Evagrius, *HE* 2.8.
61. Zacharias, *HE* 3.2.
62. Timothy Aelurus even acknowledges this general continuity when he offers easy terms of repentance and no loss of office to anti-Chalcedonian clergy who continued ministering under Proterius and Timothy Salofacialos *(Letter Six).* John Rufus claims that none of the faithful openly performed liturgies (*Vit. Pet. Ib.* 82), but the focus of his comment seems to be on the orthodoxy of the services that were conducted and not their frequency. As an opponent of both Chalcedon and Proterius, John saw all services conducted by priests affiliated with Proterius to be heterodox.
63. There is some indication that Timothy Aelurus tried to pressure clergy to abandon Chalcedon. This is suggested by letters to Leo and Anatolius from former supporters of Proterius (A.C.O. II.5, p. 15). For discussion of this see Blaudeau, *Alexandrie et Constantinople,* 153.

physically distant anti-Chalcedonian leadership. Indeed, Timothy Aelurus himself recognized this problem. When he returned to Alexandria in 475, he felt compelled to plunder tax revenues to bestow large donatives upon clerics and elite lay supporters in an attempt to reestablish real authority in the city and its church, a gift perhaps designed to mimic those often given by new bishops to their subordinates.[64] Despite Timothy's efforts, however, this devolution of episcopal power proved extremely durable.

PETER MONGUS AND RESISTANCE IN AN AGE OF COMPROMISE

Timothy Aelurus died in July of 477, after the emperor Zeno had "uttered severe threats" against him but before he could order his deposition.[65] He was succeeded "canonically" by Peter Mongus, the archdeacon who had presided at Timothy's funeral and immediately faced up to the problems that Timothy had left.[66] Peter enjoyed the impeccable anti-Chalcedonian pedigree that this task demanded. He had been ordained by Dioscorus, elevated to archdeacon by Timothy Aelurus, and, if later sources are to be believed, even shared Dioscorus's exile.[67] His role in Timothy's funeral, a reprise of Timothy's actions commemorating Dioscorus two years earlier, allowed Peter to assert a spiritual authority that derived from his connections to the first generation of Alexandrian anti-Chalcedonian bishops.

The emperor Zeno responded to Peter's elevation with alarm. He ordered Timothy Salofacialos to come out of his retirement in Canopus and resume his position as the bishop of Alexandria. Zeno also ordered the arrest of Peter Mongus. Peter had been tipped off and, like Athanasius in the fourth century, he escaped arrest by hiding among his supporters in Alexandria.[68] Peter spent most of the next five years in this fashion, encouraging his followers and frustrating Timothy Salofacialos. Peter's success in fueling anti-Chalcedonian resistance can be seen in Salofacialos's increasingly desperate countermeasures. Not only did Salofacialos plead for the emperor Zeno to order the formal exile of Peter Mongus,[69] but he also adapted his preaching. Instead of upholding Chalcedon, Salofacialos "preached

---

64. In large cities, new bishops sometimes gave their new subordinate clergy a customary ordination "gift." On this, see C. Rapp, *Holy Bishops in Late Antiquity: The Nature of Christian Leadership in an Age of Transition* (Berkeley, 2005), 212.

65. Zacharias, *HE* 5.5.

66. Zacharias, *HE* 5.5.

67. Eutychius, *Annales* 105, col. 1056; Liberatus, *brev.* 16; *History of Dioscorus*, 6. For discussion of Peter's biography, see as well, Haas, "Peter Mongus," 300; Davis, *Early Coptic Papacy*, 93; F. Nau, "Histoire de Dioscore, patriarche d'Alexandrie," *Journal Asiatique* 10 (1903), 1.

68. Zacharias, *HE* 5.5; Evagrius, *HE* 3.11. For discussion, see Haas, "Peter Mongus," 303.

69. Liberatus, *brev.* 16.

the faith of Nicaea and of the one hundred and fifty; he confessed and agreed to the transactions of Ephesus; he anathematized Nestorius; and he wrote in the diptych the names of Cyril and Dioscorus, and read them out; and he did more besides, and yet he was unable to draw the people to himself."[70]

Matters stood this way for as long as Timothy Salofacialos squared off against Peter Mongus. As the heir of Timothy Aelurus and Dioscorus, Peter Mongus claimed a spiritual authority that Salofacialos could never match. Peter could then rely upon the inertia of the lower rungs of the church hierarchy to continue the state of affairs that Timothy Aelurus had created. With a true successor to Dioscorus present in the city, Salofacialos's efforts to identify with and officially rehabilitate the legacy of Dioscorus looked like the hollow acts of desperation they were. The strong imperial embrace of Timothy Salofacialos, however, meant that neither could Peter expect any imperial recognition nor could Salofacialos be allowed to cede the stage to his anti-Chalcedonian challenger.

In late 481, Alexandria's ecclesiastical paralysis lifted. Salofacialos's health started to fail and Chalcedonian and anti-Chalcedonian ascetics began to compete for the imperial endorsement that his death would free up. The Chalcedonian ascetics of Canopus sent a delegation to the emperor asking that he recognize a monk named John Talaias as Timothy Salofacialos's legitimate successor.[71] When Salofacialos died in the spring of 482, John succeeded him as the imperially-recognized bishop of Alexandria. This did not end matters, however. During this time of transition, a delegation of monks and rhetoricians arrived in Constantinople and spoke before the emperor on behalf of Peter Mongus. Their embassy evidently argued two things. First, it presented Zeno with "written documents" detailing "the sad afflictions which, time after time, had occurred in Alexandria, and in Egypt, and in the other adjacent districts, on account of the Synod (of Chalcedon)."[72] Second, Peter's messengers also seem to have been charged with negotiating a compromise with the emperor that would end this state of affairs.

Their embassy crafted an agreement with the emperor according to which Zeno would depose John and recognize Peter Mongus as the legitimate patriarch of Alexandria. In return, Peter was to endorse a document of theological compromise. This document, Zeno's Henotikon, was drawn up by the emperor and bishop of Constantinople for circulation in the territories under the authority of the

---

70. Zacharias, *HE* 5.5. On Timothy Salofacialos during this time, note Haas, "Peter Mongus," 303–305; Davis, *Early Coptic Papacy*, 93–94. It is important to see, too, the similarity between Salofacialos's approach and the more successful efforts of Martyrius of Jerusalem (Zacharias, *HE* 5.6). For the symbolic importance of diptychs in the fifth century see Blaudeau, *Alexandrie et Constantinople*, 347–49.

71. Zacharias, *HE* 5.6–7; Evagrius, *HE* 3.12; Theophanes, *chron.* AM 5973. Note as well Haas, "Peter Mongus," 304–5; Davis, *Early Coptic Papacy*, 94.

72. Zacharias, *HE* 5.7.

bishop of Alexandria.⁷³ If restored, Peter would have to agree to "receive and hold communion with all the other bishops who would agree to the Henotikon" including those who had identified with his Chalcedonian opponents.⁷⁴ To formalize this agreement, the emperor asked the new prefect to carry the Henotikon to Alexandria and submit it to Peter's review. When Peter read the document, he deemed it righteous. Although troubled that there was "no clear and express anathema of the Synod and the Tome in it," Peter signed it and agreed to hold communion with all others who did so.⁷⁵

Both emperor and patriarch saw the need for this compromise. In 482, the emperor Zeno had only a tenuous handle on imperial power. He had already been deposed once (in 475 by Basiliscus) and the leaders of that coup used their control of the state to shift towards a policy that favored anti-Chalcedonianism. Although Zeno's restoration had led to the dismissal of most of the bishops that Basiliscus favored,⁷⁶ the empire's political and religious situation remained unsettled. Indeed, another significant insurrection was already taking form in 482. When it erupted, it too drew upon the resentments of disfavored religious groups.⁷⁷ For Zeno, an agreement with the anti-Chalcedonian patriarch of Alexandria, the most influential bishop in the movement, could eliminate this particular source of resentment.

Peter Mongus similarly stood to benefit from an agreement with the emperor. While the anti-Chalcedonian hierarchy had continued to enjoy the support of the Alexandrian and Egyptian populations, the exiles of Dioscorus and Timothy Aelurus, as well as the quasi-exile of Peter Mongus, meant that its leadership had effectively been absent from Alexandrian public life for twenty-seven of the previous thirty-one years. Despite the powerful spiritual authority that Peter Mongus could claim, it was reasonable to wonder whether his church could sustain this level of popular enthusiasm indefinitely, especially when it found itself cut off from imperial resources and forced to cede significant practical autonomy to its priests, ascetics, and laity. Both sides then had much to gain from an agreement.

When Peter signed the Henotikon, it led to a spectacle not often seen in Alexandria. At a prearranged time, Peter emerged from hiding and "the prefect, and the duke, and the chief men, and the clergy, and the monks, and the sisters, and

---

73. Zacharias, *HE* 5.7; this area of initial distribution is confirmed by the text of the Henotikon preserved by Zacharias, *HE* 5.8, and Evagrius, *HE* 3.14; cf. Liberatus, *brev.* 17; Nicephorus Callistus, *HE* 16.12. The Henotikon affirmed the faith agreed to at Nicaea, Constantinople, and Ephesus, while offering a vague anathema of those who held any different beliefs.

74. Zacharias, *HE* 5.7; cf. Evagrius, *HE* 3.12.

75. Zacharias, *HE* 5.7.

76. Zacharias, *HE* 5.5. Timothy Aelurus was the main anti-Chalcedonian exception.

77. This was the revolt of Illus and Leontius, a movement that enjoyed substantial pagan as well as Christian support. On this rebellion, see chapter 3.

the believing people assembled together at the place where he was."[78] These Christian and secular dignitaries set Peter "upon a chariot, and with pomp and praise as one who kept the true faith, and doing homage before him, they brought him to the great church."[79] The prefect also brought a group of Chalcedonians to the church to be received into communion with Peter. While Peter did not recoil from this, he wisely paused to explain to his flock how they were to understand the reconciliation they were witnessing.

Peter gave a short sermon in which he tried to frame the event in terms that would make it seem acceptable to the assembled imperial officials, clergy, monks, and lay Christians.[80] According to the most detailed surviving account of this spectacle, Peter expertly used this moment to transform his theological compromise into a political triumph. He claimed that the Henotikon grew out of the emperor's agreement with all of the main elements that defined Egyptian anti-Chalcedonian resistance. Zeno had accepted the spiritual authority of Cyril, Dioscorus, and Timothy Aelurus and had anathematized Nestorius, Eutyches, and the Tome of Leo. Just as crucially, the emperor had also heard, believed, and been moved by accounts of the sufferings of Egyptian anti-Chalcedonians told to him by Egyptian monks. As if to show how complete his victory had been, Peter displayed its fruits before his ecstatic congregation. Both imperial officials and leaders of the Alexandrian Chalcedonian faction now stood waiting to be accepted into communion with Peter.

Peter's assembly transformed his endorsement of Zeno's Henotikon into a formal acceptance of the emperor's theological surrender. To make this more persuasive, Peter also quoted from a set of symbolically important historical examples. His arrival evoked the public processions that had greeted Athanasius upon his returns from exile in 346 and 366[81] and, more recently, the grand celebration for Timothy Aelurus when he came back to Alexandria carrying the remains of Dioscorus.[82] This emphasized that, while resistance to the empire had ended, Peter had not turned away from the legacy of his predecessors. Despite his agreement with Zeno, Peter's spiritual authority as a successor of Athanasius, Dioscorus, and Timothy Aelurus remained intact.

These powerful symbolic and rhetorical statements convinced most of the Al-

---

78. Zacharias, *HE* 5.7.
79. Zacharias, *HE* 5.7; cf. Evagrius, *HE* 3.13. For discussion, see Haas, "Peter Mongus," 306–7.
80. Zacharias, *HE* 5.7, claims to reproduce Peter's sermon. In it, Peter explained that the Henotikon was sent to Zeno by God after "chaste monks presented a petition to him concerning the reformation of the faith, and informed him of the occurrences here, and of the tumults from which our people had suffered time after time." Evagrius Scholasticus, who uses Zacharias as his primary source for these events, does not record anything about the oration that Peter gave.
81. *Festal Index* 18 for 346; *Hist. Aceph.* 5.7 for 366. For discussion of these incidents, see chapter 6.
82. Zacharias, *HE* 5.4.

exandrian populace to understand the Henotikon as Peter wanted, but the document left some individuals disconcerted. A number of Chalcedonians, most notably the Pachomian monks at Canopus, refused to come into communion with Peter.[83] Even more troubling for the bishop, "some of the more ardent spirits [within the anti-Chalcedonian movement] were very indignant because in the king's document, the Henotikon, there was no express anathema of the additions imposed at Chalcedon."[84] Over time, their resistance to the document hardened, as bishops with no convincing anti-Chalcedonian identifications also endorsed it. The group of separatists soon included two Alexandrian presbyters, two deacons, the bishop of Antinoe, and a collection of prominent archimandrites and ascetics.[85]

The identity of these dissenters made their objections particularly troublesome for Peter. Not only had the Henotikon broken the inertia that had sustained the anti-Chalcedonian coalition for the previous generation, but it also caused one of the most active (and consequently most important) anti-Chalcedonian subgroups to oppose Peter openly.[86] From the time of Athanasius, Alexandrian bishops had positioned themselves as champions of the needs of ascetics and had claimed that much of their spiritual authority derived from this alliance.[87] This claim had been particularly important for the anti-Chalcedonian patriarchs Dioscorus, Timothy Aelurus, and Peter Mongus. Egyptian and Palestinian ascetics had spearheaded the initial opposition to Chalcedon. They had suffered persecution for this, and, in Timothy Aelurus, Theodosius of Jerusalem, and Peter the Iberian, their monasteries even provided a number of the most prominent early anti-Chalcedonian bishops. Furthermore, during the exiles of Dioscorus and Timothy Aelurus, monks became the most vocal public champions of the anti-Chalcedonian cause within Egypt. The anti-Chalcedonian community that Peter headed owed its survival and power to these ascetics. Their defection potentially portended a broader set of questions about his spiritual leadership.

Unfortunately, the small problem that Peter had failed to anticipate in 482 only grew. By 484, large numbers of monks were coming to identify with Peter's anti-Chalcedonian opponents.[88] Sensing trouble, Peter began to make more powerful public criticisms of Chalcedon. News of this soon reached Acacius, the bishop of Constantinople, and, doubting the sincerity of Peter's commitment to the emperor's compromise, Acacius sent a presbyter to Alexandria to investigate. The

---

83. Zacharias, *HE* 5.9.
84. Zacharias, *HE* 5.9.
85. Zacharias, *HE* 6.1.
86. On this effect see the comments of Blaudeau, *Alexandrie et Constantinople*, 227.
87. Rapp, *Holy Bishops* 147–49. For Alexandria in particular, note the basic arguments of D. Brakke, *Athanasius and Asceticism* (Baltimore, 1998); cf. the discussion of Athanasius in chapter 6, above.
88. Zacharias, *HE* 6.1.

presbyter determined that Peter had never "expressly anathematised" Chalcedon and recommended that he continue in his post.[89] While this finding placated Constantinople, it further angered the Egyptian dissident anti-Chalcedonians. For their part, they asked the revered anti-Chalcedonian monks Peter the Iberian and Elijah, both of whom were visiting the city, to investigate whether Peter Mongus remained opposed to Chalcedon. The two venerable monks then summoned Peter Mongus to an examination before a council of ascetics.

Although Acacius's investigation brought with it the threat of imperial punishment, Peter the Iberian's inquiry posed a different challenge to Peter Mongus's position. As one of the last surviving members of the first anti-Chalcedonian generation, Peter the Iberian was a living icon of ascetic resistance.[90] If Peter Mongus failed to impress him as sufficiently orthodox, his support among Alexandrian anti-Chalcedonians would quickly erode. Peter Mongus, however, won over this ascetic tribunal. In their meeting, "they selected four of Peter [the Iberian]'s discourses concerning the faith, and they said to him, 'If you agree to these, sign them;' and he signed them."[91] Peter the Iberian deemed this sufficient proof of Peter Mongus's anti-Chalcedonian convictions and his judgment led some monks to return to Peter's communion. A core group, however, still refused. In response, the bishop "took away the monastery of Bishop Theodore of Antinoë," a known miracle worker.[92] With this action against Theodore, Peter Mongus had unambiguously broken with the old anti-Chalcedonian ascetic and lay coalition that Timothy Aelurus and Dioscorus had assembled. Peter desperately needed to define his spiritual authority in a new way.

PETER MONGUS AND THE BEATING OF PARALIUS

Paralius's beating provided Peter with the opportunity to show a different sort of spiritual authority to his flock. We must depend entirely upon the Paralius material contained in Zacharias Scholasticus's *Life of Severus* to understand how Peter capitalized upon Paralius's beating. Fortunately, Zacharias gives a credible description of Peter's actions and achievements.[93] In Zacharias's retelling, Paralius

89. Zacharias, *HE* 6.1.
90. On Peter's career see chapter 5, above.
91. Zacharias, *HE* 6.1. The implication is that these were to be Peter the Iberian's writings, but the text is not entirely clear on this point.
92. Zacharias, *HE* 6.1; cf. Zacharias, *Vit. Sev.*, 100–102; Evagrius, *HE* 3.22.
93. Zacharias would have been disinclined to exaggerate Peter Mongus's achievements. As argued in appendix 2, the Paralius text was written to claim student-*philoponoi* ownership of the riot, not to glorify the bishop. In addition, Zacharias probably had a mixed view of Peter Mongus, a man who had memorably clashed with Theodore of Antinoë. In the *Life of Severus*, Zacharias claims that he would not be in communion with any bishop who was not himself in communion with Theodore

first came to Peter's attention when Salomon, the *koinobiarch* of a community at Enaton, petitioned Peter to intervene on Paralius's behalf.[94] Salomon evidently had two goals in making this trip. First, he wanted to persuade Peter to use his influence with the prefect to involve imperial officials in the matter. Perhaps suspicious of Peter's intentions, Salomon also used his visit to the city to rouse leading Alexandrian Christians against the city's pagan teachers.[95]

Salomon's appeal offered Peter a rare opportunity to demonstrate his attentiveness to the concerns of a prominent anti-Chalcedonian ascetic community without engaging in a conversation about Chalcedon. He responded positively and in a way that accorded perfectly with established procedures. After listening to Paralius's account, he sent his notary and his archdeacon to accompany the petitioners to the office of Entrechius, the prefect.[96] When the delegation reached Entrechius's office, his assessor cleared the building of all but Paralius and the four other students who had witnessed the event. He ordered them to draw up a complaint in which certain people were accused of "having offered pagan sacrifices and to have fallen upon him like brigands."[97] When he received this document, the prefect summoned the accused to answer the charges. But Salomon's efforts to rouse the city had succeeded too well. A mob of leading Christians and their supporters quickly converged on the prefect's office. They demanded that his assessor (who, they claimed, openly sacrificed to pagan gods) be forced out of office. Others among them began calling for the violent punishment of the pagan teachers whose students had attacked Paralius. This led to Horapollon's flight and the apparent resolution of the situation.

The actions of Entrechius and Peter Mongus deserve a bit more attention. Because of his behavior during this hearing, Zacharias accused Entrechius of being a secretly practicing pagan who used his office to protect his pagan assessor as well as Horapollon and his colleagues. Entrechius may well have been a pagan, but his conduct during this hearing does not reveal this. Throughout the proceedings, Entrechius tried to follow established procedure and keep events under control. He cleared his courtroom of all but the immediate witnesses to Paralius's beating in order to limit confusion. In accordance with legal protocol, he asked Paralius to put his complaints in writing and then ordered the accused to be brought forth.[98] This incited the anger of the "clergy and members of the order

---

(*Vit. Sev.* 78). Although Theodore and Peter would later reconcile, their history makes it hard to believe that Zacharias would look to celebrate unduly the achievements of Theodore's one-time adversary.

94. *Vit. Sev.* 24–25.
95. *Vit. Sev.* 25. His target was ܐܟܣܢܕܪܝܐ ܕܒܝܬ ܡܠܦܢܐ.
96. The date of Entrechius's prefecture cannot be determined for certain, though 486 seems the best estimate. For discussion of this see appendix 1, below.
97. *Vit. Sev.* 25.
98. For this procedure see *CTh* 9.1.5; 9.1.11.

called the *philoponoi*,"⁹⁹ who felt that this legally defined response was insufficient. Then, when Horapollon and his associates escaped, Zacharias volunteered that the prefect "averted his eyes out of sympathy for them."¹⁰⁰ Entrechius's fault was presumably his failure to offer his assessor and the pagan teachers up to a Christian mob. Despite Zacharias's creative spin, Entrechius's actions do not reveal a cryptopagan. Instead, they show a prefect successfully preventing the lynching of a government official and a pagan teacher.

Intriguingly, Peter Mongus did not respond to the loud calls of the excitable monks, clergy, and *philoponoi*. A partial cause of this may have been the cooperative relationship that he had established with imperial officials after agreeing to the Henotikon, but Peter also may have realized that he had little to gain from encouraging this sort of mob violence against a teacher. Peter, then, did no more than play his proper role as a Christian leader. His name and support had gotten Paralius in to see the prefect that afternoon, but he had no involvement in the demonstration that threatened to disrupt the city. In the end, he had neither gained nor lost much.

On Friday, Peter Mongus played a secondary role in the confrontation. The Enaton monks and their student associates had orchestrated the Christian response to Paralius's beating, to little real effect. While Horapollon and his associates had fled the city, they could easily return when things settled down with no restrictions placed upon their conduct. The ascetics had won the battlefield because their adversaries had melted away without a fight. But to change the dynamics in Alexandria's pagan-run schools the Enaton monks needed a champion who could apply constant pressure to the pagan teachers.

Peter Mongus could serve as this champion, but he needed to be convinced that this was a fight worth undertaking. He also needed to believe that his response would not be seen as disproportionately violent. This was the purpose of Paralius's second visit to the patriarch. After the flight of Horapollon, Stephen, a former sophist and current monk of the Enaton, summoned Paralius to the monastery. Stephen served as the most important liaison between the Enaton and its student associates, and he understood the need to take greater advantage of the opportunity presented by Paralius's beating. When Paralius arrived at the monastery, Stephen asked if he could show where pagan idols were hidden in Menouthis. Paralius responded that he could do this and even offered to find the altar on which sacrifices were performed.¹⁰¹ Stephen informed his *koinobiarch*, Salomon, of this

---

99. *Vit. Sev.* 26; the Syriac (ܐܠܟܐ ܐܢܗ ܐܝܟܢܐ ܗܘ ܠܒܪ) here seems to distinguish the *philoponoi* in the mob from the student *philoponoi*-like group with which Zacharias was associated.

100. *Vit. Sev.* 27.

101. *Vit. Sev.* 27.

and the two monks led Paralius, Zacharias, and the other student associates of the Enaton back to Peter Mongus.

Saturday's audience proceeded much differently. On Friday, Paralius stood before Peter as a victim offering a somewhat dubious story about a scholastic beating. He now came to the bishop promising to uncover the idols, altar, and priest associated with a functioning Isaic temple.[102] Like Stephen and Salomon, Peter understood the difference between these two complaints. The first required one to believe that a pagan had become a "confessor before his baptism" because of a scholastic beating.[103] This idiosyncratic situation provided an excuse for Christian students, Christian teachers, and their ascetic patrons to vent against pagan influence but offered no great benefit to Peter Mongus. Paralius's offer to show the bishop an operational pagan temple in an Alexandrian suburb provided Peter with the chance to direct a significant anti-pagan attack that evoked the examples of Theophilus and Cyril but did not result in any dead bodies or pagan martyrs. In fact, Peter could claim even to outdo the two of them because, by eliminating the Isaic shrine in Menouthis, he would eradicate an important site that survived despite the efforts of both Cyril and Theophilus.

According to Zacharias, Peter responded to Paralius's new information in a way that recalled the example of Theophilus a century earlier. Peter sent some members of the clergy to accompany the students and their anti-Chalcedonian ascetic supporters. He then sent a messenger to summon Chalcedonian monks from the Pachomian monastery of Metanoia in Canopus.[104] Like Theophilus, a band of ascetics would form Peter's anti-pagan shock troops and, again like his predecessor, Pachomian monks would play a leading role in the assault.[105] This mixed group of anti-Chalcedonian and Chalcedonian ascetics had additional symbolic significance. The violent suppression of militant paganism so excited Christians that it could bridge even the Chalcedonian and anti-Chalcedonian divide. Peter evidently hoped to use the occasion to advertise his success in bringing together competing elements of the Alexandrian Christian community.[106]

After a prayer, the anti-Chalcedonian monks of the Enaton traveled east and met up with their Chalcedonian compatriots from Canopus. The two groups then

---

102. *Vit. Sev.* 27.
103. *Vit. Sev.* 25.
104. *Vit. Sev.* 27. The involvement of Pachomians helped convey the message of Christian unity that Peter sought to send, but there was also a practical concern. Enaton lay nine miles west of the city and a reinforcement of monks from there would have taken nearly a day to reach Menouthis. Canopus, however, was on the east side of the city and monks from there could join up with Paralius and his anti-Chalcedonian enablers during their journey.
105. For Theophilus's use of Pachomian monks to clear pagan spaces around Alexandria, see *Storia della Chiesa* II.12.21–24.
106. For this idea, see as well Haas, *Alexandria in Late Antiquity*, 328–29.

proceeded to Menouthis. Paralius pointed out the building in which the Isaic shrine was located. Hieroglyphics adorned the house but the entrance to the shrine was blocked by a false wall and a large piece of pottery.[107] After Paralius moved the pottery to the side, he asked the Pachomian monks to take an axe to the wall and smash through the plaster. Their blows revealed a hidden room filled with idols and a blood-stained altar.[108]

The monks seized all of the objects in the building including a large statue of Kronos,[109] images of dogs, cats, monkeys, crocodiles, and reptiles, as well as something described as an idol of "the rebellious dragon."[110] Some of these idols, it was reported, had been taken from the great temples in Memphis and hidden in Menouthis by priests concerned about their safety. Many had deteriorated. These the monks burned in Menouthis. The monks then assembled the rest of the material, wrote up an inventory, and sent a messenger to Peter Mongus asking for instructions.[111] Most of the afternoon had been spent taking objects from the temple and, consequently, the messenger did not reach Peter until Saturday evening. With no time left for the bishop to reply, the students and their ascetic compatriots found themselves forced to spend the night in the church of Menouthis alongside the large cache of pagan idols they had plundered. Zacharias describes a night filled with the recitation of psalms that mocked the power of the old gods and the credulity of those who worship them. In the morning, the Christians left the church flanked by a guard of Pachomian monks, and returned to the temple of Isis. They "pulled down" the building and waited for further instructions.[112]

In Alexandria, Sunday's dawn brought the beginning of a spectacle unlike

---

107. For the house as a center of private pagan practice into late antiquity see K. Sessa, "Christianity and the Cubiculum: Spiritual Politics and Domestic Space in Late Antique Rome," *JECS* 15 (2007), 179n28. See as well, Frankfurter, "Iconoclasm and Christianization in Late Antique Egypt: Christian Treatments of Space and Image" in *From Temple to Church: Destruction and Renewal of Local Cultic Topography in Late Antiquity*, ed. J. Hahn, S. Emmel, and U. Gotter (Leiden, 2008), 141. It is important to note that the Menouthis shrine is somewhat distinct because, despite its domestic location and hidden idols, it was accessible to a wider pagan public.

108. On the blood-stained altar, one should note the doubts expressed by A. Cameron, "Poets and Pagans in Byzantine Egypt," in *Egypt in the Byzantine World, 300–700*, ed. R. Bagnall (Cambridge, 2007), 27. It is also an interesting parallel to the remains of the "Mithraeum" unearthed by Theophilus in 391 (cf. Rufinus, *HE* 5.16).

109. This is, at any rate, the identification made by Zacharias. For the significance of Kronos in Alexandrian pagan intellectual circles at this time one should note the interesting discussion found in Olympiodorus, *Commentary on the Gorgias*, 47.2–3.

110. *Vit. Sev.* 29.

111. *Vit. Sev.* 30.

112. *Vit. Sev.* 32. If Zacharias's description is not exaggerated, the building must have been small. This seems closer to the house-temple described by David Frankfurter (*Religion in Roman Egypt: Assimilation and Resistance* [Princeton, 1998], 164) than the temple converted into a house posited by Alan Cameron ("Poets and Pagans," 26–27).

anything the city had seen for nearly a century. In the cathedral, the student *philoponos* Menas helped his senior *philoponoi* colleagues lead chants mocking Horapollon and the pagan teachers who had fled the city on Friday. Peter had a clear answer to the chants of the crowd. "In his sermon, the patriarch of God read the description we had sent of the idols, in which he indicated the material they were made from and the number of idols we had found."[113] Like Theophilus following the destruction of the Serapeum, Peter then encouraged his congregation to collect all of the idols that they could find in bathhouses or private residences, pull them off of their mountings, and burn them.[114]

In the meantime, Peter's messengers reached Menouthis with a team of camels. The monks loaded twenty camels with various types of pagan paraphernalia, kidnapped the priest of Isis, and began the short trip into Alexandria.[115] Peter had ordered the procession to go to the Tychaion, a former pagan temple at the center of the city, which Theophilus had turned into a tavern in the 390s.[116] The Tychaion itself would have been too small for this gathering, but it occupied an ideal location. It stood on the Via Canopica, the main east-west axis of the city and the road on which the caravan from Menouthis would have entered the city. It was about three city blocks south of the cathedral along the north or northwestern edge of the garden adjoining the Kom el-Dikka auditoria.[117] If Horapollon did teach in one of these auditoria, the Tychaion then may have been only a few hundred meters away from the location of the initial assault upon Paralius. This symmetry may well have further influenced Peter's choice.

---

113. *Vit. Sev.* 32–33.

114. *Vit. Sev.* 33. Cf. the description of mob actions following the destruction of the Serapeum in Rufinus, *HE* 11.29.

115. *Vit. Sev.* 33.

116. On the Tychaion and its transformation, note Pallades, *Anth. Pal.* 9.180–83; J. Hahn, *Gewalt und religiöser Konflikt: Studien zu den Auseinandersetzungen zwischen Christen, Heiden, und Juden im Osten des Römischen Reiches (von Konstantin bis Theodosius II)* (Berlin, 2004), 95; and the studies of C. Gibson, "Alexander in the Tychaion: Ps.-Libanius on the Statues," *GRBS* 47 (2007), 431–54; and "The Alexandrian Tychaion and the date of Ps.-Nicolaus *Progymnasmata*," (forthcoming). In addition, see J. McKenzie, *The Architecture of Alexandria and Egypt, 300 B.C.–A.D. 700* (New Haven, 2007), 245–46 and "The Place in Late Antique Alexandria 'Where the Alchemists and Scholars Sit...Was Like Stairs,'" in *Alexandria: Auditoria of Kom el-Dikka and Late Antique Education*, ed. T. Derda, T. Markiewicz, and E. Wipszycka (Warsaw, 2007), 67, 79.

117. The exact location of the Tychaion is unknown but fourth-century sources locate it in the "middle of the city" (Ps.-Libanius, *Prog.* 12.25.2) with gates that open onto the "temenos of the Muses" (Ps.-Libanius, *Prog.* 12.25.8). This suggests a location near the intersection of the Via Canopica and street R4, a spot that borders on the large open space next to the Kom el-Dikka auditoria. For discussion of this location see McKenzie, "The Place in Late Antique Alexandria," 67, 79; and C. Haas, "Kôm el-Dikka in Context: The Auditoria and the History of Late Antique Alexandria," in *Alexandria: Auditoria of Kom el-Dikka and Late Antique Education*, ed. T. Derda, T. Markiewicz, and E. Wipszycka (Warsaw, 2007), 89, 94–95.

When the caravan arrived, it found Peter waiting. Seated around him were "the prefect of Egypt, the chief of the corps of guards, and those who were under his command, as well as the municipal senate, and the wealthy property owners of the city."[118] A large crowd of less important onlookers had gathered below, probably in the *temenos* of the Muses south of the temple.[119] Peter ordered the Isaic priest to come and stand on a podium while the idols were brought in to the assembly. A fire was lit and Peter ordered the priest to "give the names of all the demons and say why each one was represented by this specific form."[120] As he did this, the audience pressed in close to see the images and hear the priest's explanations of them. The excited crowd began a set of raucous chants that made fun of the various stories the priest told. They continued for some time until all of the images of the gods had been displayed, mocked, and burned. The event concluded with a set of acclamations, first to the pious emperor Zeno, then to Peter "the great patriarch," and the nobles of the city.[121]

While Peter had been largely uninvolved in the first two days of the riot, he dominated events on its third day. Indeed, from the moment that Paralius volunteered to lead the bishop to a pagan temple, Peter wrote the script that all of the participants followed. Peter had already displayed a particular flair for staging novel public events that put his leadership in the best possible light. In this case, however, he chose to do something deliberately derivative. The order of events differed, but at each step Peter Mongus drew upon the actual and symbolic rhetoric that had defined the first and most dramatic stage of Theophilus's anti-pagan campaign. Just as Theophilus had used Pachomian monks to destroy the temples of Canopus, Peter Mongus called upon their heirs to dismantle the temple of Menouthis. Peter also ensured that his followers treated the plundered pagan images in the same way that Theophilus had a century before. Theophilus had touched off the violence that led to the destruction of the Serapeum by parading bloody cultic images taken from an abandoned temple and encouraging Christians to mock them.[122] Following the destruction of the Serapeum, he had also encouraged his flock to pull down and destroy the representations of pagan gods

---

118. *Vit. Sev.* 34. Haas's suggestion ("Kôm el-Dikka in Context," 95) that the assembly of notables may have taken place in the theater at Kom el-Dikka is an intriguing one, though at a slight variance with what Zacharias describes.

119. The size of the crowd and the fact that a large number of objects were burned suggest that this event probably took place in the *temenos* outside of the Tychaion building. Further supporting this was the discovery of a burned fragment of a marble statue in the open space adjoining the Kom el-Dikka complex. This fragment, some have posited, is debris from Peter's spectacle. For the findings, see McKenzie, "The Place in Late Antique Alexandria," 79; for their association with Peter Mongus, note Haas, "Kôm el-Dikka in Context," 94–95.

120. *Vit. Sev.* 34.

121. *Vit. Sev.* 35.

122. Rufinus, *HE* 11.22; Socrates, *HE* 5.16; Sozomen, *HE* 7.15.

that adorned public and private spaces in the city.[123] Finally, he had arranged for a sort of public cleansing in which the cult statue of Serapis was ceremonially burned.[124] Though other practical and symbolic concerns certainly influenced his thinking, Peter's decision to stage this event in the Tychaion and not the amphitheater (the larger space where Theophilus had burned the torso of the chryselephantine statue of Serapis)[125] also emphasized a Theophilan connection. It was, after all, Theophilus who had transformed this space from a pagan shrine into desecrated public space.

The most notable evocation of Theophilus came at the end of this Sunday spectacle. The assembly concluded with a set of acclamations celebrating the piety and excellence of the patriarch, the local elite, and the emperor Zeno. These were, of course, as well choreographed as the rest of the day's events, but these acclamations also underlined the message that Peter hoped that the day's activities would communicate. He had completed Theophilus's work by assembling the same powerful coalition of supporters. Egyptian traditions emphasized that Theophilus had destroyed the Serapeum and remade the Alexandrian sacred landscape because God had enabled him to cooperate with the emperor.[126] Although Chalcedon and its aftermath had forced Alexandrian patriarchs to move away from this sort of rhetoric, the regular celebration of Theophilus and his achievements meant that Egyptian Christians remained aware of what ecclesiastical and imperial cooperation could achieve. Peter Mongus's assembly harkened back to this earlier era by bringing together imperial officials, monks, clergy, and notable Alexandrians in a common celebration of Christian triumph. It showed that, under Peter, bishop and emperor could again work collaboratively to influence the spiritual direction of the city.

The relationship between Peter Mongus and imperial authorities was important, but one should not discount the gesture that Peter made by seating members of the city council and other Alexandrian notables next to the prefect. It is much more difficult to reconstruct the networks and personal ties that joined Alexan-

123. Rufinus, *HE* 11.29.
124. Rufinus, *HE* 11.23. Both Peter Mongus and Theophilus here follow the general outlines of Alexandrian rituals of civic purification (for a discussion of these see Haas, *Alexandria in Late Antiquity*, 87–89), but Theophilus's actions against pagan images from the Serapeum represent a distinct version of this longstanding idiom. A standard Alexandrian purification called for the object to be removed from the city and then destroyed (e.g., the case of Agathocles described in Polybius, 15.33.9; the Christian martyrs described by Eusebius, *Ecclesiastical History*, 6.51.1ff). Theophilus, however, destroyed the Serapeum materials within the city and never removed them. Peter Mongus, for his part, actually imported spiritual pollution from Menouthis in order to destroy it within Alexandria. For the powerful message sent by leaving desecrated cultic images exposed in the city, see D. Frankfurter, "Iconoclasm and Christianization," 146–48.
125. Rufinus, *HE* 11.23.
126. E.g., *Storia della Chiesa*, 2.14.12–14.

drian bishops to local notables than it is, say, to trace those binding bishops of Rome to the Roman and Italian elite,[127] but councilors and other Alexandrian notables do turn up in narrations of Alexandrian episcopal triumphs. They appear among the crowds that greeted Athanasius upon his return from exile in both 346 and 366,[128] they received gifts from the bishop at the assembly that welcomed Timothy Aelurus back to Alexandria in 475,[129] and they were featured prominently in the ceremony that marked Peter Mongus's acceptance of the Henotikon in 482.[130] All of these moments show members of the local political and economic elite participating in a sort of episcopal adventus that marked the symbolic reconciliation of a divided Alexandrian Christian community.

Perhaps just as interesting as the cases where bishops assembled members of the local elite in order to demonstrate Alexandrian unity are the occasions when elite interests diverged from those of the bishop. In 365, for example, the emperor Valens succeeded in dividing the Alexandrian council from Athanasius by subjecting it to an onerous financial penalty if it did not exile the bishop.[131] Perhaps more interesting, if less clearly documented, is the conflict between Alexandrian notables and Cyril in 414/5.[132] Intriguingly, both Athanasius and Cyril managed to overcome these problems by mobilizing other groups of Christians against the policies of Alexandria's councilors. This strategy had real risks and offered no guarantee of success. Athanasius used the crowds to noisily petition civic leaders and imperial officials, but this tactic only managed to delay his exile.[133] Cyril, notoriously, encouraged a climate that resulted in mob violence and the lynching of the philosopher Hypatia.[134] He succeeded in cowing the council but his reputation outside of the city suffered as a result.[135]

Recognizing that the Alexandrian elite could (and sometimes did) oppose the patriarch adds another layer of meaning to Peter's Sunday spectacle. Sources tell us very little about either the composition of the Alexandrian council in 486 or the particular civic issues it confronted. It is clear, however, that the bishop could

127. For relationships between late antique bishops of Rome and Roman notables see the detailed treatment of K. Sessa, *The Household and the Bishop in Late Antique Rome, ca. 400–600*, chapter 4, forthcoming.

128. 346: *Festal Index* 18; cf. *Historia Acephala* 1.1–2.366: *Historia Acephala* 5.7.

129. Zacharias, *HE* 5.4.

130. Zacharias, *HE* 5.7.

131. Socrates Scholasticus, *HE* 4.13; Sozomen, *HE* 6.12.5. This is discussed in more detail above.

132. The circumstances are described by Socrates, *HE* 7.13–14. For a discussion of the opposition role of the civic elite see Haas, *Alexandria in Late Antiquity*, 312–13; Dzielska, *Hypatia of Alexandria*, trans. F. Lyra (Cambridge, MA, 1995), 88–90; E. Watts, *City and School in Late Antique Athens and Alexandria* (Berkeley, 2006), 197–98.

133. *Historia Acephala* 5.2.

134. Socrates, *HE* 7.14.

135. For discussion, see chapter 7, above.

not spontaneously conjure the symbolic unity displayed on that Sunday by the notables, prefect, and military commanders. Some Christian notables would have obeyed his summons because, as representatives of the city of Alexandria, they wanted collectively to show support for the bishop and his actions.[136] But not all of the civic leaders sat there simply as living and breathing symbols of an Alexandrian municipal consensus. At least one group of notables probably came to be placated. They had been summoned by the Enaton monks to protest Paralius's beating on Friday[137] and could not have been happy with the modest outcome of Peter's efforts on Paralius's behalf. Their participation in Sunday's display would have shown their satisfaction with the bishop's continued attentiveness to their concerns. This event, the product of careful episcopal efforts to acknowledge elite concerns, again showed Peter's considerable political skill. It did not, however, necessarily suggest that his temple attack had inspired universal enthusiasm among the leaders of the city.

A RIOT'S AFTERMATH

Despite his expert staging, Peter's first attempt to present his reconciliation with Zeno as a vindication of anti-Chalcedonian resistance had failed to persuade all of his audience. Now, Peter put on a new public spectacle that defined his position in Theophilan terms. Nevertheless, Peter's evocation of Theophilus proved no more successful than his earlier star turn as a new Athanasius. The events of 486 quickly passed into memory, to be replaced by a new outbreak of ascetic opposition to Peter.

The separatist monks had not forgotten Peter's seizure of Theodore's monastery in 484 and, probably in 486, the displaced monks sent an embassy to Constantinople complaining that Peter "had plundered them, and ejected them, and taken away their monasteries."[138] This news incensed Zeno, who had given official recognition to Peter "with the object of uniting the people together, and not keeping them divided into two parts." The emperor then sent an envoy, the *spatharius* Cosmas,[139] to investigate the complaints and try to facilitate a solution. Cosmas

---

136. Some pagans known to have senatorial standing lived in Alexandria in the later fifth century (e.g., the former consul Severus; Horapollon would later attain this) and, presumably, there were also pagan members of the city council. For obvious reasons, it is hard to believe that men like these attended Peter's display (or, for that matter, the other spectacles arranged by Alexandrian bishops).

137. *Vit. Sev.* 25 indicates that Salomon stirred up the "leaders of the city" (ܪ̈ܝܫܐ ܕܗܕܐ ܡܕܝܢ̄ܬܐ) before approaching Peter.

138. Zacharias, *HE* 6.2.

139. Cosmas was a eunuch of the emperor (Zacharias, *Vit. Sev.* 101; *Vit. Isaiae* 9; *Vit. Pet. Ib.* 98). His trip to Alexandria appears to have been in early 487. For the date, see F. Cumont, "L'Astrologue Palchos," *Revue de l'instruction publique en Belgique* 40 (1897), 1–12, esp. 7, 9–10.

traveled to Alexandria along with the leader of the Separatist embassy and, when they disembarked, they found a crowd of thirty thousand monks and ten bishops waiting to enter the city with them.[140] They were cautioned not to enter Alexandria so as to avoid inciting violence. Instead, a delegation of a bishop, three presbyters, two deacons, two monastic heads and two hundred archimandrites was selected to represent this group.[141]

This delegation followed Cosmas into the church to meet Peter Mongus and the prefect. After Cosmas delivered Zeno's letter, Peter addressed the assembled group "anathematising, in their ears, the Synod and the Tome" and writing a declaration of faith to that effect. But the monks still did not accept his legitimacy because "Peter associated in communion with the chief priests, who had uttered no express anathema against the Synod and the Tome."[142] Peter responded that he remained in communion with all who accepted the Henotikon because, he explained, it "nullified the Synod of Chalcedon."[143] Despite Peter's declaration of faith, most of the dissidents returned unmollified to their monasteries. Some even began talking about the appointment of a rival patriarch. When Cosmas returned to Zeno, his report indicted the Separatist monks for their hard-headedness. The emperor then ordered that, if these monks did not join in communion with Peter, they were to be forcibly expelled from their monasteries.[144] Arsenius, the newly appointed prefect, carried these orders to Alexandria in late 487 and read them out before an assembly of Separatist leaders. Peter Mongus joined the assembly and "readily repeated to them his explanation and anathema, at the same time entreating them to join in communion with himself."[145] Again they refused to do so. The prefect then detained them and brought them to Constantinople for a hearing before the emperor.

The detention and transport of these separatist leaders seems to have taken place in 488 and they remained in Constantinople until the fall of 489. While they were away, Peter initiated a second round of actions designed to reinforce his anti-pagan credentials. This began with a request that the emperor investigate the pagan teachers who had supervised Paralius's study and encouraged his involvement with the Menouthis cult of Isis.[146] When Nicomedes, the imperial official

---

140. Zacharias, *HE* 6.2. On this, see Davis, *Early Coptic Papacy*, 96; Haas, "Peter Mongus," 309.
141. Zacharias, *HE* 6.2.
142. Zacharias, *HE* 6.2; cf. Severus of Antioch, *Letters* 4.2, 254–55; Evagrius, *HE* 3.22.
143. Zacharias, *HE* 6.2.
144. Zacharias, *HE* 6.4; cf. Evagrius, *HE* 3.22. This message was sent with the prefect Arsenius (*PLRE* 2.152, s.v. Arsenius 2). Arsenius must have come to the city in late 487 because Theodorus was serving as the Augustal prefect on March 23 of that year (Palchus, *Apotelesmata* 7; Zacharias, *HE* 6.1; *Vit. Isaiae* 9ff; cf. *PLRE* 2.1092, s.v. Theodorus 32).
145. Zacharias, *HE* 6.4.
146. This is suggested by Damascius, who calls Peter "the leader of those in charge of the state, appointed to oversee their creed" and "a reckless and truly evil man" (*Vit. Is.* 113 I). The revolt of Illus

charged with leading the investigation, arrived in Alexandria, it seems that Peter set his agenda. Damascius suggests that Peter encouraged Nicomedes to direct his attention towards the classroom conduct of these teachers.[147] Nicomedes apparently found something distressing because he soon ordered them to suspend their teaching. Not long after this, Nicomedes uncovered some incriminating information about the philosopher Ammonius that was serious enough to prompt a larger investigation of the pagan teachers. [148]

Although Nicomedes' investigation put considerable pressure on Alexandrian pagan intellectuals, it failed to produce a second act to Peter's great Theophilan performance. Instead of uncovering more hidden pagan temples, Nicomedes managed to discover only a faint-hearted teacher of Aristotle with questionable religious practices and some suspicious behavior by his colleagues. This may have impressed the Enaton monks and student-*philoponoi,* but it did not lead to any more processions of idols or public displays of Christian unity before boisterous crowds. When the investigation did not deliver what he had hoped, Peter decided to cut his losses and arranged a compromise with Ammonius.

Ammonius's interest in coming to such an agreement is obvious. Without it, he faced bankruptcy, imprisonment, torture, and possibly even death.[149] For Peter, the agreement needed simply to address the most basic concerns of the monks and students who took the greatest interest in the Alexandrian schools. Zacharias Scholasticus (whose views may be taken as representative of this group) outlines two main complaints. The first concerned Ammonius's affirmation of the eternity of the cosmos, a doctrine that conflicted with fundamental anti-Chalcedonian ideas.[150] The agreement seems not to have affected this teaching.[151] The general religious atmosphere of the Alexandrian schools also troubled Zacharias. Peter's deal with Ammonius does seem to have addressed this, probably by limiting his ability to present some of the more objectionable theological elements of the Neoplatonic curriculum.[152] This agreement then allowed Peter to reward his supporters and walk away from an unproductive investigation.

---

and the pagan support it had generated virtually guaranteed Zeno's support for this initiative. For discussion of the larger context of this investigation see Watts, *City and School,* 220–22.

147. This is consistent with P. Athanassiadi's idea (*Damascius: The Philosophical History* [Athens, 1999], 29) that Nicomedes was sent to look into the school of Horapollon.

148. *Vit. Is.* 117B–C describes the expansion of the investigation.

149. For these possibilities, see Watts, *City and School,* 222–25.

150. For this set of complaints see Watts, "Creating the Ascetic and Sophistic Mélange," *ARAM* 17/18 (2006–7), 153–64, as well as chapter 5, above.

151. This is suggested by Zacharias's dialog, *Ammonius.* On that text, see Watts, "Sophistic Mélange," 162–63 and chapter 5, above.

152. Note here Watts, *City and School,* 224–25; R. Sorabji, "Divine Names and Sordid Deals in Ammonius' Alexandria," in *The Philosopher and Society in Late Antiquity,* ed. A. Smith (Swansea,

The historical representation of Ammonius's deal reveals how little excitement Peter's second tilt at Alexandria's diminished pagan community generated among Christians. While pagan sources tar Peter as "a reckless and truly evil man" and grieve because of the suffering he caused, no Christian source mentions this incident. It would devastate the Alexandrian pagan intellectual community, but the limited scope of Nicomedes' investigation and its unimpressive results merited no mention in the Christian treatments of Peter's career. Even Zacharias Scholasticus fails to note it in either his *Life of Severus* or his *Ecclesiastical History*. Peter's efforts to style himself a new Theophilus had failed.

By the end of 488, Peter had deployed two distinct models of Alexandrian episcopal authority to try to build support for his compromise with the emperor Zeno. Each one had failed to convince a significant segment of Egyptian Christians that Peter could assent to Zeno's Henotikon and not betray the principles upon which anti-Chalcedonian resistance was founded. Neither of Peter's approaches had been particularly revolutionary; indeed, their appeal lay in their clear evocation of the well-known communal history of the Alexandrian church. In the last year of his life, however, Peter stumbled into a truly revolutionary public position that would enable his anti-Chalcedonian successors to cooperate with imperial power for most of the next generation. It would also make most of his Christian contemporaries forget Paralius and the riot he provoked.

This transformation occurred in large part because of the separatist monks who had been taken to Constantinople after angering the prefect of Egypt. While they waited for the chance to make their case directly before the emperor Zeno, Acacius, the Constantinopolitan bishop, died and was succeeded by Fravitta, a candidate with mildly anti-Chalcedonian views. Upon his appointment, Fravitta wrote a letter to Peter and Peter responded with an epistle that "expressly anathematised the Synod and the Tome of Leo."[153] Unfortunately, Fravitta died before the letter arrived. Instead of reaching the anti-Chalcedonian Fravitta, Peter's message instead reached his indignant successor, the Chalcedonian bishop Euphemius.

Euphemius circulated Peter's letter publicly and, using it as a justification, immediately severed communion with Peter. He then began proceedings to bring Peter before a council of bishops in order to depose him.[154] Peter responded by threatening to organize a council of his own. Before these events could play out, however, Peter died in October of 489. This unexpected (and unresolved) conflict

---

2005), 203–14. See, however, R. M. van den Berg, "Smoothing Over the Differences: Proclus and Ammonius on Plato's *Cratylus* and Aristotle's *De Interpretatione*," in *Philosophy, Science and Exegesis in Greek, Arabic, and Latin Commentaries*, 191–201.

153. Zacharias, *HE* 6.4; cf. Evagrius, *HE* 3.23. The letter of Fravitta is reproduced in Zacharias, *HE* 6.5, and Peter's reply is Zacharias, *HE* 6.6.

154. Zacharias, *HE* 6.4; Evagrius, *HE* 3.23.

had an unanticipated effect. Peter's Alexandrian anti-Chalcedonian opponents witnessed its outbreak while in Constantinople and returned to Alexandria convinced of their bishop's orthodoxy. When they arrived, Peter's successor Athanasius II performed an interesting public test. He gave a sermon in which he mentioned the names of Dioscorus and Timothy, but he purposely omitted the name of Peter. The crowd then "became greatly excited (and they would not be quiet) until he named Peter."[155] In a bit of public ceremonial that Peter would no doubt have appreciated, Athanasius forced the public and the separatist monks to call for Peter's inclusion in the diptychs. This represented a symbolic resolution of the monks' conflict with Peter. It also bound them to an unspoken promise to remain in communion with Athanasius if he followed Peter's example.

Peter struggled for most of his episcopate to draft words and choreograph actions that showed him to be the spiritually authoritative heir of bishops like Athanasius, Theophilus, Cyril, Dioscorus, and Timothy Aelurus.[156] Ultimately Peter's legacy would be determined not by sermons and planned public spectacles but by the accidental publication of his letters to Fravitta. Evagrius Scholasticus deemed him an "opportunist and unstable, a man who adapted himself to the occasion" in part because he felt that Peter's correspondence with Fravitta revealed that the bishop had taken one set of theological positions before the court and another in private.[157]

Anti-Chalcedonian tradition saw Peter somewhat differently. The biography of Peter in the *History of the Patriarchs* centers upon his correspondence, its vigorous rejection of Chalcedon, and the misguided opposition this provoked in Egypt.[158] The *Synaxary,* too, makes Peter's letters the centerpiece of its commemoration of the bishop and places far more emphasis upon them than on Peter's earlier exile.[159] Zacharias Scholasticus provides perhaps the most remarkable presentation of Peter. Peter features prominently in both Zacharias's *Ecclesiastical History* and in his *Life of Severus.* In the former text, Peter's correspondence with Fravitta evinces both his orthodoxy and the propriety of his agreement to the Henotikon.[160] The

---

155. Zacharias, *HE* 6.4.

156. For Peter's efforts to tie himself to Cyril see the documents contained in Cod. Vat. Gr. 1431. This collection may have been connected to Peter Mongus, though perhaps not directly. For discussion see P. Blaudeau, *Alexandrie et Constantinople (451-491): de l'Histoire à la Géo-Ecclésiologie* (Rome, 2006), 370–79.

157. For this assessment of Peter, see Evagrius, *HE* 3.17.

158. Severus, *Hist. Pat.* 13, Peter Mongus. The account is somewhat confused because the letters it describes are between Acacius and Peter, not Fravitta.

159. Hathor 2. This account too confuses Acacius and Fravitta.

160. Blaudeau (*Alexandrie et Constantinople,* 592) correctly sees Zacharias distinguishing between those who held to the letter of the Henotikon and those, like Peter Mongus, who understood its true, anti-Chalcedonian spirit.

presentation of Peter in the *Life of Severus* is less consistent. In the Paralius section of the *Life*,[161] Zacharias emphasizes the activities at Menouthis. Intriguingly, when Zacharias composed the *Life of Severus* around this earlier Paralius material in the 510s, his perspective on Peter Mongus had changed. As the text approached its close, Zacharias described a monk named Nephalius who had opposed Peter because he had come into communion with Acacius.[162] Zacharias then makes clear that Peter's correspondence with Fravitta demonstrated his spiritual authority to such a degree that Nephalius was forced to back down.[163] Although some of this shift in focus may have been due to the different thematic needs of the Paralius material and the larger *Life of Severus*, the passing of time evidently gave Zacharias a new perspective on the career of Peter Mongus.[164]

Zacharias seems to have understood that, while Peter's anti-pagan efforts had failed to create any sort of permanent impression, his epistolary discussion with Fravitta came to define his legacy. It also provided a new, extremely influential model for imperial and episcopal interaction in Alexandria. The reason was simple. Stripped of the symbolic language and ritual historical evocations that had typified many of his public appearances, Peter's letter to Fravitta defined his opposition to Chalcedon in the bishop's own words. When Peter stood by these ideas and appeared willing to begin ecclesiastical warfare with the bishop of Constantinople, he demonstrated that he had not compromised his principles when he agreed to the Henotikon. Indeed, he was willing to accept whatever consequences his beliefs brought upon him.

With these letters, Peter showed that it was possible to engage with imperial power without provoking it through the aggressive assertion of theological distinctiveness. Far from a carefully articulated plan, these letters bore the residue of Peter's bold failures. They showed the path to episcopal peace but they robbed the Alexandrian patriarchate of the influence that two centuries of aggressive and uncompromising theological and political advocacy had earned for it. Despite his best attempts to build a Henoticist patriarchate on previous Alexandrian models, Peter had failed to articulate a way for an anti-Chalcedonian bishop to remain both politically assertive and cooperative with the emperor.

---

161. On the nature of this text and the context in which its earlier components were assembled, see Watts, "Winning the Intracommunal Dialogs: Zacharias Scholasticus' *Life of Severus*," *JECS* 13 (2005), 437–64.
162. *Vit. Sev.* 100–102. Consistent with his habit of reusing material, Zacharias's account of Nephalius and his opposition to Peter strongly resembles that which appears in his *Ecclesiastical History* (e.g., 6.2–3). Both include the figure of thirty thousand separatist monks and describe the arrival of the imperial eunuch Cosmas.
163. *Vit. Sev.* 101–102.
164. It is notable that, while much of the fifth and sixth books of Zacharias's *Ecclesiastical History* focus upon Peter Mongus, the sacking of Menouthis merits no mention at all in the text.

His failure ended the leadership role that the Alexandrian patriarchate had played since the age of Constantine. The next two generations of Alexandrian patriarchs would prove to be nonentities who were more interested in ecclesiastical peace than in determined leadership. Their biographies are studies in meekness. Athanasius II "was a good man, full of faith and the Holy Ghost; and he accomplished that with which he was entrusted; and in his days there was no disorder or persecution in the holy Church."[165] His successor, John I, "walked according to the lives of the excellent fathers who preceded him. The Church and the people and the inhabitants of the country-districts were in his days in security and peace through the grace of the Lord Christ."[166]

John I was in turn succeeded by two more patriarchs whose main contribution was to assent softly as Severus of Antioch grabbed the reins of the anti-Chalcedonian movement.[167] Indeed, in a letter penned early in his episcopate, Severus tried to rouse the Egyptian church by railing against the "mention of Peter in the sacred tablets" because he "embraced the communion of those who did not write the same things as he did."[168] Later in the letter Severus makes clear that Peter had come to symbolize the theological policy of Athanasius II and John too.[169] In another letter sent to the newly enthroned Alexandrian patriarch Dioscorus II in 516, Severus pushed (without great success) for the bishop to embrace the old and aggressive legacy of Timothy Aelurus.[170]

Although early sixth-century Alexandrian bishops gradually moved away from the quiet policies of Peter's immediate successors, even Severus could not succeed in rousing them to restart the spirited attacks on Chalcedon typical of the generation before Peter. By the 520s, Alexandrian patriarchs had become so quiescent that they could not effectively intervene in the Julianist conflict when it erupted in their own city.[171] But it need not have been so. Peter had tried to chart a course towards an assertive and imperially approved model of episcopal government. It

165. Severus of Al'Ashmunein, *History of the Patriarchs* 13.448 (trans. Evetts).

166. Severus of Al'Ashmunein, *History of the Patriarchs* 13.448–49 (trans. Evetts).

167. For the career of Severus as bishop note the still vital study of R. Darling, "The patriarchate of Severus of Antioch, 512–518," (PhD diss., University of Chicago, 1982).

168. Severus of Antioch, *Epistle to Ammonius, Presbyter of Alexandria*, (E. W. Brooks, ed. and trans., *The Sixth Book of Select Letters of Severus* [London, 1904], 1.2.287, 2.2.253).

169. Severus of Antioch, *Epistle to Ammonius*, 1.2.288.

170. Severus of Antioch, *Epistle to Dioscorus* (ed. and trans. Brooks, *Sixth Book of Select Letters*, 1.2.290–93).

171. For the rise of the Julianist heresy, see Ps.-Zacharias, *Chronicle* 9.9–16 and, less accurately, *The History of the Patriarchs* (Timothy III). For modern accounts, J. Maspero, *Histoire des Patriarches d'Alexandrie: depuis la mort d'Empereur Anastase jusqu'à la reconciliation des églises jacobites* (Paris, 1923), 88–93, puts the details together well, while a less detailed account is found in W. H. C. Frend, *Rise of the Monophysite Movement*, 253–54. Note as well R. Draguet, *Julien d'Halicarnasse et sa controverse avec Sévère d'Antioche sur l'incorruptibilité du corps du Christ* (Louvain, 1924).

failed because Peter had promised things that the age could not deliver. The 480s offered neither resounding Athanasian theological victories nor large Egyptian pagan areas ripe for Theophilan urban renewal. The next generation of Alexandrian anti-Chalcedonian leadership would continue to celebrate the resistance of Athanasius, the anti-pagan zeal of Theophilus, and the ardent anti-Chalcedonianism of Dioscorus and Timothy Aelurus, but the exemplar who most influenced their behavior was Peter Mongus. His odd commemorations, then, accurately reflect his enduring and accidental revolutionary legacy.

Bishops enjoyed a complicated relationship with their congregations that required them to serve as both intimate acquaintances and remote representatives of divine power. Unlike those of ascetic and scholastic leaders, the words of bishops could reach thousands of hearers immediately and, in the larger cities of the Roman Empire, hundreds of thousands more in a matter of hours. The ability of bishops to shape the perspectives and behaviors of large numbers of Christians came from the particular sort of spiritual authority that they claimed and that the community usually granted to them. In principle, the bishop guided all of the Christians under his charge along a spiritual path that led to eternal life. He welcomed newcomers into the community, baptized them, and celebrated the Eucharist that regularly affirmed their place within the church. Perhaps most importantly, the bishop also took responsibility for teaching his followers. In both personal communication with his flock and in the sermons he delivered, the bishop examined Scripture, explained Christian doctrine, and instructed his congregation how to avoid sin. Like the lectures of a philosopher or the teachings of a leading ascetic, the sermons of a bishop offered practical applications of the often abstract ideas expressed in Christian texts. Sermons also enabled a bishop to explain to his congregation how contemporary events ought to be understood and how Christians ought to respond to them.

Like oral communication in other environments, the force of a sermon depended upon the particular faith that listeners had in the person of the bishop. All bishops claimed that the Holy Spirit inspired their words, but only truly authoritative bishops behaved in ways that displayed this spiritual inspiration. Like a respectable teacher of philosophy, an effective and persuasive bishop needed to live according to the standards of conduct he advocated. If he failed to do so, the bishop could expect his congregation to doubt his inspiration.

As Christian communities grew, ideas about the appropriate way in which a bishop ought to behave became more specific. The careers of some notable bishops even served as paradigms of episcopal behavior. Some bishops served as villains in Christian communal histories. Egyptian tradition remembered the Alexandrian Proterius for the hypocrisy he showed when he abandoned Dioscorus at

Chalcedon and accepted the episcopate in his stead.[172] Juvenal of Jerusalem received even worse treatment. He too failed to support Dioscorus at Chalcedon and, for this, anti-Chalcedonians attacked him for hypocrisy, apostasy, and even Satanic inspiration.[173] Within Egypt, Athanasius stood out among the positive exemplars because of his anti-Arian activities, his resistance to imperial pressure, and his connection to prominent ascetics.[174] Theophilus provided a different sort of paradigm that highlighted the benefits of imperial cooperation and celebrated his remaking of the Alexandrian sacred landscape.[175]

As the *Synaxary* of the Coptic Church suggests, Egyptian Christians who routinely attended church heard about these figures regularly during services. Simply by listening to liturgy, a Christian would find himself armed with a developed knowledge of the careers of Athanasius, Theophilus, Cyril, and a large number of other significant figures. This Christian communal history had its own unique form and taught Christians to focus more upon what an exemplar represented than upon what he or she had specifically done. Like a Plutarchan biography, the details of each individual life added up to a specific, thematically defined historical identity. The stories told about Athanasius, for example, reinforced his status as a model of theological and political resistance. Those that featured Proterius, by contrast, highlighted his unprincipled opportunism. In rare cases, the thematic identity of past figures could be expanded (as when the sermons of Theophilus and Cyril created anti-pagan credentials for Athanasius),[176] but most of the time these were fixed identities that served as common points of reference for Egyptian Christians.

These common points of historical reference proved important because, like leaders of intellectual and monastic circles, bishops could use them to generate a particular sort personal affection for themselves. Implicit in the relationship between a bishop and his congregation were the same sorts of promised benefits and personal attachments that gave meaning to teacher-student and ascetic master-disciple interactions. However, because a bishop could not possibly develop a personal relationship with all of his followers, his bond with his congregation took a different form. Instead of building intimate connections with tens of thousands of people through conversations and shared experiences, the bishops of large cities relied upon a preexisting sense of community to build trust in their personal spiritual authority. A bishop's evocation of a shared Christian past allowed him to connect with the expectations of his congregation and demonstrate his fidelity to the historical standards of their community. Because Christians thought of the

---

172. *Panegyric on Macarius of Tkow* 15; *History of Dioscorus* 15; *Plerophories* 68.
173. E.g., *Panegyric on Macarius of Tkow* 7; *History of Dioscorus* 1, 7, 11, 13; *Plerophories* 25, 56, 58.
174. On this see the discussion of chapter 6, above.
175. See chapter 7, above.
176. See the discussion in chapter 7, above.

past thematically, an astute bishop could also use this shared history to shape the way that his followers thought about contemporary events and figures.

Peter Mongus understood this dynamic as well as (and perhaps better than) any other Alexandrian bishop. When considered simplistically, Peter's career bears a stronger resemblance to that of Juvenal of Jerusalem than it does to that of Athanasius or Theophilus. Peter began his episcopate in hiding as the loyal successor of the aggressively anti-imperial bishops Dioscorus and Timothy Aelurus. Like Juvenal, he would end his life as an imperially endorsed prelate who had used the power of the state to silence critics, attack monks, and seize monasteries. And yet, Peter understood how to frame this transformation effectively in historical terms that many of his followers would accept. Unlike Juvenal, who endorsed Leo's Tome at Chalcedon, or Proterius, who signed the same document in Alexandria,[177] Peter largely managed to redefine his subscription to the Henotikon as an anti-Chalcedonian theological and political victory. Had Peter been less astute, however, he could have expected to find himself associated with the unfortunate examples of Juvenal of Jerusalem and Proterius rather than revered bishops like Athanasius and Timothy.

The aftermath of Paralius's beating shows Peter's great skill in shaping public perceptions of events as they unfolded. When Paralius offered Peter the opportunity to raid a shrine of Isis in Menouthis, Peter used it to make a number of important symbolic statements. Although Peter had tried to present himself as a conciliator who could bring together Alexandrian Christian communities, ascetic opposition centered in the Chalcedonian monastery of Metanoia and anti-Chalcedonian monasteries like the Enaton had made this impossible. Peter understood that a Christian attack on a pagan shrine would cause these two groups of ascetics to embrace a common cause. If presented correctly, this attack could bring ordinary Christians of these two theological persuasions together in public. Peter further understood the unique power that his position as bishop gave him to publicly define the parade of plundered pagan idols as a celebration of the common features that joined all Alexandrian Christians together.

While neither Peter nor his supporters ever seem to have mentioned Theophilus by name, Alexandrian Christians would immediately have associated Peter's actions against paganism with those undertaken by Theophilus. Perhaps most importantly, they also seem to have known how to respond to these stimuli. By tapping into the shared history of Alexandrian Christians, Peter both instructed them how they were to behave in the present and allowed them to trust that the Holy Spirit inspired his instructions. Peter had slipped carefully into a leadership role defined neither by the specific time nor by the circumstances in which he

---

177. On these events, note the anti-Chalcedonian views of the *History of Dioscorus* 9 (Juvenal), 15 (Proterius); *Plerophories* 20.

lived. Because they had been taught to revere bishops who filled this role, Peter's congregation listened.

While this riot shows the impressive capacity of a most skilled bishop to shape opinion and influence behavior among his followers, its aftermath shows the disadvantages associated with channeling a timeless avatar. Peter counted, quite rightly, on the existence of a Christian mentality in which the saints of the past remained both relevant to and active in a sort of eternal present. The legacies of the saints could always be evoked but, if they were evoked too frequently or in an inappropriate context, they could distort the bishop beyond recognition. Peter could dress himself up as a second Athanasius, Theophilus, or Timothy Aelurus, but the Egyptian separatists rightly recognized that his career did not parallel that of any of these exemplars. They could not trust a bishop they did not know. Not surprisingly, their reconciliation with Peter came only when his letter to Fravitta revealed a Peter who had shed symbolic gestures and ritual historical invocations to speak clearly and plainly about his objection to Chalcedon. It took this, the naked sentiments of a careful patriarch, to convince anti-Chalcedonian monks of his true spiritual authority. Ultimately, even the most powerful symbolism depended upon a perceived personal connection to resonate with a Christian audience.

9

Conclusion

On first glance, the riot that inflamed Alexandria for a long weekend in the spring of 486 looks like yet another eruption of the pagan-Christian violence that often troubled this notoriously excitable city in the fourth and fifth centuries. In the previous century and a half, Alexandria had been the site of religious conflict on many occasions. Unfortunately, the large numbers of individuals involved, the opacity of our sources, and the difficulty in determining the order of events make it possible to reconstruct the social tensions that catalyzed these violent incidents in only the most general terms. The Paralius riot, however, arose out of a set of tensions that are far better attested than those which fed other late antique Alexandrian riots. As both pagan and Christian sources suggest, the initial fuel for the violence came from a conflict between the beliefs and personal identifications of individual students studying philosophy, rhetoric, and grammar in the city's large complex of auditoria. Many students in these classrooms felt a strong connection to their teachers and an obligation to defend their reputations. The most skilled and devoted students enjoyed an even stronger bond with their mentors. They often styled professors their intellectual "fathers" and shared meals and personal conversations with them.

In many cases, these discussions evoked the memories of the teacher's own intellectual family. Sources ranging in date from the early fourth century B.C. to the later sixth century A.D. show that philosophers and rhetoricians frequently sprinkled anecdotes about intellectual ancestors into the conversations that they had with students. These stories helped students to identify with the scholarly genealogy that they now shared with their teacher, they allowed students to bask in their ancestors' reflected glory, and they gave meaning to often abstract ethical teaching. Many of the students offered this information came to treasure both these intimate exchanges and the stories passed along during them. For this reason, devoted students responded aggressively to any outside criticism of these traditions.

These interactions joined students and their professors in a shared intellectual patrimony, but the realities of late antique education meant that a significant portion of those attending classes did not develop a strong identification with their scholastic families. Some of these students would sample the offerings of a range of teachers and may have enjoyed only a casual association with any one particular school. Others may not have remained affiliated with a circle long enough to develop any strong ties. Most late antique evidence suggests that only a minority of those attending lectures at any one time would complete even a three-year course of study.[1] Each of these problems almost certainly affected the Alexandrian schools out of which the riot of 486 developed, but they served only to dilute the passion felt and expressed by the more devoted members of a school. Responsibility for the riot cannot lie at their feet.

In Alexandria in the 480s, another group of students also refused to associate themselves with the intellectual family of their teachers. They did this not because of their dispassion for the scholastic environment or the short time they spent within it, but because of their stronger attachment to anti-Chalcedonian ascetic leaders. Like pagan schools, the ascetic communities with which these students were associated depended upon intimate personal relationships that joined leading monks and their followers. In monasteries, as in pagan schools, ideals of conduct were both explained abstractly and illustrated tangibly by historical anecdotes. In addition, sources describing the apprenticeships through which communal elders individually supervised the spiritual development of junior monks suggest that ascetic master-disciple relationships often facilitated the transmission of particularly potent historical traditions.[2] Personal ties and shared communal experiences, then, helped monks to accept these stories and the ideals they illustrated.

Texts as diverse as the sermons of Shenoute and the *Historia Monachorum* show that some of the same illustrative anecdotes that circulated among monks also reached visitors to their monasteries. These oral testimonies exercised particular power over the lay Christians who came to see leading monks as their spiritual mentors. Personal interactions like these encouraged laymen to become invested in the historical traditions that defined the ascetic communities with which they

1. R. A. Kaster, *Guardians of Language: The Grammarian and Society in Late Antiquity* (Berkeley, 1988), 26–27; based upon P. Petit, *Les Étudiants de Libanius* (Paris, 1957), 62–65. See Libanius, *Ep.* 379, for a case of a student who left his care before completing his course. Note, however, the cautions of R. Cribiore, *The School of Libanius in Late Antique Antioch* (Princeton, 2007), 177.

2. For discussion of cases when these relationships did not work out see B. Bitton-Ashkelony and A. Kofsky, *The Monastic School of Gaza* (Leiden, 2006), 202–203.

were affiliated and also shaped their behavior in the outside world. However, outside factors limited the influence of even the most powerful spiritual fathers. Lay associates often struggled to balance their devotion to an ascetic mentor and the demands of their secular life.

Some students in Alexandria found themselves similarly torn between the expectations of their student life and the teaching of anti-Chalcedonian ascetic masters in Alexandria and Gaza. These Christian students, Zacharias Scholasticus foremost among them, were affiliates of the Enaton monastery in Alexandria and related ascetic communities in Gaza. By the 480s, the Alexandrian and Gazan monasteries to which these students were tied had become important centers of resistance to the Council of Chalcedon. The anecdotes heard by students and other visitors to these anti-Chalcedonian ascetic circles celebrated monastic resistance to imperial pressure and described divinely inspired visions that associated the Council of Chalcedon with the imminent end of the world. These eschatological ideas conflicted directly with the important Neoplatonic teaching that the world was eternal and forced students to choose between the ascetic discourse to which they had become attached and the ideas presented by their teachers. This choice provoked the Alexandrian student-*philoponoi* to become extremely hostile towards pagan professors whose teachings they thought pulled people away from Christianity.[3]

When Paralius arrived at the school of Horapollon in the fall of 485 he entered a complicated social environment in which groups of students shared the same teachers, the same classrooms, and many of the same experiences but understood each of these things in dramatically different ways. Paralius had the misfortune of revealing these gaps in perception. Although Horapollon had apparently made efforts to draw Paralius into the social environment of his school, the young man felt more affection for his brother and his brother's friends at the Enaton than he did for his peers. Paralius began to spend more and more time at the monastery. Eventually he decided to attack the integrity of his teachers and the Menouthis Isaic shrine that they and their students visited. Horapollon's students reacted as they felt they should. They found an appropriate moment to defend their teachers' honor, reassert the proper scholastic hierarchy, and put Paralius in his place. They understood Paralius's beating to be a punitive action that was perfectly acceptable within the context of an intellectual circle.

The anti-Chalcedonian ascetic affiliates who attended classes in the same space saw the beating differently. Their own experiences had conditioned them to see anti-Christian activity throughout the scholastic environment. When they saw a student beaten for criticizing the religious credulity of pagan teachers, these students immediately understood this as a "persecution," not as the defense of the

---

3. Zacharias, *Ammonius*, ll. 357–60.

integrity of a scholar. Their vigorous response to Paralius's beating grew out of a fundamental conflict between the values promoted by the Alexandrian scholastic social environment and the beliefs sustained by their personal relationships with anti-Chalcedonian ascetics.

Both Paralius's attackers and his defenders responded to this situation in ways that reflected the personal relationships that they held dear and the values that their mentors had taught them. For the students of Horapollon, the beating manifested the loyalty to teacher that they had been taught to place on the same level as loyalty to family and country. For the anti-Chalcedonian student-*philoponoi*, their rescue of Paralius and the prosecution of his assailants and teacher represented the same sort of uncompromising combat for Christ that their mentors in Enaton and Gaza encouraged. Like Horapollon's students, the student-*philoponoi* acted according to the fundamental values of the social group with which they most closely identified.

When Peter Mongus learned of the assault on Paralius, he reacted more as an opportunistic outsider than as a person with a particular concern for Alexandria's schools. Unlike Horapollon's students and the student-*philoponoi*, Peter Mongus occupied a position of authority from which he could try to define the way that others would first understand Paralius's beating. He could also encourage people to respond to it in specific ways. Peter enjoyed this remarkable ability to shape public opinion because, for centuries, Christians had been taught to accept that their bishops possessed a particular sort of influence. Bishops presented themselves as spiritual mediators to whom the Holy Spirit had given responsibility for the salvation of their congregation. Inspired by the Holy Spirit, they supervised every aspect of a Christian's religious growth and offered regular guidance about how a Christian ought to behave. This involved not only the explanation of Scripture and Christian doctrine but also weekly sermons that instructed a congregation how these teachings ought to be applied in their lives.

This immense influence carried with it an important obligation. The Christian community granted bishops power to shape their views and influence their behaviors because it trusted that these men had been divinely invested by the Holy Spirit. They required repeated assurances that the bishop possessed the sort of spiritual authority that he claimed. Unlike smaller communities where the intimate bond between a leader and his followers could be reaffirmed through regular personal contact, practical limitations prevented the bishop from reaching most of his flock in this way. Instead, bishops in large cities depended upon public sermons and actions that displayed, in symbolic terms, their continued spiritual authority over the community. From the time of Paul, Christians had determined a set of general behaviors that suggested the divine inspiration of their bishops. As Christian history developed over the next four hundred years, the wider church and its various local communities regularly commemorated individual exemplars who manifested these general virtues in particular ways. The deeds of these figures and the virtues they exemplified became a part of the communal history with which Christians identified. As such, they provided a rich set of historical parallels that a bishop could draw upon to show how his own behavior and the actions he advocated remained consistent with the authority he claimed.

Peter Mongus faced a particular challenge because, midway through his episcopate, the historical parallels upon which he chose to stake his claim to spiritual authority no longer matched his conduct. Peter had succeeded Timothy Aelurus, a bishop who had deliberately and modestly claimed to be doing little more than fighting to preserve the political and theological legacy of Dioscorus and his revered predecessors. Like Timothy, Peter began his episcopate by highlighting his qualification to lead an ascetic and episcopal coalition in theological resistance against imperial power. However, in 482, Peter changed course and accepted a theological compromise endorsed by the emperor Zeno. Instead of resisting imperial power, Peter had now embraced it. He could provide no universally acceptable justification for this change of course and, as a result, his anti-Chalcedonian coalition soon began to fragment.

Peter did not find himself in a particularly secure position at the moment of Paralius's beating. Peter enjoyed the support of the emperor and a majority of the Alexandrian population but, while substantial, this support also appears to have been shallow. By 486, ascetic resistance to Peter's theological compromise had metastasized across Egypt and become a significant threat to his position. Peter had, in part, created this very problem for himself. After endorsing the Henotikon, Peter continued to base his authority upon his fidelity to an Athanasian, Dioscoran, and Timothy Aeluran model of episcopal behavior. This model, however, required both theological rigidity and close cooperation with ascetics. In his Henoticist incarnation, Peter Mongus could claim neither of these things.

Peter Mongus's decision to intervene decisively against scholastic paganism in 486 represents an attempt to change the conversation. Instead of asserting his connection to the resistance legacy of Athanasius, Dioscorus, and Timothy Aelurus, Peter could now symbolically position himself as an heir to the anti-pagan legacy of Theophilus. The fact that Paralius offered him the opportunity to sack a pagan shrine in Menouthis only heightened the appeal of such a shift. Paganism had survived in Menouthis despite the efforts of Theophilus and Cyril; Peter could use this occasion to simultaneously tie himself to his illustrious predecessors and succeed in a task that they had been unable to complete. Peter then took advantage of the power of his pulpit to define before his congregation, in the clearest terms, the larger meaning of the actions he ordered.

Just as Horapollon's students, Enaton's student-*philoponoi* affiliates, and Peter Mongus each drew upon their own particular understanding of the past to shape their behavior during the riot, so too did that weekend's violence refashion their communal histories. Among pagan teachers, the riot and the imperial investigation it ultimately set in motion caused a significant shift in both their teaching and their presentation of the past. Teachers like Isidore ceased to glorify efforts to overthrow the Roman political order (which current conditions made impossible) and began advocating a more passive response to political pressure. In the final years of the Athenian Neoplatonic school, the behavior of Damascius and his colleagues reflected their fidelity to this ideal. Paralius's beating and its aftermath helped to ensure that, when Damascius's school came under political pressure in the 520s, he disastrously chose to disengage from political life instead of adapting to new realities.

The riot pushed the anti-Chalcedonian student-*philoponoi* to become more personally assertive within the schools. These students produced a series of texts, both oral and written, that attacked the integrity of pagan teachers while celebrating the achievements of their Christian student opponents. The riot eventually came to occupy a central position in the communal narratives underpinning this new Christian assertiveness.

Peter Mongus's intervention in the riot, his decision to expand the violence to include a pagan shrine in Menouthis, and his call for an additional imperial investigation into Alexandrian paganism had an important short-term symbolic consequence. These events, however, had little lasting effect on his broader historical legacy. While Peter temporarily established himself as a Christian anti-pagan champion, this triumph did not define his historical legacy. Instead, Peter's correspondence with the Constantinopolitan patriarch Fravitta and his conflict with Fravitta's successor Euphemius overshadowed his actions against paganism. These interactions revealed Peter to be a new sort of historical exemplar for an age that valued principled Christological stands but did not require them to be displayed through constant theological combat.

Peter Mongus perhaps represents the most interesting character in this entire event because, while he had the ability and opportunity to use this violence to make a statement about the nature of his leadership, the riot had no appreciable influence upon his broader legacy. He appears in both pagan philosophical descriptions of Nicomedes' investigation and in the student-*philoponoi* celebration of Paralius, but in each case the authors have rendered him a character who serves to push along events whose larger course has already been determined. In Damascius's narrative, Peter simply hastens the moral decline already set in motion by Pamprepius. For Zacharias Scholasticus, Peter enables the student-*philoponoi* to achieve their most significant victory over the leaders of the Alexandrian schools. Indeed, the omission of any reference to this event in Zacharias's *Ecclesiastical History* suggests quite strongly that he did not see the Paralius riot as a defining (or even particularly significant) moment in Peter Mongus's larger career. It merited retelling not because of its general significance to Christians but because of its specific importance to one small part of the Alexandrian Christian community.

The riot and its aftermath also show that intellectuals, ascetic groups, and ecclesiastical leaders interpreted contemporary circumstances and incorporated them into their communal histories in different fashions. For Alexandrian intellectuals (and philosophers in particular) the events of the later 480s came to be understood through the prism of Neoplatonic and Epitectan ethical teachings. Works like Epictetus's *Encheiridion* played an important role in abstractly instructing students how a philosopher should act in the world. Not surprisingly, they also offered an interpretative framework through which the various responses to the trials brought about by Pamprepius, Paralius, and Nicomedes could be explained. In the Neoplatonic retelling, Ammonius's greed, Horapollon's cowardice, Gessius's unexpected heroism, and Isidore's principled exile overshadow many of circumstantial details surrounding their actions. We must not assume that this occurred because of deliberate deception on the part of Damascius or other members of his community. Instead, we must remember that the accounts of these events played a functional role in modeling philosophical behavior and shaping the behaviors of Damascius's followers. But the interpretative connections between philosophic doctrine and philosophical behavior flowed both ways. In the same way that oral testimony and oral traditions describing the actions of philosophers could enhance a student's understanding of a complicated text, so too did the texts at the core of philosophical study serve as a sort exegetical tool through which philosophers could distill clear meaning from a complicated set of real events. It is also important to note that neither the choice nor the interpretation of these doctrinal texts and illustrative traditions remained static. Reading curricula, communal traditions, and their mutually dependent exegeses evolved in tandem with the needs and circumstances of an intellectual community.

Ascetic communities and their affiliates used a different set of tools to interpret events and institutionalize their meaning in communal traditions. Christian ethical and theological teaching shaped these groups and the way in which they understood the world around them. Biblical materials always ranked as the most authoritative texts, but contemporary theology and the controversies it engendered also deeply influenced the ideals of ascetics. The powerful opposition that Gazan and Alexandrian anti-Chalcedonian ascetic communities had to the Tome of Leo and the Chalcedonian creed that it supported affected their understanding of the events around them. Perhaps the best example of this was the interpretative loop that connected Roman theology, the city's terrible political circumstances in the 450s and 470s, and notions that the Tome of Leo played an important role in determining the city's fate. The nature of ascetic life meant that these ideas and others like them circulated widely among anti-Chalcedonians. As John Rufus's

Plerophories show, they also rapidly reinforced one another. At the same time, however, the hierarchical nature of monastic society meant that the maintenance and interpretation of tradition was, to a greater or lesser degree, controlled by the most authoritative figures in the community.

The student affiliates of these anti-Chalcedonian monasteries saw in the paganism of their teachers and fellow students a threat that demanded combating as much as Chalcedonian heresy. It had produced a hostile spiritual environment that required them to mount a continuous and vigorous defense of their Christianity. The pre-riot attitudes of this group of students are somewhat difficult to recover[4] but it is clear that the beating of Paralius and its aftermath changed the way that these students understood their ability to influence Alexandria's scholastic environment. This change seems to have grown organically out of the sensibilities of the students themselves. Consciously or unconsciously, the student-*philoponoi* seem to have undertaken this process of communal redefinition on their own. Because they had no defined hierarchy, no one figure or group of figures seems to have controlled the communal interpretation of Paralius's beating or the activist ethos that it supported.

The Alexandrian episcopate had the most efficient and effective mechanisms for interpreting contemporary events and incorporating them into communal historical traditions. Bishops naturally combined Christian doctrinal instruction with illustrative historical traditions in their sermons. In addition, the liturgical calendar that they superintended regularly celebrated exemplars of Christian piety. This formalized and stabilized a communal history that catechumens could learn and baptized Christians could recall. These sorts of commemorations had a formal role in the common experience of Christians and, unlike the oral traditions that circulated informally among intellectuals and ascetics, Christian liturgy regularly presented them to the community. This meant that these traditions preserved a broader and more detailed history than the illustrative anecdotes shared by teachers and monks.

By the later fifth century, the large and diverse set of historical examples known to Christians made it difficult for a bishop to craft completely new explanatory idioms. The student-*philoponoi*, for example, were a small group with a short collective history and no structures for determining what elements of that history would become authoritative. Bishops, however, superintended a long, well-known history that was shared by millions of Christians and had conditioned Christian audiences to expect a range of acceptable behaviors. This had two clear effects on the way in which contemporary events were interpreted and institutionalized as shared traditions. First, as the experience of Peter Mongus shows, bishops often struggled to

---

4. Our only access to this comes from the *Life of Severus*'s descriptions of the student-*philoponoi* before the riot. For further analysis of this material see chapter 5, above.

create new paradigms of episcopal action to explain their deeds. Second, even if a bishop did succeed in temporarily defining himself in a new or surprising way, the inertia of Christian history and the initiative of individual minds could eventually reinterpret his actions so that they fit back into a familiar slot.

Ultimately, it is important for us to recognize that the specific concerns of two small groups and one urban leader created three distinct views of the causes and three unique memories of the consequences of this riot. This has important implications for our broader understanding of late antique society. It suggests the need to consider the internal dynamics of smaller communities when exploring the larger social and religious changes that spread across the Roman world in late antiquity. The individuals living through this period identified intensely with social and religious groups that were tied together by personal intimacy and shared histories. These communities did not eliminate individual initiative, but they affected the way that individuals saw the world, influenced the ideas that they believed, and shaped the manner in which they interacted with other people. Paying greater attention to their unique structures enhances our appreciation of the human elements that propelled the immense social changes of late antiquity.

Adjusting our historical focus in this way has two important implications. First, it reveals with greater acuity the importance that oral communication had in the circulation of influential ideas in late antiquity. All three of the communities involved in this riot learned their common history and the ideals of conduct it illustrated primarily through oral communication. Second, paying attention to the mechanisms through which ideas became influential allows one to understand why they came to affect the way that people behaved. There can be no doubt that texts influenced the way that people thought and acted in late antiquity, but personal communication like that which occurred during a student-teacher dinner, an ascetic master-disciple conversation, or a bishop's sermon proved equally (and perhaps more) powerful. The affection that an audience felt for a speaker invariably made it more receptive to the information and anecdotes that he or she shared.

This study has examined how three distinct and important social elements of the late antique world preserved their past, shaped it into a set of illustrative stories, and tried to live according to the values this history emphasized. History was not the only or even the most important type of formative discourse within late antique communities. Historical traditions, however, provided tangible examples of behaviors to be emulated and avoided. As such, they provide perhaps the best chance to connect the words that described the communities of the later Roman Empire with the actions that shaped them. As the Alexandrian riot shows, new ideas remade the Roman world in late antiquity, but they did it on the back of the personal relationships and larger communal structures that gave them meaning.

APPENDIX ONE

Dating the Riot

It is impossible to date the riot precisely because the prefect involved, Entrechius, is known only from Zacharias's *Life of Severus.* The two secure chronological brackets within which the riot can be placed are the revolt of Illus in August of 484 and the death of Peter Mongus in October of 489. It is possible to narrow the date down further, however, based upon a number of clues found in Zacharias's text. Paralius was certainly still in Aphrodisias when Illus's revolt failed in the late summer of 484.[1] Furthermore, Zacharias tells us that Paralius spoke to Isidore about philosophical questions during his first year of study. It is known that Isidore was in Athens at the time of Proclus's death on April 17, 485; as the sailing season lasted from approximately March 10 to November 10, it is probable that he had been there since the previous autumn.[2] Isidore then likely returned to Alexandria for the beginning of the fall term in 485, with Paralius conceivably arriving soon afterwards either in the fall of 485 or for the spring term of 486.[3]

The events described by Zacharias could not, however, have taken place in 487. Two prefects are known for that year. The first, Theodorus, was serving as the Augustal prefect on 23 March of that year.[4] The second, Arsenius, arrived later that

---

1. *Vit. Sev.* 40–41.
2. For the date of the death of Proclus, see *Vit. Proc.* 36. For Isidore's presence, note *Vit. Is.* 125A–B. On the sailing season, see L. Casson, *Ships and Seamanship in the Ancient World* (Princeton, 1971).
3. Most students arrived in the fall, but some did come for the spring term. On this see R. Cribiore, *The School of Libanius in Late Antique Antioch* (Princeton, 2007), 117.
4. Palchus, *Apotelesmata* 7; cf. F. Cumont, "L'Astrologue Palchos," *Revue de l'instruction publique en Belgique* 40 (1897), 1–12.

year.[5] The Athanasian festal letters suggest that the average tenure of an Egyptian prefect from 328–73 was about eighteen months.[6] If this pattern held into the fifth century (and there is no reason to think that it did not), it is unlikely that three prefects would have held office in 487. It is more reasonable to think that Entrechius held the position sometime either between 485 and mid-486 or in 488. If Entrechius held office in 488, however, this would have greatly compressed the timeline for Paralius's beating and Nicomedes's subsequent investigation of the philosophers (all of which took place while Peter Mongus was still alive).[7] This is not impossible, but it seems more likely that the beating took place in 486 and Nicomedes' investigation in late 487 or early 488, possibly following the final suppression of Illus's revolt. This would, incidentally, fit with the likelihood that Severus of Antioch moved to the law school of Berytus in the fall of 486 or 487.[8]

If the beating of Paralius took place during the 485/6 school year, it seems that spring 486 would be the most likely time. This would have given Paralius sufficient time to grow disenchanted with his fellow students and begin his relationship with the Enaton. Zacharias's description of the riot's third day may be taken to imply that the events coincided with Easter weekend (April 4–6, 486),[9] though, as Jan Eric Steppa has pointed out to me, subsequent references to Easter in the text do not particularly match this description.[10] If Paralius's baptism is to be placed in the same year as his beating, the riot then must have taken place around the New Year.[11] Given the catechetical process that Paralius seems to have undergone, it is not unreasonable to think that his baptism may instead have occurred the following Easter.

To conclude, the riot probably dates to the spring of 486, perhaps even April 4–6 of that year. Certainty remains elusive, however. Barring additional evidence for the date of Entrechius's prefecture, dates between late 485 and spring 486 or the spring of 488 remain possibilities.

5. Zacharias, *HE* 6.4; cf. Evagrius, *HE* 3.22; *PLRE* 2.152, s.v. Arsenius 2.
6. A. H. M. Jones, *The Later Roman Empire 284–602* (Norman, 1964), 381.
7. For additional reasons to disentangle the two events see E. Watts, *City and School in Late Antique Athens and Alexandria* (Berkeley, 2006), 220n96.
8. H. I. MacAdam, "*Studia et Circenses:* Beirut's Roman Law School in its Colonial, Cultural Context", *ARAM* 13–14 (2001–2002), 211. I thank Jan Eric Steppa for this reference
9. *Vit. Sev.*, 32 ll. 10ff., terms the Sunday of the riot "the first day of the week, on which the Lord Jesus rose from his grave and loosened the power of death."
10. E.g., *Vit. Sev.* 37, 57.
11. This is described in *Vit. Sev.* 37.

APPENDIX TWO

How Much Should We Trust Zacharias Scholasticus?

The basic narrative upon which I base my reconstruction of Paralius's beating and the riot it touched off derives from one source, Zacharias Scholasticus's *Life of Severus*. There are two different factors that suggest that modern scholars should exercise caution when drawing upon this particular work. In a thought-provoking 2007 article, Alan Cameron outlined a set of arguments against an over-credulous reading of Zacharias's text.[1] Cameron argues that triumphalist Christian texts like the *Life of Severus* are often unreliable, but Zacharias's text has particular problems because its author uses the text to lie about Severus's religious affiliation. Instead of the life-long Christian that Zacharias claims, Severus himself admits to experimenting with paganism while a student—and mentions that his friend "the scholasticus" knew this.[2]

From this starting point, Cameron critically examines many of the details within the text. First, Cameron argues that Zacharias's claim that Asclepiodotus's baby was purchased cannot be true. He gives a number of reasons. The priest who admitted this was coerced into doing so, the question of whether Asclepiodotus's wife was lactating was a red herring that did not take into account the possible use of wet-nurses, and Asclepiodotus need not have come all the way to Egypt if he wanted to adopt.[3] Beyond this, Cameron argues that the idea of Menouthis as a pagan stronghold is difficult to support if we accept Sophronius's testimony that Cyril

---

1. A. Cameron, "Poets and Pagans in Byzantine Egypt," in *Egypt in the Byzantine World, 300–700*, ed. R. Bagnall (Cambridge, 2007), 21–46.
2. Cameron, "Poets and Pagans," 23.
3. Cameron, "Poets and Pagans," 23–25.

destroyed the city's Isis shrine and replaced it with the shrine to Cyrus and John.[4] Instead, Cameron proposes that Zacharias's account was taken entirely from the words of Paralius. This was, Cameron asserts, an exercise in self-promotion that overstated (or even fabricated) the significance of the Menouthis Isis shrine, obscured the role of the church founded by Cyril, and offered a sensationalized account of a pagan temple and mountains of pagan religious statuary.[5]

A study based upon the Paralius materials in the *Life of Severus* withstands these objections. First, one must distinguish between the material connected with Paralius and the larger text of the *Life of Severus*.[6] Not only is the Paralius discussion structurally distinct from the rest of the *Life of Severus,* Zacharias very much sets it apart within the text as well. He introduces it with the statement, "A little while after this, the events relating to Paralius and the grammarian Horapollon took place."[7] A thirty-page discussion of Paralius's birth, childhood, education, involvement with Horapollon, conversion to Christianity, mission work in Caria, and death follows this. It contains no mention of Severus. Zacharias then concludes simply by saying, "Let no one think that this story is too far off from our subject," before returning to Severus.[8] It seems much more reasonable to consider this a self-contained work that has rhetorical concerns and a thematic structure distinct from the *Life of Severus*.[9] Indeed, given its particular focus on the Alexandrian schools and the ideas advocated by their pagan teachers, it seems much more relevant to the specific Alexandrian student and alumni concerns of the 490s than to Zacharias's broader projects of the 510s.

The nature of Zacharias's discussion of Paralius does not excuse the fact that Zacharias was capable of hiding the truth from his readers, but it should encourage us to consider whether he tried to be more forthcoming here than in, say, his account of Severus's studies in Berytus. There is a good reason to think that Zacharias has generally tried to describe Alexandrian events as he thought that they occurred. As argued in chapter 5, the Paralius text was written to claim student-*philoponoi* ownership of the riot. Zacharias's task was difficult enough without also having to render persuasive a fictionalized sequence of events that conflicted with people's own memories. Instead, it is more likely that Zacharias tweaked his narrative to emphasize the roles played by Menas, Paralius, and the other student-*philoponoi* in the events leading up to and following Paralius's beating. Zacharias's

---

4. Cameron, "Poets and Pagans," 25.
5. Cameron, "Poets and Pagans," 26–27.
6. E. Watts, "Winning the Intracommunal Dialogues: Zacharias Scholasticus' *Life of Severus*," *JECS* 13 (2005), 437–64.
7. *Vit. Sev.* 14.
8. *Vit. Sev.* 44.
9. The different views of Peter Mongus expressed in the Paralius section of the text and later in the work reinforce this point. For further analysis of this material see chapter 8, above.

broader defense of Severus required him to lie; his presentation of Paralius, however, worked only if Zacharias remained generally true to details.

What then are we to make of the specific objections raised by Cameron? Some of these have merit. The absence of the Menouthis shrine to Cyrus and John from Zacharias's narrative is puzzling. This was, however, a Chalcedonian shrine in the late sixth century and may well have been one in the late fifth. We know that Zacharias hesitated to frequent Chalcedonian sites in Phoenicia in the 480s and 490s; perhaps he and his colleagues showed a similar resistance in Egypt.[10] Second, the Cyrus and John shrine was a healing shrine that had no ascetic garrison associated with it. While its construction by Cyril could have eliminated a larger shrine to Isis, there is no reason to think that its mere existence would prevent the continued activity of a smaller Isis cult at a time when religious sampling occurred at other healing shrines in the city.[11]

In the case of Asclepiodotus's baby, Cameron highlights a number of significant problems that also cannot be adequately resolved. It is certainly possible, for example, that Asclepiodotus's wife Damiane conceived naturally and used a wetnurse. It is also possible that Asclepiodotus tried to furtively adopt a child after an appropriately long stay in Alexandria in order to fool people in Aphrodisias. This question simply cannot be resolved satisfactorily.

Cameron does give Paralius more responsibility for the contents of Zacharias's narrative material than he deserves, however. Zacharias was present with Paralius for most of the events that took place after the initial beating. The descriptions and interpretations of the Isis temple in Menouthis and of the objects found there are more likely to be Zacharias's own observations than a simple record of things described by Paralius. He does depend upon Paralius for events before the beating, but there is reason to be more confident in this account than Cameron suggests. Aside from the terrified priest, Paralius is the only person we know of who spoke to Zacharias about the functions of the Isis shrine. He was not, however, the only figure to use it. Cameron acknowledges that Asclepiodotus probably used the shrine in some fashion. Zacharias also mentions that one of Paralius's fellow-students received an oracle that directly contradicted something the goddess told Paralius. This youth spoke to Paralius about the oracle, evidently with others present.[12] Although Zacharias never makes this explicit, Paralius's account of his pre-riot experiences may have been confirmed by Stephen, the Enaton monk who helped to convert Paralius and whom Zacharias describes as "a teacher to us all."[13]

---

10. *Vit. Sev.* 77–78.

11. E.g., *Miracles of Cyrus and John* 30, a miracle that involves one of Zacharias's pagan contemproraries visiting the shrine of Cyrus and John.

12. *Vit. Sev.* 20.

13. *Vit. Sev.* 43.

Zacharias probably tried to recount events truthfully in his discussion of Paralius's life, but, regardless of an author's intentions and skill, social circumstances influence the way that he or she packages and disseminates a narrative.[14] This is a much more difficult problem to address, but there is some reason for optimism. Zacharias wrote about the riot and its aftermath not too long after the events occurred. Given the use to which Zacharias's recollections have been put, some distortion is inevitable even in this short span of time. The loose structure of the student-*philoponoi* also meant that no dominant collective memory likely existed to influence Zacharias. This limits (but does not eliminate) distortion. So, for example, the outrage felt by Zacharias and his associates because of Entrechius's perceived unwillingness to respond aggressively to Paralius's complaint probably contributed to Zacharias's misleading and one-dimensional profile of the prefect. So too must we imagine that some of the emotional and intellectual nuance now missing from Zacharias's account of Paralius's religious wanderings washed away as Paralius became a friend and member of Zacharias's community of anti-Chalcedonian students. None of this renders the larger narrative unusable, however. In fact, the broader picture of the personalities and physical layout of the Alexandrian scholastic environment that Zacharias presents is consistent not just with his other works (which, as the product of the same mind, have little probative value in this case), but also with Damascius's profile of the same community and with the physical remains uncovered at Kom el-Dikka.[15] This does not resolve the question of his reliability, of course, but it does give additional reason to be confident in the general accuracy of Zacharias's account.

14. For this process see J. Vansina, *Oral Tradition as History* (Madison, 1985), 91–94.
15. In this context it is worth noting Vansina's comment (*Oral Tradition as History,* 91) that incidental details tend to be the elements of oral tradition least susceptible to manipulation or distortion.

BIBLIOGRAPHY

Alexander, P. J. *The Oracle of Baalbek: The Tiburtine Sibyl in Greek Dress*. Dumbarton Oaks Studies 10. Washington, D. C., 1967.
Allen, P. "Zachariah Scholasticus and the *Historia Ecclesiastica* of Evagrius Scholasticus." *Journal of Theological Studies*, n.s., 31 (1980): 471–88.
Ambjörn, L., trans. *The Life of Severus by Zachariah of Mytilene*. Piscataway, NJ, 2008.
Antonini, L. "La chiese cristiane nell'Egitto dal IV a IX secolo secondi i documenti dei papyri greci." *Aegyptus* 20 (1940): 129–208.
Assmann, J. *Das kulturelle Gedächtnis: Schrift, Erinnerung und politische Identität in frühren Hochkulturen*. Munich, 1992.
Athanassiadi, P. "Dreams, Theurgy and Freelance Divination: The Testimony of Iamblichus." *Journal of Roman Studies* 83 (1993): 115–30.
———. "Persecution and Response in Late Paganism: The Evidence of Damascius." *Journal of Hellenic Studies* 113 (1993): 1–29.
———. "The Oecumenism of Iamblichus: Latent Knowledge and its Awakening." *Journal of Roman Studies* 85 (1995): 244–50.
———, ed. and trans. *Damascius: The Philosophical History*. Athens, 1999.
———. "The Chaldean Oracles: Theology and Theurgy." In *Pagan Monotheism in Late Antiquity*, edited by P. Athanassiadi and B. Frede, 149–83. Oxford, 1999.
———. "Philosophy and Power: The Creation of Orthodoxy in Neoplatonism." In *Philosophy and Power in the Graeco-Roman World*, edited by G. Clark and T. Rajak, 271–91. Oxford, 2002.
———. *La Lutte pour L'Orthodoxie dans le Platonisme Tardif: Du Numénius á Damascius*. Paris, 2006.
Bagnall, R. S., et al. *Consuls of the Later Roman Empire*. Atlanta, 1987.
Baltussen, H. "From Polemic to Exegesis: The Ancient Philosophical Commentary." *Poetics Today* 28 (2007): 247–81.

———. *Philosophy and Exegesis in Simplicius. The Methodology of a Commentator.* London, 2008.
Banchich, T. "Julian's School Laws: *Cod. Theod.* 13.3.5 and *Ep.* 42." *The Ancient World* 24 (1993): 5–14.
Barnes, R. "Cloistered Bookworms in the Chicken-Coop of the Muses: The Ancient Library of Alexandria." In *The Library of Alexandria: Centre of Learning in the Ancient World*, edited by R. McLeod, 61–77. New York, 2000.
Barnes, T. D. "The *Epitome de Caesaribus* and its Sources." *Classical Philology* 71 (1976): 258–68.
———. "Himerius and the Fourth Century." *Classical Philology* 82 (1987): 206–25.
———. *Athanasius and Constantius: Theology and Politics in the Constantinian Empire.* Cambridge, MA, 1993.
Baudy, G. J. "Die Wiederkehr des Typhon. Katastrophen-Topoi in nachjulianischer Rhetorik und Annalistik: zu literarischen Reflexen des 21 Juli 365 n. C." *Jahrbuch für Antike und Christentum* 35 (1992): 47–82.
Bauer, A. and J. Strzygowski. *Eine alexandrinische Weltchronik: Text und Miniaturen eines griechischen Papyrus des Sammlung W. Goleniscev. Denkschriften der kaiserlichen Akademie der Wissenschaften in Wien, Phil.-hist., Klasse,* Bd. 51, Abh. 2. Vienna, 1905.
Behlmer, H. "Visitors to Shenoute's Monastery." In *Pilgrimage and Holy Space in Late Antique Egypt,* edited by D. Frankfurter, 341–71. Leiden, 1998.
Bell, H. I. *Jews and Christians in Egypt: The Jewish Troubles in Alexandria and the Athanasian Controversy Illustrated by Texts from Greek Papyri in the British Museum.* London, 1924.
———, ed. *The Abinnaeus Archive: Papers of a Roman Officer in the Reign of Constantius II.* Oxford, 1962.
Bitton-Ashkelony, B., and A. Kofsky, eds. *Christian Gaza in Late Antiquity. Jerusalem Studies in Religion and Culture,* Vol. 3. Leiden, 2004.
———, eds. *The Monastic School of Gaza.* Leiden, 2006.
Blaudeau, P. *Alexandrie et Constantinople (451–491): de l'Histoire à la Géo-Ecclésiologie.* Rome, 2006.
Bloomer, M. "Schooling in Persona: Imagination and Subordination in Roman Education." *Classical Antiquity* 16.1 (1997): 57–78.
Blumenthal, H. J. "529 and its Sequel: What Happened to the Academy." *Byzantion* 48 (1978): 369–85.
Bonneau, D. *La crue du Nil, divinité égyptienne à travers mille ans d'histoire, 332 av. – 641 ap. J.-C.* Paris, 1964.
Boter, G. *The Encheiridion of Epictetus and its Three Christian Adaptations: Transmission and Critical Editions.* Philosophia Antiqua 82. Leiden, 1999.
Bowersock, G. *Julian the Apostate.* Cambridge, MA, 1978.
———. *Hellenism in Late Antiquity.* Ann Arbor, 1990.
Bradbury, S. "A Sophistic Prefect: Anatolius of Berytus in the Letters of Libanius." *Classical Philology* 95 (2000): 172–86.

Brakke, D. "Shenoute: On Cleaving to Profitable Things." *Orientalia Lovaniensia Periodica* 20 (1989): 115–41.

———. *Athanasius and Asceticism*. 2nd ed. Baltimore, 1998.

———. "'Outside the Places, Within the Truth': Athanasius of Alexandria and the Localization of the Holy." In *Pilgrimage and Holy Space in Late Antique Egypt*, edited by D. Frankfurter, 445–81. Leiden, 1998.

———. "The Lady Appears: Materializations of 'Woman' in Early Monastic Literature." *Journal of Medieval and Early Modern Studies* 33 (2003): 387–402.

———. *Demons and the Making of the Monk: Spiritual Combat in Early Christianity*. Cambridge, MA, 2006.

Brennan, T., and C. Brittain, trans. *Simplicius: On Epictetus' Handbook 1–26*. Ithaca, 2002.

Brooks, E. W., and F. Hamilton, trans. *The Syriac Chronicle Known as that of Zachariah of Mitylene*. London, 1899.

Brooks, E. W., ed. and trans. *The Sixth Book of Select Letters of Severus*. London, 1904.

———. *Fragmentum Vitae Petri Iberi*. In *Vitae virorum apud monophysitas celeberrimorum*, CSCO vol. 7–8. Paris, 1907.

———. *Historia Ecclesiastica Zachariae Rhetori vulgo adscripta*, CSCO vol. 83–4; 87–8. Louvain-Paris, 1919–1924.

Brown, P. "The Rise and Function of the Holy Man in Late Antiquity." *Journal of Roman Studies* 61 (1971): 80–101.

———. *The Making of Late Antiquity*. Cambridge, MA, 1978.

———. *Power and Persuasion: Towards a Christian Empire*. Madison, WI, 1992.

———. "The Rise and Function of the Holy Man in Late Antiquity, 1971–1997." *Journal of Early Christian Studies* 6.3 (1998): 353–76.

———. *Poverty and Leadership in the Later Roman Empire*. Hanover, 2002.

Brunt, P. A. Review of P. Garnsey, *Social Status and Legal Privilege in the Roman Empire*. *Journal of Roman Studies* 62 (1972): 166–70.

———. "The Bubble of the Second Sophistic." *Bulletin of the Institute of Classical Studies* 39 (1994): 25–52.

Buck, D. F. "Eunapius' *Lives of the Sophists*: A Literary Study." *Byzantion* 62 (1992): 141–57.

Cameron, Alan. "Palladas and Christian Polemic." *Journal of Roman Studies* 55 (1965): 17–30.

———. "The Last Days of the Academy at Athens." *Proceedings of the Cambridge Philological Society* 195 (1969): 7–29.

———. "Poets and Pagans in Byzantine Egypt." In *Egypt in the Byzantine World, 300–700*, edited by R. Bagnall, 21–46. Cambridge, 2007.

——— and J. Long. *Barbarians and Politics at the Court of Arcadius*. Berkeley, 1993.

Camplani, A. *Le Lettre festali di Atanasio di Alessandria*. Rome, 1989.

Carile, A. "Giovanni di Nikius, cronista bizantino-copto del VII secolo." *Felix Ravenna* 121-122 (1981): 103–55.

Casson, L. *Ships and Seamanship in the Ancient World*. Princeton, 1971.

Castelli, E. *Martyrdom and Memory: Early Christian Culture Making*. New York, 2004.
Chalmers, R. "Eunapius, Ammianus Marcellinus, and Zosimus on Julian's Persian Expedition." *Classical Quarterly*, n.s., 10 (1960): 152–60.
Charles, R., trans. *The Chronicle of John, Bishop of Nikiu*. Oxford, 1916.
Chilton, C. W. *Diogenes of Oenoanda, The Fragments: A Translation and Commentary*. Oxford, 1971.
Chitty, D. "Abba Isaiah." *Journal of Theological Studies* 22 (1971): 47–72.
Chuvin, P. *Chronicle of the Last Pagans*. Translated by B. A. Archer. Cambridge, MA, 1990.
Clark, E. *The Origenist Controversy: The Cultural Construction of an Early Christian Debate*. Princeton, 1992.
Clark, G., trans. *Iamblichus: On the Pythagorean Life*. Liverpool, 1989.
Cole, T. *The Origins of Rhetoric in Ancient Greece*. Baltimore, 1991.
Connerton, P. *How Societies Remember*. New York, 1989.
Coquin, R-G. "Saint Constantin, évêque d'Asyūt." *Studia Orientalia Christiana Collectanea* 16 (1981): 151–70.
———. "Discours attribué au patriarche Cyrille, sur la dédicace de l'Église de Raphaël, rapportant les propos de son oncle, le patriarche Théophile." *Bulletin de la Société d'archéologie Copte* 33 (1994): 25–56.
Countryman, L. W. *The Rich Christian in the Church of the Early Empire: Contradictions and Accommodations*. New York, 1980.
Cox, P. *Biography in Late Antiquity: A Quest for the Holy Man*. Berkeley, 1983.
Cox Miller, P. "Strategies of Representation in Collective Biography: Constructing the Subject as Holy." In *Greek Biography and Panegyric in Late Antiquity*, edited by T. Hägg and P. Rousseau, 209–54. Berkeley, 2000.
Cribiore, R. *Gymnastics of the Mind: Greek Education in Hellenistic and Roman Egypt*. Princeton, 2001.
———. "Spaces for Teaching in Late Antiquity." In *Alexandria: Auditoria of Kôm el-Dikka and Late Antique Education*, edited by T. Derda, T. Markiewicz, and E. Wipszycka, 143–50. Warsaw, 2007.
———. *The School of Libanius in Late Antique Antioch*. Princeton, 2007.
Croke, B. "Reinventing Constantinople: Theodosius I's Imprint on the Imperial City." In *From the Tetrarcks to the Theodosians*, edited by S. McGill, C. Sogno, and E. Watts. Cambridge, 2010.
Crum, W. E. *Coptic Ostraca from the Collection of the Egypt Exploration Fund, the Cairo Museum, and Others*. London, 1902.
———, ed. *Theological Texts from Coptic Papyri*. Oxford, 1913.
———. "Some Further Melitian Documents." *Journal of Egyptian Archeology* 13 (1927): 19–26.
Cumont, F. "L'Astrologue Palchos." *Revue de l'instruction publique en Belgique* 40 (1897): 1–12.
Darling, R. A. "The patriarchate of Severus of Antioch, 512–518." PhD diss., University of Chicago, 1982.
Darling Young, R. A. "Zacharias: *The Life of Severus*." In *Ascetic Behavior in Greco-Roman Antiquity*, edited by V. Wimbush, 312–38. Minneapolis, 1990.

Davis, S. *The Early Coptic Papacy: The Egyptian Church and Its Leadership in Late Antiquity*. Cairo, 2004.

Delia, D. "The Population of Roman Alexandria." *Transactions and Proceedings of the American Philological Association* 118 (1988): 275–92.

Delmas, F. "Zacharie le Rhéteur d'après un ouvrage recent." *Echos d'Orient* 3 (1899): 36–40.

Derda, T., T. Markiewicz, and E. Wipszycka, eds. *Alexandria Auditoria of Kôm el-Dikka and Late Antique Education. Journal of Juristic Papyrology*, Supplement 8. Warsaw, 2007.

De Romilly, J. *Les grands sophistes dans l'Athènes de Périclès*. Paris, 1988.

Dickie, M. "Hermeias on Plato *Phaedrus* 238D and Synesius *Dion* 14.2." *American Journal of Philology* 114 (1993): 421–40.

Dillon, J. "Iamblichus of Chalcis." *Aufstieg und Niedergang der römischen Welt* 2.36.2 (1987): 862–909.

———. *The Middle Platonists, 80 B.C. to A.D. 220*. 2nd ed. Ithaca, 1996

———. *The Heirs of Plato: A Study of the Old Academy (347–274 B.C.)*. Oxford, 2002.

Dix, G., and rev. H. Chadwick, ed. and trans. *The Treatise of the Apostolic Tradition of St. Hippolytus of Rome*. London, 1968.

Draguet, R. *Julien d'Halicarnasse et sa controverse avec Sévère d'Antioche sur l'incorruptibilité du corps du Christ*. Louvain, 1924.

Drake, H. A. *Constantine and the Bishops: The Politics of Intolerance*. Baltimore, 2000.

Dzielska, M. *Hypatia of Alexandria*. Translated by F. Lyra. Cambridge, MA, 1995.

Ebied, R. Y. and L. R. Wickham. "Collection of Unpublished Syriac Letters of Timothy Aelurus." *Journal of Theological Studies*, n.s., 21.2 (1970): 321–69.

———. "Timothy Aelurus: Against the Definition of the Council of Chalcedon." In *After Chalcedon: Studies in Theology and Church History Offered to Professor Albert van Roey for his Seventieth Birthday*, 115–66. Leuven, 1985.

Edwards, M. "Two Episodes in Porphyry's *Life of Plotinus*." *Historia* 40 (1991): 456–64.

———. "Birth, Death, and Divinity in Porphyry's Plotinus." In *Greek Biography and Panegyric in Late Antiquity*, edited by T. Hägg and P. Rousseau, 52–71. Berkeley, 2000.

———, trans. *Neoplatonic Saints: The Lives of Plotinus and Proclus by their Students*. Liverpool, 2001.

El-Abbadi, M. "Demise of the Daughter Library." In *What Happened to the Ancient Library of Alexandria?*, edited by M. El-Abbadi and O. Fathallah, 89–94. Leiden, 2008.

Elm, S. *Virgins of God: The Making of Asceticism in Late Antiquity*. Oxford, 1994.

Elton, H. "Illus and the Imperial Aristocracy Under Zeno." *Byzantion* 70 (2000): 393–407.

Emmel, S. "The Historical Circumstances of Shenute's Sermon 'God is Blessed'." In θεμελια: *Spätantike und koptologische Studien Peter Grossmann zum 65 Geburtstag*, edited by M. Krause and S. Schaten, 81–96. Wiesbaden, 1998

———. "From the Other Side of the Nile: Shenute and Panopolis." In *Perspectives on Panopolis: An Egyptian Town from Alexander the Great to the Arab Conquest*, edited by A. Egberts, B. Muhs, and J. van der Vliet, 95–113. Leiden, 2002.

Eshleman, K. "Defining the Circle of Sophists: Philostratus and the Construction of the Second Sophistic." *Classical Philology* 103 (2008): 395–413.
Evelyn White, H. G. *New Texts from the Monastery of Saint Macarius: The Monasteries of Wadi 'n Natrûn*. Vol. 1. New York, 1926.
Fernandez Marcos, N. *Los Thaumata de Sofronio. Contribucion al estudio de la incubatio cristana*. Madrid, 1975.
Festugière, A. J. *Antioche païenne et chrétienne: Libanius, Chrysostome et les moines de Syrie*. Paris, 1959.
Foat, M. "Shenute: Discourse in the Presence of Eraklammon." *Orientalia Lovaniensia Periodica* 24 (1994): 113–32.
Fornara, C. "Julian's Persian Expedition in Ammianus and Zosimus." *Journal of Hellenic Studies* 111(1991): 1–15.
Fournet, J.-L. and J. Gascou. "Moines pachômiens et batellerie." *Alexandrie médiévale* 2, *Études alexandrines* 8 (2002): 23–45.
Fowden, G. "The Platonist Philosopher and his Circle in Late Antiquity." *Philosophia* 7 (1977): 359–83.
———. "The Pagan Holy Man in Late Antique Society." *Journal of Hellenic Studies* 102 (1982): 33–59.
Frank, G. "Miracles, Monks and Monuments: The *Historia Monachorum in Aegypto* as Pilgrims' Tales." In *Pilgrimage and Holy Space in Late Antique Egypt*, edited by D. Frankfurter, 483–505. Leiden, 1998.
Frankfurter, D., ed., *Pilgrimage and Holy Space in Late Antique Egypt*. Leiden, 1998.
———. *Religion in Roman Egypt: Assimilation and Resistance*. Princeton, 1998.
———. "The Consequences of Hellenism in Late Antique Egypt: Religious Worlds and Actors." *Archiv für Religionsgeschichte* 2 (2000): 162–94.
———. "'Things Unbefitting Christians': Violence and Christianization in 5th century Panopolis." *Journal of Early Christian Studies* 8.2 (2000): 273–95.
———. "Iconoclasm and Christianization in Late Antique Egypt: Christian Treatments of Space and Image." In *From Temple to Church: Destruction and Renewal of Local Cultic Topography in Late Antiquity*, edited by J. Hahn, S. Emmel, and U. Gotter, 135–59. Leiden, 2008.
Fraser, P. M. "A Syriac Notitia Urbis Alexandrinae." *Journal of Egyptian Archaeology* 37 (1951): 103–8.
Frend, W. H. C. *The Rise of the Monophysite Movement*. Cambridge, 1972.
Gaddis, M. *There Is No Crime for Those Who Have Christ: Religious Violence in the Christian Roman Empire*. Berkeley, 2005.
Galvão-Sobrinho, C. R. "The Rise of the Christian Bishop; Doctrine and Power in the Later Roman Empire, AD 318–80." PhD diss., Yale University, 1999.
Garitte, G. "Constantin, évêque d' Assiout." In *Coptic Studies in Honor of W. E. Crum, Bulletin of the Byzantine Institute* 2 (1950): 287–304.
———. "Textes hagiographiques orientaux relatifs à S. Leonce de Tripoli: II. L' homélie copte de Sevère d'Antioche," *Le Muséon* 79 (1966): 335–86.
Garnsey, P. *Social Status and Legal Privilege in the Roman Empire*. Oxford, 1970.

———. *Famine and Food Supply in the Greco-Roman World: Responses to Risk and Crisis.* Cambridge, 1988.
Gascou, J. "Les origines du culte des saints Cyr et Jean." *Analecta Bollandiana* 125 (2007): 1–35.
Gibbon, E. *The Decline and Fall of the Roman Empire.* 7 vols. Edited by J. B. Bury. London, 1909–14.
Gibson, C. "Alexander in the Tychaion: Ps.-Libanius on the Statues." *Greek Roman and Byzantine Studies* 47 (2007): 431–54.
———. "The Alexandrian Tychaion and the date of Ps.-Nicolaus *Progymnasmata*." Forthcoming.
Gigante, M. *Polemonis Academici Fragmenta.* Naples, 1977.
Gilsenan, M. *Saint and Sufi in Modern Egypt: An Essay in the Sociology of Religion.* Oxford, 1973.
Gleason, M. *Making Men: Sophists and Self-Presentation in Ancient Rome.* Princeton, 1995.
Glucker, J. *Antiochus and the Late Academy.* Göttingen, 1978.
Goehring, J. "New Frontiers in Pachomian Studies." In *The Roots of Egyptian Christianity*, edited by B. A. Pierson and J. Goehring, 236–57. Philadelphia, 1986.
———. "Monastic Diversity and Ideological Boundaries in Fourth-Century Christian Egypt." *Journal of Early Christian Studies* 5 (1997): 61–84.
Gottwald, J. "Die Kirche und das Schloss Paperon in Kilikisch-Armenien." *Byzantinische Zeitschrift* 36 (1936): 86–100.
Gruen, W. C. "The Compilation and Dissemination of 'The Life of Antony' (Saint Athanasius, Patriarch of Alexandria)." PhD diss., University of Pennsylvania, 2005.
Haas, C. "Patriarch and People: Peter Mongus of Alexandria and Episcopal Leadership in the Late Fifth Century." *Journal of Early Christian Studies* 1 (1993): 297–316.
———. *Alexandria in Late Antiquity: Topography and Social Conflict.* Baltimore, 1997.
———. "Alexandria and the Mareotis Region." In *Urban Centers and Rural Contexts in Late Antiquity*, edited by T. S. Burns and J. W. Eadie, 47–62. East Lansing, 2001.
———. "John Moschus and Late Antique Alexandria." In *Alexandrie Medievale II, Études alexandrines 8*, edited by C. Décobert, 47–59. Cairo, 2002.
———. "Kôm el-Dikka in Context: The Auditoria and the History of Late Antique Alexandria." In *Alexandria: Auditoria of Kom el-Dikka and Late Antique Education*, edited by T. Derda, T. Markiewicz, and E. Wipszycka, 85–96. Warsaw, 2007.
Hadot, I. *Le Problème du Néoplatonisme Alexandrin: Hiéroclès et Simplicius.* Paris 1978.
———. *Simplicius: Commentaire sur le Manuel d'Épictète.* Leiden 1996.
———. "Dans quel lieu le néoplatonicien Simplicius a-t-il fondé son école de mathématiques, et où a pu avoir lieu son entretien avec un manichéen?" *International Journal of the Platonic Tradition* 1 (2007): 42–107.
Hahn, J. *Gewalt und religiöser Konflikt: Studien zu den Auseinandersetzungen zwischen Christen, Heiden, und Juden im Osten des Römischen Reiches (von Konstantin bis Theodosius II).* Berlin, 2004.
———. "The Conversion of the Cult Statues: The Destruction of the Serapeum 392 A.D. and the Transformation of Alexandria into the 'Christ-Loving' City." In *From Temple*

to Church: Destruction and Renewal of Local Cultic Topography in Late Antiquity, edited by J. Hahn, S. Emmel, and U. Gotter, 335–63. Leiden, 2008.
Halbwachs, M. *Les Cadres Sociaux de la Mémoire.* Paris, 1925.
Hall, A. "Who was Diogenes of Oenoanda?" *Journal of Hellenic Studies* 99 (1979): 160–63.
Harries, J. "The Roman Imperial Quaestor from Constantine to Theodosius II." *Journal of Roman Studies* 78 (1988): 148–72.
———. *Law and Empire in Late Antiquity.* Cambridge, 1999.
Hartmann, U. "Geist im Exil: Römische Philosophen am Hof den Sasaniden." In *Grenzüberschreitungen: Formen des Kontakts zwischen Orient und Okzident im Altertum*, edited by M. Schuol, U. Hartmann, and A. Luther, 123–60. Stuttgart, 2002.
Hartney, A. *John Chrysostom and the Transformation of the City.* London, 2004.
Hevelone-Harper, J. *Disciples of the Desert: Monks, Laity, and Spiritual Authority in Sixth-Century Gaza.* Baltimore, 2005.
Hirschfeld, Y. *The Roman Thermae at Hammat-Gader: Final Report.* Jerusalem, 1997.
Honigmann, E. "Juvenal of Jerusalem." *Dumbarton Oaks Papers* 5 (1950): 209–79.
———. *Patristic Studies.* Studi e Testi 173. Vatican City, 1953.
Horn, C. *Asceticism and Christological Controversy in Fifth-Century Palestine: The Career of Peter the Iberian.* Oxford, 2006.
———, and R. Phenix, ed. and trans. *John Rufus: The Lives of Peter the Iberian, Theodosius of Jerusalem, and the Monk Romanus.* Atlanta, 2008.
Isnardi Parente, M. "Per la biografia di Senocrate." *Rivista di Filologia e Instruzione Classica* 109 (1981): 129–62.
Jackson, R., K. Lycos, and H. Tarrant, trans. *Olympiodorus' Commentary on Plato's Gorgias.* Leiden, 1998.
Jacques, F. "Le défenseur de la cité d'après la Lettre 22* de Saint Augustin." *Revue des études augustinienne* 32 (1986): 56–73.
Jansen, H. L. *The Coptic Story of Cambyses' Invasion of Egypt.* Oslo, 1950.
Johnson, D. W., trans. *Panegyric of Macarius, Bishop of Tkow, Attributed to Dioscorus of Alexandria*, CSCO 416, Scriptores Coptici 42. Louvain, 1980.
Johnson, S. F. *The Life and Miracles of Thekla: A Literary Study.* Washington, D. C., 2006.
Jones, A. H. M. *The Later Roman Empire 284–602.* Norman, 1964.
Kaldellis, A. *Procopius of Caesarea: Tyranny, History, and Philosophy at the End of Antiquity.* Philadelphia, 2004.
Kaster, R. A. *Guardians of Language: The Grammarian and Society in Late Antiquity.* Berkeley and Los Angeles, 1988.
Kayser, F. "Oreilles et couronnes: à propos des cultes de Canope." *Bulletin de l'Institut français d'Archéologie Orientale* 91 (1991): 207–17.
Kelly, G. "Ammianus and the Great Tsunami." *Journal of Roman Studies* 94 (2004): 141–67.
Kennedy, G. *Greek Rhetoric under Christian Emperors.* Princeton, 1983.
Kiss, Z. "Les auditoria romains tardifs." In *Fouilles Polonaises à Kôm el-Dikka (1986–1987), Alexandrie VII*, edited by Z. Kiss, G. Majcherek, H. Meyza, H. Rysiewski, and B. Tkaczow, 8–33. Warsaw, 2000.

Kötting, B. "Wallfahrten zu lebenden Personen in Altertum." In *Wallfahrt kennt keine Grenzen,* edited by L. Kriss-Rettenbeck and G. Mohler, 226–34. Munich/Zurich, 1984.
Krautheimer, R. *Three Christian Capitals: Topography and Politics.* Berkeley, 1983.
Krüger, G. and K. Ahrens. *Die sogenannte Kirchengeschichte des Zacharias Rhetor.* Leipzig, 1899.
Krusch, B., ed. *Studien zur christlich-mittelalterlichen Chronologie. Der 84 jährige Ostercyclus und seine Quellen.* Leipzig, 1880.
Kugener, M. A. "Observations sur la Vie de l'Ascète Isaïe et sur les Vies de Pierre l'Ibérien et de Théodore d'Antinoé par Zacharie le Scholastique." *Byzantinische Zeitschrift* 9 (1909): 464–70.
———, ed. and trans. Zacharias of Mytilene, *Vie de Sévère, Patrologia Orientalis* II. Paris, 1907; rev. ed., Belgium, Turnhout, 1971.
Lameer, J. "From Alexandria to Baghdad: Reflections on the Genesis of a Problematic Tradition." In *The Ancient Tradition in Christian and Islamic Hellenism,* edited by G. Endress and R. Kruk, 181–91. Leiden, 1997.
Lamoreaux, J. C. "Episcopal Courts in Late Antiquity." *Journal of Early Christian Studies* 3 (1995): 143–67.
Lane Fox, R. "Harran, the Sabiens, and the late Platonist 'Movers.'" In *The Philosopher and Society in Late Antiquity,* edited by A. Smith, 231–44. Swansea, 2005.
Lang, D. M. "Peter the Iberian and his Biographers." *Journal of Ecclesiastical History* 2.2 (1951): 158–68.
Laniado, A. *Recherches sur les notables municipaux dans l'empire protobyzantin.* Paris, 2002.
Layton, B. "Social Structure and Food Consumption in an Early Christian Monastery: The Evidence of Shenoute's Canons and the White Monastery Federation A.D. 385–465." *Le Muséon* 115 (2002): 25–55.
———. "Rules, Patterns, and the Exercise of Power in Shenoute's Monastery: The Problem of World Replacement and Identity Maintenance." *Journal of Early Christian Studies* 15 (2007): 45–73.
Layton, R. *Didymus the Blind and His Circle in Late-Antique Alexandria: Virtue and Narrative in Biblical Scholarship.* Urbana, 2004.
Lebon, J. *Le Monophysitisme Sévérien.* Louvain, 1909.
———. "Version arménienne et version syriaque de Timothée Élure." *Handes Amsorya* 41 (1927): 713–22.
Leeman, T. *The Rites of Passage in a Student Culture.* New York, 1972.
Lefort, L. T., ed. *Oeuvres de s. Pachôme et de ses disciples,* CSCO 159. Louvain, 1956.
Lenski, N. *Failure of Empire: Valens and the Roman State in the Fourth Century* A.D. Berkeley, 2002.
Leo, F. *Die griechisch-römische Biographie nach ihrer literarischen Form.* Leipzig, 1901.
Lewis, S. *News and Society in the Greek Polis.* London, 1996.
Liebeschuetz, J. H. W. G. "Why Did Synesius Become Bishop of Ptolemais?" *Byzantion* 56 (1986): 180–95.
———. *Barbarians and Bishops: Army, Church, and State in the Age of Arcadius and Chrysostom.* Oxford, 1990.

Lowenthal, D. *The Past is a Foreign Country*. Cambridge, 1985.
Luna, C. Review of R. Thiel, *Simplikios und das Ende der neuplatonischen Schule in Athen*. *Mnemosyne* 54 (2001): 482–504.
Lynch, J. P. *Aristotle's School: A Study of a Greek Educational Institution*. Berkeley, 1972.
MacAdam, H. I. "*Studia et Circenses*: Beirut's Roman Law School in its Colonial, Cultural Context." *ARAM* 13–14 (2001–2): 193–226.
MacCoull, L. "Philosophy in its Social Context." In *Egypt in the Byzantine World, 300–700*, edited by R. Bagnall, 67–82. Cambridge, 2007.
MacGeorge, P. *Late Roman Warlords*. Oxford, 2002.
Magdalino, P. "The History of the Future and Its Uses: Prophecy, Policy, and Propaganda." In *The Making of Byzantine History*, edited by R. Beaton and C. Roueché, 3–34. Aldershot, 1993.
Majcherek, G. "Kôm el-Dikka. Excavations and Preservation Work, 2002/2003." *Polish Archaeology in the Mediterranean* 15 (2004): 25–38.
———. "Kom el-Dikka. Excavation and Preservation Work, 2003/2004." *Polish Archaeology in the Mediterranean* 16 (2005): 17–30.
———. "The Late Roman Auditoria: An Archeological Overview." In *Alexandria: Auditoria of Kôm el-Dikka and Late Antique Education*, edited by T. Derda, T. Markiewicz, and E. Wipszycka, 11–50. Warsaw, 2007.
Marrou, H. ΜΟΥΣΙΚΟΣ ΑΝΗΡ: *Étude sur les scenes de la vie intellectuelle figurant sur les monuments funéraires romains*. Grenoble, 1938.
Maspero, J. "Horapollon et la fin du paganisme égyptien." *Bulletin de l'Institut français d'Archéologie Orientale* 11 (1914): 163–95.
———. *Histoire des Patriarches d'Alexandrie: depuis la mort d' Empereur Anastase jusqu' à la reconciliation des églises jacobites*. Paris, 1923.
Matthews, J. *The Roman Empire of Ammianus*. London, 1989.
———. *Laying Down the Law: A Study of the Theodosian Code*. New Haven, 2000.
Maxwell, J. *Christianization and Communication in Late Antiquity: John Chrysostom and his Congregation in Antioch*. Cambridge, 2006.
Mayer, W. "John Chrysostom: Extraordinary Preacher, Ordinary Audience." In *Preacher and Audience: Studies in Early Christian and Byzantine Homeletics*, edited by M. Cunningham and P. Allen, 105–38. Leiden, 1998.
Mazza, M. "Cataclismi e calamità naturali: la documentazione letteraria." *Kôkalos* 36–37 (1990–91, 1994): 307–30.
McGuckin, J. A. "The Influence of the Isis Cult on St. Cyril of Alexandria's Christology." *Studia Patristica* 24 (1993): 291–99.
———. *St. Cyril of Alexandria: The Christological Controversy*. Leiden, 1994.
McKenzie, J., S. Gibson, and A. T. Reyes. "Reconstructing the Serapeum in Alexandria from the Archaeological Evidence." *Journal of Roman Studies* 94 (2004): 73–121.
McKenzie, J. *The Architecture of Alexandria and Egypt, 300 B.C.–A.D 700*. New Haven, 2007.
———. "The Place in Late Antique Alexandria 'Where the Alchemists and Scholars Sit... Was Like Stairs.'" In *Alexandria: Auditoria of Kom el-Dikka and Late Antique Education*, edited by T. Derda, T. Markiewicz, and E. Wipszycka, 53–83. Warsaw, 2007.

McLynn, N., "Moments of Truth: Gregory Nazianzen and Theodosius I." In *From the Tetrarchs to the Theodosians*, edited by C. Sogno, S. McGill, and E. Watts. Cambridge, 2010.

Meier, M. *Das andere Zeitalter Justinians. Kontingenzerfahrung und Kontingenzbewältigung im 6. Jht. N. Chr.*, Hypomnemata 147. Göttingen, 2003.

Minniti Colonna, M. *Zacaria Scolastico, Ammonio: Introduzione, testo critico, traduzione, commentario*. Naples, 1973.

Mitchell, S. "Festivals, Games, and Civic Life in Roman Asia Minor." *Journal of Roman Studies* 80 (1990): 183–93.

Moberg, A. *On Some Syriac Fragments of the Book of Timothy Ailuros against the Synod of Chalcedon*. Lund, 1928.

Momigliano, A. *The Development of Greek Biography*. 2nd ed. Cambridge, MA, 1993.

Montserrat, D. "Pilgrimage to the Shrine of SS Cyrus and John at Menouthis in Late Antiquity." In *Pilgrimage and Holy Space in Late Antique Egypt*, edited by D. Frankfurter, 257–79. Leiden, 1998.

Most, G. "A Cock for Asclepius." *Classical Quarterly* 43 (1993): 96–111.

Nasson, B. "Abraham Esau's War, 1899–1901: Martyrdom, myth, and folk memory in Calvinia, South Africa." In *The Myths We Live By*, edited by R. Samuel and P. Thompson, 111–26. London and New York, 1990.

Nau, F., ed. and trans. "Histoire de Dioscore, patriarche d'Alexandrie." *Journal Asiatique* 10 (1903): 5–108 (text), 241–310 (trans.).

———, ed. *Jean Rufus, Évêque de Maïuma, Plérophories*. Patrologia Orientalis 8.1. Paris, 1911.

———, ed. *Textes Syriaques Édites et Traduit*. Patrologia Orientalis 13.2. Paris, 1916.

Nedungatt, G. "The Covenanters of the Early Syriac-Speaking Church." *Orientalia Christiana Periodica* 39 (1973): 191–215.

Nuwer, H. *Wrongs of Passage*. Bloomington, 1999.

O'Meara, D. *Pythagoras Revived: Mathematics and Philosophy in Late Antiquity*. Oxford, 1989.

———. "Simplicius on the Place of the Philosopher in the City (*In Epictetum* Chap. 32)." *Mélanges de l'Université de Saint Joseph* 57 (2004): 89–98.

Orlandi, T. *Testi copti: 1. Encomio di Atanasio. 2. Vita di Atanasio*. Testi e Documenti per lo Studio dell'Antichita 21. Milan, 1968.

———. "Uno scritto di Teofilo di Alessandria sulla distruzione del Serapeum." *La Parola del Passato* 23 (1968): 295–304.

———. *Storia della Chiesa di Alessandria*. Vol. I, Milano, 1968. Vol. II, Milano, 1970.

———. "Un frammento copto di Teofilo di Alessandria." *Rivista degli Studi Orientali* 44 (1970): 23–26.

———. *Constantini episcopi urbis Siout, Encomia in Athanasium Duo*. 2 vols. CSCO 349–350. Louvain, 1974.

———. "Giovanni Rufo di Maiuma, Pleroforie (K 2502a-b; [appendice] K 7343; K 2502c-e)," in *Koptische Papyri theologischen Inhalts, Mitteilungen aus der Papyrussammlung der Österreichischen Nationalbibliothek*. Vienna, 1974.

———, ed., *Vite dei Monaci Phif e Longino*, Testi e Documenti per lo Studio dell'Antichita 51. Milan, 1975.

———. "Un frammento delle Pleroforie in Copto." *Studi e Ricerche sull'Oriente Cristiano* 2 (1979): 3–12.
———. "Theophilus of Alexandria in Coptic Literature." *Studia Patristica* 16 (1985): 100–104.
Patlagean, E. *Pauvreté économique et pauvreté sociale à Byzance: 4e-7e siècles*. Paris, 1977.
Penella, R. *Greek Sophists and Philosophers: Studies in Eunapius of Sardis*. Leeds, 1990.
———. *Man and the Word: The Orations of Himerius*. Berkeley, 2007.
Pépin, J. *Théologie cosmique et théologie chrétienne*. Paris, 1964.
Perrone, L. "The Necessity of Advice: Spiritual Direction as a School of Christianity in the Correspondence of Barsanuphius and John of Gaza." In *Christian Gaza in Late Antiquity, Jerusalem Studies in Religion and Culture, Vol. 3*, edited by B. Bitton-Ashkelony and A. Kofsky, 131–49. Leiden, 2004.
Petit, P. *Les Étudiants de Libanius*. Paris, 1957.
Pettersen, A. "'To Flee or Not to Flee': An Assessment of Athanasius *De Fuga Sua*." In *Persecution and Toleration*, edited by W. J. Shiels, 29–43. Oxford, 1984.
Praechter, K. "Die griechischen Aristoteleskommentatoren." *Byzantinische Zeitschrift* 18 (1909): 516–38.
Price, R., and M. Gaddis, trans. *The Acts of the Council of Chalcedon*, 3 vols. Liverpool, 2005.
Raabe, R. *Petrus der Iberer, ein Charakterbild zur Kirchen und Sittengeschichte des fünften Jahrhunderts*. Leipzig, 1895.
Rapp, C. *Holy Bishops in Late Antiquity: The Nature of Christian Leadership in an Age of Transition*. Berkeley, 2005.
Rappe, S. "The New Math: How to Add and to Subtract Pagan Elements in Christian Education." In *Education in Greek and Roman Antiquity*, edited by Y. L. Too, 405–32. Leiden, 2001.
Regnault, L. "Moines et laïcs dans la region de Gaza au VIe Siècle." In *Christian Gaza in Late Antiquity, Jerusalem Studies in Religion and Culture, Vol. 3*, edited by B. Bitton-Ashkelony and A. Kofsky, 165–72. Leiden, 2004.
Rémondon, R. "L'Église dans la société égyptienne à l'époque Byzantine." *Chronique d'Égypte* 47 (1972): 254–77.
Riedel, W., and W. E. Crum, ed. and trans. *The Canons of Athanasius*. Amsterdam, 1973.
Riginos, A. S. *Platonica: The Anecdotes concerning the Life and Writings of Plato*. Leiden, 1976.
Rouche, M. "Le matricule des pauvres. Evolution d'une institution de charité du Bas-Empire jusqu'à la fin du Haut Moyen Age." In *Études sur l'histoire de la pauvreté*, edited by M. Mollat, 83–110. Paris, 1974.
Roueché, C. *Aphrodisias in Late Antiquity*. London, 1989.
Rousseau, P. *Pachomius: The Making of a Community in Fourth-Century Egypt*. 2nd ed. Berkeley, 1999.
———. "Pachomius." In *Late Antiquity: A Guide to the Postclassical World*, edited by G. W. Bowersock, P. Brown, and O. Grabar, 624–25. Cambridge, MA, 1999.
Rubenson, S. "Philosophy and Simplicity: The Problem of Classical Education in Early Christian Biography." In *Greek Biography and Panegyric in Late Antiquity*, edited by T. Hägg and P. Rousseau, 110–39. Berkeley, 2000.

Russell, N. *Theophilus of Alexandria*. London, 2007.
Sbordone, F., ed. *Hori Apollinis Hieroglyphica*. Naples, 1940.
Schroeder, C. "Purity and Pollution in the Asceticism of Shenute of Atripe." *Studia Patristica* 35 (2001): 142–47.
Schwartz, E. *Johannes Rufus, ein monophysitischer Schriftsteller*. Heidelberg, 1912.
———, ed. *Acta Conciliorum Oecumenicorum*. Berlin, 1927.
Schwartz, J. "La fin du Serapeum d'Alexandrie." In *American Studies in Papyrology*, vol. 1, *Essays in Honor of C. Bradford Welles*, 97–111. New Haven, 1966.
Sessa, K. "Christianity and the Cubiculum: Spiritual Politics and Domestic Space in Late Antique Rome." *Journal of Early Christian Studies* 15 (2007): 171–204.
———. *The Household and the Bishop in Late Antique Rome, ca. 400–600*. Forthcoming.
Shaw, G. "Theurgy: Rituals of Unification in the Neoplatonism of Iamblichus." *Traditio* 41 (1985): 1–28.
———. *Theurgy and the Soul: The Neoplatonism of Iamblichus*. University Park, Pennsylvania, 1995.
Sheppard, A. "Proclus' Attitude to Theurgy." *Classical Quarterly* 32 (1982): 212–24.
Siniossoglou, N. *Plato and Theodoret: The Christian Appropriation of Platonic Philosophy and the Hellenic Intellectual Resistance*. Cambridge, 2008.
Siorvanes, L. *Proclus: Neo-platonic Philosophy and Science*. New Haven, 1996.
Smith, A.. *Porphyry's Place in the Neoplatonic Tradition: A Study of Post-Plotinian Neoplatonism*. The Hague, 1974.
Smith, M. F. *The Philosophical Inscription of Diogenes of Oinoanda*. Vienna, 1996.
———. *Supplement to Diogenes of Oinoanda The Epicurean Inscription*. Naples, 2003.
Sorabji, R. "Divine Names and Sordid Deals in Ammonius' Alexandria." In *The Philosopher and Society in Late Antiquity*, edited by A. Smith, 203–14. Swansea, 2005.
Stead, G. C. "Was Arius a Neoplatonist?" *Studia Patristica* 32 (1997): 39–52.
Stein, E. and J. M. Palanque. *Histoire du Bas-Empire*. Vol. II. Paris, 1949.
Steppa, J. E. *John Rufus and the World Vision of Anti-Chalcedonian Culture*. Piscataway, NJ, 2002.
Stock, B. *The Implications of Literacy: Written Language and Models of Interpretation in the Eleventh and Twelfth Centuries*. Princeton, 1983.
Swain, S. "The Reliability of Philostratus' *Lives of the Sophists*." *Classical Antiquity* 10.1 (1991): 148–63.
Tarán, L. *Speusippus of Athens: A Critical Study with a Collection of the Related Texts and Commentary*. Leiden, 1981.
Tardieu, M. "Sābiens Coraniques et Sābiens' de Harrān." *Journal Asiatique* 274 (1986): 1–44.
———. *Les Paysages reliques. Routes et haltes syriennes d'Isidore à Simplicius*. Bibliothèque de l'École des Hautes Études, Sciences Religieuses, vol. 94. Louvain, 1990.
Ter-Mekertsschian, K., and E. Ter-Minassiantz. *Timotheus Älurus, des Patriarchen von Alexandrien, Widerlegung der auf der Synode zu Chalcedon festgesetzten Lehre, Armenischer Text*. Leipzig, 1908.
Thissen, H.-J., *Vom Bild Zum Buchstaben–Vom Buchstaben Zum Bild. Von Der Arbeit an Horapollons Hieroglyphika*. Stuttgart, 1998.

Thomas, J. *Private Religious Foundations in the Byzantine Empire.* Dumbarton Oaks Studies 24. Washington, 1987.
Thomas, R. *Oral Tradition and Written Record in Classical Athens.* Cambridge, 1989.
Tkaczow, B. *Topography of Ancient Alexandria: An Archaeological Map.* Warsaw, 1993.
Trombley, F. *Hellenic Religion and Christianization AD 320–529.* 2 vols. Leiden, 1993–94.
van Bladel, K. *The Arabic Hermes: From Pagan Sage to Prophet of Science.* Oxford, 2009.
van Cauwenbergh, P. *Étude sur les moines d'Égypte: depuis le Concile de Chalcédoine, jusqu'à l'invasion arabe.* Paris-Louvain, 1914.
van den Berg, R. M. "Smoothing over the Differences: Proclus and Ammonius on Plato's *Cratylus* and Aristotle's *De Interpretatione.*" In *Philosophy, Science and Exegesis in Greek, Arabic, and Latin Commentaries,* vol. 1, edited by P. Adamson, H. Baltussen and M. W. F. Store, 191–201. London, 2004.
van Gennep, A. *The Rites of Passage.* Translated by M. B. Vizedom and G. Caffee. 2nd ed. Chicago, 1960.
Vansina, J. *Oral Tradition: A Study in Historical Methodology.* Harmondsworth, 1973.
———. *Oral Tradition as History.* Madison, 1985.
Veilleux, A. *La Liturgie dans le cénobitism pachômien au quatrième siècle.* Studia Anselmiana 57. Rome, 1968.
———. *Pachomian Koinonia. The Lives, Rules, and Other Writings of Saint Pachomius and his Disciples.* Vols. 1–3 (*Cistercian Studies Series* 45–47). Kalamazoo, MI, 1980–83.
Virlouvet, C. *Tessera frumentaria: Les procédures de la distribution du blé public à Rome à la fin de la République et au début de l'Empire.* Rome, 1995.
Vivian, T. *St. Peter of Alexandria: Bishop and Martyr.* Philadelphia, 1988.
———. "Humility and Resistance in Late Antique Egypt: The *Life of Longinus.*" *Coptic Church Review* 20 (1999): 2–30.
Volbach, W. F. *Elfenbeinarbeiten der Spätantike und des frühen Mittelalters.* 3rd ed. Mainz/Rhein, 1976.
von Haehling, R. "Damascius und die heidnische Opposition im 5 Jahrhundert nach Christus." *Jahrbuch für Antike und Christentum* 23 (1980): 82–95.
von Wilamowitz-Möllendorf, U. *Antigonos von Karystos.* 2nd ed. Berlin, 1965.
Vööbus, A. *Syriac and Arabic Documents Regarding Legislation Relative to Syrian Asceticism.* Estonian Theological School in Exile. Stockholm, 1960.
———. "The Institution of the *Benai Qeiama* and *Benat Qeiama* in the Ancient Syrian Church." *Church History* 30 (1961): 19–27.
———, ed. and trans. *The Didascalia Apostolorum,* CSCO vol. 401/2, 407/8. Louvain, 1979.
Walker, J. "The Limits of Late Antiquity: Philosophy between Rome and Iran." *Ancient World* 33 (2002): 45–69.
Watts, E. "Justinian, Malalas, and the End of the Athenian Philosophical Teaching in A.D. 529." *Journal of Roman Studies* 94 (2004): 168–82.
———. "Student Travel to Intellectual Centers: What was the Attraction?" In *Travel, Communication and Geography in Late Antiquity,* edited by L. Ellis and F. Kidner, 13–23. Aldershot, 2004.
———. "An Alexandrian Christian Response to Fifth-century Neoplatonic Influence." In *The Philosopher and Society in Late Antiquity,* edited by A. Smith, 215–29. Swansea, 2005.

———. "Orality and Communal Identity in Eunapius' *Lives of the Sophists and Philosophers*." *Byzantion* 75 (2005): 334–61.
———. "The Student Self in Late Antiquity." In *Religion and the Self in Antiquity*, edited by D. Brakke, M. Satlow, and S. Weitzman, 234–52. Bloomington, 2005.
———. "Where to Live the Philosophical Life in the Sixth Century? Damascius, Simplicius, and the Return from Persia." *Greek Roman and Byzantine Studies* 45 (2005): 285–315.
———. "Winning the Intracommunal Dialogues: Zacharias Scholasticus' *Life of Severus*." *Journal of Early Christian Studies* 13 (2005): 437–64.
———. *City and School in Late Antique Athens and Alexandria*. Berkeley, 2006.
———. "The Murder of Hypatia: Acceptable or Unacceptable Violence?" In *Violence in Late Antiquity*, edited by H. A. Drake, 333–42. Aldershot, 2006.
———. "Creating the Ascetic and Sophistic Mélange." *ARAM* 17/18 (2006-7): 153–64.
———. "Creating the Academy: Historical Discourse and the Shape of Community in the Old Academy." *Journal of Hellenic Studies* 127 (2007): 106–22.
———. "The Enduring Legacy of the Iatrosophist Gessius." *Greek Roman and Byzantine Studies* 49 (2009): 113–34.
———. "Dioscorus as a Paradigm of Resistance in Syriac and Coptic Anti-Chalcedonian Literature." Forthcoming.
———. "John Rufus, Timothy Aelurus and the Fall of the Western Roman Empire." In *Romans, Barbarians, and the Transformation of the Roman World*, edited by R. Mathisen and D. Shanzer. Forthcoming.
Welch, K. "Some Architectural Prototypes for the Auditoria at Kom el-Dikka and Three Late Antique (fifth century AD) Comparanda from Aphrodisias in Caria." In *Alexandria: Auditoria of Kôm el-Dikka and Late Antique Education*, edited by T. Derda, T. Markiewicz, and E. Wipszycka, 115–33. Warsaw, 2007.
Wessel, S. *Cyril of Alexandria and the Nestorian Controversy: The Making of a Saint and of a Heretic*. Oxford, 2004.
Westen, D. and G.O. Gabbard. "Developments in Cognitive Neuroscience: 1. Conflict, Compromise, and Connectionism." *Journal of the American Psychoanalytic Association* 50 (2002): 53–98.
Westerink, L. G., ed. *The Greek Commentaries on Plato's Phaedo, Vol. II, Damascius*. Amsterdam, 1977.
———, ed. and trans. *Prolégomènes à la Philosophie de Platon*. Paris, 1990.
Wheeler, E., trans. *Dorotheus of Gaza: Discourses and Sayings*. Kalamazoo, MI, 1977.
Whitby, Michael. "Maro the Dendrite: An Anti-Social Holy Man?" In *Homo Viator: Classical Essays for John Bramble*, edited by Michael Whitby, Philip Hardie, and Mary Whitby, 309–17. Bristol, 1987.
———, trans. *The Ecclesiastical History of Evagrius Scholasticus*. Liverpool, 2000.
Wildberg, C. "Philosophy in the Age of Justinian." In *The Cambridge Companion to the Age of Justinian*, edited by M. Maas, 316–40. Cambridge, 2005.
Williams, R. "The Logic of Arianism." *Journal of Theological Studies* 34 (1983): 56–81.
———. *Arius: Heresy and Tradition*. London, 1987. [Arius1]
———. *Arius: Heresy and Tradition*. 2nd ed. Grand Rapids, 2002. [Arius2]

Wipszycka, E. "Les confréries dans la vie religeuse de l'Egypte chrétienne." In *Proceedings of the Twelfth International Congress of Papyrology,* edited by R. Samuel, 511–25. Toronto, 1970.

———. "Contribution à l'étude de l'économie de la congrégation Pachômienne." *Journal of Juristic Papyrology* 26 (1996): 167–210.

Wolf, P. *Vom Schulwesen der Spätantike: Studien zu Libanius.* Baden, 1952.

Wright, W. *Catalogue of the Syriac Manuscripts in the British Museum.* Vol. 2. London, 1871.

Zintzen, C. *Damascii Vitae Isidori Reliquae.* Hildesheim, 1967.

Zotenberg, M. H. *La Chronique de Jean, Évêque de Nikiou.* Paris, 1879.

INDEX

Acacius (bishop of Constantinople), 233, 234, 246, 248
Academy, 26, 27, 29–34, 50, 57, 63, 183
Aedesius, 38, 41, 86
Aelianus, 117–18, 126–27
Aeneas of Gaza, 139; *Theophrastus*, 140–42
Alexander (of Macedon), 31
Alexander (bishop of Alexandria), 172, 173, 213, 222, 223
Alexandria, 1, 9, 13, 14, 16, 20, 22, 23, 25, 56, 131, 132, 139–40, 147, 163, 169, 173, 175, 178, 180, 183, 208, 220, 225, 227, 233, 238, 244, 252, 254, 263, 267; Alexandrian exceptionalism, 20–21; ascetic communities of, 21, 93, 123, 128, 133, 136, 256, 260; bishops of, 12, 15, 21, 73, 91, 133, 135, 155–253, 261; Caesareum of, 157; city council of, 158, 182, 241–43; clergy of, 221, 228–29, 231; destruction of pagan temples in, 191–205, 211, 214, 240–41, 251–52; intellectuals of, 27, 53–88, 154, 245–46, 260; Peter the Iberian in, 132–33; *philoponoi* in, 91–93, 115, 127, 256, 259; reception of Henotikon in, 231–33; schools of, 2–11, 44, 130, 137, 143–47, 149, 151, 153, 236, 255, 257, 266, 268; support for Illus in, 72–73; tsunami of, 365, 185; Tychaion of, 155, 158, 195, 239, 241; visit of Antony to, 177
Amelius, 46

Ammianus Marcellinus, 40
Ammonius (philosopher, c. 435/445–c. 517/526), 5, 10, 11, 23, 61–63, 65, 66, 69, 83, 85, 130, 140, 143, 145, 154, 260; compromise of, 70–71, 74–77, 81, 87, 144, 245–46
Ammonius (monk, d. 415), 208
Ammonius Saccas, 8
Amoun, 111
Anatolius, 42
Anthemius, 55
Antichrist, 135, 136, 141
Antigonus of Carystus, 32
Antiochus of Ascalon, 34
Antony, 105, 106, 112, 177, 181, 223
Apelles, 111, 113
Aphrodisias, 1–3, 20, 60, 63, 72, 263, 267
Apollo (monk), 112–13
Apollo (god), 204
Aphthonius, 128, 144
Apophthegmata Patrum, 109n86, 198, 200
Arcesilaus, 29
Arians, 172, 179, 187
Arius, 172–74, 177,
Aristotle, 8, 30n5, 33, 92, 139, 245
Aristoxenus, 32, 33
Arsenius (Melitian), 173
Arsenius (prefect), 244, 263
Asclepiades, 5, 57–58, 60, 62, 65; death of, 70

286   INDEX

Asclepiodotus of Alexandria, 2–3, 5, 9–11, 25, 60, 66, 69–70, 130, 144; conception of his child, 3, 10, 63–65, 67–68, 149, 265–67
Asclepius, 49
Athanasius (brother of Paralius), 10, 66, 68
Athanasius (bishop of Alexandria, 328–73), 105, 159–60, 163–89, 190, 191, 198, 216, 251, 252; and Constanius, 175–82 ; and Constantine, 172–74; exiles of, 164–65, 174, 178–81; historical legacy of, 182–89; relationship with ascetics, 177, 181, 184, 190, 199; rhetorical use of persecution, 176–80, 186; use by anti-Chalcedonians, 217, 222–25, 227–29, 250; use by Cyril, 212–14; use of imperial resources, 174–75; use of legacy by Theophilus, 191, 200–205, 210, 214; use by Peter Mongus, 232–33, 242–43, 253, 258; and Valens, 163–64, 169, 182
Athanasius II (bishop of Alexandria, 489–96), 247, 249
Athens, 2, 4, 35, 36, 42, 50, 75, 80, 83, 84, 88, 263
Augustine, 168

Barsanuphius, 93, 116–21, 123, 132n55; lay followers of, 117–18, 126–27
Basil of Caesarea, 142, 168–69, 171
Basiliscus, 231
Berytus, 9, 67, 129, 130, 131, 140, 147, 264, 266
Besa, 212
Bessarion, 199, 200
bishops, 19–20, 165–72; patronage activities of, 166–67; practical limitations on power, 228–29; spiritual authority of, 20, 165, 170–72, 175, 180, 182, 187, 189, 191, 192n4, 197–99, 200, 202, 207, 210, 215, 218, 222, 223, 226–27, 229, 230–34, 247, 248, 250–51, 253, 257–58; support of poor, 167–70; wealth available to, 165–66
Brasidas, 164
Brown, Peter, 171

Calandion, 139
Cameron, Alan, 265–67
Canopus, 13, 211, 229, 230, 240; Pachomian community of, 230, 233, 237; Serapeum of, 160, 196–98, 214
Caria, 1, 3, 20, 266

Chrysanthius, 27, 37–39, 41, 43, 86
Clement of Alexandria, 171
Constans, 36, 180, 181
Constantine I, 20, 165, 172, 174, 175, 249
Constantine of Siout, 184–88, 205
Constantinople, 131, 132, 146, 174, 175, 182, 192, 219, 230, 233, 234, 243, 244, 246, 247, 248
Copres, 113–14
Corinth, 43
Cosmas (spatharius), 243, 244
Council of Chalcedon, 20, 93, 219–20; opposition to, 132–38, 217, 220–29, 231; supporters of, 65, 72
Council of Ephesus I (431), 212, 218, 221, 230, 231n71
Council of Ephesus II (449), 218, 219, 222,
Crantor, 29
crocodiles, 97, 238
Cyril, 159, 160, 191, 197, 204, 207–15, 217–18, 219, 228, 230, 232, 242, 247, 251; anti-Chalcedonian evocation of, 222–26, 237; anti-pagan actions, 161, 191, 210–11, 258, 265–67; *contra Julianum*, 212–13; evocation of Athanasius, 160, 191, 212–14; evocation of Theophilus, 160, 191, 209–12; and Hypatia, 208–10; and Shenoute, 212

Damascius, 27, 60, 64, 79–85, 144, 245, 259, 260, 268; *Life of Isidore*, 27, 53n1, 54–60, 71–78, 80, 82, 149n130; view of rhetoric, 64
Damascus, 2
Damiane, 267
David, 184, 213
Democharus, 1, 9
Didymus the Blind, 105
Diocletian, 211
Diogenes of Oenoanda, 34, 35
Dionysius, tyrant of Sicily, 31
Dionysius, bishop of Alexandria, 159n5, 223, 224
Dioscorus I, 135, 160, 161, 217–19, 228, 229, 230, 231, 232, 233, 234, 247, 252; anti-Chalcedonian representation of, 221–27, 250–51, 258; break with family of Cyril, 217
Dioscorus II, 249
Dorotheus of Gaza, 119

INDEX 287

Edwards, Mark, 49
Egypt, 10, 20, 108, 116, 132,165, 167, 192, 205, 207, 227, 230, 247, 258; anti-Chalcedonianism in, 132–34, 136, 217, 220–22, 227–29, 231; ascetics of, 108–14, 134, 181, 184, 192, 212, 214, 218, 233; Athanasius's appeal to, 175–82, 189, 251; exceptionalism, 20–21; Melitians in, 174, 177n83; prefect of, 12, 13, 144, 155, 178, 179, 208, 231, 240, 246, 264, 265, 267; traditional religion of, 59, 64, 137, 197
Elias (bishop of Jerusalem), 147
Elisha, martyrium of, 196, 200–203, 221, 226
Enaton, 9, 12–14, 66–68, 87, 89, 91, 123, 144, 217, 235–37, 243, 245, 252, 264; center of anti-Chalcedonianism, 12, 133, 136, 151, 153, 220; ties to Alexandrian students, 10–11, 20, 93, 128, 142–43, 154, 256–58, 267
Entrechius, 235, 236, 263, 264, 268
Epictetus, 56, 78, 79, 260
Epicureans, 33, 34, 35
Epiphanius (pagan), 64
Epiphanius (monk), 198
eschatology, 135–37, 141
eternity of the world, 8, 138, 140–43, 145, 151, 245
Eubulus, 46
Eulogius, 110
Eunapius, 37, 51, 54, 86, 87, 196 ; *Lives of the Sophists*, 37–45, 54, 57
Euphemius (bishop of Constantinople), 246, 259
Euprepius, 64
Eusebius of Nicomedia, 174, 178
Eustochius (follower of Plotinus), 48–50
Eustochius (bishop of Jerusalem), 119–20
Eutyches, 187, 218, 232
Evagrius (law student), 129–30
Evagrius Scholasticus, 119–20, 247

Firmicus Maternus, 47
Flavian, prefect of Alexandria, 163, 164
Flavian, bishop of Constantinople, 218, 219
Fravitta, bishop of Constantinople, 246, 247, 248, 253, 259

Gadara, 38
Gangra, 221, 222, 224, 225, 226, 227

Gaza, 2, 72, 91, 93, 139, 151, 153, 256; ascetic life around, 116, 119, 123, 130–36, 256–57, 260
George of Cappadocia, 169, 183, 184, 198n38
Gesius (nemesis of Shenoute), 109, 197n37
Gessius (iatrosophist), 76, 78, 81, 210n117, 260
Gibbon, Edward, 17
Gregory (Arian bishop of Alexandria), 169, 178–80
Gregory Nazianzen, encomium of Athanasius,183–85, 187, 205

Harran, 85n166
Hegias, 78
Henotikon, 230–33, 236, 242, 244, 246, 247, 248, 252, 258
Heraiscus, 5, 10, 11, 23, 57–59, 65–66, 69–70, 76, 78
Hermes Trismegistus, 49
Hermippus, 32
Herodes Atticus, 60
Hierocles, 57, 59, 78
Himerius, 36
Historia Monachorum in Aegypto, 92, 109–14, 119, 121, 255; oral traditions preserved in, 109, 113
History of Dioscorus, 222–26, 227
Horapollon, 3, 5, 8–13, 20, 23, 27, 33, 65, 69, 74, 87, 143–44, 150, 154, 157, 235–36, 239, 256, 258, 266; Christian conversion of, 70–71; *Hieroglyphica*, 59n41; students of, 11, 15, 25, 26, 63, 66, 70, 87, 143–44, 257
Horsiesios, 95, 97, 98, 106, 107
Hypatia, 8; murder of, 57, 208–10, 214, 242

Iamblichus, 27, 38, 39, 41, 44, 86
Ignatius (bishop of Antioch), 223
Illus: revolt of, 3, 63, 72–74, 77, 88, 139, 148, 263–64
Isaiah, 132, 137–40; *Life of Isaiah*, 138–40, 142, 148–49
Ischyras, 173
Isis, 13, 20, 58, 60, 65, 158, 197, 266, 267; iconography of, 11n51; Menouthis shrine of, 3, 8, 10–14, 63, 68–70, 72, 144, 149, 196, 238, 244, 252, 267
Isidore, 5, 10, 11, 23, 54, 57–60, 62, 64–66, 69, 80, 87, 130, 144, 259, 263; as a philosophical exemplar, 74–75, 80–81, 84 ; flight from

Isidore *(continued)*
    Alexandria, 64, 70, 82–83, 144, 260.
    See also Damascius, *Life of Isidore*

Jerome, 105
Job, 183
John (Gazan hermit), 93, 114, 116–19, 121;
    lay followers of, 117, 118, 126–27
John (Christian law student), 67
John I (Alexandrian patriarch), 249
John Chrysostom, 170n41, 171, 207, 224n36
John of Lycopolis, 111–13, 121
John of Nikiu, 203–4, 209–10
John Philoponus, 151
John Rufus, 92, 134, 141; *Plerophories*, 92,
    134–37, 260–61
John Semeiographos, 5
John Talaias, 139, 230
John the Baptist, martyrium of, 196, 200–
    203, 221, 226
Jovian, 201
Julian (emperor), 37n45, 40, 41, 163, 164, 184,
    200; *Contra Galilaeos*, 212–13;
Julian (brother of Damascius), 60
Julian of Halicarnassus, 187, 249
Julianus of Cappadocia, 41, 42
Juvenal of Jerusalem, 133–35, 141, 153, 219,
    220, 251, 252

Kom el-Dikka, 5–7, 62–63, 158n2, 239–40,
    268
Kronos, 238

Leo I (pope), 135, 218, 219, 225. *See also* Tome
    of Leo
Leo I (emperor), 224
Leonas, 60
Libanius, 36, 69, 87, 142
liturgy, 144; as historical instruction, 160,
    184, 188, 202, 251, 261
Longinus (philosopher), 46
Longinus (archimandrite of the Enaton), 133,
    136n80, 221; *Life of Longinus*, 220
Lucius, 169

Macarius, 173
Macarius of Tkow, 220, 221
Magnentius, 181
Maiuma, 129, 130, 132, 133, 134, 135, 224

Mani, 187
Marcellinus of Dalmatia, 55n15, 77, 82
Marcian, 219, 221, 222
Marcion, 187
Marinus, 50, 51
Mark (Apostle), 159n5, 195, 223, 224
Maximus of Ephesus, 40, 41, 44
Melitians, 172–75, 187
Memphis, 191, 203, 238
Menas, 127, 239, 266; funeral of, 145–47
Menedemus, 33
Menouthis, 8, 13, 15, 150, 157–58, 217, 236–
    41, 248, 259, 265–67; Christianization of,
    161, 197, 210–11, 240, 258; church of Holy
    Evangelists in, 197, 211; Isis shrine of, 3,
    8, 10–14, 63, 68–70, 72, 144, 149, 196, 238,
    244, 252, 267; shrine of Cyrus and John
    in, 8, 115, 197
Moses, Athanasius as, 183–85

Nebuchadnezzar, 176
Nephalius, 248
Nestorius, 212–14, 218, 223, 230, 232; and
    Shenoute, 212
Nicomedes, 244, 245, 260; investigation
    of, 70–78, 80, 82, 83, 88, 144, 145, 246,
    259, 264
Nikiu, 204
Nile, 20, 58, 60, 113
Noah, 183, 185
Novatians, 208, 209
Numenius, 46, 54n1

Olympiodorus, 61–63, 66
Olympus, 57
Oral traditions, 262; in ascetic environ-
    ments, 92–93, 103, 106, 107–9, 113–14,
    134n67, 136, 141, 144, 255, 259; communi-
    cation in sermons, 250, 261; in schools,
    38–39, 41, 44–46, 49, 50, 54, 61, 62–65, 72,
    149, 193n8, 260
Orestes, 208
Oribasius, 37
Origen, 171, 223

Pachomians, 92, 95–107, 119, 121, 125–26, 152,
    238; community at Canopus, 223, 233, 237;
    community structure, 95, 99–100, 102–3;
    daily routines, 92, 101–2, 107; historical

traditions among, 103–6, 108; and Theophilus, 197, 211, 240
Pachomius, 95, 97–100, 103–8, 126, 152; and Antony, 105–6; biographers of, 103; synod at Latopolis, 108
Paideia, 17
Palamon, 104, 105
Palestine, 34, 110, 113, 114, 141, 200 ; intellectual environment in, 139, 142; monasteries of, 21, 110, 114, 141, 147, 197, 233; reaction to Chalcedon, 133–35, 220, 233
Palladas, 193, 195
Palladius, 109
Pamprepius, 59n38, 72–78, 82, 139, 143, 259, 260
Paphnutius, 223
Paralius, 16, 17, 20, 44, 53, 63, 72, 73, 80, 82, 87, 91, 128, 217, 244, 246, 256, 260, 263; in Alexandria, 5, 9–15; beating of, 11–12, 23, 27, 65–71, 87, 93, 123–24, 127, 143–44, 154, 157, 216, 234–43, 252, 254, 257–59, 264; childhood, 1–3; textual representation of, 14–15, 77, 146–51, 248, 259, 265–68
Paul (Apostle), 170, 177, 183, 188, 257
Paul (ascetic), 112
Paul (Alexandrian *philoponos*), 115–16
Paul of Samosata, 223
Peripatetics, 26, 32, 33
Peter I of Alexandria, 159n5, 223
Peter II of Alexandria, 191, 216, 224
Peter III Mongus, 73, 77, 155, 216–18, 229–53, 261, 263–64; acceptance of the Henotikon, 230–33, 242; conflict with Egyptian anti-Chalcedonians, 12, 233–34, 243–48, 258; evocation of Athanasius, 232–33, 242–43, 253, 258; evocation of Theophilus, 15, 237, 239–41, 252–53, 258; exile of, 229–30; historical legacy of, 249–50, 259; and Nicomedes, 244–46; role in riot, 12–15, 157–61, 234–43, 257
Peter the Iberian, 129, 131–38, 151, 153–54, 221, 224; source for the *Plerophories*, 137, 141
Petronius, 95, 223
Phbow, 95, 96, 98
Philagrius, 178–80
Philodemus, 34
Philostratus, 35, 69
Photius, 53n1, 54
Pisidia, 2

Plato, 8, 26–27, 29, 32–34, 47, 92, 139, 184; Academy of, 29–34
Plotinus, 45–51, 86, 139; *Enneads* of, 46, 49
Plutarch of Athens, 50
Polemo, 31–34
Porphyry, 45–51, 86
poverty, 166–68
Proclus (brother of Paralius), 1, 9
Proclus (Athenian philosopher), 50–51, 60–61, 81, 137, 263
Procopius of Gaza, 151
Prohaeresius, 36, 37, 41–44, 86
Proterius, 134, 135, 220, 227, 228, 250, 251, 252; death of, 224–25
Pulcheria, 219
Pythagoreanism, 58, 59, 78

Rome, 48, 49, 219, 242; fall to barbarians 135n72, 260
Rufinus of Aquileia, 109, 192–93, 202, 203

Salomon, 128, 143, 235, 236, 237
Salustius, 77, 82
Schools, 2, 15, 17–18, 25, 26, 34, 37, 45, 51–52, 65, 91, 92; dining customs of, 60–61; hierarchy of, 3–5, 62, 86, 255; initiation of new students, 3–5; of law, 9, 67, 129, 147, 264; physical locations of, 5–7, 62–63; of Platonic philosophy, 25–27, 29–33, 38–41, 73, 78–85, 86, 259; of Plotinus, 46–50; religious dynamic in, 64, 66, 93, 129, 137–46, 148–54, 236. ; of rhetoric, 2, 35–36, 41–44, 86, 153; Serapis, 194, 195, 198, 201, 206, 210, 214, 241. See also Alexandria, school of
Serapeum, 14, 57, 160, 192–98, 200, 202, 203, 210, 214, 239–41; of Canopus, 160, 196–98, 214
Serapio (philosopher), 58, 59, 74
Serapion (monk), 110
Severianus, 56, 60, 64, 77, 82
Severus, Flavius Messius Phoebus (cos. 470), 55, 56, 77, 82, 243n136
Severus, bishop of Antioch (512–18), 67, 129, 130, 147, 148, 249, 264, 266; alleged paganism of, 147, 265; *Life of Severus*, 13n57, 64–69, 127–28, 142–52, 234–36, 246–48, 263, 265–68
Severus of Al'Ashmunein, 226
Shenoute, 19, 108, 109, 124–26, 212, 223, 255

290 INDEX

Simplicius, 61n53, 78, 80–83, 85n166; *Commentary on Encheiridion*, 79
Socrates, 33, 47, 75
Socrates Scholasticus, 210
Sopater (fifth-century Alexandrian rhetorician), 5
Sosipatra, 41
Speusippus, 29, 32, 34, 184
Stephen (former sophist and Enaton monk), 10, 66–69, 128, 236, 237, 267
Steppa, Jan Eric, 264
Stoics, 33, 34, 78, 79
Storia della Chiesa di Alessandria, 200, 203, 212, 213
Suda, 53n1, 54
Synaxary of the Coptic church, 187, 188, 226, 247, 251
Syria, 2, 19, 20, 34, 58, 220; ascetics from, 136

Tawatha, 116–120
Theodore (Pachomian monk), 95–99, 102, 104, 107, 126, 223; visit with Antony, 105–6
Theodore of Antinoe, 234, 243
Theodore of Mopsuestia, 171
Theodorus (prefect of Egypt), 263
Theodosius (effective bishop of Jerusalem, 451–53), 133, 221, 233
Theodosius I, 111, 190, 193, 214
Theodosius II, 209, 218, 219, 223
Theon (monk), 110–11
Theonas, 223; church of, 178
Theophilus, 14, 15, 159, 161, 190–208, 213, 216, 217, 224, 237, 240–41, 250, 251; *de aedificatione Martyrii Iohannis Baptistae*, 203; attack on Serapeum, 14, 160, 192–96, 210, 214, 239; evocation of Athanasius, 191, 200–205, 210, 214; evoked by Cyril, 209–12; evoked by Peter Mongus, 15, 237, 239–41, 252–53, 258; Origenist controversy, 199
Theosebius, 56, 57, 59, 78, 82; source for Damascius, 57

Theurgy, 39, 41, 42
Thmoušons, 95
Thomas (sophist), 89, 91
Timothy I (bishop of Alexandria), 191, 205, 224
Timothy Aelurus, 133, 137, 138, 153, 154, 160, 161, 217, 224–30, 231, 232, 233, 234, 247, 249, 250, 252, 253, 258; funeral of, 229; historical writing, 221–22; return from exile, 225, 242; as source for *Plerophories*,134–36; use of *florilegia* by, 225
Timothy Salofacialos, 225, 227–30
Tome of Leo, 135, 218–20, 231, 232, 244, 246, 252, 260; anti-Chalcedonian rejection of, 221–23
Trypho, 46
Tuscianus, 43, 51n116

Valens, 40, 163, 182, 214, 242
Valentinus, 187
Via Canopica, 239

Xenocrates, 30–34, 57, 63, 184

Zacharias Scholasticus, 12, 62, 70, 87, 91, 92, 130–34, 136–54, 237–38, 245, 259, 264; *Ammonius*, 62, 138, 140–42, 146, 148–49, 151; and anti-Chalcedonian monasteries, 93, 123–24, 131, 136, 143, 256; *Ecclesiastical History*, 16n69, 246–48, 259; narration of riot, 15–16, 25–26, 53, 142; *Life of Isaiah*, 138–40, 142, 148–49; *Life of Severus*, 13n57, 64–69, 127–28, 142–52, 234–36, 246–48, 263, 265–68
Zaccheus, 105
Zeno, 13, 56, 60, 72, 76, 77, 83, 139, 155, 158, 161, 229, 230, 240, 241, 243, 244, 246; Henotikon of, 138n91, 217, 230–33, 246, 258
Zenodotus of Lesbos, 89, 91
Zethus, 48

TEXT
10/12.5 Minion Pro

DISPLAY
Minion Pro

COMPOSITOR
Integrated Composition Systems

CARTOGRAPHER
Bill Nelson

PRINTER AND BINDER
Maple-Vail Book Manufacturing Group

www.ingramcontent.com/pod-product-compliance
Lightning Source LLC
Chambersburg PA
CBHW030524230426
43665CB00010B/763